T0328863

The Capital Asset Pricing Model in the 21st Century
Analytical, Empirical, and Behavioral Perspectives

The Capital Asset Pricing Model (CAPM) and the mean-variance (M-V) rule, which are based on classic expected utility theory (EUT), have been heavily criticized theoretically and empirically. The advent of behavioral economics, prospect theory, and other psychology-minded approaches in finance challenges the rational investor model from which CAPM and M-V derive. Haim Levy argues that the tension between the classic financial models and behavioral economics approaches is more apparent than real. This book aims to relax the tension between the two paradigms. Specifically, Professor Levy shows that although behavioral economics contradicts aspects of EUT, CAPM and M-V are intact in both EUT and Cumulative Prospect Theory (CPT) frameworks. There is, furthermore, no evidence to reject CAPM empirically when *ex-ante* parameters are employed. Professionals may thus comfortably teach and use CAPM and behavioral economics or CPT as coexisting paradigms.

Haim Levy is Miles Robinson Professor of Business Administration at the Hebrew University of Jerusalem and Dean of the Academic Center of Law and Business, Israel. He is the author of hundreds of articles in leading academic journals and nineteen books. Based on publications in sixteen core journals in finance, he has obtained the ranking of the most prolific researcher in finance covering the fifty-year period through 2002. A coauthor with Nobel Laureates Harry Markowitz and Paul Samuelson, Professor Levy's major research contributions have been in the field of stochastic dominance in financial economics, which sets forth the criteria for decision making under conditions of uncertainty. He has also developed economic models for risk management. Professor Levy received Hebrew University's Prize for Excellence in Research in 1996 and the EMET Prize in 2006. He has served as economic adviser to the Bank of Israel and has held academic positions at the University of California, Berkeley, and the Wharton School, University of Pennsylvania. He received his Ph.D. from Hebrew University in 1969 and has held a full professorship there since 1976.

The Capital Asset Pricing Model in the 21st Century

Analytical, Empirical, and Behavioral Perspectives

HAIM LEVY

Hebrew University, Jerusalem

CAMBRIDGE
UNIVERSITY PRESS

Shaftesbury Road, Cambridge CB2 8EA, United Kingdom

One Liberty Plaza, 20th Floor, New York, NY 10006, USA

477 Williamstown Road, Port Melbourne, VIC 3207, Australia

314–321, 3rd Floor, Plot 3, Splendor Forum, Jasola District Centre, New Delhi – 110025, India

103 Penang Road, #05–06/07, Visioncrest Commercial, Singapore 238467

Cambridge University Press is part of Cambridge University Press & Assessment, a department of the University of Cambridge.

We share the University's mission to contribute to society through the pursuit of education, learning and research at the highest international levels of excellence.

www.cambridge.org
Information on this title: www.cambridge.org/9780521186513

First published 2012
Reprinted 2012

A catalogue record for this publication is available from the British Library

Library of Congress Cataloging-in-Publication data
Levy, Haim.
The capital asset pricing model in the 21st century : analytical, empirical, and behavioral perspectives / Haim Levy.
p. cm.
Includes bibliographical references and index.
ISBN 978-1-107-00671-3 – ISBN 978-0-521-18651-3 (pbk.)
1. Capital asset pricing model. I. Title.
HG4636.L48   2012
332´.0414–dc22   2011015049

ISBN   978-1-107-00671-3   Hardback
ISBN   978-0-521-18651-3   Paperback

Contents

Preface

Modern finance is relatively new. Before the breakthrough "Portfolio Selection" article was published by Markowitz in 1952, research in finance was basically nonquantitative and the use of quantitative models in teaching and in research was rare. A glance at finance textbooks that were used in teaching before 1952 and textbooks that are currently used suffices to reveal the revolution induced in the finance profession by the publication of this 1952 Mean-Variance (M-V) article. The next revolutionary papers in portfolio selection and equilibrium pricing were published by Sharpe, Lintner, and Black in 1964, 1965, and 1972, respectively. These three papers use Markowitz's M-V model as a springboard in developing equilibrium prices of risky assets in the capital market and in identifying beta rather than sigma as the risk measure of an individual asset in a portfolio context. The model developed by Sharpe and Lintner, known as the Capital Asset Pricing Model (CAPM), is used in virtually all research studies that deal with risk and return and occupies a substantial portion of textbooks on investments and corporate finance.

The other pillars of modern finance are the papers published by Modigliani and Miller in 1958, which focus on the optimal capital structure, and the two breakthrough papers published by Black and Scholes and by Merton on option pricing in 1973. No wonder Markowitz, Sharpe, Scholes, Merton, Modigliani, and Miller have all been awarded the Nobel Prize in Economics for their revolutionary contributions (the other researchers mentioned were not alive in relevant years when the prizes were awarded). Because this book focuses on portfolio selection and the CAPM, we mainly discuss and analyze the contributions of Markowitz, Sharpe, Lintner, and Black to the financial literature.

The publication of the Prospect Theory (PT) article by Kahneman and Tversky in 1979, for which Kahneman won the Nobel Prize in Economics in 2002, has shaken the foundations of the Expected Utility Theory (EUT); and, as the M-V framework and the CAPM have been developed within the EUT framework, PT indirectly has also shaken the foundations of these two models.

PT's criticism of EUT is based on experimental findings. Additional criticism of the CAPM is based on empirical findings, showing that beta has very little or even no explanatory power at all. Leading this criticism is the 1992 empirical study of Fama and French, revealing that the coefficient of the CAPM's beta is statistically insignificant; hence, in contradiction to the CAPM, beta does not explain the cross section of stock returns. Therefore, this finding allegedly casts doubt on the validity of beta as a measure of risk.

Thus, we have the M-V and the CAPM, which are widely used in teaching, in research, and by practitioners on the one hand, and PT's experimental findings and empirical studies that criticize these two models on the other hand. Because PT has been known since 1979 and the empirical studies that criticize the M-V and the CAPM models have also been known for decades, one must wonder why academics as well as professional investors keep adhering to the M-V and the CAPM and why virtually all curriculums in finance still heavily rely on these two models. We devote this book to this question. We show that PT and M-V and the CAPM can coexist, even though PT and EUT cannot. We also show that although the CAPM is rejected with *ex-post* parameters, it cannot be rejected with *ex-ante* parameters.

We hope that after reading this book, professors of finance can comfortably teach the M-V and the CAPM, as well as the behavioral PT model, as we show that there is no contradiction between these two frameworks. Also, this book provides a somewhat different interpretation of the CAPM's empirical studies, which, in a nutshell, asserts that the M-V and the CAPM cannot be rejected with the *ex-ante* parameters. Similarly, professional investors and consulting firms can continue relying on the M-V and the CAPM models, although some modifications may be needed.

In this book, we present all the material needed to achieve the integration of the M-V, CAPM, and Cumulative PT (CPT). For example, EUT and stochastic dominance rules are discussed, as we employ both to show that the M-V and the CAPM do not contradict CPT. Of course, we could refer the reader to this material in other books or articles but, to facilitate the reading of this book, we prefer to have all the relevant material contained in one place. The same principle is valid regarding PT and CPT material needed to prove that the behavioral model and the classical portfolio models can coexist. Finally, although we rely on the CPT, which is the modified version of PT, realizing the growing role of behavioral finance in recent years, we also devote a chapter to the original PT.

This book is mainly written for professors of finance and professional investors who use the M-V framework and the CAPM and who are also certainly aware of the criticisms of these two models. We hope that this book will resolve some conflicts and increase their confidence in the employed models. The book can be used in advanced courses in economics and finance and in Ph.D. classes in these two areas.

The book could not achieve its present form and level without the help of many people. I would like to thank Turan Bali, Rob Brown, Harry Markowitz, Richard Roll, William Sharpe, Jim Yoder, and an anonymous reader for their many helpful comments. It is a pleasure for me to thank Moshe (Shiki) Levy and Michal Orkan, who read the whole manuscript and provided me with many detailed comments.

Finally, I would like to thank Scott Parris and Adam Levine at Cambridge University Press and Peggy Rote at Aptara, Inc., for their great assistance in making writing and producing this book a pleasure.

1

Introduction

Harry Markowitz and William Sharpe were awarded the Nobel Prize in Economics in 1990 for the development of the Mean-Variance (M-V) framework and the Capital Asset Pricing Model (CAPM), respectively. In 2002, this prize was awarded to Daniel Kahneman for the development of Prospect Theory (PT), which contradicts Expected Utility Theory (EUT), on which the M-V framework and the CAPM are based. Is the Economics Nobel Committee inconsistent?

The PT criticism of EUT, which indirectly also criticizes the M-V model and the CAPM, is just one of the mounting empirical and theoretical criticisms of the M-V framework in general, and, in particular, the CAPM, criticisms that imply that one cannot conduct theoretical research or implement practical investment strategies *with them*. However, the observed extensive academic research and investment strategies, which rely on the M-V and the CAPM, indicate that by the same token, academics and practitioners cannot conduct their research, teaching, and financial analysis and services *without them* either.

Indeed, as we shall see in the forthcoming chapters, the M-V rule and, in particular, the CAPM are heavily criticized both theoretically and empirically. Briefly, the CAPM is empirically rejected because the risk index – beta – does not explain the cross-section variability of returns. In addition, the CAPM is rejected because the hypothesis

1

of normal distribution of returns – which is an essential component of this model – is empirically rejected.

Regarding the M-V rule, there are three main approaches to justify its use. The first approach, like the CAPM, assumes risk aversion and normal distribution of returns. With this assumption, the M-V rule is optimal and is consistent with expected utility maximization (for the proof of this claim, see Tobin[1] and Hanoch and Levy[2]). By the second approach the normality assumption is relaxed, and one assumes expected utility maximization with quadratic utility function (for this approach, see Tobin[3] and Hanoch and Levy[4]). These two approaches are criticized because the normal distribution is empirically rejected and the quadratic utility function is too specific and, in addition, has several unaccepted characteristics. The third approach to justify the M-V rule is the one suggested by Markowitz[5] in his 1959 book: he shows that one can use the quadratic approximation to expected utility for a wide class of utility functions (see also Levy and Markowitz[6]). Markowitz[7] recently wrote:

I never – at any time – assumed that return distributions are Gaussian. . . . Nor did I ever assume that the investor's utility function is quadratic. Rather, I noted that quadratic approximation to traditional utility function is often quite good over a surprisingly large range of returns.

To the best of our knowledge, this approach has not been criticized. However, having an approximation to expected utility rather than a precise expected utility has a vague implication to the validity of the CAPM.

---

[1] J. Tobin, "Liquidity Preference as Behavior towards Risk," *Review of Economic Studies*, 1958.

[2] G. Hanoch and H. Levy, "The Efficiency Analysis of Choices Involving Risk," *Review of Economic Studies*, 1969.

[3] See Tobin, *op. cit.*

[4] G. Hanoch and H. Levy, "Efficient Portfolio Selection with Quadratic and Cubic Utility," *Journal of Business*, 1970.

[5] H. M. Markowitz, *Portfolio Selection: Efficient Diversification of Investments*, 2nd edition, Cambridge, MA: Basil Blackwell.

[6] H. Levy and H. M. Markowitz, "Approximating Expected Utility by a Function of Mean and Variance," *American Economic Review*, 1979.

[7] H. M. Markowitz, "Portfolio Theory: As I Still See It," *Annual Review of Financial Economics*, 2010.

The M-V and the CAPM are also experimentally rejected, as EUT, on which these models are based, is rejected. Therefore, it is puzzling why the M-V rule and the CAPM are extensively employed by academics as well as professional investors despite all these criticisms.

The M-V rule and the M-V efficiency analysis were published in 1952 by Markowitz,[8] and the CAPM was published by Sharpe[9] and Lintner[10] in 1964 and 1965, respectively. Although the M-V analysis was slightly criticized after its publication in 1952, the CAPM, as an equilibrium model, has been heavily criticized. The first phase of empirical tests of the CAPM revealed mixed results: most studies support the CAPM at least partially because beta and cross-section average returns have been found to be positively correlated, as predicted by the CAPM. However, the model has also been found to be incomplete because some other variables – for example, the individual stock's variance, σ^2, skewness, and β^2 – also substantially explain the cross section of mean returns, in contradiction to the CAPM. People who use beta realize that it provides an explanation for a relatively small portion of the cross-section variation of returns. Therefore, to have better explanatory power of the cross section of returns by beta, some econometric models have been employed to account for possible measurement errors and some other errors in the variables.

In the second phase of the empirical studies, the tests reveal that when explaining cross-section returns with the CAPM, some anomalies stubbornly emerge. The most profound anomalies reported in the empirical studies are the Weekend Effect, the Small Firm Effect (SFE), the Value Premium, and the Momentum Effect. All these effects imply that cross-section returns are not fully explained by beta and that some other variables, which are not included in the CAPM, also explain the variation in cross-section market returns. Because the CAPM does not explain these phenomena, the effects mentioned here are called *market anomalies*. It is worth noting, however, that some of these anomalies (e.g., the Monday Effect) have vanished in recent

[8] H. M. Markowitz, "Portfolio Selection," *Journal of Finance*, 1952.
[9] W. F. Sharpe, "Capital Asset Prices: A Theory of Market Equilibrium," *Journal of Finance*, 1964.
[10] J. Lintner, "Security Prices, Risk and the Maximal Gain from Diversification," *Journal of Finance*, 1965.

years[11] (probably because once they became well known to the public, they were exploited by professional investors).

The highly cited study of Fama and French,[12] which was published in 1992 (and many other studies that followed), presents the most severe empirical criticism of the CAPM. Fama and French have claimed that beta has no explanatory power at all! Thus, their study constitutes a much more severe criticism of the CAPM than the criticisms of previous studies, which revealed that beta and the cross-section returns are positively and significantly associated – albeit beta provides only partial explanatory power.

Specifically, in the various regressions reported by Fama and French, the regression coefficient corresponding to beta is insignificant and other variables – not related to the CAPM – turn out to be significant factors in explaining the cross section of returns. Therefore, Fama and French suggest the Three-Factor Model as a substitute to the CAPM. The Three-Factor Model can be theoretically justified by the Arbitrage Pricing Theory (APT) with three factors. However, the selected factors are not motivated by theory, as is the explanatory factor, beta, in the CAPM. The selected three factors rather rely on the observed empirical connection between the cross-section returns and several variables. The Three-Factor Model of Fama and French includes the following three explanatory variables: (1) beta, (2) the SMB (a variable that is related to firm size difference, where SMB stands for "small minus big" size of firms), and (3) the HML (a variable related to the differences in the book/market value of firms, where HML stands for "high minus low" book-to-market values). Thus, it is interesting to note that even the Three-Factor Model, which reveals that beta is insignificant, does not give it up! This implies that beta is considered to be an important explanatory variable, albeit not the *main* explanatory variable, even by this model, which criticizes the CAPM.

Despite these severe empirical criticisms of the CAPM, this model – and particularly beta – and the CAPM's alpha are probably

---

[11] See G. W. Schwert, "Anomalies and Market Efficiency," in G. Constantinides, M. Harris, and R. M. Stulz (editors), *Handbook of the Economics of Finance*, North Holland, 2003.

[12] E. F. Fama and K. R. French, "The Cross–Section of Expected Stock Returns," *Journal of Finance*, 1992.

the most widely employed financial measures used by academic researchers, and it is even more intensively used by investment firms and practitioners. If, as according to the CAPM's first severe criticisms published decades ago, beta and alpha are economically meaningless, why are they still so intensively employed? How then can one explain the heavy use of these two models in the face of the overwhelming reported evidence rejecting them or rejecting the assumptions that underline these models? This tension is precisely the focus of this book. Specifically, we address the following related issues:

a) The CAPM is stated with *ex-ante* parameters, whereas the empirical tests are conducted with *ex-post* parameters. This difference is of particular importance when measuring beta. Can this be the source of the contrast between the widely employed CAPM and the empirical criticisms?

b) Most empirical tests that refute the CAPM employ monthly (or even shorter horizon) rates of returns, whereas the typical investment horizon is about one year. Can this gap in the two investment horizons explain some of the observed anomalies that constitute evidence against the CAPM? Can the SFE be explained by this horizon difference?

c) Can the seemingly unrealistic assumptions that underline the M-V efficiency analysis and the CAPM be the reason for the empirical rejection of these two models?

d) The M-V and the CAPM have been derived in the expected utility framework. EUT assumes that people are rational. However, psychologists and behavioral economists reveal that in many cases people make irrational investment decisions. The criticisms of expected utility (and hence of the M-V and CAPM) in this regard have mounted after the publication of the highly influential PT study by Kahneman and Tversky[13] and the Cumulative Prospect Theory (CPT) by Tversky and Kahneman.[14] Can the M-V rule and the CAPM coexist along

[13] D. Kahneman and A. Tversky, "Prospect Theory: An Analysis of Decision under Risk," *Econometrica*, 1979.

[14] A. Tversky and D. Kahneman, "Advances in Prospect Theory: Cumulative Representation of Uncertainty," *Journal of Risk and Uncertainty*, 1992.

with the suggested irrational behavior, specifically with CPT, whereas expected utility cannot? Because these behavioral economic criticisms of the M-V rule, and, in particular, of the CAPM, have been well known for years, the following nagging question arises: Do all the people who use the CAPM simply ignore the experimental criticisms of the EUT, which is the theoretical foundation of the CAPM?

In this book, we show that people who continue to use the M-V and the CAPM, albeit with some statistical modifications, are not, in fact, irrational. In the following chapters, we demonstrate the fact that the M-V and the CAPM are still being used extensively and probably will continue to be pillars in investment decision making for many more years to come, and for good reason. First, it is explained that the M-V and the CAPM cannot be empirically rejected with *ex-ante* parameters. Second, we show that the M-V and the CAPM can coexist with the modified version of the PT, the CPT.

This does not mean that the stable CAPM should be used. On the contrary, because the *ex-ante* parameters are unknown, efforts should be made by academics and practitioners alike to employ sophisticated methods to improve the estimates of the *ex-ante* beta, as well as the *ex-ante* risk premium, for example, by relying on the Conditional CAPM, which assumes that current information may affect the various parameters in some systematic way. This search for a better estimate does not contradict the M-V analysis and the CAPM, which are theoretically stated with *ex-ante* parameters.

Thus, we claim that investors and researchers are well aware that relying on *ex-post* parameters in a world with many dynamic and drastic changes may lead to wrong decisions. However, they are equally aware of the fact that the M-V and the CAPM are probably the best available investment tools and hence continue to employ these investment vehicles, albeit not naively. Namely, because the *ex-post* parameters are not ideal estimates of the *ex-ante* parameters, investors and researchers try to use all the information they have to improve the relevant estimates, thereby improving the effectiveness of these tools. This is accomplished by using various methods, including reliance on additional market and accounting supplement variables that may serve as proxies for the *ex-ante* parameters.

The purpose of the rest of this introductory chapter is to show that nowadays the CAPM and, in particular, alpha and beta, are widely used among academics and even more intensively employed among practitioners, despite the well-known criticisms. Thus, the evidence clearly shows that neither academics nor practitioners are willing to give up the M-V analysis and the CAPM as viable investment frameworks. One possible explanation for this behavior may be because these models cannot be easily rejected or perhaps because no better models exist. This evidence of the wide use of the M-V and the CAPM, despite the surrounding empirical and experimental criticisms, is the raison d'être for writing this book.

1.2. THE INTENSIVE USE OF THE MEAN-VARIANCE AND THE CAPITAL ASSET PRICING MODEL AMONG PRACTITIONERS

In this section, we demonstrate the widespread use of the M-V and the CAPM and, in particular, the CAPM's beta. To support our claim, we provide several case samples. This small sample of cases is sufficient to show the important role that the M-V and the CAPM play in the financial arena. However, a word of caution is called for: when one talks about beta, it is generally referring to beta derived from the CAPM. However, when one talks about alpha, it could be the CAPM's alpha or the alpha corresponding to any other model – for example, the Fama and French Three-Factor Model – because alpha measures the abnormal profit (or loss) beyond what is expected by the suggested model. In this chapter, however, when we discuss or report *alpha* we mean the CAPM's alpha.

We begin our analysis with extracts of a standard financial website. PracticalStockInvesting.com offers definitions and clarifications of a number of basic concepts. A substantial part of the article given in this website is dedicated to defining and giving a brief explanation of Markowitz's main investment principle. Alpha and beta are also widely discussed.[15] From the discussion and information given in this website, it is clear that practitioners consider the CAPM's alpha and beta very important investment tools. For example, it asserts:

---

[15] See http://practicalstockinvesting.com/category/basic-concepts/academic-theories/alpha-and-beta/.

β is a commonly-used tool. Value Line, among others, lists calculations in its publications, so they're easy to find.

Although alpha and beta are commonly employed, the view is that beta is more intensively employed than alpha:

You can often hear an investment professional say, "That's a high-Beta stock." Less frequently, you may see the claim, normally in writing, that someone "is searching for alpha."

Thus, it is more common to classify stocks as high (or low) beta stocks than to classify stocks using alpha.

However, the article also presents some reservations related to the implementation of these tools in practice:

There's a practical problem, though. If the universe has only two or three stocks in it, calculating this information is straightforward. If the universe is the S&P 500, however, figuring out all the interrelationships among all the stocks becomes a real pain in the neck....There's a much bigger problem, though. The virtues of short-term price volatility as a measure of risk is that the data are easily available for many stocks and that variance is part of an established mathematical framework. So it has been widely adopted by academics and consultants. Unfortunately, it's otherwise not very informative, I think. It's like saying that the risk in an airplane flight should be measured by the amount of air turbulence en route. By this measure, the plane that recently took a smooth ride into the Hudson River would be classified as a safe flight.

Thus, it is obvious from this article that beta and alpha occupy the minds of professional investors, even though they raise legitimate questions regarding the implementation of the M-V optimization model:

True, CAPM has crazy "simplifying" assumptions...although it's still taught to MBAs, nobody much believes in it anymore. Still, CAPM would be a lot easier to make fun of if we could produce more people with credible claims to have achieved positive α over long periods of time. On the other hand, if you could do this, why in the world would you ever tell someone else?

Sharpe[16] realizes the technical difficulty of handling many assets and therefore suggests the Single Index Model (SIM), which facilitates the investment diversification task when a relatively large number of assets are involved. In addition, it is well known that "a little

---

[16] W. F. Sharpe, "A Simplified Model for Portfolio Analysis," *Management Science*, 1963.

diversification goes a long way";[17] hence, most of the risk-reduction benefits are obtained by holding only a few assets.[18] Thus, one can adhere to the article's argument and invest in only a small number of assets without losing the main gain derived from diversification. Indeed, the segmented market CAPM (which is a generalization of the CAPM, obtained by relaxing one of the assumptions that underline the CAPM) fits the case presented in the article: it allows for the holding of an optimal portfolio containing only a small number of assets. The good news is that this segmented market model also suggests a risk-return equilibrium, whose structure is similar to the CAPM.

Capital market researchers recognize that there are many real-world impediments to achieving perfect diversification. These impediments include transaction costs, constraints on short selling, and taxations, among many others. Considering these impediments to efficiency, Sharpe[19] suggests a model to determine asset prices without negative holdings. According to this model, a portfolio containing only a small number of assets may be optimal, which is in line with the segmented-market CAPM and in agreement with the argument raised in the preceding article regarding the difficulties in handling the risk-reduction processes with many assets. Of course, with a model implying less than perfect diversification, the market portfolio may be M-V inefficient and the maximal gain from diversification may not be achieved. However, in regard to this matter, Sharpe concludes[20]:

Happily, technological advances and a greater understanding of the principles of financial economics are reducing costs and constraints of this type at a rapid pace. As a result, capital markets are moving closer to the conditions assumed in some of the simpler types of financial theory.

[17] See H. Levy and H. M. Markowitz, "Approximating Expected Utility by a Function of Mean and Variance," *American Economic Review*, 1979, p. 314.

[18] It has been shown empirically that increasing the number of assets in the portfolio beyond ten only slightly affects the reduction in the portfolio's risk. See J. L. Evans and S. H. Archer, "Diversification and Reduction in Dispersion: An Empirical Analysis," *Journal of Finance*, 1968. However, a more recent study reveals that the idiosyncratic risk tends to increase over time; hence, the number of stocks needed to obtain any given amount of portfolio diversification has also increased. See J. Y. Cambell, M. Lettau, B. G. Malkiel, and Y. Xu, "Have Individual Stocks become More Volatile? An Empirical Exploration of the Idiosyncratic Risk," *Journal of Finance*, 2001.

[19] W. F. Sharpe, "Capital Asset Prices with and without Negative Holdings," *Journal of Finance*, 1991.

[20] See Sharpe, *op. cit.*, p. 508.

One of the preceding citations also makes a valid point regarding the investment horizon: we agree that for, say, the one-year horizon investor, the beta calculated with weekly rates of returns is irrelevant and may be misleading. However, recall that the M-V and the CAPM assume that some investment horizon exists, and these two models are derived based on the assumed investment horizon. Indeed, we show in this book that using a shorter horizon than the actual holding period in the empirical tests may be a source of many biases in these tests.

We shall demonstrate the extent to which the M-V, the CAPM, and particularly beta, are employed. Table 1.1 presents a sample page of the standard financial analysis provided by Value Line. Specifically, the page provides financial information on the stock of American Medical Systems Holdings Inc., which trades on the NASDAQ. From this typical page, we can conclude two things. First, beta, which is reported at the top left corner of Table 1.1 (see zoom-in box), is a standard reported parameter as an index of risk. Second, professional investors recognize that the *ex-post* beta may be a misleading indicator of the *ex-ante* risk; thus, they add many other parameters that may aid in measuring the risk involved with the investment in the stock under consideration (e.g., see the SAFETY index and various financial ratios).

This is in line with our claim asserting that the relevant *ex-ante* beta (risk) is unknown; hence, academic and professional investors alike employ many other variables, presumably as a proxy to the *ex-ante* beta.

Tables 1.2.a and 1.2.b present sample financial analyses of some indexes, as well as individual stocks, respectively, supplied by Merrill Lynch's *Security Risk Evaluation*, also known as the "beta book." Unlike in Table 1.1, here the entire table is concerned with the CAPM: it reports the CAPM's alpha and beta, as well as some statistical information regarding these two CAPM variables.

The beta parameter is calculated by using the S&P 500 index as a proxy to the market portfolio. Thus, as expected, the S&P 500 index beta is 1, and the corresponding alpha is 0 with a correlation of $+1$ (see Table 1.2.a). Let us now demonstrate the given information in these pages with ATC HEALTHCARE INC given at the end of Table 1.2.b. As we can see, the beta of this stock is equal to 0.68; hence,

Table 1.1. *Value Line Beta*

AMER. MEDICAL SYS. NDQ-AMMD	RECENT PRICE 10.72	P/E RATIO 16.8 (Trailing: 19.5 Median: NMF)	RELATIVE P/E RATIO 1.24	DIV'D YLD Nil	VALUE LINE 175

TIMELINESS	2	Lowered 12/12/08
SAFETY	3	New 8/29/08
TECHNICAL	3	Raised 2/27/09
BETA	.85	(1.00 = Market)

| High: | 10.7 | 11.5 | 13.0 | 12.0 | 21.8 | 24.4 | 23.5 | 22.2 | 18.4 | 12.0 |
| Low: | 5.4 | 3.6 | 6.4 | 6.5 | 10.6 | 15.0 | 14.9 | 11.9 | 8.0 | 8.7 |

LEGENDS
18.0 x "Cash Flow" p sh
.... Relative Price Strength
2-for-1 split 3/05
Options: Yes
Shaded area: prior recession
Latest recession began 12/07

2012-14 PROJECTIONS

	Price	Gain	Ann'l Total Return
High	30	(+180%)	30%
Low	20	(+85%)	17%

Insider Decisions

	A	M	J	J	A	S	O	N	D
to Buy	0	0	0	0	1	0	0	0	0
Options	0	2	0	0	0	0	0	0	2
to Sell	0	2	0	0	1	0	0	0	2

Institutional Decisions

	1Q2008	2Q2008	3Q2008
to Buy	67	71	93
to Sell	72	59	56
Hld'd(000)	94092	91793	89206

Percent shares traded: 75 50 25

Target Price Range
2012 | 2013 | 2014

% TOT. RETURN 1/09

	THIS STOCK	VL ARITH. INDEX
1 yr.	-25.1	-39.3
3 yr.	-52.8	-36.6
5 yr.	-23.0	-18.3

American Medical Systems Holdings, Inc. was incorporated in Delaware in 1972. It began trading on the NASDAQ market August 15, 2000. 6,250,000 shares were offered at $5.50 by lead underwriter US Bancorp Piper Jaffray. A secondary offering followed in June 2001 with 7,000,000 shares priced at $8.20 again with US Bancorp Piper Jaffray as lead underwriters.

CAPITAL STRUCTURE as of 9/27/08
Total Debt $591.6 mill. Due in 5 Yrs. $217.8 mill.
LT Debt $591.6 mill.
Includes $373.8 mill. 3.25% sub notes ('36) cv. into 51.5318 shs. at $19.406.
(61% of Cap'l)
Leases, Uncapitalized Annual rentals $2.6 mill.
Pension Obligation $3.2 million

Preferred Stock None

Common Stock 73,290,774 shares as of 11/3/08
MARKET CAP: $775 million (Small Cap)

CURRENT POSITION

(\$MILL.)	2006	2007	9/27/08
Cash Assets	29.5	35.2	35.8
Receivables	91.3	106.5	92.4
Inventory (FIFO)	38.0	60.7	44.9
Other	74.8	23.0	14.0
Current Assets	233.6	225.4	187.1
Accts Payable	15.4	13.4	8.6
Debt Due	--	--	--
Other	87.1	68.7	41.5
Current Liab.	102.5	82.1	50.1

ANNUAL RATES

of change (per sh)	Past 10 Yrs.	Past 5 Yrs.	Est'd '05-'07 to '12-'14
Revenues	--	21.0%	11.0%
"Cash Flow"	--	1.0%	NMF
Earnings	--	-12.0%	NMF
Dividends	--	--	Nil
Book Value	--	10.5%	14.5%

Fiscal Year Begins	QUARTERLY REVENUES (\$ mill.)				Full Fiscal Year
	Mar.Per	Jun.Per	Sep.Per	Dec.Per	
2006	73.6	78.8	90.5	115.4	358.3
2007	108.4	116.5	109.0	130.0	463.9
2008	120.4	129.7	117.4	134.1	501.6
2009	120.0	128.0	125.0	132.0	505
2010	131.0	134.0	132.0	138.0	535

Fiscal Year Begins	EARNINGS PER SHARE A				Full Fiscal Year
	Mar.Per	Jun.Per	Sep.Per	Dec.Per	
2006	.16	d.12	d.82	.15	d.63
2007	.06	.10	.09	.08	.33
2008	.11	.19	.08	.20	.58
2009	.11	.17	.16	.21	.65
2010	.13	.18	.17	.22	.70

Cal-endar	QUARTERLY DIVIDENDS PAID				Full Year
	Mar.31	Jun.30	Sep.30	Dec.31	
2005					
2006	NO CASH DIVIDENDS BEING PAID				
2007					
2008					
2009					

	1999	2000	2001	2002	2003	2004	2005	2006	2007	2008	2009	2010	© VALUE LINE PUB., INC. 12-14	
	--	1.81	1.85	2.18	2.54	3.09	3.78	5.04	6.42	6.80	6.85	7.40	Revenues per sh	8.90
	--	.22	.31	.50	.60	.52	.75	d.38	.70	1.00	1.05	1.20	"Cash Flow" per sh	1.45
	--	.01	.10	.37	.43	.33	.55	d.63	.33	.58	.65	.70	Earnings per sh A	1.00
	--	--	--	--	--	--	--	--	--	--	Nil	Nil	Div'ds Decl'd per sh	Nil
	--	.03	.04	.03	.10	.05	.07	.31	.20	.10	.15	.15	Cap'l Spending per sh	.15
	--	1.97	2.72	3.14	3.63	3.69	4.36	3.96	4.54	5.05	5.65	6.30	Book Value per sh C	8.90
	--	55.53	63.92	65.00	66.27	67.48	69.53	71.06	72.26	73.50	74.00	74.50	Common Shs Outst'g B	76.00
	--	NMF	77.2	--	21.9	47.5	35.3	--	54.3	24.4	Bold figures are Value Line estimates		Avg Ann'l P/E Ratio	25.0
	--	NMF	3.96	--	1.25	2.51	1.88	--	2.88	1.51			Relative P/E Ratio	1.65
	--	--	--	--	--	--	--	--	--	--			Avg Ann'l Div'd Yield	Nil
	--	100.3	117.9	141.6	168.3	208.6	262.6	358.3	463.9	501.6	505	535	Revenues (\$mill)	675
	--	18.5%	25.2%	32.3%	31.1%	32.2%	29.6%	2.4%	22.3%	25.0%	26.0%	26.0%	Operating Margin	26.0%
	--	12.1	13.2	7.7	10.6	12.8	13.0	17.1	26.9	30.0	31.0	32.0	Depreciation (\$mill)	35.0
	--	.1	6.5	24.9	29.1	22.6	39.3	d43.9	23.5	42.5	48.0	52.5	Net Profit (\$mill)	76.5
	--	NMF	47.3%	38.7%	34.1%	60.0%	40.7%	--	47.4%	38.3%	39.0%	39.0%	Income Tax Rate	39.0%
	--	.1%	5.5%	17.6%	17.3%	10.8%	15.0%	NMF	5.1%	8.5%	9.5%	9.8%	Net Profit Margin	11.3%
	--	18.7	50.9	97.3	89.6	79.5	69.5	131.1	143.3	100	85.0	120	Working Cap'l (\$mill)	275
	--	38.5	24.0	18.0	9.2	--	--	713.5	666.2	560	475	435	Long-Term Debt (\$mill)	315
	--	109.5	174.1	204.3	240.3	249.2	302.9	281.2	328.2	370	420	470	Shr. Equity (\$mill)	675
	--	2.4%	4.3%	11.8%	12.0%	9.1%	13.0%	NMF	4.3%	6.0%	6.5%	7.0%	Return on Total Cap'l	8.5%
	--	.0%	3.8%	12.2%	12.1%	9.1%	13.0%	NMF	7.2%	11.5%	11.5%	11.5%	Return on Shr. Equity	11.5%
	--	.0%	3.8%	12.2%	12.1%	9.1%	13.0%	NMF	7.2%	11.5%	11.5%	11.5%	Retained to Com Eq	11.5%
	--	--	--	--	--	--	--	--	--	--	Nil	Nil	All Div'ds to Net Prof	Nil

BUSINESS: American Medical Systems Holdings, Inc. provides medical solutions to physicians treating men's and women's pelvic health conditions. It manufactures and markets surgical products to urologists, gynecologists, and urogynecologists for erectile restoration, benign prostatic hyperplasia, male urethral stricture, urinary and fecal incontinence, and pelvic organ prolapse. 2007 foreign sales, 28%. 2007 depr. rate: 29.1%. Has 1239 employees. Officer/directors own 5.8% of stock; Neuberger Berman, 14.3%, Franklin Resources, Inc., 10.4%, FMR LLC, 9.6%. (4/08 Proxy) President & Chief Executive Officer: Anthony Bihl III. Inc.: Delaware. Address: 10700 Bren Road West, Minnetonka, MN 55343. Tel.: (952) 930-6000. Internet: www.americanmedicalsystems.com.

American Medical Systems finished 2008 with a soft landing. Share earnings performance in the December interim was one third weaker than our estimate of $0.30 likely owing to the recession. Pelvic health procedures while not altogether elective, are somewhat deferrable, and an increase in postponements has been noted. Further, capital spending by hospitals and health care professionals has been clipped, with economic concerns at the forefront of many budgetary decisions. We look for a stagnant top-line in 2009 and have pared our bottom line by $0.15 to just a $0.07 improvement over the 2008 tally.

A healthy pipeline ought to enhance its long-term performance. The company has launched several new products since the last half of 2008 that are garnering interest, such as *Spectra*, a penile prosthesis and *Elevate*, a treatment for vaginal prolapse. In addition to these rollouts, product line extensions are in the works as well, such as additional applications of its Laser Therapy. Not all projects have gone smoothly. AMMD stopped development efforts on Ovion, its permanent contraception project. The company has

maintained its 10% budget for R & D, similar to previous years, despite a bleary economic picture.

Extension of its geographic footprint provides strong growth potential. Foreign sales now encompass 30% of total revenues and the company is gearing to expand that share with a push into new locations. Product acceptance, usage, and growth rates are increasing faster abroad than in the more mature domestic market. Its GreenLight Therapy has been approved for distribution in Brazil and China, both densely populated. Though the global economy has sputtered as well, the diversification ought to provide a buffer to weakness in AMMD's home market.

Short-term investors may want to consider this stock. AMMD shares have slipped a notch in Timeliness to (2), but are still a good choice in the coming year. We foresee a longer recovery due to slower top- and bottom-line growth given the recession. This curtails our 3- to 5-year outlook. Consequently, these shares now offer below average price performance to 2012-2014.

Mary Beth Wiedenkeller February 27, 2009

(A) Diluted earnings. Next earnings report due late April.
(B) In millions.
(C) Incl. intangibles. At 1/3/09: $799.7 million.

Company's Financial Strength	B
Stock's Price Stability	45
Price Growth Persistence	60
Earnings Predictability	10

To subscribe call 1-800-833-0046.

		ALPHA
		January 2007
		Price As of December 2006 Month End

Table 1.2.a. *Merrill Lynch, Pierce, Fenner & Smith, Inc. Market Sensitivity Statistics*

Ticker Symbol	Security Name		2006/12 Close Price	Beta	Alpha	R-Sqr	Resid. Std. Dev-n	Std. Error Beta	Std. Error Alpha	Adjusted Beta	No. of Observ.
DOWI	DOW JONES & CO	30 INDUSTRIALS	12,463.150	0.96	0.03	0.91	1.09	0.04	0.14	0.98	60
DJ 20	DOW JONES & CO	20 TRANS ACTUAL	4,560.200	0.94	0.65	0.42	3.86	0.14	0.50	0.96	60
DJ 15	DOW JONES & CO	15 UTIL ACTUAL	456.770	0.57	0.60	0.19	4.12	0.15	0.54	0.72	60
DJ 65	DOW JONES & CO	65 STOCK COMPOSITE	4,120.960	0.89	0.28	0.86	1.29	0.05	0.17	0.93	60
SPAINS	S & P 500	500 STOCKS	14,18.300	1.00	0.00	1.00	0.00	0.00	0.00	1.00	60

b. *Merrill Lynch, Pierce, Fenner & Smith, Inc. Market Sensitivity Statistics*

Ticker Symbol	Security Name		2006/12 Close Price	Beta	Alpha	R-Sqr	Resid. Std. Dev-n	Std. Error Beta	Std. Error Alpha	Adjusted Beta	No. of Observ.
AJSB	AJS BANCORP INC IIL		26.150	0.15	1.17	0.00	4.23	0.15	0.55	0.44	60
AKS	AK STL HLDG CORP		16.900	2.51	1.82	0.16	19.68	0.72	2.56	2.00	60
AMB	AMB PROPERTY CORP		58.610	0.19	1.40	0.00	4.75	0.17	0.62	0.46	60
AMB PL	AMB PROPERTY CORP	PFD SER L 6.50%	25.060	0.11	-0.03	-0.02	2.48	0.18	0.42	0.41	42
AMB PM	AMB PROPERTY CORP	PFD M 6.75%	25.760	0.09	0.03	-0.02	2.26	0.18	0.40	0.40	38
AMB PO	AMB PROPERTY CORP	PFD 7.0% SER O	25.940	0.11	0.08	-0.08	2.03	0.36	0.67	0.41	13
ACFL	AMC FINL HLDGS INC		1.750	-0.25	3.49	-0.01	18.57	0.68	2.41	0.17	60
ADL	ANDL INC	COM PAR 2006	4.070	2.67	1.48	0.06	32.74	1.19	4.26	2.11	60
AMCS	AMICAS INC		2.940	0.18	-0.20	-0.01	13.16	0.48	1.71	0.46	60
AMLJ	AML COMMUNICATIONS INC		0.900	2.09	3.69	0.02	36.31	1.32	4.72	1.72	60
AHN	**ATC HEALTHCARE INC**	**CLASS A**	**0.340**	**0.68**	**-1.66**	**0.00**	**17.53**	**0.64**	**2.28**	**0.79**	**60**

Source: http://newarkwww.rutgers.edu.

Figure 1.1. Beta of Google Inc. in Google Finance. *Source:* www.google.com/ finance.

it is considered to be a defensive stock because it has a lower beta than that of the market portfolio. The alpha is negative (–1.66); therefore, this stock underperformed, or graphically it is located below the Security Market Line (SML). The table also provides the standard deviation of these estimates; thus, one can test whether the estimates are significantly different from zero.

The important conclusion derived from Table 1.2 is that Merrill Lynch considers this CAPM information very relevant to investors and therefore has been supplying it for years. Another conclusion that can be drawn is that although beta is calculated based on the last 60 months, it is clear, once again, that the *ex-post* beta may not represent the *ex-ante* beta well. As a result, the financial service provider also suggests the "adjusted beta," which allegedly corrects for some biases and thus better represents the future beta.

Value Line and Merrill Lynch are far from being the only reporters of the CAPM's variables. Beta, for example, is a very popular measure provided in numerous top financial news and research websites. Figures 1.1, 1.2, 1.3, and 1.4 provide a screenshot of Google Finance, Yahoo! Finance, Reuters, and the *Financial Times*, respectively, reporting key financial information on the stock of Google Inc., which was chosen randomly for illustration purposes. In all

Figure 1.2. Beta of Google Inc. in Yahoo! Finance. *Source:* http://finance.yahoo.com.

four websites, beta is reported, strengthening the assertion that investors view it as an important parameter in investment decision making.

Furthermore, not only does beta appear in many websites, but many pages that guide users on how and where to find beta also exist. Figures 1.5 and 1.6 are extracts of a library guide on how to find beta, taken from the library website of Babson College in Wellesley, Massachusetts. Figure 1.5 presents an explanation on how to find beta in Value Line reports.

Similarly, Figure 1.6 presents an explanation on how to find beta with Bloomberg. This figure illustrates the process of obtaining the Goldman Sachs Group Inc. beta using the regression technique.

The figures accompanying this graph show the CAPM's alpha and beta, the R^2, along with some other statistical data. It is interesting to see that this figure also reports the adjusted beta and provides the

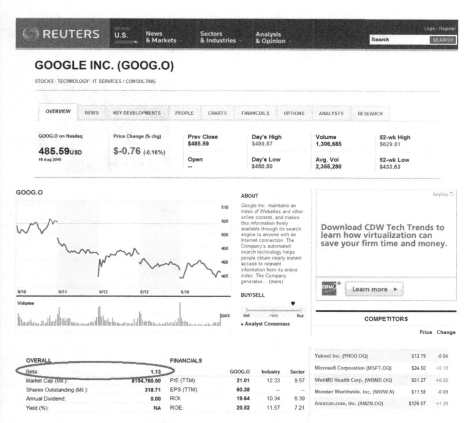

Figure 1.3. Beta of Google Inc. in Reuters. *Source:* http://www.reuters.com.

formula for calculating it. In the explanation to the adjusted beta, the following quote appears:

Bloomberg reports both the Adjusted beta and Raw beta. The adjusted beta is an estimate of the security's future beta. It uses the historical data of the stock, but assumes that a security's beta moves toward the market average over time.

This emphasizes the notion that practitioners, albeit not all of them, accept the CAPM as a useful investment tool, yet consider this model to be unstable over time. Hence, for investment purposes, the *ex-post* beta should be adjusted to obtain a better estimate of the *ex-ante* beta.

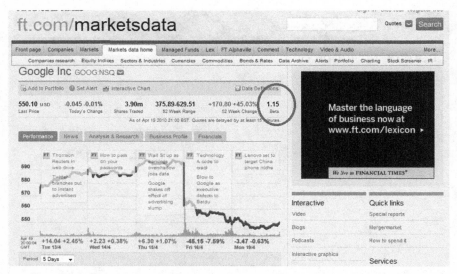

Figure 1.4. Beta of Google Inc. in the *Financial Times. Source:* http://markets. ft.com.

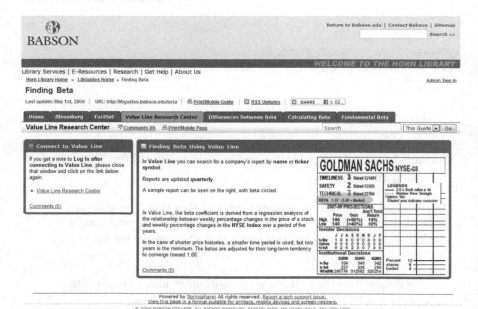

Figure 1.5. Finding Beta with Value Line Research Center. *Source:* http:// libguides.babson.edu taken from the Library Guides of Babson College in Wellesley, Massachusetts.

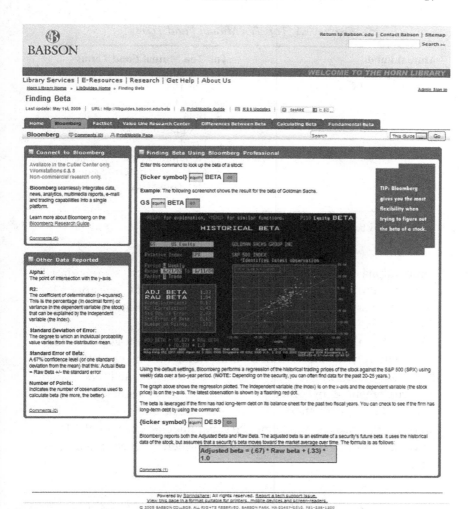

Figure 1.6. Finding Beta with Bloomberg. *Source:* http://libguides.babson. edu taken from the Library Guides of Babson College in Wellesley, Massachusetts.

Another standard financial website is BankRate.com, a provider of aggregate financial rate information as well as personal finance stories. Like PracticalStockInvesting.com, it also points out important financial terms, specifically, ten terms one should know when selecting a mutual fund.[21]

---

[21] See http://www.bankrate.com/finance/personal-finance/top-10-mutual-fund-terms-1.aspx.

Extract 1.1. *Top Ten Mutual Fund Terms*

Mutual Funds	Top Ten Mutual Fund Terms
Here's our guide to the 10 terms most likely to trip you up.	1. Expense ratio
	2. 12b-1fee
	3. Alpha
	4. Beta
	5. R-squared
	6. Load
	7. Redemption fee
	8. Contingent deferred sales load
	9. Net asset value
	10. Turnover

Source: www.bankrate.com, written by S. Brodrick.

Three (alpha, beta, and R-squared) of the ten terms are related to the CAPM, and professionals recommended that investors who consider investing in mutual funds be better acquainted with these terms.

Once again, we reach two conclusions: the first is that professionals heavily rely on the CAPM's parameters, and the second is that they realize that for investment purposes, these parameters should be complemented by other parameters (e.g., the stock turnover) because the *ex-post* beta on its own is not sufficient. One can always interpret the use of supplementary parameters as a method for adjusting the *ex-post* beta, such that it will better reflect the *ex-ante* beta.

1.3. THE ROLE OF THE MEAN-VARIANCE AND THE CAPITAL ASSET PRICING MODEL IN ACADEMIA

Virtually every finance professor who teaches a corporate finance course, and particularly one who teaches an investments course, devotes a substantial part of these courses to the M-V analysis and to the CAPM. Although providing a survey of the portions of the various finance textbooks devoted to these two topics is unnecessary, we would like to now report on the role that these two topics play in the two leading textbooks; one is a corporate finance textbook, and the other is an investments textbook.

The ninth edition of the *Investments* textbook, written by Bodie, Kane, and Marcus,[22] is divided into seven sections, each covering several chapters. Altogether the book contains twenty-eight chapters. About one-third of the book deals directly with topics related to the CAPM and the M-V analysis: namely, portfolio theory, performance measures, active portfolio management, and international diversification. Moreover, some other chapters of the book that deal with other subjects often refer to the CAPM's beta as well. Although we report here on one leading textbook, we stress that the preceding description of the specific investment textbook is typical to most popular textbooks used in the leading business schools in most countries in the Western world.

Let us now turn to the corporate finance textbooks, which have naturally been devoted mainly to other topics (e.g., net present value, capital structure, dividend policy, and so forth) rather than to the M-V efficiency analysis and the CAPM. Yet, even in corporate finance textbooks, a substantial portion is devoted to the M-V, the CAPM, and their implications to corporate finance, particularly to measuring the cost of capital. For example, in the tenth edition of the leading corporate finance textbook, *Principles of Corporate Finance*, written by Brealey, Myers, and Allen,[23] two full chapters are devoted to risk and return, portfolio theory, and the CAPM. Chapter 7, entitled "Introduction to Risk and Return," presents the concepts and the way to calculate portfolio risk and return. Chapter 8, called "Portfolio Theory and the Capital Asset Pricing Model," provides the basic principles of these two topics, as well as tests of the CAPM and alternative models.

Moreover, the CAPM also appears in other chapters. For example, an important application of the CAPM in corporate finance, which almost every corporate finance textbook covers, is related to the estimation procedure of the firm's cost of capital. In this textbook, this issue is addressed in chapter 9, entitled "Risk and the Cost of Capital." Brealey, Myers, and Allen suggest estimating the cost of equity as follows (using their notations):

$$r_{equity} = r_f + \beta_{equity}(r_m - r_f)$$

[22] Z. Bodie, A. Kane, and A. J. Marcus, *Investments*, 9th edition, McGraw-Hill, 2010.
[23] R. A. Brealey, S. C. Myers, and F. Allen, *Principles of Corporate Finance*, 10th edition, McGraw-Hill, 2011.

Namely, the estimate of the cost of equity is equal to the riskless interest rate, plus the difference between the average rate of return on the market portfolio and the riskless interest rate multiplied by the relevant CAPM's beta. Thus, the CAPM beta is employed in estimating the firm's cost of capital.

From these two sample textbooks, which have been very widely used and are very influential, we learn that the M-V efficiency analysis and the CAPM both play a major role in the academic education system, despite the criticisms published decades ago.

Finally, it is notable to mention that the preceding two textbooks also devote one chapter to behavioral finance, which plays a central role in the present book. In the investment book, this appears in chapter 12, entitled "Behavioral Finance and Technical Analysis." In the corporate textbook, this subject is discussed in chapter 13, entitled "Efficient Markets and Behavioral Finance." The inclusion of the behavioral finance topic in the latest editions of these two leading finance textbooks reflects, without a doubt, the recent evidence showing that investors sometimes make irrational investment decisions, casting doubt on the theoretical models, which assume rationality and market efficiency. The addition of behavioral finance chapters in finance textbooks is in the spirit of this book, which attempts to integrate the M-V rule and the CAPM, both of which assume that investors are rational, with experimental evidence and behavioral models suggested by psychologists, particularly Kahneman and Tversky,[24] revealing irrational investment choices.

The important role of the M-V and the CAPM, however, is not confined to textbooks. These two models also play a prominent role in academic research. Once again, a sample of the three leading academic journals in finance – namely, the *Journal of Finance*, the *Journal of Financial Economics*, and the *Review of Financial Studies* – is sufficient to reveal that the M-V analysis and the CAPM, and beta in particular, are also cornerstones in academic research, despite empirical and theoretical criticisms. Table 1.3 summarizes this sample's results. For each one of the three journals, a current issue was chosen randomly. Each issue contains eight to eleven articles. We can see that, on average, in each issue, almost 50% of the articles either

[24] See Kahneman and Tversky, *op. cit.*

Table 1.3. *Academic Journals Sample*

Journal	Year	Month	Volume	Issue	Total No. of Articles in Issue	No. of Articles Related to M-V & CAPM	Percentage of Articles Related to M-V & CAPM
Journal of Finance	2010	August	65	4	11	4	36
Journal of Financial Economics	2010	July	97	1	9	5	56
Review of Financial Studies	2010	August	23	8	8	4	50
						Mean	47

Source: http://newarkwww.rutgers.edu.

mention or more heavily rely on the CAPM, beta, the M-V analysis, or other related subtopics (e.g., the Sharpe ratio). Not surprisingly, this is in line with the previous sample results provided earlier in this chapter, implying that researchers are also not ready to let these two models go, despite their many criticisms.

At this point, it is simply impossible not to wonder how the M-V and the CAPM have served for years as pillars in the field of finance within the education system and of academic research in finance, despite the empirical, theoretical, and experimental criticisms of these two models. We devote this book to better understanding this challenging query.

1.4. SUMMARY

In this introductory chapter, we have briefly discussed the tension that probably every professor of finance experiences: on the one hand, there is well-documented empirical and experimental evidence against the M-V, and particularly against the CAPM. Yet, on the other hand, textbooks that devote a substantial amount of pages to these topics are still popularly used for teaching. This uneasiness is particularly felt by those professors who teach investment courses devoted mainly to the M-V and the CAPM but, in the same breath, discuss the Three-Factor Model, showing that the CAPM's beta has no explanatory power of the cross-section mean returns and suggesting other explanatory factors instead of beta. Furthermore, professors who teach corporate finance courses face a similar dilemma; if they teach that beta has zero explanatory power, how can they also teach that the CAPM's beta, which they have just rendered irrelevant, should be employed in estimating the firm's cost of equity? Editors of academic journals face the same problem: on one hand, they accept articles showing that beta has no explanatory power for publication while also accepting many papers that rely on the CAPM.

In this chapter, we show that despite the empirical and experimental evidence against the M-V and the CAPM, these two models are still "alive and kicking." We bring sample evidence from the practical world, as well as from the academic world, including the arenas of both research and teaching. We show that not only academics but also professional investors use these models. In addition, investment consultant firms widely employ these two models. However, it appears that both practitioners and academics do not ignore the criticisms of these two models but rather attempt to make adjustments and employ additional information to improve their M-V/CAPM–based estimates. Nonetheless, from both aspects, namely, the practitioners' and the academics' perspective, we reach the same conclusion: The M-V analysis and the CAPM play a prominent role in both worlds – a role that thus far has not been successfully replaced by another better model.

And yet, how can one explain the extensive use of these two models, despite all the evidence against them? This question, among others, will be answered in this book. Further on, we shall see that although PT contradicts EUT, the M-V model and the CAPM are intact in both EUT and CPT (which is the modified version of PT) frameworks. Hence, no contradiction exists between M-V and the CAPM normative models and the behavioral modified version of the PT model. Thus, we conclude that the Economic Nobel Committee did not make inconsistent decisions!

Finally, we hope that after reading this book, professors of finance will feel more comfortable teaching the M-V model and the CAPM and practitioners will feel more confident when implementing them in their business.

2

Expected Utility Theory

2.1. INTRODUCTION

Investors generally face many prospects available in the capital market to choose from (e.g., stocks, bonds, portfolios of assets, and mutual funds), where only one portfolio (which may contain one or many assets) of these prospects is selected. To be able to make systematic choices, one needs a method for ranking the various investments. Finding the appropriate method for ranking the various prospects is not an easy task. Moreover, many methods are available, each with its pros and cons, and researchers generally disagree on the appropriate ranking method to be employed. This chapter is devoted to the expected utility ranking method and to the existing criticisms of this method. In subsequent chapters, we show the relation of the Mean-Variance (M-V) analysis and the Capital Asset Pricing Model (CAPM) to the Expected Utility Theory (EUT), and we also show how deviations from the expected utility paradigm affect the M-V and the CAPM.

In the trivial and unrealistic situation in which certainty prevails, the prospects' ranking is a simple task, and the optimal prospect is the one with the highest monetary outcome. Thus, when certainty prevails, there is no dispute among researchers regarding the method for ranking the various prospects under consideration. However, things become more complex and less agreeable when the outcomes of the various prospects are uncertain. Moreover, to be able to rank prospects under uncertainty, one first needs to establish a measure characterizing the profitability (and maybe the risk) of each prospect

23

that technically enables us to rank the various prospects in an unambiguous way. Technically, this can be done, for example, by calculating the expected outcome of each prospect. By the mean outcome criterion, we have an unambiguous ranking: the prospect with the highest mean outcome should be selected. This does not mean that this ranking is optimal. For example, this ranking criterion ignores risk, which is a severe drawback. Suppose, for example, that prospect F yields $5 or $15 with equal probability; hence, the mean is $10. Prospect G yields –$10 or $40 with equal probability, and hence the mean is $15. By the expected outcome criterion, G should be selected. However, many would disagree with this choice because prospect G has the disadvantage of being exposed to losses, whereas prospect F does not.

Realizing this drawback (and others) of the expected outcome criterion, which is particularly extreme in the well-known St. Petersburg Paradox, Bernoulli and Cramer[1] suggested in the eighteenth century that investors derive some well-being or "utility" from each outcome and that they should select the prospect with the highest expected utility rather than the one with the highest expected monetary outcome. They suggested an ad hoc solution to the previously mentioned paradox, but no general new method was available for many years to come – until the expected utility model was formulated. Although several general formulations to the expected utility framework are available, this model is attributed mainly to von Neumann and Morgenstern,[2] who developed the EUT. They proved that under some mild axioms, every rational investor should select the prospect with the highest expected utility. Thus, they suggest that every investor would rank the various prospects by the expected utility criterion. Because each investor may have a different utility function, the ranking of the various prospects may vary across investors. Investment decision rules developed in finance and economics try to find some agreement regarding the ranking of the various prospects among a partial group of investors. Of course, the larger this partial group of investors, the more valuable the suggested investment

[1] For more details on this paradox and the various suggested solutions, see H. Levy, *Stochastic Dominance*, 2nd edition, Springer, United States, 2006.
[2] See J. von Neumann and O. Morgenstern, *Theory of Game and Economic Behavior*, 3rd Edition, Princeton University Press, N.J., 1953.

ranking criterion. For example, investment criteria, including the M-V rule, to which a large portion of this book is devoted, are nothing but special cases of the expected utility maximization principle, where under some assumption (e.g., a normal distribution), all risk-averse investors agree on the ranking of all available prospects composed solely from the risky assets.

In this chapter, we discuss the expected utility paradigm and its implication to risk-aversion and risk-seeking attitudes. We also discuss several alternative utility functions (preferences) suggested in the literature. In subsequent chapters, we discuss under what specific cases the expected utility criterion and the M-V criterion coincide. In the analysis that follows, "the pleasure of gambling" of the investor, if it exists, is not taken into account.

2.2. THE AXIOMS AND EXPECTED UTILITY THEORY

Suppose the investor faces two prospects, denoted by L_1 and L_2, respectively. These prospects are given by

$$L_1 = \{p_1 A_1, p_2 A_2 \ldots \ldots p_n A_n\}$$
and
$$L_2 = \{q_1 A_1, q_2 A_2, \ldots \ldots q_n A_n\} \tag{2.1}$$

where A_i is the ith monetary outcome, and it has a probability of occurring of p_i and q_i under prospects L_1 and L_2, respectively.

By the EUT, every rational investor should select the prospect with the highest expected utility, as long as some axioms hold. Therefore, we first present the axioms and then prove the expected utility maximization principle, and finally we discuss the meaning of the utility function.

a) The Axioms

One can prove the EUT by several sets of axioms. We prefer to present here the relatively large set of axioms (six axioms) because with this set, the proof is relatively simple.

Axiom 1: Comparability
Facing two monetary outcomes, say, A_i and A_j, the investor must be able to assert whether he or she prefers A_i to A_j, denoted by $A_i \succ A_j$ (when the sign $\succ$ means "prefer"); prefers A_j to A_i, denoted by $A_j \succ A_i$; or is indifferent about the two, denoted by $A_i \sim A_j$ (when the sign $\sim$ means "indifferent"). Thus, one of these three alternatives must exist.

Axiom 2: Continuity
If $A_3 \succ A_2 \succ A_1$, then there must be a probability, denoted by $U(A_2)$, such that the investor will be indifferent toward obtaining A_2 with certainty or an uncertain prospect composed from the other two outcomes. To be more specific, there must be a probability, $U(A_2)$, for which the following holds:

$$L = \{(1 - U(A_2))A_1, (U(A_2))A_3\} \sim A_1. \qquad (2.2)$$

First, note that this axiom is called the continuity axiom. The reason is that if one selects a probability $U(A_2)$ that is equal to zero, then by the monotonicity axiom (i.e., more money is preferred to less money; see the following), $L \prec A_2$, and if one selects this probability to be equal to 1, then $L \succ A_2$. Therefore, by *continuously* increasing this probability from zero to one, we must hit a probability such that $L \sim A_2$; hence, equation (2.2) holds. Of course, this probability is a function of the outcome A_2 and varies from one investor to another, reflecting the specific preference of each investor. Indeed, as we shall see, this probability is nothing but the utility attached to the outcome A_2.

Axiom 3: Interchangeability
Suppose you have a prospect given by

$$L_1 = \{p_1 A_1, p_2 A_2, p_3 A_3\}.$$

Furthermore, suppose also that you are indifferent regarding having A_2 and having prospect B, given by

$$B = \{q A_1, (1 - q)A_3\},$$

then, by this axiom, the following also must hold:

$$L_1 \sim L_1^C = \{p_1 A_1, p_2 B, p_3 A_3\},$$

where the superscript c indicates that the prospect is *complex*, as one of the outcomes (B) is by itself an uncertain prospect.

Axiom 4: Transitivity

Suppose that $L_1 \succ L_2$ and $L_2 \succ L_3$, then we must have that $L_1 \succ L_3$. Similarly, we have transitivity regarding the indifference property,

$$L_1 \sim L_2 \quad \text{and} \quad L_2 \sim L_3 \Rightarrow L_1 \sim L_3.$$

Axiom 5: Decomposability

As defined already, a *complex prospect* is one such that the outcomes are also prospects with uncertain returns, for example, L_1 and L_2, whereas a *simple prospect* is one in which the outcomes are monetary values, for example A_1 and A_2.

Suppose you face a complex prospect L given by

$$L^C = \{q L_1, (1 - q)L_2\}.$$

Also, it is given that $L_1 = \{p_1 A_1, (1 - p_1)A_2\}$ and $L_2 = \{p_2 A_1, (1 - p_2)A_2\}$.

Then the complex prospect can be rewritten as a simple prospect, namely,

$$L^C \sim L^S = \left\{ p^S A_1, (1 - p^S)A_2 \right\},$$

where

$$p^S = q p_1 + (1 - q)p_2,$$

and the superscripts s and c are added to indicate simple and complex prospects, respectively. The intuition of this axiom is that in the complex prospect, we have, after all, only two basic outcomes, A_1 and A_2 (hidden in L_1 and L_2); therefore, one can collect all probabilities of each of these two outcomes and write the complex prospect as a simple one. For example, suppose you face the following game: A dice is rolled and you get $100 if an even number or a five appears. Thus, you have a probability of getting $100 of 3/6 plus 1/6. Realizing that, you can collect these probabilities, having a probability of 4/6 to win $100.

Axiom 6: Monotonicity

With certainty, this axiom asserts that

$$A_2 > A_1 \Leftrightarrow A_2 \succ A_1.$$

Suppose now that the investor faces two uncertain prospects containing two outcomes, A_1 and A_2, where $A_2 > A_1$. These two prospects are given by

$$L_1 = \{(1-p)A_1, pA_2\}, \quad L_2 = \{(1-q)A_1, qA_2\}.$$

Then, by the monotonicity axiom, we have

$$p > q \Rightarrow L_1 \succ L_2.$$

Namely, the prospect with the higher probability assigned to the higher outcome (A_2) is preferred.

b) The Expected Utility Principle

Accepting these axioms, the principle of expected utility maximization follows, as given in Theorem 2.1.

Theorem 2.1: Facing uncertain (or certain) prospects that are mutually exclusive, the optimal prospect is the one with the largest expected utility.

Proof: Suppose one has to choose one of the following two prospects as given in equation (2.1):

$$L_1 = \{p_1 A_1, p_2 A_2 \ldots \ldots p_n A_n\} \quad \text{and} \quad L_2 = \{q_1 A_1, q_2 A_2 \ldots \ldots q_n A_n\},$$

when the outcomes are ordered such that $A_1 < A_2 < \ldots \ldots < A_n$ and the probabilities are p_i and $q_i,$ respectively.

First, note that by the comparability axiom, we can compare each pair of returns, and by the monotonicity axiom, we can conclude that, for example, with A_1 and A_2 the following holds:

$$A_2 \succ A_1 \Leftrightarrow A_2 > A_1.$$

The same relation holds corresponding to any two outcomes taken from these two prospects. Second, in practice, one may face two prospects that do not contain the same outcomes, in contrast to what is given in equation (2.1). However, one can easily overcome this seeming difficulty by simply taking all the outcomes of the two prospects under consideration, order them by size, and assign a probability of zero to outcomes that are irrelevant under the prospect under consideration.

Define the following simple prospect, $A_i^S = \{(1 - U(A_i)A_1, U(A_i)A_n\}$, where $U(A_i)$ is a probability assigned to A_i, namely, $0 \leq U(A_i) \leq 1$. By the monotonicity axiom, as A_i increases, $U(A_i)$ also increases. This is an important property, as we shall see later on; U serves not only as probability, but it also serves as the utility function, and it is important that the larger the outcome, the larger the utility of this outcome. By the continuity axiom for each A_i, there is a probability $U(A_i)$ such that $A_i \sim A_i^S$. By the interchangeability axiom we have

$$L_1 \sim L_1^C = \{p_1 A_1, p_2 A_2 \ldots \ldots p_i A_i^S \ldots \ldots p_n A_n\}.$$

Using the continuity, the interchangeability, and the transitivity axioms again and again, we replace all values A_i by A_i^S to obtain

$$L_1 \sim L_1^C = \{p_1 A_1^S, p_2 A_2^S \ldots \ldots, p_n A_n^S\},$$

where the superscript C indicates complex and simple prospects, respectively. (Note that for A_1, $U(A_1) = 0$; hence, $A_1 = A_1^S$ and for A_n, $U(A_n) = 1$; hence, $A_n = A_n^S$).

Finally, because all A_i^S are composed of A_1 and A_n, one can express this complex prospect as a simple prospect. Namely,

$$L_1 \sim L_1^C \sim L_1^S = \{(1 - p^S)A_1, p^S A_n\},$$

where

$$p^S = \Sigma p_i U(A_i).$$

We follow the same steps with prospect L_2 to obtain

$$L_2 \sim L_2^C \sim L_2^S = \{(1 - q^S)A_1, q^S A_n\},$$

where

$$q^S = \Sigma q_i U(A_i).$$

Finally, by the monotonicity axiom, we have

$$p^S = \Sigma p^i U(A_i) > q^S = \Sigma q^S U(A_i) \Leftrightarrow L_1^S \succ L_2^S,$$

and by the transitivity axiom, it implies that $L_1 \succ L_2$. To summarize, we proved that

$$\Sigma p_i U(A_i) > \Sigma q_i U(A_i) \Rightarrow L_1 \succ L_2.$$

If U is a utility function, it implies that the prospect with the larger expected utility is preferred, which completes the proof. Although this is the common way to present the EUT, a more precise way to assert this theorem is as follows: If there are two prospects, and the investor prefers one prospect over the other, one can always find a monotonic nondecreasing function such that the preferred prospect has a higher expected value of this function. We call this function a utility function because it represents the investor's preference.

We turn next to discuss the meaning of U and its interpretation as a utility function, reflecting the investor's preference.

2.3. IS $U(A)$ A PROBABILITY OR A UTILITY?

In the proof of the expected utility principle, we assume that $U(A)$ is a probability function (see the continuity axiom). Yet we claim that this function is also the utility function reflecting the investor's preference. So is it a probability or a utility function? Actually, this function is both a probability and a utility function. It is a probability function by construction; see the continuity axiom (equation 2.2). To see why U also reflects preference, recall that by the continuity axiom, we are looking for a probability $U(A_2)$ such that the investor is indifferent toward getting the uncertain prospect or getting A_2 with certainty (see equation 2.2). Because the value $U(A_2)$ varies across the various investors depending on the inventors' tastes regarding the uncertainty of the prospect under consideration, it actually reflects the investor's preference function or the investor's utility function.

The fact that this function is bound between zero and one (see equation 2.2) is not confining because the utility function can be changed by a positive linear transformation without affecting choices. To see this, suppose x and y are random variables (financial outcomes; for simplicity, we assume here zero initial wealth) corresponding to two prospects, and the investor has to choose one of them. By theorem 2.1, we look at the expected utility of $U(x)$ and $U(y)$, where each of these two functions is a probability function; hence, they are bound between zero and one. However, one can conduct the following positive linear transformation:

$$U^\bullet(x) = a + bU(x) \quad \text{and} \quad U^\bullet(y) = a + bU(y),$$

where $b > 0$. Then, it is obvious that the following holds:

$$EU^\bullet(x) > EU^\bullet(y) \Leftrightarrow EU(x) > EU(y),$$

because the parameter a is cancelled out and b is positive. Thus, if x is preferred over y with the utility function U, which is bound between zero and one, the same preference is intact also with the unbound utility function $U^\bullet$. Therefore, one can switch from the "probability" function U, by a linear transformation, to any function that is not a probability function, which depends on the selected parameters a and b. Both functions U and $U^\bullet$ can serve as utility functions for ranking choices, and both provide the same ranking. Namely, given *any* set of choices, an individual characterized by a utility function U and another individual characterized by a utility function $U^\bullet$ will always have the same ranking and make the same choices. Thus, economically, they are indistinguishable. In fact, the utility can be even negative (choose negative parameter a) because what is important in an expected utility paradigm is the ranking of the numbers attached to each investment, not the absolute size of the expected utility.

Finally, note that U is a monotonic nondecreasing function (see the proof of theorem 2.1, in which we show that the higher the monetary outcome, A_j, the higher the $U(A_j)$). This implies that $U'(x) \geq 0$. Because the parameter $b > 0$, we have that also after the transformation that $U^{\bullet\prime}(x) \geq 0$. To sum up, the probability function is also the utility function and both, as well as all transformed preferences, have non-negative first derivative, implying that more wealth is always preferred to less wealth.

2.4. VARIOUS ATTITUDES TOWARD RISK

We first discuss the commonly assumed risk aversion and the implied risk premium, and then we discuss risk seeking, which is unlikely to prevail in the whole range of wealth; finally, we discuss mixed preference-revealing risk seeking in some ranges of possible wealth and risk aversion in other ranges. In all cases, we assume that the utility function is monotonic nondecreasing in wealth.

First note that by the monotonicity axiom, $U'(x) \geq 0$. We define the following basic risk attitudes for all monotone nondecreasing utility functions:

a) Risk neutral: $U''(x) = 0$.
b) Risk averter: $U''(x) \leq 0$ and for some x, $U''(x) < 0$.
c) Risk seeker: $U''(x) \geq 0$ and for some value x, $U'' > 0$.

These three utility functions are demonstrated in Figure 2.1. Suppose the investor faces an uncertain prospect with outcomes x_1 and x_2 (for simplicity of presentation, these values include the initial wealth, or the initial wealth is assumed to be zero) with a mean of $E(x)$; see Figure 2.1. The risk-averse investor is indifferent about obtaining the uncertain prospect or obtaining the certain amount of x^*, because both options yield the same expected utility. Thus, to get rid of the risk, a risk averter is willing to give up, on average, the positive amount of dollars of:

$$\pi = E(x) - x^*,$$

where π is called the *risk premium* (see Figure 2.1).

To demonstrate the concept of risk premium in practice, let us provide some figures. An investment in the New York Stock Exchange index for a long period yields on average (arithmetic average) about 11% per year, whereas the annual rate of return on safe U.S. Treasury bills, on average, is only about 4%. Why do investors invest in such a low-return financial vehicle when an investment with an average of 11% per year is available? The reason for such investment behavior is that one cannot guarantee that the 11% will be earned every year. Moreover, although the average is 11% per year, a return of –50% may be realized, as occurred in the economic crises of 2008. Thus, the investment in stocks is risky, and some, albeit not all, investors are ready to give up, on average, 7% in return to get rid of the risk. Indeed, the difference between the average return on the risky asset and the riskless asset is called the "market-risk premium."

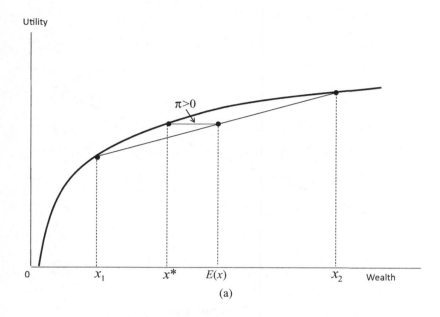

(a)

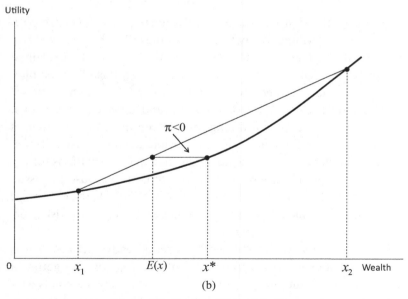

(b)

Figure 2.1. Various Risk Attitudes.

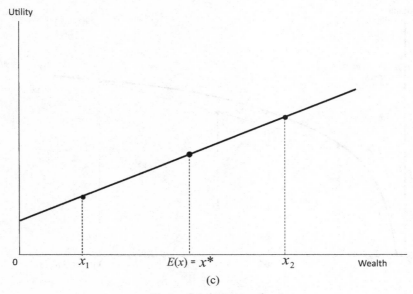

(c)

Figure 2.1 (*continued*)

Of course, the higher the degree of risk aversion, the higher the risk premium one is willing to pay to get rid of the risk. The observed risk premium in the United States is much larger than can be explained by a plausible degree of risk aversion. Therefore, this observed phenomenon is called the *equity premium puzzle*.[3] Although there are decades with a quite low-risk premium and even decades with a negative-risk premium, for a long time (a century), the premium is relatively high, and one needs an implausible degree of risk aversion to justify it – hence, an economic puzzle. Several explanations for the observed risk premium have been suggested, but because this issue constitutes a deviation from the main topic of this book, the only point we would like to make here is that the higher the degree of risk aversion, the higher the expected risk premium.

In contrast to a risk averter, as discussed already, a risk seeker is indifferent about getting a certain amount of dollars of x^* or getting a lower expected value, $E(x)$; see Figure 2.1b. Thus, this person is willing, on average, to pay π for the privilege to be exposed to the risk.

---

[3] See R. Mehra and E. Prescott, "The Equity Premium: A Puzzle," *Journal of Monetary Economics*, 1985.

Between these two extremes, we have the risk-neutral investor, who is indifferent to the risk exposure: He or she is neither willing to pay to get rid of the risk nor willing to pay for the privilege to be exposed to the risk. Thus, a risk-neutral investor is indifferent about choosing a risky prospect or obtaining its expected return with certainty.

A "utility function" is a function of wealth, denoted as w. Arrow[4] and Pratt[5] analyzed the relation between the utility function and the risk premium. It is assumed that an investor, who has an initial wealth denoted as w, faces additional random income, with a small variance denoted by σ^2. Namely, a small risk is assumed. They have shown that with "small risks," the risk premium is, approximately, given by

$$\pi \cong -\frac{\sigma^2}{2} \frac{U''(w)}{U'(w)}, \tag{2.3}$$

where w is the investor's wealth and the variance measures the dispersion of the outcomes (i.e., it measures the risk involved). It can be easily shown from equation (2.3) that the risk premium that a risk-neutral investor is willing to pay to get rid of risk is zero ($U'' = 0$) (see Figure 2.1.c), that a risk-averter investor ($U'' < 0$) is willing to pay a positive amount to get rid of the risk (hence, this investor tends to buy an insurance policy) (see Figure 2.1.b), and that for a risk seeker ($U'' > 0$), the premium is negative (hence, this investor is willing to have a lower expected wealth than the certain available wealth as long as he or she has the privilege to be exposed to risk, and this investor tends also to buy lottery tickets) (see Figure 2.1.b). Obviously, the investor's behavior may change with wealth. For example, an investor with moderate wealth may decide to insure her house, but the same investor who becomes rich may decide not to insure. This is consistent with the fact that risk premium is a function of wealth.

Because the variance is a constant number that does not include the wealth (it is the variance of the random variable added to the initial wealth), it is common to have the following two measures of

---

[4] K. J. Arrow, *Essays in the Theory of Risk Bearing*, North-Holland, Amsterdam, 1971.
[5] J. W. Pratt, "Risk Aversion in the Small and in the Large," *Econometrica*, 1964.

risk aversion: absolute risk aversion (ARA) and relative risk aversion (RRA):

$$\text{ARA measure: } r_u = -\frac{U''(w)}{U'(w)} \tag{2.4}$$

and

$$\text{RRA measure: } R_u = -w\frac{U''(w)}{U'(w)}. \tag{2.5}$$

Most economists agree that investors reveal a decreasing ARA. The implication is that the more wealth the investor has, the less he or she is willing to pay to get rid of a given risk. Regarding the RRA characteristics, there is less disagreement. However, it is common to use in research the Constant Relative Risk Aversion (CRRA) utility function. The implication of this function is that as the investor becomes wealthier, he or she keeps the same *proportion* of risky asset and the riskless asset in the portfolio.

The common utility functions employed by researchers are as follows:

1. $U(w) = -e^{-\alpha w}$, exhibiting CARA, which is equal to α.
2. $U(w) = \frac{w^{1-\alpha}}{1-\alpha}$, exhibiting CRRA, which is equal to α. The log function $U(w) = \log(w)$ is a specific case of this function when $\alpha = 1$.[6]
3. It is also common to use the quadratic utility function given by:
4. $U(w) = w - \alpha w^2$, where $\alpha > 0$. This utility function has the undesired property of increasing ARA (denoted by IARA), yet it is widely employed because it implies the M-V rule and because it is relatively easy to handle mathematically, obtaining results that are otherwise impossible to achieve.

---

[6] Note that this claim is intact, despite the fact that the function is not defined at the point $\alpha = 1$. At this point, we have that the function is equal to the derivative of the numerator divided by the derivative of the denominator at point $\alpha = 1$. Namely, $(\partial(w^{1-\alpha})/\partial\alpha)/\partial(1-\alpha)/\partial\alpha$. Define $y = w^{1-\alpha}$ to obtain $\log y = (1-\alpha)\log w$; hence, $y'/y = -\log w$, and $y' = -(w^{1-\alpha})\log w$, which at point $\alpha = 1$ is equal to $-\log w$. Because the derivative of the denominator is -1, we finally get that at this point the function is equal to $\log w$.

As additional and more diverse research is published on decision making under uncertainty (theoretical as well as experimental), and because some research supports EUT and some refutes it, we conclude that there is no one theory that fits all situations. It is possible that EUT fits well in some situations, but in other situations, this model reveals paradoxes: the theoretical predictions of EUT are in contrast to what most people would experimentally select.

In this book, we rely on EUT as well as other theoretical frameworks that contradict expected utility; therefore, we now discuss some paradoxes of expected utility paradigm and briefly present the Prospect Theory (PT) and Cumulative Prospect Theory (CPT), which compete head to head with the traditional EUT. Later in this book, we expand CPT and show that under very weak conditions, the M-V efficient frontier and the CAPM are intact in both the EUT and the CPT frameworks.

2.5. PREFERENCE WITH RISK AVERSION AND RISK SEEKING

So far, we assume either risk aversion or risk seeking, but these are not the only two possibilities. Actually, to be able to explain some economic behavior and subjects' choices, it is suggested in the literature that the utility function has a risk-seeking as well as a risk-aversion segment or segments. In Chapter 3, we discuss the preferences suggested by Markowitz[7] as early as 1952 and the CPT preference suggested by Kahneman and Tversky in 1979.[8] As we shall see, both these preferences have risk-seeking and risk-aversion segments.

This type of function was suggested by Friedman and Savage[9] in 1948, which probably inspired the other nonconcave utility function suggested later in the literature. Figure 2.2 demonstrates this utility function. It is concave in relatively low-modest wealth, which explains why the people belonging to this group purchase insurance, which is an "unfair" gamble. It is an unfair gamble because, on average, the insured pays the insurer more than what he or she ever gets back as

---

[7] H. M. Markowitz, "The Utility of Wealth," *Journal of Political Economy*, 1952.

[8] D. Kahneman and A. Tversky, "Prospect Theory of Decisions Under Risk," *Econometrica*, 1979.

[9] M. Friedman and L. J. Savage, "The Utility of Choices Involving Risk," *Journal of Political Economy*, 1948.

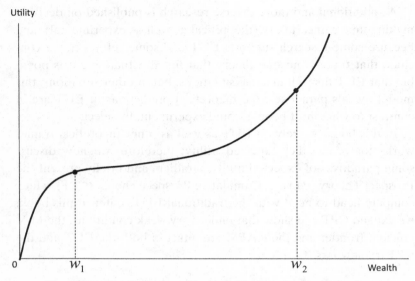

Figure 2.2. The Preference Suggested by Friedman and Savage.

compensation. Then we have a convex segment, which explains why people are willing to purchase lottery tickets. People with wealth in the middle range may buy insurance policies and lottery tickets simultaneously.

Thus, this preference explains observed phenomena regarding people's choices in practice to distinguish from subjects' choices in laboratories. This preference emphasizes the importance of the initial wealth to EUT. A person with initial wealth below W_1 may decide to purchase insurance, and the same person being richer, with wealth above W_1, say W_2, will reject the suggested insurance. Thus, the initial wealth plays an important role in decisions made in EUT's framework. As we shall see, by CPT, the initial wealth does not play any role. Actually, this is one of the main criticisms of CPT on EUT – that it is claimed that experimentally people make decisions based on the *change* of wealth rather than on the *total* wealth.

2.6. CRITICISMS OF THE EXPECTED UTILITY THEORY

The criticisms of EUT are divided into two categories. First, it is claimed that EUT in general, and particularly the commonly used specific utility functions, lead to paradoxical results. Second, it is demonstrated experimentally that subjects make choices that contradict EUT. We discuss these two categories as follows:

a) Allais Paradox

Allais[10] points out the following paradox. Suppose that an investor has to select between prospects A and B given as follows:

$$A = \{\$ 1 \text{ million with probability } 1\}$$

and

$$B = \{\$0, \$1 \text{ million, or } \$5 \text{ million with probabilities}$$
$$\text{of } 0.01, 0.89, \text{ and } 0.10, \text{ respectively}\}$$

In this case, most investors choose prospect A, implying that (all monetary figures are in millions):

$$1U(1) > 0.01U(0) + 0.89U(1) + 0.1U(5)$$
$$\Rightarrow 0.01U(0) + 0.1U(5) < 0.11U(1). \tag{2.6}$$

Now suppose that investors face prospects C and D given by:

$$C = \{\$0 \text{ or } \$1 \text{ million with probabilities}$$
$$\text{of } 0.89 \text{ and } 0.11, \text{ respectively}\}$$

and

$$D = \{\$0 \text{ or } \$5 \text{ million with probabilities}$$
$$\text{of } 0.9 \text{ and } 0.1, \text{ respectively}\}.$$

In this case, most investors prefer prospect D, implying that

$$0.9U(0) + 0.1U(5) > 0.89U(0) + 0.11U(5)$$
$$\Rightarrow 0.01U(0) + 0.1U(5) > 0.11U(1). \tag{2.7}$$

Of course, equations (2.6) and (2.7) are in contradiction, raising doubt about the validity of EUT. The choice of A in the first decision and D in the second decision by the same person violates EU; that is, one

---

[10] M. Allais, "Le Comportement de l'Homme Rationnel devant le Risque: Critique des Postulats et Axiomes de l'Ecole Americaine," *Econometrica*, 1953.

(or more) of the axioms described in Section 2.2 are violated. This suggests that maybe investors make decisions by other criteria, and not by the EUT.

b) Criticism of the Commonly Employed Utility Functions

As mentioned, the quadratic preference is not acceptable because of the following two drawbacks: First, it reveals an IARA, implying that the wealthier the investor is, the larger the amount of money he or she is willing to pay to get rid of a given risk. To see this, note that the quadratic utility function is given by

$$U(x) = x + bx^2, \quad \text{where} \quad b < 0.$$

The ARA corresponding to this function is given by

$$\pi = -\frac{U''(x)}{U'(x)} = -\frac{2b}{1+2bx} \quad \text{and} \quad \partial\pi/\partial x = \frac{4b^2}{(1+2bx)^2} > 0.$$

Thus, the wealthier the investor is, the larger the risk premium. This is an unacceptable result because, in practice, we observe the opposite: the wealthier the investor is, the smaller the risk premium she is willing to pay to get rid of a given risk.

Another drawback of this function is that beyond a certain point, where the quadratic function reaches its maximum, it starts to decline, implying negative marginal utility, which contradicts the monotonicity axiom, asserting that the more wealth the investor has, the better off that investor is.

The expressed utility function with a CARA also has a severe drawback: Markowitz, Reid, and Tew[11] show that an investor with such preference would turn down a prospect yielding an infinite outcome, a case well known as a prospect with a "blank check." To demonstrate this idea, consider a prospect yielding zero outcome or a "blank check," each event with a 50:50 chance. A simple calculation with the exponential utility function reveals that the expected utility of the "blank check" prospect is:

$$EU(x) = -1/2e^{-0} - 1/2e^{-\infty} = -1/2(1) - 1/2(0) = -1/2,$$

[11] H. M. Markowitz, D. W. Reid, and B. V. Tew, "The Value of a Blank Check," *Journal of Portfolio Management*, 1994.

where for simplicity, and without loss of generality, we assume in the calculation that $\alpha = 1$. Now suppose that the subject is offered to obtain a certain amount of money. What is the certain amount of money, x, the investor is willing to get so that he or she is exactly indifferent between getting the uncertain prospect given previously and the certain amount? A simple calculation reveals that:

$$-e^{-x} = -1/2,$$

and hence the certainty equivalent is $0.69.

This is a paradox: presumably, no investor would say that he or she is indifferent about getting $0.69 for sure and getting zero and an infinite amount of money with a 50:50 chance.

Finally, risk aversion for relatively modest stakes also leads to a paradox, casting doubt on the validity of the EUT with risk aversion. Hansson[12] shows that a person who is exactly indifferent about gaining $7 with certainty or a gamble with a 50:50 chance yielding either $0 or $21, for all possible initial wealth, would prefer a certain gain of $7 to any gamble, where the chance of winning a positive amount of money is less than 40% – no matter how large the monetary gain. This, of course, is an unacceptable result. In a similar argument, Rabin[13] shows that if an investor turns down gambles where he or she loses $100 or gains $110, each with 50% probability, and if this decision is intact for all levels of wealth, the investor will also turn down a prospect with a loss of $1,000 or a gain of any sum of money. This is, of course, unacceptable because most, if not all, investors would not turn down a 50:50 bet of losing $1,000 or winning a million dollars, let alone winning an even larger amount. Therefore, Rabin suggests that the CPT, rather than the EUT, may better explain people's choice without having such paradoxes. In particular, Rabin's paradox does not exist when one makes decisions based on the change of wealth rather than on the total wealth. As we shall see in this book, the M-V rule, as well as the CAPM, is intact also when the initial wealth is ignored as well as for nonconcave utility functions. Thus, Rabin's

[12] B. Hansson, "Risk Aversion as a Problem of Conjoint Measurement," *Decision, Probability, and Utility*, P. Gardenfors and N. E. Sahlin (editors), Cambridge University Press, 1988.

[13] M. Rabin, "Risk Aversion and Expected Utility Theory: A Calibration Theorem," *Econometrica*, 2000.

paradox questions the validity of EUT with risk aversion. However, it does not contradict the M-V criterion and the CAPM, because these two paradigms are intact with total wealth and change of wealth alike. We discuss these issues in detail in the coming chapters.

To sum up, the objections to EUT listed so far are as follows: Allais shows that investors do not behave according to EUT when small probabilities are involved, one of the outcomes is zero monetary value, and other outcomes are very high (e.g., $1 million). As we see later in this book, when a zero outcome and small probabilities are involved, indeed, deviation from EUT may occur. The specific utility function, $-e^{-\alpha x}$, is rejected because it leads to the "blank check" paradox. Risk aversion in the whole range is rejected because it leads to rejection of a prospect with any amount of positive reward. Of course, this is true only if the modest prospect suggested by Rabin is rejected at all levels of hypothetical wealth. The quadratic preference is rejected because it reveals increasing ARA. Thus, we find mainly that some specific preferences are rejected; or, under some conditions, risk aversion is rejected; and, with some specific and unique prospects, EUT is also rejected.

We shall see in this book that the M-V and the CAPM do not rely on the preceding specific preferences. Moreover, under some mild conditions, these models are theoretically valid, even when risk aversion is rejected; that is, preference has some risk-seeking segment.

c) Cumulative Prospect Theory: Experimental Findings that Contradict Expected Utility Theory

Kahneman and Tversky[14] (K&T) and Tversky and Kahneman[15] (T&K) have conducted many experiments in which the subjects have to choose between two prospects. They find that investors maximize the expected value of some preference that is neither concave nor convex. Moreover, they find that the following points characterized the choices of the subjects:

1. The investor makes investment decisions based on the *change* of wealth rather than the *total* wealth, contradicting EUT. Thus,

---

[14] D. Kahneman, and A. Tversky, *op. cit.*
[15] A. Tevrsky and D. Kahneman, "Advances in Prospect Theory: Cumulative Representation of Uncertainty," *Journal of Risk and Uncertainty*, 1992.

according to K&T, the investor is seeking maximization of the expected value of some function $V(x)$, whereas by EUT the investor should maximize the expected value of some function $U(w + x)$, where w is the initial wealth and x is the change of wealth. Moreover, if indeed the change of wealth rather than total wealth is relevant for investment decision making, the concepts of ARA and RRA lose ground because these two concepts are related to the relevant point on the utility function, which is determined by the investor's wealth.

2. The investors do not employ objective probabilities but rather decision weights. Specifically, investors overweigh small probabilities – which contradicts EUT – and can explain paradoxes such as that suggested by Allais.

3. Unlike what is assumed in most economic models, K&T claim that risk aversion does not prevail in the whole range of outcomes: rather, risk seeking prevails in the negative domain (losses), whereas risk aversion prevails in the positive domain (gains).

4. Loss aversion: The segment of the utility function corresponding to the negative domain is steeper than the segment corresponding to the positive domain.

Whereas points 1 and 2 strictly contradict EUT, points 3 and 4 are not in contradiction to EUT: They are in contradiction to the commonly employed concave utility functions but not in contradiction to EUT. Moreover, points 3 and 4 can explain some paradoxes within EUT. For example, the loss aversion and the change in wealth rather than total wealth arguments can explain Rabin's paradox and the risk premium paradox.[16] Indeed, although it is common to assume risk aversion in the whole domain of wealth, not all economists claim that risk aversion prevails. To give only a few examples, recall that as early as 1948, Friedman and Savage[17] suggested that to be able to explain the existence of insurance and lotteries, investors typically have a utility function with a concave as well as convex segment. Also Markowitz[18] suggests that the utility function is not concave in

---

[16] See S. Benartzi and R. Thaler, "Myopic Loss Aversion and the Equity Risk Premium Puzzle," *Quarterly Journal of Economics*, 1995, and Mehra and Prescott, *op. cit.*

[17] M. Friedman and L. J. Savage, *op. cit.*

[18] H. M. Markowitz, *op. cit.*

the whole domain. Moreover, he suggests loss aversion (although not using this term) because the segment of the preference corresponding to the losses is steeper than the segment corresponding to the gains.

Thus, having a nonconcave utility function with loss aversion as suggested by K&T is not in contradiction to EUT: On the contrary, such utility functions are employed by economists, as we shall see in the book, to explain investor's choices within EUT framework. Furthermore, such preference is not in contradiction to the M-V and the CAPM paradigms.

d) Roy's Safety-First Rule

Roy[19] raises strong objection to EUT. When risk and returns are considered, Roy suggests that there is some disaster level, denoted by d, and the primary goal of the investor is to minimize the probability of having an outcome below d. Thus, according to Roy, the goal of the investor is not to maximize expected utility but rather to minimize the following probability:

$$P_r(x < d),$$

where d is some level of outcome such that any outcome below it is considered a disaster. Of course, the disaster level is a subjective measure. The objection to EUT by Roy is strong, and he writes:

In calling in a utility function to our aid, an appearance of generality is achieved at the cost of a loss of practical significant and applicability in our results. A man who seeks advice about his actions will not be grateful for the suggestion that he maximizes expected utility. (Roy, p. 433)

We show later in the book that Roy's Safety-First Rule does not contradict EUT; rather, it implies a specific preference. With this specific preference, the M-V frontier and the CAPM analysis are intact.

2.7. SUMMARY

The St. Petersburg paradox was no doubt the main trigger for the development of EUT. Bernoulli and Cramer suggested an ad hoc

---

[19] A. D. Roy, "Safety First and Holding of Assets," *Econometrica*, 1952.

solution to the paradox. After many years, a formal EUT has been established. After making some reasonable axioms, it has been proved that any rational investor should select the prospect with the highest expected utility. By EUT, the utility function must be nondecreasing in wealth, but no claim is made as to whether the utility is concave or convex.

Most economic models of decision making under uncertainty assume that expected utility theory is intact. Moreover, risk aversion is commonly assumed in these models, and Arrow and Pratt have developed risk aversion measures. Yet some economists claim that EUT is intact, but to explain people's behavior, the utility function must have convex as well as concave segments.

The barrage of criticisms of EUT started as early as 1952. Roy conceptually rejects EUT as not being practical. Allais demonstrates with a unique example that EUT is contradicted. Some specific preferences (the exponential and the quadratic functions) are criticized for inducing paradoxes in choices. Rabin claims that EUT with risk aversion also leads to paradoxical choices. K&T show experimentally that people's choices contradict expected utility. Moreover, by accepting their paradigm, many of the paradoxes, including Rabin's paradox, are solved.

To summarize, EUT and, particularly risk aversion, in the whole range of wealth is criticized. We shall see in this book that although EUT may not be intact in some cases, under some mild conditions, the M-V and the CAPM are intact. Moreover, these models are also intact under CPT (i.e., even when the preference is not concave in the whole range of wealth).

3

Expected Utility and Investment Decision Rules

3.1. INTRODUCTION

In this chapter, we discuss several stochastic dominance (SD) investment criteria, of which some are quite old and well known and some are relatively new and therefore not as widely known. As we see later in this book, we employ some of these SD investment criteria in the analysis of the Capital Asset Pricing Model (CAPM) in the Prospect Theory (PT) framework.

We discuss First-degree SD (FSD), Second-degree SD (SSD), Prospect SD (PSD), and Markowitz's SD (MSD). All these SD rules are derived in the expected utility framework. The FSD criterion is a cornerstone also in the Cumulative Prospect Theory (CPT) framework and is, in fact, imperative to all the relevant competing investment decision paradigms. Actually, to derive the FSD rule, one needs only to assume monotonicity: the more wealth one has, the better off one is. This is a reasonable assumption, and almost all economic models of decision making assume monotonicity. In terms of the utility function, this assumption implies that U' is non-negative. Indeed, in some of the proofs of expected utility theory (EUT), the FSD requirement replaces the monotonicity axiom.

To derive the SSD rule, one needs only to add the risk aversion assumption to the monotonicity assumption. Namely, U'' is nonpositive. To drive the PSD rule, one needs to assume that the preference is S-shaped, with risk seeking in the negative domain and risk aversion in the positive domain, as suggested by CPT. Finally, in employing the MSD investment criterion, one assumes a preference with risk aversion in the negative domain and risk seeking in the positive domain (a reverse S-shape, which is opposite to the CPT preference).

All these investment decision rules are important as they relate to various assumptions regarding preference – assumptions regarding which there is a disagreement among researches from different disciplines. Figure 3.1 illustrates four typical preferences corresponding to FSD, SSD, PSD, and MSD, respectively.

In the next section, we state the four SD criteria and prove the sufficiency of the FSD and SSD rules without proving the necessity side of the proofs. PSD and MSD rules are stated without the proofs, which are very similar to the SSD proof. We emphasize the FSD and SSD rules because we employ mainly these two rules in the rest of this book. The detailed proofs of the necessity of the FSD and SSD rules, as well as the full proofs of the PSD and MSD, with ample of numerical examples, can be found in Levy.[1]

3.2. STOCHASTIC DOMINANCE RULES

We first formulate expected utility in terms of the cumulative distributions, and then, based on this formulation, we derive the various SD decision rules. Graphical illustrations and intuitive explanations are given at the end of the chapter.

a) Expected Utility and the Cumulative Distributions

Denote by $U(w + x)$ the utility of initial wealth w plus a random cash flow x. Then the expected utility of $w + x$ is given by

$$EU(w + x) = \int_a^b U(w + x) f(w + x) d(w + x)$$

where $f(w + x)$ is the density function of $w + x$. Note that even when w, the initial wealth, is constant, $w + x$ is a random variable because x is a random variable. The values a and b stand for the lower

---

[1] See H. Levy, *Stochastic Dominance: Investment Decision Making Under Uncertainty*, 2nd edition, Springer, United States, 2006. For the proof of SD criteria see also G. Hanoch and H. Levy, "The Efficiency Analysis of Choices Involving Risk," *Review of Economic Studies*, 1969, J. Hadar and W. Russell, "Rules for Ordering Uncertain Prospects," *American Economic Review*, 1969, M. Rothschild and J. Stiglitz, "Increasing Risk: I. A Definition," *Journal of Economic Theory*, 1970.

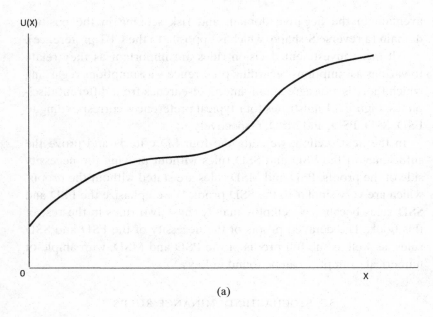

(a)

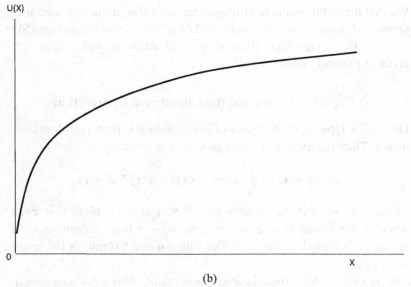

(b)

Figure 3.1. Four Utility Functions.

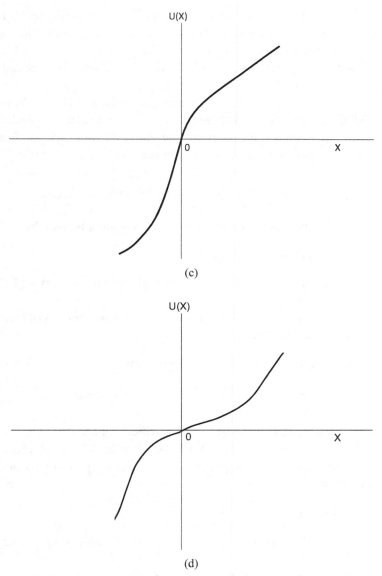

(c)

(d)

Figure 3.1 *(continued)*

and upper bounds of the value $w + x$. However, in some cases, it is assumed that the distributions are unbounded; hence, the values a and b are not finite. For example, if the distributions are assumed to be normal, then the random variable is unbounded with $a = -\infty$ and $b = +\infty$.

For simplicity, we confine our proofs to bounded variables; however, all the proofs can be easily generalized to the case of unbounded variables. By a similar formulation, the expected utility of another random variable, whose density function is $g(x)$, is given by

$$EU(w + x) = \int_a^b U(w + x)g(w + x)d(w + x).$$

The difference between the expected utility of f and g is given by

$$
\begin{aligned}
\Delta &\equiv E_F U(w + x) - E_G U(w + x) \\
&= \int_a^b [U(w + x)((f(w + x) - g(w + x)]d(w + x) \quad (3.1)
\end{aligned}
$$

Integrating by parts and denoting the cumulative distributions of f and g by F and G, respectively, yields

$$
\begin{aligned}
\Delta &= \{U(w + x)[F(w + x) - G(w + x)]\}\big|_a^b \\
&\quad - \int_a^b [F(w + x) - G(w + x)]U'(w + x)d(w + x)
\end{aligned}
$$

Recalling that F and G are cumulative distribution functions with $F(w + b) = G(w + b) = 1$ and $F(w + a) = G(w + a) = 0$, the first term on the right-hand side of the preceding equation is equal to zero, and we remain with

$$
\begin{aligned}
&EU_F(w + x) - EU_G(w + x) \\
&= \int_a^b [G(w + x) - F(w + x)]U'(w + x)d(w + x) \quad (3.2)
\end{aligned}
$$

To simplify the proofs and the presentation given in the following, we use the following definitions, which will be used in the various theorems:

Monotonic Preference: Utility that is nondecreasing in wealth. Formally, $U'(x) \geq 0$ with a strict inequality for at least one x (see Figure 3.1a).

Monotonic Concave Preference: Utility that is nondecreasing and concave. Formally, $U'(x) \geq 0$, and $U''(x \leq 0)$ with a strict inequality for at least one x (see Figure 3.1b).

Monotonic Convex Preference: Utility that is nondecreasing and convex. Formally, $U'(x) \geq 0$ and $U''(x \geq 0)$ with a strict inequality for at least one x.

S-Shape Preference: Utility that is concave in the positive domain and convex in the negative domain (see Figure 3.1c).

Markowitz's Preference: Utility that is convex in the positive domain and concave in the negative domain (see Figure 3.1d).

Using these basic definitions, we can now turn to the FSD rule.

b) The First-Degree Stochastic Dominance Decision Rule

Having equation (3.2), which accounts for the difference in expected utility of the two prospects, we now turn to derive the FSD rule. The FSD rule corresponds to all monotonic preferences.

Theorem 1 (FSD): Prospect F dominates prospect G for all monotonic utility functions if and only if $F(x) \leq G(x)$ for all values x, with a strict inequality for at least one x. Thus, the preference can be concave, convex, with convex as well as concave segments, as long as the first derivative is always non-negative and in some segments it is strictly positive (see Figure 1a).

Proof: The sufficiency condition of the proof is simple. Suppose that for all values of x $F(x) \leq G(x)$ and for some value of x, a strict inequality holds. Because w is the initial wealth, which is not a random variable, we have

$$F(w + x) \leq G(w + x) \Leftrightarrow F(x) \leq G(x). \tag{3.3}$$

Thus, by the theorem's condition, F is always below (or equal) to G. By the assumption of $U' > 0$, the integrand in equation (3.2) is non-negative. Therefore, the integral on the right-hand side of equation (3.2) must be non-negative because an integral of a non-negative term is non-negative. The requirement that there is at least one strict inequality implies that one can find at least one utility function for which the expected utility of F is strictly larger than the expected utility of G (e.g., take $U(x) = x$, for which the expected utility of F is larger than the expected utility of G); hence, the expected utility of F is always equal or larger than the expected utility of G for all monotonic preferences U. Thus, F dominates G by FSD. Finally, two comments that will save time and space are called for:

1) Note that to prove the necessity condition of this theorem, one needs to show that if all investors with a non-negative U' prefer F to G, then $F(x) \leq G(x)$ must hold. This can be easily proved by employing some counterexample. However, to save space, we will not prove this here. Similarly, in all the other SD criteria discussed subsequently, we focus on the sufficiency. The necessity condition of all the proofs, extensions, and ample examples can be found in Levy.[2]

2) All the SD criteria are based on the relative location of F and G. Adding w to x shifts both distributions under consideration by a constant, w, without changing the relative location of the two distributions; so one can conduct all the proofs with or without the initial wealth w and without affecting the dominance relationship. Thus, if F is preferred to G with some initial wealth, it is preferred to G with any other initial wealth. Namely, the SD efficient set is unaffected by the initial wealth. Therefore, in the rest of this book, without loss of generalization, we ignore the initial wealth w.

We now turn to the SSD rule.

c) The Second-Degree Stochastic Dominance Decision Rule

The SSD rule corresponds to all monotonic concave preferences.

Theorem 2 (SSD): Let F and G be defined as before. Then prospect F dominates prospect G for all concave utility functions if and only if

$$\int_a^x [G(t) - F(t)]dt \geq 0 \qquad (3.4)$$

for all values x and there is at least one strict inequality.

[2] See H. Levy, *op. cit.*

Proof: Integrating by parts once again the right-hand side of equation (3.2) (and ignoring w) yields

$$E_F U(x) - E_G U(x) = \left\{ U'(x) \int_a^x [G(t) - F(t)]dt \right\} \Big|_a^b$$
$$- \int_a^b U''(x) \int_a^x [G(t) - F(t)]dt\,dx.$$

Because $G(a) = F(a) = 0$, the first term in the last equation can be simplified as follows:

$$E_F U(x) - E_G U(x) = U'(b) \int_a^b [G(t) - F(t)]dt$$
$$- \int_a^b U''(x) \int_a^x [G(t) - F(t)]dt\,dx$$

Because by assumption the SSD integral condition holds, we have that for all values of x the following holds:

$$\int_a^x [G(t) - F(t)]dt \geq 0, \tag{3.5}$$

and, therefore, this inequality is intact also for the particular value $b = x$. Because U' is non-negative (by the monotonicity of the preference), the first term on the right-hand side of the preceding equation is non-negative. The contribution of the second term is also non-negative because the second integral on the right-hand side is non-negative (see equation (3.5)), U'' is negative, and there is a minus sign in front of the integral.

Thus, the two terms on the right-hand side are non-negative, implying that the left-hand side of the equation is non-negative, and, therefore, the expected utility of F is equal or larger than the expected utility of G. Of course, to get dominance by SSD, it is sufficient to find one risk averse preference such that the expected utility of F is strictly larger than the expected utility of G. This can be easily done. We now turn to the PSD rule.

d) The Prospect Stochastic Dominance Decision Rule

This rule corresponds to all S-shape preferences as suggested by the PT and with a typical structure as given in Figure 1c. Namely, the preference is concave in the positive domain and convex in the negative domain.

Theorem 3 (PSD): Prospect F dominates prospect G for all S-shape preferences if and only if

$$\int_x^0 [G(t) - F(t)]dt \geq 0 \quad \text{for all } x \leq 0$$

and   (3.6)

$$\int_0^x [G(t) - F(t)]dt \geq 0 \quad \text{for all } x \geq 0$$

and, once again, to avoid trivial cases, we need at least one strict inequality.

To avoid repetition, we skip the proof because it is similar to the previous SSD proof.

e) The Markowitz Stochastic Dominance Decision Rule

We now turn to the last SD criterion employed in this book, the MSD. The MSD corresponds to all reverse S-shape preferences, that is, with risk seeking in the positive domain and risk aversion in the negative domain as suggested by Markowitz (see Figure 1d).

Theorem 4 (MSD): Prospect F dominates prospect G for all Markowitz's preferences if and only if

$$\int_a^x [G(t) - F(t)]dt \geq 0 \quad \text{for all } x \leq 0$$

and   (3.7)

$$\int_x^b [G(t) - F(t)]dt \geq 0 \quad \text{for all } x \geq 0$$

3.3. GRAPHICAL ILLUSTRATIONS OF THE STOCHASTIC DOMINANCE CRITERIA

Figure 3.2 illustrates a case where F dominates G by FSD. Note that the cumulative distribution of F is below or coincides with G for the whole domain of x. Also note that in the range (x_1, x_2), we have $F = G$. However, to avoid the trivial case where $F = G$ in the whole

Cumulative
Distribution

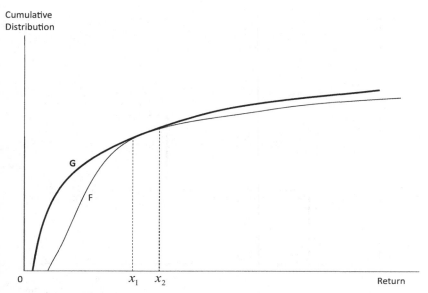

Figure 3.2. First-Degree Stochastic Dominance Illustration.

range, to have FSD dominance, we must have some range or a point x where $F < G$.

We now turn to the intuitive explanation of the FSD rule. For simplicity and without loss of generalization, we will provide the FSD intuition by assuming a strict inequality in the FSD condition. If $F(x) < G(x)$ for all x, it implies that

$$1-F(x) > 1 - G(x) \quad \text{for all values of x.} \tag{3.8}$$

But this means that the probability of obtaining an income x or more under distribution F is larger than under distribution G, a desired property. And because this property holds for any value x, F dominates G.

To explain this FSD intuition further, suppose that an investor has to select between prospects F and G. By prospect G, the variable x can get the values 1, 2, or 3 with an equal probability of 1/3, and by prospect F, the random variable can get the values 2, 4, or 6 with an equal probability of 1/3. The probability of getting 1 or more is the same under both distributions (which is equal to 1). The probability

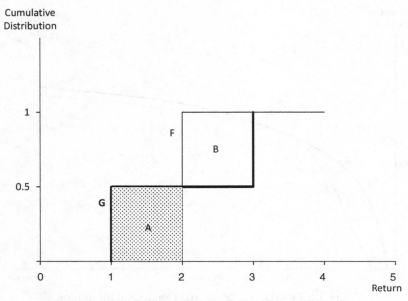

Figure 3.3. Second-Degree Stochastic Dominance Illustration.

of getting 2 or more is 2/3 under G and 1 under F. The probability of getting 3 or more is 1/3 under G and 2/3 under F. The probability of getting the higher possible values or more (in our example, 5 or 6) is positive under F and zero under G. Thus, for any value x, the probability of getting this value or more is higher (or equal) under F – hence, the superiority of F over G. In other words, as the event "to obtain some certain income or more" for any given income is desirable, the prospect that provides a higher probability for all these events is preferred by all investors who prefer more to less wealth. As when F is below G the probability to obtain any income x or more is higher under F than under G, we say that if F is below G, F dominates G by FSD.

We now turn to the intuitive explanation of SSD. Consider Figure 3.3. Distribution F yields 2 with a probability of 1, and distribution G provides 1 or 3 with an equal probability of 0.5 each.

We can rewrite equation (3.2) as follows:

$$E_F U(x) - E_G U(x) = A \times (\text{average } U' \text{ in the range } 1-2)$$
$$- B \times (\text{average } U' \text{ in the range } 2-3).$$

To see areas A and B, refer to Figure 3.3. Notice that by construction of this specific example, $A = B$. Because U' is declining (because risk aversion is assumed by SSD), we obtain the right-hand side of the preceding equation as positive; hence, $E_F U(x)$ is larger than $E_G U(x)$ for all risk averse preferences. Therefore, F dominates G by SSD.

This is a technical explanation in terms of the SSD integral condition. To provide a more intuitive explanation, suppose that a risk averter holds prospect G, namely, holds a prospect that yields either 1 or 3 with an equal probability. Would this investor be better off switching to F, which provides 2 with certainty? This means that if this investor gets 3, he or she would give up 1; if this investor gets 1, he or she will get another 1, such that in any event he or she ends up with 2. Thus, by shifting from G to F, he or she gives up the marginal prospect, which yields $+1$ and -1 with an equal probability. Would a risk averter who holds prospect G benefit from giving up this marginal prospect? Because the marginal utility is declining (recall the risk aversion assumption, $U'' < 0$), the disutility of losing 1 is greater than the utility of gaining 1; hence, every risk averter would benefit from giving up this marginal prospect, namely, by shifting from G to F. In other words, a risk averter will always reject a lottery that provides an equal probability to gain or lose the same amount of money (such a lottery game is called a "fair gamble").

Of course, this is a simplistic case in which the SSD dominance is transparent. In the general case, F and G can cross each other many times. However, if F dominates G by SSD, it implies that for any range of outcomes, x, where F is above G (like area B in Figure 3.2), in the range of x preceding it, F is below G (like area A in Figure 3.2), and this positive area is larger than (or equal to) the subsequent negative area. Thus, before any negative area (where F is above G), there is a larger (or equal) positive area (where F is below G), and because the marginal utility of x corresponding to the positive area is larger than the marginal utility of x corresponding to the negative area, all risk averse inventors would prefer F over G.

The intuitive explanations of PSD and MSD are similar and are based on the fact that by assumption, U' is either declining or increasing in the various ranges of outcomes under consideration.

3.4. STOCHASTIC DOMINANCE RULES AND THE DISTRIBUTION'S MEAN AND VARIANCE

We first discuss the role that the mean and the variance play in SD criteria, and then we show the role these parameters play for some risk-averse investors, but not for all risk averters.

a) Mean, Variance, and Stochastic Dominance Rules

This book is devoted to the Mean-Variance (M-V) rule and the CAPM. However, bridging between expected utility and the PT, we need to employ some of the SD rules that are discussed in this book. Therefore, as a first step, we investigate in this section the relationship between SD rules and the M-V rule. We show that the mean return plays a crucial role in all SD rules, whereas the variance of returns plays a relatively minor role. To be more specific, if prospect F dominates prospect G by any one of the SD criteria, then it must be that the mean return of F is greater than or equal to the mean return of G. However, by all rules, the variance of F may generally be larger than the variance of G; hence, it does not play a crucial role in the dominance relationship. Because we can ignore the initial wealth, w, equation (3.2) can be rewritten as follows:

$$E_F U(x) - E_G U(x) = \int_a^b [G(x) - F(x)]U'(x)dx. \qquad (3.2')$$

Equation (3.2') is intact for any value U; hence, it holds also for the specific linear utility function $U(x) = x$. Therefore, equation (3.2') becomes in this specific case:

$$E_F U(x) - E_G U(X) = E_F(x) - E_G(x)$$
$$= \int_a^b [G(x) - F(x)]dx. \qquad (3.2'')$$

(Recall that $U' = 1$ in this specific case of a linear utility function.)

Using equation (3.2''), one can easily see that FSD of F over G implies that the mean return of F must be larger than the mean of G. By FSD, $F(x) \leq G(x)$ and a strict inequality must hold for some value x; hence, the integral in equation (3.2) is positive.

Therefore, if F dominates G by FSD, this implies that $E_F(x) > E_G(x)$. Thus, if we have a dominance of F over G, by FSD it is *necessary* that the mean of F be larger than that of G. Stated alternatively, because the linear preference $U(x) = x$ is monotonic, and because with such utility one always prefers the prospect with the higher mean, if F is preferred to G by *all* monotonic preferences, it must be that F has a higher mean.

We now discuss the role that the variance plays in *FSD* criterion. Suppose that F assumes the values of 5 and 10 with equal probability, and G assumes the values of 4 and 6 with an equal probability. One can easily check that F dominates G by FSD, yet it has a larger variance. From this simple example, we conclude that the dominating prospect does not necessarily have a smaller variance.

We now turn to SSD. We show here that if F dominates G by SSD, then F must have a larger (or equal) mean than that of G. To see this, recall that by SSD, equation (3.5) holds for any value x; hence, it must hold also for the specific value $x = b$. Thus, SSD of F over G implies that

$$\int_a^b [G(t) - F(t)]dt \geq 0,$$

and from this requirement and from equation (3.2″), we can conclude that $E_F(x) \geq E_G(x)$. Note that although with FSD the requirement is that the dominating prospect will have higher mean than the inferior one, with SSD the requirement is that the superior prospect has a higher or an equal mean.

Regarding the variance, once again, a dominance of F over G by SSD does not imply that the variance of F must be smaller, despite the fact that risk aversion is assumed. To see this, let us go back to the FSD example. F has a larger variance than G does, and it dominates G by FSD. Because FSD dominance implies SSD dominance (to see that, recall that if equation (3.3) holds, it implies that equation (3.4) holds), F dominates G also by SSD, despite F having a larger variance.

To summarize, for FSD dominance, the superior prospect must have a larger mean; for SSD dominance, the superior prospect must have a larger or equal mean; and for both FSD and SSD, the variance of the superior prospect is not necessarily larger. Although we elaborate in this chapter on the role of the mean and the variance on FSD and SSD, by similar arguments and proofs one can show that for PSD and MSD dominance, the mean of the superior prospect must be equal to or larger than the mean of the inferior one, but the variance is not necessarily smaller. Thus, in all the SD rules, the mean plays a crucial role in the dominance relationship, whereas the variance does not.

b) Mean, Variance, and Risk Aversion

Suppose it is given that some investor is risk averse. Furthermore, suppose that this investor faces two prospects, one with a higher mean and a lower variance. Would he or she necessarily select this seemingly superior prospect? The answer to this question, quite surprisingly, is negative. We show this claim by the following intriguing example.

Consider the following two prospects F and G with the following means and variances:

$$E_G(x) > E_F(x),$$

and

$$\text{Variance }_G(x) < \text{Variance }_F(x).$$

One is tempted to conclude that every risk averter would prefer G over F because G has a higher mean and a lower variance. However, this is not the case and, counterintuitively, a risk averter with non-pathological preference may prefer G, which by the M-V rule is inferior.

To see this, consider the following example taken from Hanoch and Levy.[3] Suppose that prospect F yields 10 and 1,000 with probabilities of 0.99 and 0.01, respectively, and prospect G yields 1 and 100 with probabilities of 0.80 and 0.20, respectively. A simple calculation reveals:

$$E_G(x) = 20.8 > E_F(x) = 19.9$$

$$\text{Variance }_G(x) = 1,468 < \text{Variance }_F(x) = 9,703$$

Thus, as required by the example, G dominates F by the M-V rule. To show that a risk averter may prefer F, consider the following utility function $U(x) = Log_{10}(x)$. With this function, we have that the

---

[3] See G. Hanoch and H. Levy, *op. cit.*

expected utility of F is 1.02 and the expected utility of G is 0.4. Thus, this specific risk averter prefers the prospect with the lower mean and higher variance, revealing quite surprising results. (*Hint:* Prospect F has a much larger "skewness" than prospect G does, and most risk averse investors prefer a positive skewness.[4])

3.5. SUMMARY

Given that investors act to maximize expected utility, in this chapter, we derive and discuss various investment decision rules that are consistent with this goal. The various decision rules depend on the partial information assumed on preference. The more assumptions one is ready to make, the sharper the obtained investment criterion. The decision rules we discuss in this chapter are quite general and assume nothing on the shape of the distribution of returns, whereas in Chapter 4, we assume "normality" when we derive the M-V rule.

We focus in this chapter on FSD and SSD because these criteria are employed later in the book to justify the M-V rule in the case of "normal" distributions and to bridge between CPT and the CAPM, which is the core of this book.

The FSD assumes only monotonic nondecreasing preferences. To obtain SSD, the risk-aversion assumption (concavity of preferences) is added. To derive PSD, one needs to add to the monotonicity assumption the assumption that risk aversion (concavity) prevails in the positive domain and risk seeking (convexity) prevails in the negative domain. Finally, to obtain MSD, one needs to add to the monotonicity assumption the assumption that risk aversion (concavity) prevails in the negative domain and risk seeking prevails in the positive domain.

Obviously, FSD dominance implies SSD, PSD, and MSD. Generally, there is no obvious relationship between SD rules and the

---

[4] Expanding the utility function to Taylor's series and taking expected utility of both sides, we see that if the third derivative of the utility function is positive, there is a preference for skewness. Indeed, most preferences commonly employed in economics and finance reveal a positive third derivative. Skewness preferences and positive third derivative are related to third-degree Stochastic Dominance (TSD). See G. A. Whitmore, "Third Degree Stochastic Dominance," *American Economic Review*, 1970.

M-V rule. Regarding the mean of returns, FSD implies that the superior prospect must have a larger mean than the inferior one, whereas SSD, PSD, and MSD imply that the superior prospect must have a greater or equal mean compared with that of the inferior prospect. Regarding the variance of returns, the superior prospect may have a larger or a smaller variance than that of the inferior prospect. Thus, although the mean return plays a crucial role in SD rules, the variance does not.

4

The Mean-Variance Rule (M-V Rule)

4.1. INTRODUCTION

The Mean-Variance (M-V) rule is employed mainly when ranking various prospects and when constructing efficient portfolios out of the individual risky assets that are available. Most important, the M-V rule is the foundation of the Capital Asset Pricing Model (CAPM), particularly of beta as a measure of risk. The M-V rule, the CAPM, and particularly beta are probably the most commonly employed investment criteria by academics and practitioners alike.

Is there a theoretical or an empirical justification to the widespread employment of the M-V rule? Under what conditions is it safe to employ the M-V rule, and under what conditions may doing so lead to paradoxical results? We devote this chapter to these issues. We first define the M-V rule, and then we show cases in which it is consistent with expected utility and cases in which it leads to paradoxical results. Specifically, we show that when the utility function is quadratic (with no need to require that returns be normally distributed) or, alternatively, when one is ready to assume a normal distribution with risk aversion, it is legitimate to employ the M-V rule. The word *legitimate* rather than *optimal* is employed to emphasize that the M-V rule is not always the optimal one. To be more specific, in the quadratic case, the M-V rule is sufficient but not necessary and hence can be improved. Indeed, in the quadratic utility function case, we suggest in this chapter sharper investment decision rules than the M-V rule. In contrast to the quadratic case, in the normal case, the M-V rule is sufficient and necessary; hence, it is optimal. Therefore, unlike in the quadratic preference case, in the normal case, one cannot establish a better rule than the M-V rule. Finally, we illustrate that even when one cannot theoretically justify employment of the M-V rule (i.e., neither quadratic preference nor normality prevail), in a wide spectrum of cases, it can serve as an excellent approximation to expected utility maximization. Thus, in the last part of this chapter, we answer (accompanied with an empirical demonstration) the question raised by Markowitz[1] in his Nobel Laureate speech:

The crucial question is: if an investor with a particular single period utility function acted only on the basis of expected return and variance, could the investor achieve almost maximum expected utility? Or put it another way, if you know the expected value and variance of the probability distribution of return on a portfolio can you guess fairly closely its expected utility? (p. 471)

We would like to add the following question:

Selecting an investment portfolio by some function of the mean and variance, $f(\mu, \sigma^2)$, which is an approximation to expected utility (as suggested by Markowitz), is it certain that an M-V efficient portfolio is chosen? If the answer is a negative one, it implies that an M-V inefficient, or an interior, portfolio may be selected by the suggested approximation, which could be a severe drawback of this approximation.

We show in this chapter that the answer to Markowitz's question is positive, whereas the answer to our added question is that in some cases, the answer is negative, but in the most relevant economic case, the answer is positive. When investors are willing to add to the risk aversion assumption also decreasing absolute risk aversion (DARA), they will always choose a portfolio from the M-V efficient frontier when choosing according to the suggested approximation to the expected utility. Hence, the market portfolio must be located on this frontier, and the CAPM is intact (see also Chapters 5 and 6).

The structure of this chapter is as follows: We first define the M-V rule and show that in some cases it may lead to paradoxical results; hence, the M-V rule cannot be employed in all scenarios. We then show the conditions under which the M-V rule can be safely employed. Finally, we report on the various quadratic approximations.

[1] H. M. Markowitz, "Foundation of Portfolio Theory," *The Journal of Finance*, 1991, p. 471.

4.2. THE MEAN-VARIANCE RULE: PARTIAL ORDERING

Comparing two prospects whose returns are given by x and y, respectively, we say that x dominates y by the M-V rule if the following two conditions hold:

$$\text{a) } E(x) \geq E(y) \quad \text{and} \quad \text{b) } \sigma_x^2 \leq \sigma_y^2 \tag{4.1}$$

and there is at least one strict inequality.

Conversely, if the following holds:

$$\text{a) } E(x) > E(y) \quad \text{and} \quad \text{b) } \sigma_x^2 > \sigma_y^2 \tag{4.2}$$

there is no dominance by the M-V rule, and we conclude that both investments, x and y, are included in the M-V *efficient set*, as long as there is no other investment, say z, which dominates one of the prospects, x or y, or dominates them both. Thus, it is possible that out of N available prospects, n will be in the M-V efficient set and $(N-n)$ will be in the inefficient set, when $n \leq N$. Because we generally have more than one prospect in the efficient set, we name this M-V division of prospects to the *efficient set* and the *inefficient set-partial ordering*, distinguishing it from *complete ordering*, under which only one prospect is included in the efficient set.

To illustrate these concepts, suppose we have 100 available prospects. Furthermore, conducting all pairwise M-V comparisons, by employing equations (4.1) and (4.2), suppose that twenty prospects are included in the efficient set (i.e., for each prospect included in the efficient set, no prospect, of the other ninety-nine prospects, dominates it by the M-V rule), and eighty prospects are relegated to the inefficient set (i.e., for each prospect included in the inefficient set, there is at least one prospect included in the efficient set that dominates it by the M-V rule).[2] Then, we say that we have a partial ordering, and all M-V investors should select their optimal prospect from those twenty prospects included in the efficient set, but we cannot

---

[2] Actually, it is sufficient that one of the other ninety-nine prospects dominates a prospect that is included in the inefficient set. However, the M-V rule is transitive, implying that if prospects x and y are in the inefficient set, and z, which dominates x, is included in the efficient set, then if x dominates y, z must also dominate y. Therefore, we assert that for each inefficient prospect, there is *at least* one prospect included in the efficient set that dominates it by the M-V rule.

tell which prospect should be selected. The reason for this is that different investors may select different prospects from the efficient set according to their preferences. However, we can safely assert with the M-V partial ordering that no one should select a prospect from the other eighty prospects that constitute the inefficient set. Of course, the smaller the efficient set, the more effective the M-V division to the two sets is. The effectiveness of the M-V rule depends on the data set, and no general assertion can be made regarding the relative size of these two prospect sets.

However, if we are willing to assume that all investors have some specific utility function, for example, a log–function, we can calculate the expected utility of each prospect and order all prospects by one dimension, the expected utility, yielding a complete ordering, when the prospect with the highest expected utility is the optimal choice. Note, however, that in this case investors do not employ the M-V rule, but rather they directly maximize expected utility, which is assumed to be known and common to all investors. Moreover, with a different assumed utility function, we may have a different optimal prospect. Because generally the specific preference is unknown, virtually all investment decision analyses are focused on the partial ordering procedure.

When constructing the investment efficient set by the M-V rule, it is assumed that the expected value of the outcomes measures the prospect's profitability, and the variance (or the standard deviation)[3] of the outcomes measures the risk involved. Is it always true that these two indices measure profitability and risk, respectively? Although this is the common view among many investors, which in turn explains the popularity of the M-V rule, the M-V rule may be misleading in some cases.

Let us first illustrate the failure of the M-V rule to provide optimal investment decision making in certain cases by using a number

---

[3] Because the standard deviation is defined as the positive square root of the variance, it is obvious that if the variance of one prospect is larger than that of the other, the same is intact when we compare the standard deviations of the two prospects. Whereas the standard deviation is economically more meaningful (because it is measured by, say, dollars, unlike the variance, which is measured in dollars squared), the variance is easier to handle mathematically and therefore is employed as a measure of risk in many cases. We will use both measures of risk, the variance and the standard deviation, interchangeably.

of examples. These examples emphasize the importance of examining whether the characteristics of the prospects under consideration allow the employment of the M-V rule before widely using it. Accordingly, the M-V rule should not be employed in all situations, and in some specific cases, better investment rules avoid the paradoxical results.

Suppose one has to choose between prospect *F*, which yields $5 or $10 with an equal probability to each outcome, and prospect *G*, which yields $10 or $20 with an equal probability. Prospect *G* dominates prospect *F* by the First-Degree Stochastic Dominance (FSD) rule (see Chapter 3); hence, any investor – risk seeker and risk averter alike – should select *G*. Nevertheless, it is easy to show that given that prospect *G* has a higher mean and a higher variance than prospect *F* that is, equation (4.2) holds – and we therefore have no M-V dominance, implying that both *F* and *G* are included in the M-V efficient set. This means that by the M-V rule, some investors may choose prospect *F* and some may choose prospect *G*. Thus, the M-V rule in this case is not sharp enough; it may be misleading in the sense that it is unable to distinguish between the two prospects when there is a clear preference for prospect *G* by all investors, regardless of their preferences. This example demonstrates that the M-V rule may produce a relatively large efficient set. The smaller the efficient set, the better the investment criterion because investors have to choose from a small number of prospects. We thus conclude that in some cases, as in the case presented here, the M-V rule is ineffective, or not sharp enough.

This simple example naturally gives rise to the following questions: When can one safely employ the M-V rule? Are there cases in which the M-V rule is effective and no further reduction of the efficient set is possible? In the next sections of this chapter, we analyze the precise conditions under which it is allowed to employ the M-V rule with no fear that such paradoxical results emerge. We discuss scenarios in which the M-V rule may lead to paradoxical results, such as the one given in the example. We examine situations where the other distribution's moments (e.g., skewness) are also relevant for investment decision making, constituting a deviation from the M-V rule. We also show under what restrictions on the probability distribution of outcomes the M-V rules coincide with the SD rules. Finally, we look at cases in which there is no theoretical justification to employ the M-V rule, yet it serves as an excellent approximation to the maximization of expected utility.

4.3. EXPECTED UTILITY AND DISTRIBUTION'S MOMENTS: THE GENERAL CASE

We show in this section that, generally, the M-V rule does not capture all the relevant information regarding the prospects' features, and some other distribution's moments, apart from the first two, should also be considered. To see this claim, recall that by Taylor expansion, we have the following general relation:

$$
f(t) = f(a) + f'(a)(t - a) + f''(a)(t - a)^2/2! \\
+ f'''(a)(t - a)^3/3! + \cdots \cdots \quad (4.3)
$$

where the function $f(t)$ is expanded about some constant value a and the derivatives are at point a. Consider now a utility function $U(w + x)$, when w denotes the initial wealth (constant) and x is the uncertain income from the investment. Expanding this utility function about the value $w + E(x)$ and employing the rule given in equation (4.3) yields

$$
U(w + x) = U(w + E(x)) + U'(\cdot)(x - E(x)) + U''(\cdot)(x - E(x))^2/2! \\
+ U'''(\cdot)(x - E(x))^3/3! \cdots \cdots + U^i(\cdot)E(x - E(x))^i/i! \\
+ \cdots \cdots \cdots \cdots
$$

where the derivatives are at the point $(\cdot)$ where this point is given by $w + E(x)$. Note that the various values given in this equation are written in terms of x, because we have in our specific case $t - a = w + x - (w + Ex) = x - Ex$. Taking the expected value of both sides of this equation and recalling that the derivatives are at a given constant point, and are therefore not random variables, yields

$$
EU(w + x) = U(w + E(x)) + \frac{U''(\cdot)}{2!}\sigma_x^2 + \frac{U'''(\cdot)}{3!}\mu_{3,x} \\
+ \cdots \cdots \frac{U^i(\cdot)}{i!}\mu_{i,x} + \cdots \cdots \quad (4.4)
$$

where in the derivation of equation (4.4), we use the following relations:

$$
E(x - E(x)) = 0, \quad E(x - E(x))^2 = \sigma_x^2, \quad E(x - E(x))^3 = \mu_{3,x},
$$

where the last term given is the third moment of the probability distribution, which measures the distribution skewness. Of course, for symmetrical distributions, this term is equal to zero. Similarly, the ith moment of the distribution is given by

$$\mu_{i,x} = E(x - E(x))^i$$

Equation (4.4) explicitly asserts that *all* distributions' moments are relevant for decision making because they all determine the expected utility. Thus, relying solely on the mean and variance may be generally misleading. For example, it is possible that when two prospects x and y are compared, the mean of x is higher than that of y, and the variance of x is smaller than that of y, so by the M-V rule x dominates y. But this may not be true in the expected utility framework because the skewness of x may be smaller than that of y, and if an investor prefers a large skewness, he or she may choose y because it yields a higher expected utility (such a case is demonstrated in Chapter 3, Section 3.4).

Does it mean that in the general case the mean and variance are not important factors in the decision making process? Absolutely not! The mean and the variance are strongly related to the monotonicity axiom and to risk aversion, respectively. Nevertheless, we claim that unless some assumptions are made, these two parameters do not paint the full picture and other moments may also be important. Let us elaborate.

Equation (4.4) sheds light on the relation between the derivatives of the utility function and the distribution moments. For example,

$$\partial EU(w + x)/\partial \sigma_x^2 = U''(\cdot)/2!$$

Given this example, if an investor is a risk averter ($U'' < 0$), increasing the variance (other parameters held constant) decreases the investor's expected utility. Thereupon we can say that risk averters dislike large variance. Although it cannot be seen from equaton (4.4), increasing the mean while keeping other parameters unchanged increases expected utility. The reason for this is that by increasing the mean (and not changing the other parameters), the cumulative distribution of returns is shifted to the right and, as a result, the distribution with the higher mean dominates the one with the lower mean by FSD. Hence, the distribution with the higher mean provides a higher expected utility for all possible preferences, with risk aversion and risk seeking alike. In this chapter, we show that by the monotonicity axiom, the higher the mean, other parameters held constant, the higher the expected utility, and with risk aversion, the lower the variance, the higher the expected utility. These two properties are the raison d'être for the importance of the mean and variance in investment decision making.

However, recognizing the importance of the M-V rule for investment decision making does not imply that the other distribution's moments can be ignored. For example, by equation (4.4),

$$\partial EU(w + x)/\partial \mu_{3,x} = U'''(\cdot)/3!$$

implying that if the third derivative of the utility function is positive, the larger the skewness, the larger the expected utility (provided that other moments are kept constant). Indeed, most utility functions employed in economics and finance reveal a positive third derivative; suitably, at least for these functions, increasing skewness (other parameters held constant) increases the expected utility.

A theoretical justification for skewness preference exists. Specifically, the observation that risk premium is generally decreasing with wealth, a characteristic called DARA (decreasing absolute risk aversion), also implies that the third derivative is positive; that is, investors like large skewness. To see this, recall that risk premium is given by

$$\pi = -\frac{U''(w)}{U'(w)}$$

and, therefore,

$$\frac{\partial \pi}{\partial w} = -\frac{U'(w)U'''(w) - [U''(w)]^2}{[U'(w)]^2}$$

If the left-hand side of this equation is negative, as required by DARA, it must be that

$$U'(w)U'''(w) - [U''(w)]^2 > 0,$$

which can hold only if $U'''(w) > 0$. Thus, we proved that

$$\partial \pi/\partial w < 0 \Rightarrow U'''(w) > 0.$$

Namely, DARA implies that investors like skewness. Because the most commonly employed preferences reveal a positive third derivative, we conclude that generally, the third moment cannot be ignored in prospect selection. This, in turn, implies that unless some restrictions are imposed on the distributions of the prospects under consideration, one cannot choose among prospects solely by the M-V rule because skewness must also be taken into account. As we shall see when we discuss the quality of the suggested approximation function to expected utility, DARA is needed to make sure that by the approximation function an M-V efficient prospect is selected.

The following additional conclusions can be drawn from equation (4.4):[4]

1. If all derivatives but the first one are equal to zero, all terms apart from the first one on the right-hand side of equation (4.4) are equal to zero, and we are then left only with the mean outcome. Because the utility function is monotonic, we can conclude that in this specific case, the investment ranking is done only by the mean outcome. This is not a surprising result because if all derivatives but the first one are equal to zero, we have the following linear utility function:

$$U(x) = a + bx$$

where $b > 0$. Thus, we have $U' = b > 0$, and all other derivatives are equal to zero. Clearly, in this specific case, the expected utility is determined solely by the mean outcome; see equation (4.4).

2. Similarly, for the quadratic utility function of the form

$$U(x) = a + bx + cx^2,$$

all moments but the first two are irrelevant for decision making because all derivatives apart from the first two are zero; see equation (4.4). Therefore, in this case, as we shall see later on in the chapter, only the mean and the variance of returns are relevant for investment decision making.

3. By a similar argument, with the cubic function of the form

$$U(x) = a + bx + cx^2 + dx^3,$$

all moments apart from the first three are irrelevant, and so on for utility functions of a higher power.

---

[4] For simplicity, we denote by x the total wealth. However, because the M-V rule is invariant to the initial wealth, in the M-V analysis, the initial wealth can be ignored.

4. However, if the function is not given as a polynomial (a sum of the various terms) but is of the form such as

$$U(x) = \log(x) \quad \text{or} \quad U(x) = \sqrt{x},$$

then all derivatives are not equal to zero and therefore by equation (4.4), all the moments of the probability distribution of outcomes are relevant for decision making, a clear case of when the M-V rule may be misleading.

From these examples and analysis, particularly from equation (4.4), we conclude that the M-V rule cannot be safely employed because other distributions' moments may also count. Yet, as we shall see, when some assumptions are made, it is justified to ignore the higher moments. Let us turn to the cases where the M-V rules can be legitimately used without worrying about the effects of the higher distribution's moments on the expected utility.

4.4. THE QUADRATIC UTILITY FUNCTION AND THE MEAN-VARIANCE RULE

One of the popular employed utility functions in economics and finance is the quadratic function. Its popularity stems from its mathematical tractability, not from its superior theoretical features. On the contrary, it is widely employed despite its two major drawbacks.

The quadratic utility function depends only on the mean and variance because all derivatives higher than the second one are equal to zero; see equation (4.4). Therefore, with this preference, the M-V rule may provide optimal choices, that is, choices that are consistent with expected utility. Indeed, Tobin[5] employs the quadratic preference in his M-V analysis. We show in the following that with a quadratic function, the M-V rule is a sufficient but not a necessary rule. Namely, if prospect x dominates prospect y by the M-V rule, it must have a higher expected utility for all quadratic preferences. However, we may have situations where x does not dominate y by the M-V rule, yet all investors, including those with quadratic preferences, will prefer prospect x. This implies that for quadratic preferences, the M-V rule

[5] J. Tobin, "Liquidity Preference as Behavior Toward Risk," *Review of Economic Studies*, 1958.

produces an efficient set that is "too large" because it may include prospects that no investor with a quadratic preference would choose. In situations where we obtain by the M-V rule an efficient set that includes also inefficient prospects, we say that the M-V rule is not the optimal rule (not sharp enough) for quadratic preferences and that one can employ a better rule even when quadratic preferences are assumed.

Recall from the previous section (4.3, point 2) that the general form of the quadratic utility function is given by

$$U(x) = A + Bx + Cx^2,$$

where B is positive and C is negative (these signs are induced by the monotonicity and risk-aversion assumptions). Subtracting A and dividing by B (a positive linear transformation, which is allowed), we get the simple form

$$U(x) = x + bx^2.$$

The monotonicity axiom (see Chapter 2) asserts that the utility function must be nondecreasing. Thus, with more wealth, the investor's welfare either increases or remains unchanged. Thus, by the monotonicity axiom, risk aversion, and quadratic preference, the following two conditions must hold:

$$U'(x) = 1 + 2bx > 0 \quad \text{and} \quad U''(x) = 2b < 0.$$

We turn now to show, as claimed, that with this quadratic utility function, the M-V rule follows, yet it is not optimal in that it does not utilize all the available information of the quadratic function.

Theorem 4.1: Suppose that prospect F dominates prospect G by the M-V rule. Then the expected utility of F is larger than the expected utility of G for all quadratic utility functions.

Proof: The expected utility of x is given by

$$EU(x) = E(x) + bE(x^2) = E(x) + b[E(x)]^2 + b\sigma_x^2 \qquad (4.5)$$

where we use the relation $\sigma_x^2 = E(x^2) - [E(x)]^2$.

Taking the derivatives of the expected utility of the mean and variance, respectively, yields

$$\partial EU(x)/\partial Ex = 1 + 2bEx > 0 \qquad (4.6)$$

and

$$\partial EU(x)/\partial\sigma_x^2 = b < 0. \tag{4.7}$$

The positive derivative given in equation (4.6) stems from the monotonicity assumption, that is:

$$1 + 2bx > 0 \Rightarrow 1 + 2bEx > 0.$$

If the inequality holds for any x, it holds also for the expected value of x, and the negative derivative given in equation (4.7) reflects the risk-aversion assumption. Thus, with this preference, only the mean and variance are relevant (all higher moments are irrelevant because all derivatives of the utility function higher than the second one are equal to zero (see equation (4.4)), and the investor likes a high mean and dislikes a higher variance, leading to the M-V rule.

With these derivatives at hand, the proof of Theorem 4.1 is straightforward: The mean of prospect F is higher than (or equal to) the mean of prospect G. By shifting from G to F, the mean increases, so by equation (4.6), the expected utility increases (or remains the same). Similarly, if the variance of prospect F is lower than (or equal to) that of prospect G, once again, by shifting from G to F, by equation (4.7), the expected utility increases (or remains the same). Thus, if F dominates G by the M-V rule, the expected utility increases (because we must have at least one strict inequality in the M-V condition), as long as the preference is quadratic.

Formally, we proved that the following holds:

$$E_F(x) \geq E_G(x), \sigma_F^2(x) \leq \sigma_G^2(x), \quad \text{with at least one strict inequality}$$
$$\Rightarrow EU_Q^F(x) > EU_Q^G(x) \quad \text{for all quadratic preferences,}$$

where the subscript Q emphasizes that the theorem is valid only for all quadratic preferences.[6]

---

[6] Using the derivatives approach in this proof implies that one can move from one distribution to another by employing an infinite series of such a small number of shifts in the mean and the variance. It can be shown that indeed this is the case. However, the following simple proof is also intact; decreasing the variance, holding other parameters constant, increases the expected utility of all quadratic preferences; see eq. (4.5). Increasing the mean, holding other parameters constant, increases the expected utility of all possible preferences (because there is FSD), let alone the specific quadratic preference. Thus, if x dominates y by the M-V rule, the expected utility of x is greater than the expected utility of y for all quadratic preferences.

Note that we proved only the sufficiency side, asserting that if one prospect dominates the other by the M-V rule, then it must reveal a higher expected utility. However, we did not prove the necessity side, asserting that if one prospect yields a higher expected utility than the other for all quadratic utility functions, dominance must exist also with the M-V rule. We did not prove the necessity side simply because it is an invalid claim. To see why the necessity side does not hold, one counterexample is sufficient.

Counter example: Suppose that prospect F yields \$1 or \$2, each with a probability of .5. Prospect G yields \$1 with probability of 1. It is obvious that neither F nor G dominates the other by the M-V rule because F has a higher mean and a higher variance. Yet because F dominates G by the FSD rule, we can conclude that

$$EU_F(x) \geq EU_G(x) \Rightarrow EU_Q^F(x) \geq E_Q^G(x)$$

when the left-hand side holds for all nondecreasing utility functions, and the right-hand side holds for all nondecreasing quadratic utility.

Thus, this example reveals that F dominates G for all preferences and *a fortiori* for all quadratic preferences, despite the no-dominance by the M-V rule. Therefore, we have shown with this example that $EU_Q^F(x) \geq EU_Q^G(x)$ for all U_Q, with at least one strict inequality, does *not* imply that $E_F(x) \geq E_G(x)$ and $\sigma_F^2 \leq \sigma_G^2$.

The explanation for this result is that the M-V rule does not utilize all the information of the quadratic utility function; therefore, stronger rules can be developed by using the information available on this function. To be more specific, in the derivation of the M-V rule with quadratic preferences, we use the fact that the first derivative is positive, the second derivative is negative, and all other higher derivatives are equal to zero. But we did not use the fact that the quadratic utility function has a maximum and, after reaching this maximum, it starts to decline. By the monotonicity axiom, the utility function cannot decline; therefore, the range of the possible outcomes must be confined to the range where the quadratic utility function increases. Using this information, a stronger investment decision rule than the M-V rule can be developed. We now turn to show how exploiting the monotonicity axiom and the information that the quadratic preference is confined to the increasing range may improve the M-V rule.

4.5. QUADRATIC UTILITY: ARE THERE SHARPER RULES THAN THE MEAN-VARIANCE RULE?

Using the information that for outcomes larger than a certain outcome, the quadratic utility function declines, we can establish a decision rule that is stronger than the M-V rule.[7] It is stronger in the sense that the M-V rule may fail to distinguish between two prospects where one prospect dominates the other for all relevant quadratic preferences. In other words, the suggested rule is able to detect this dominance of one prospect over the other, whereas the M-V rule is not, making the suggested rule sharper than the M-V rule is. This superior decision rule is given in Theorem 4.2.

Theorem 4.2: Having two prospects x and y, prospect x dominates prospect y by all relevant quadratic utility functions if

$$\text{a)} \quad Ex - Ey \geq 0 \tag{4.8}$$

and

$$\text{b)} \quad (Ex - Ey)[2\,Max(x, y) - (Ex + Ey)] \geq (\sigma_x^2 - \sigma_y^2)$$

and there is at least one strong inequality.

Thus, condition a) is similar to the M-V rule's condition on the means, but condition b) replaces the M-V's required condition on the variances.

Proof: Figure 4.1 illustrates the general shape of the quadratic utility function. Recall that with this function we have

$$U'(x) = 1 + 2bx \geq 0 \Rightarrow x \leq -1/2b \equiv K,$$

where b, the parameter of the quadratic function, is negative, and K defines the maximum value the outcome x can assume without violating the monotonicity axiom (as for $x > -1/2b \equiv K \Rightarrow U'(x) < 0$). Of course, for various quadratic utility functions, we have a different parameter b and, hence, a different upper bound K. As we shall see,

---

[7] See G. Hanoch and H. Levy, "Efficient Portfolio Selection with Quadratic and Cubic Utility," *Journal of Business*, 1970.

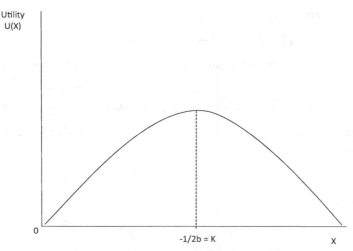

Figure 4.1. The Quadratic Utility Function.

this additional information allows us to develop an investment decision rule corresponding to the quadratic preferences that is stronger, and therefore better, than the M-V rule.

To prove the claim given in Theorem 4.2, assume that the investor faces two prospects, denoted by x and y. Having a quadratic preference, the expected utility of these two prospects is given by

$$EU(x) = Ex + b(Ex)^2 + b\sigma_x^2$$

and

$$EU(y) = Ey + b(Ey)^2 + b\sigma_y^2.$$

Subtracting the second equation from the first equation, we can assert that x dominates y for all relevant quadratic utility functions if for all relevant values b the following holds:

$$\Delta \equiv EU(x) - EU(y) = (Ex - Ey) + b[(E(x)^2 - E(y)^2] \\ + b(\sigma_x^2 - \sigma_y^2) \geq 0. \qquad (4.9)$$

Dividing all terms by $(-b)$ does not change this inequality because $-b > 0$. Thus, we assert that x dominates y for all relevant quadratic preferences if the following holds:

$$(1/-b)(Ex - Ey) - [(Ex)^2 - (Ey)^2] - (\sigma_x^2 - \sigma_y^2) \geq 0.$$

Using the rule

$$(Ex)^2 - (Ey)^2 = (Ex - Ey)(Ex + Ey),$$

the previous condition for dominance of x over y, can be rewritten as

$$(Ex - Ey)[-1/b - (Ex + Ey)] - (\sigma_x^2 - \sigma_y^2) \geq 0. \qquad (4.10)$$

Recalling that $-1/2b \equiv K$ or $-1/b = 2K$, equation (4.10) can be rewritten as

$$(Ex - Ey)[2K - (Ex + Ey)] \geq (\sigma_x^2 - \sigma_y^2). \qquad (4.11)$$

Namely,

$$(Ex - Ey)[2K - (Ex + Ey)] \geq (\sigma_x^2 - \sigma_y^2)$$
$$\Rightarrow EU_Q(x) \geq EU_Q(y) \qquad (4.12)$$

when the right-hand side of equation (4.12) is intact for all *relevant* quadratic preferences.

The claim given in Theorem 4.2 follows immediately from equation (4.12); if the conditions of the theorem hold, *a fortiori* equation (4.12) holds, implying that x has a higher expected utility than the expected utility of y. To see this claim, recall that by condition a) of the theorem, the mean of x is larger than (or equal to) the mean of y. Then, if condition b) of the theorem holds, equation (4.12) must hold, because for the relevant utility functions to avoid a violation of the monotonicity axiom, the following must hold:

$$\max(x, y) \leq K. \qquad (4.13)$$

Because by condition a) of Theorem 4.2, $(Ex - Ey) \geq 0$ by substituting K for $\max(x, y)$, we increase the positive term on the left-hand side of condition b) of Theorem 4.2 (or keep the difference unchanged). Because condition b) of Theorem 4.2 by assumption of the theorem holds, then by shifting from $\max(x, y)$ to K, we increase the positive term on the left-hand side of equation (4.12). So, if the conditions of the theorem hold, equation (4.12) must hold and we conclude that x has a higher utility than y for all relevant quadratic preferences. In short, we proved that if the conditions a) and b) hold $\Rightarrow$ equation (4.12) holds, implying that $EU_Q(x) \geq EU_Q(y)$ for all relevant quadratic utility functions.

To avoid trivial situations in the comparison of the two prospects under consideration, we require in Theorem 4.2 that there be at least one strict inequality: If $Ex = Ey$, to have a strict inequality in condition b) of the theorem, we must have that $\sigma_x^2 < \sigma_y^2$. If we have equality in condition b) of the theorem, we must have a strict inequality in condition a) of the theorem. Thus, by Theorem 4.2, either $\sigma_x^2 < \sigma_y^2$ or $Ex > Ey$ must hold.

Finally, if $Ex = Ey$, and $\sigma_x^2 = \sigma_y^2$, we always have equality in equation (4.12), implying that $EU_Q(x) = EU_Q(y)$ for all quadratic preferences. Thus, in the trivial case where the means and the variance of the two prospects are identical, there is no dominance by the M-V rule, and the M-V rule cannot be improved by the other rules suggested in the chapter.

Discussion

A few comments are called for:

1. In the preceding proof of Theorem 4.2, we refer to "all *relevant* quadratic functions." The reason for adding the word *relevant* is that the set of the quadratic preferences depends on the prospects under consideration. Thus, for each set of prospects, there is a corresponding set of relevant preferences. For example, if the highest outcome of the two prospects under consideration is 10, then only preferences with

$$10 \le -1/2b = K \quad \text{or} \quad b \le -1/20$$

   should be considered. If, however, with another set of prospects the highest outcome of the prospects under consideration is 1, then only preferences with the following parameters b should be considered:

$$1 \le -1/2b = K \quad \text{or} \quad b \le -2$$

As a consequence, the set of quadratic preferences that does not violate the monotonicity axiom depends on the prospects under consideration. This explains why we use the term *relevant quadratic utility function* in this theorem.

We stress that, generally, preference should not depend on the prospects under consideration. For example, when we discuss the

Second-Degree Stochastic Dominance (SSD) rule, we refer to the set of *all* concave preferences, and this set does not change with the possible change in the available prospects. However, with the set of quadratic preferences, we must ignore preferences that violate the monotonicity axiom; hence, the relevant preference set depends on the prospects under consideration. Indeed, the dependency of the preference set on the outcomes of the prospects is one of the deficiencies of the quadratic preference.

2. One can seemingly overcome this dependency of the preference on prospects' outcomes by choosing a parameter b that is close to zero. In this case, $-1/2b \equiv K \to \infty$, making K independent of the outcomes of prospects. Moreover, by such a parameter selection, the preference never declines – a second desirable characteristic of a preference. However, this technical solution is not satisfactory because with b close to zero, the quadratic function approaches the linear preference and risk neutrality prevails. Therefore, to keep risk-aversion behavior, this technical solution is unacceptable.

3. In Theorem 4.2, we assume that there are only two prospects under consideration. If there are z prospects, one should change condition b of Theorem 4.2. Specifically, one should replace $Max(x, y)$ with $Max(x, y, \ldots, z)$ because the highest outcome of all available prospects should not violate the monotonicity axiom.

4. One may argue that the superiority of the suggested rule over the M-V rule is not valid in cases in which only the means and variances are known and there is no information on the individual returns. Indeed, so far, we assume that all observations are available. We show that even when we have information on only the means and variances, we can construct an investment rule that is superior to the M-V rule for all quadratic preferences. Let us elaborate.

If there is information on only the means and variances, and not on the individual observations, we know that $Max(Ex, Ey)$ must be smaller than (or equal to) K, so we substitute this term with $Max(x, y)$ in condition b) of the theorem. Because we assume that $Ex \geq Ey$, the dominance condition with quadratic preferences will be in this specific case:

a) $Ex \geq Ey$ and   b) $(Ex - Ey)[2Ex - (Ex + Ey)] \geq (\sigma_x^2 - \sigma_y^2)$,

which can be rewritten also as

$$\text{a) } Ex \geq Ey \quad \text{and} \quad \text{b)} (Ex - Ey)^2 \geq \sigma_x^2 - \sigma_y^2. \tag{4.14}$$

Finally, note that dominance by the M-V rule implies dominance by the two suggested rules. This claim is intact because

if equation (4.1) holds $\Rightarrow$ equation (4.8) holds.

and because

if equation (4.1) holds $\Rightarrow$ equation (4.14) holds.

We conclude that also dominance by M-V $\Rightarrow$ dominance for all relevant quadratic preferences. Therefore, because M-V dominance implies dominance by the suggested two rules, and because dominance by the suggested rules does not necessarily imply dominance by the M-V rule, we conclude that the M-V efficient set must be larger than (or equal to) the efficient set derived by either one of the suggested rules given previously.

Examples
Example 1: Let us first go back to the numerical example given previously: Prospect F yields \$5 or \$10 with equal probability, and prospect G yields \$10 or \$20 with equal probability. For simplicity, denote the outcome of prospect G by x and the outcome corresponding to prospect F by y. A simple calculation reveals that,

$$E(x) = 15 > E(y) = 7.5$$

and

$$\sigma_x^2 = 25 > \sigma_y^2 = 6.25.$$

Therefore, neither F nor G dominates the other by the M-V rule. However, this is an unacceptable result because G dominates F by the FSD rule. Thus, not being able to reveal the superiority of prospect G is an obvious deficiency of the M-V rule.

Let us examine whether the stronger rules presented in this section overcome this shortcoming of the M-V rule and indeed reveal the superiority of G over F.

Using the conditions of Theorem 4.2, we have

$$\text{a) } E_G(x) = 15 > E_F(y) = 7.5$$

and

$$\text{b) } (Ex - Ey)[2\,Max(x, y) - (Ex + Ey)]$$
$$= (15 - 7.5)[2 \cdot 20 - (15 + 7.5)]$$
$$= 131.25 > \sigma_x^2 - \sigma_y^2 = 25 - 6.25 = 18.75.$$

Thus, with $Max(x, y) = 20$, both conditions a) and b) of Theorem 4.2 hold, and by the stronger rule given in Theorem 4.2, indeed the superiority of prospect G over prospect F is revealed. This example reaffirms that the M-V rule is sufficient but not necessary for dominance for quadratic preferences; thus, a better rule can be established. The stronger rule given in Theorem 4.2 can detect the FSD of G over F, whereas the M-V rule is unable to detect this superiority.

Assume that we have information regarding only the means and variances of the preceding two prospects. Does the investment rule given in condition (4.14) reveal the superiority of G? According to this example,

$$\text{a) } Ex = 15 > Ey = 7.5$$
$$\text{and}$$
$$\text{b) } (15 - 7.5)^2 = 56.5 > 25 - 6.25 = 18.75$$

Thus, prospect G dominates prospect F also when only the means and variances are known.

Example 2: Another example given previously reveals that the M-V rule fails to distinguish between prospect x yielding 1 and 2 with an equal probability and prospect y yielding 1 with certainty. Because x dominates y by the FSD rule, the fact that the M-V rule does not distinguish between the two prospects constitutes a deficiency of the M-V rule.

Does the stronger rule given in equation (4.14) resolve this paradoxical result? The mean of x is larger than the mean of y:

$$Ex = 1.5 > Ey = 1$$

and

$$(Ex - Ey)^2 = (1.5 - 1)^2 = .25 \geq (\sigma_x^2 - \sigma_y^2) = (.25 - 0) = .25.$$

Thus, we have at least one strong inequality; hence, by equatioin (4.14), the superiority of x is revealed. It is easy to show also that when we use in this example the information on the individual observations, a fortiori x dominates y. This stems from the fact that equation (4.8) $\Rightarrow$ equation (4.14). For brevity's sake, we do not give the detailed calculation corresponding to this case.

Example 3: In this example, there is no FSD, no SSD, and no M-V, yet there is dominance for all relevant quadratic preferences. Suppose that prospect x yields 0 or 4 with an equal probability and prospect y yields 1 with probability of 1. The mean of x is 2, and the variance is equal to 4. Obviously, there is no dominance by the M-V rule, and it is easy to see that there is also no FSD and no SSD because the two cumulative distributions corresponding to x and y intersect and the one with the highest mean also has the smallest possible return.

However, by the improved rules given in this section, there is dominance for all relevant quadratic preferences. Condition a) of Theorem 4.2 holds because x has a higher mean. Also, condition b) of Theorem 4.2 holds because

$$(2 - 1)[2 \cdot 4 - (2 + 1) = 5 > (4 - 0) = 4$$

(the parameters of x and y are inserted in condition b) of Theorem 4.2). Thus, in this case, there is no dominance by the M-V rule (and there is no FSD and no SSD), but there is dominance by the rule given in Theorem 4.2 for all relevant quadratic preferences.

Example 4: The last example illustrates how exploiting all available information can improve the decision-making process. We present here a case in which there is no M-V dominance and there is no dominance by the rule given by equation (4.14) (when only information on the mean and variances is available), but when there is also information on the individual observations, dominance is established. Thus, the more information we have on the distributions of outcomes, the stronger the decision rule that can be employed with quadratic preferences.

Suppose that prospect x yields 0, 3, or 6, each with a probability of 1/3 and that prospect y yields 1 with certainty. A simple calculation reveals that

$$Ex = 3, \sigma_x^2 = 6 \quad \text{and} \quad Ey = 1, \sigma_y^2 = 0.$$

Obviously, there is no M-V dominance (it is easy to verify that there is also no FSD and no SSD). However, assuming quadratic preference with information only on the means and variances does not change the results because still no dominance is revealed. To see this, we employ equation (4.14) to obtain

$$(3 - 1)^2 = 4 < (6 - 0).$$

Hence, condition b) does not hold, and there is no dominance.

We now turn to the strongest case, when the information on all observations is available and exploited. In this case, by condition b) of Theorem 4.2, we obtain

$$(3 - 1)[2 \cdot 6 - (3 + 1)] = 16 > (6 - 0) = 6.$$

Hence, conditions a) and b) of Theorem 4.2 hold and x dominates y. By means of this example, we show, as expected, that the more information we have, the sharper the obtained decision rule.

To sum up, the M-V rule is sufficient for dominance for quadratic preferences, implying that dominance by M-V rule means a higher expected utility for all relevant quadratic preferences. However, it is not a necessary rule, implying that one prospect may dominate the other for all preferences, let alone for all quadratic preferences, but the M-V rule is unable to detect this superiority. We suggest in this section other rules that are better than the M-V rule for the quadratic preferences because these suggested rules utilize more information on the quadratic preference that is related to the distribution of returns.

Finally, we do not advocate that the quadratic preference be recommended as a descriptive preference of investors' behavior. On the contrary, the quadratic preference reveals increasing absolute risk aversion, implying that the greater one's wealth, the higher the premium one requires to get rid of a given risk. Also, it implies that in contradiction to the observed behavior, given that the investor faces a risky asset and a riskless asset, the higher the investor's wealth, the less he or she would invest in the risky asset. This property contradicts observed behavior (see Pratt[8] and Arrow[9]) and therefore constitutes a drawback of the quadratic preference. The other two related drawbacks are that there is a range of outcomes where the first derivative is negative and that the relevant set of preferences we deal with depends of the outcomes of prospects under consideration. Despite these deficiencies, the quadratic preference is widely used in academic research. Therefore, if it is employed, we suggest the preceding ways to improve the decision rules that are based on this quadratic function.

4.6. NORMAL DISTRIBUTIONS AND THE MEAN-VARIANCE RULE

The strongest theoretical case for employment of the M-V rule is when the return distributions are normal and risk aversion prevails. Calculating the expected utility directly with the normal density function, Tobin[10] shows that the M-V rule is optimal as long as risk aversion is assumed. In this section, we choose another route: we show that in the specific case where distributions of returns are normal, the M-V rule and the SSD rule coincide. Because we have already shown in Chapter 3 that with risk aversion the SSD rule is optimal regardless of the precise shape of the distribution of returns, it is obviously optimal also in the specific case where distributions are normal. Because M-V and SSD rules coincide in such a case, we can safely conclude that when distributions are normal, the M-V is, like SSD, an optimal investment rule.

The normal distribution has some unique features that are employed in proving the optimality of the M-V rule. We discuss here only those features needed for the proof of the optimality of the M-V rule and some other features that we employ in other chapters of this book.

Property 1: The probability of any event can be calculated with the standard normal distribution with a mean of zero and a variance of 1. The density function of the normal distribution is given by

$$f(x) = \frac{1}{\sqrt{2\pi\sigma_x^2}} \exp\left[-\frac{(x - \mu_x)^2}{2\sigma_x^2}\right] dx \quad \text{for } -\infty < x < +\infty.$$

---

[8] J. W. Pratt, "Risk Aversion in the Small and in the Large," *Econometrica*, 1964.

[9] K. Arrow, *Aspects of the Theory of Risk Bearing*, Yrjo Jahnssonin Saatio, Helsinki, 1965.

[10] See J. Tobin, *op. cit.*

The cumulative distribution $F(x)$ is given by the integral of the density function up to any point x. As can be seen from this density function, it depends only on two parameters, the mean, μ_x, and the variance, σ_x^2.

Making the transformation

$$z = \frac{x - \mu_x}{\sigma_x},$$

the following density function of the standard normal distribution is obtained:

$$f(z) = \frac{1}{\sqrt{2\pi}} \exp\left[-\frac{z^2}{2}\right] dz \quad \text{for} -\infty < z < +\infty$$

This standard normal distribution has the following parameters:

$$E(z) = E\left(\frac{x - \mu_x}{\sigma_x}\right) = \frac{1}{\sigma_x} E(x - \mu_x) = 0$$

and

$$\sigma_z^2 = \frac{E(x - \mu_x)^2}{\sigma_x^2} = 1.$$

Suppose we have two normal distributions:

$$x \sim N\left(\mu_x, \sigma_x^2\right) \text{ and } y \sim N\left(\mu_y, \sigma_y^2\right).$$

The probability of any event corresponding to these distributions can be calculated by shifting to the variable z, namely, by the probability distribution $z \sim N(0, 1)$. Moreover, if we have

$$\frac{x - \mu_x}{\sigma_x} = \frac{y - \mu_y}{\sigma_y} = z,$$

then the cumulative probability up to any given value z is identical for the two distinct distributions under consideration. For example, suppose we have the following parameters corresponding to two normal distributions x and y:

$$\mu_x = 1, \sigma_x = 2 \quad \text{and} \quad \mu_y = 0, \sigma_y = 4;$$

then, for any value, say, K, for which the following holds:

$$\frac{K - 1}{2} = \frac{K - 0}{4} = z.$$

The two distributions accumulate the same probability. It is easy to see that for the value $K = 2$, we get the same value $z = 1/2$. Therefore, we have

$$F_x(2) = \Pr(X \le 2) = F_y(2) = \Pr(Y \le 2) = F_z(1/2) = \Pr(Z \le 1/2),$$

where F denotes the cumulative distributions of x, y, and z, respectively. Looking at the tables of normal distributions, indeed, we find that the probability of this event is equal to about 69.15%. Thus, the probability of a given event with any normal distribution can be calculated by means of the standard normal distribution, for which probability tables are available.

Property 2: The cumulative normal distributions intersect at most once.

By property 1, two cumulative normal distributions accumulate the same probability up to an outcome K, where K is given by

$$\frac{K - \mu_x}{\sigma_x} = \frac{K - \mu_y}{\sigma_y} = z.$$

Solving for K we obtain

$$K = \frac{\mu_x \sigma_y - \mu_y \sigma_x}{\sigma_y - \sigma_x}. \tag{4.15}$$

Because there is only one solution for K (see equation [4.15]), we can safely assert that any two cumulative normal distributions cross at most once, at the value K given in equation (4.15). Employing the parameters given previously, we indeed obtain

$$K = (1 \cdot 4 - 0 \cdot 2)/(4 - 2) = 2$$

as obtained before. In the specific case in which the two distributions have identical variances, the denominator in equation (4.15) is equal to zero, implying that the cumulative distributions never cross.

Figure 4.2 illustrates two cases, one case when the two cumulative distributions cross once (Figure 4.2a) and the other case when the two cumulative distributions do not cross (Figure 4.2b). The value K is the outcome corresponding to the intersection point of the two cumulative distributions.

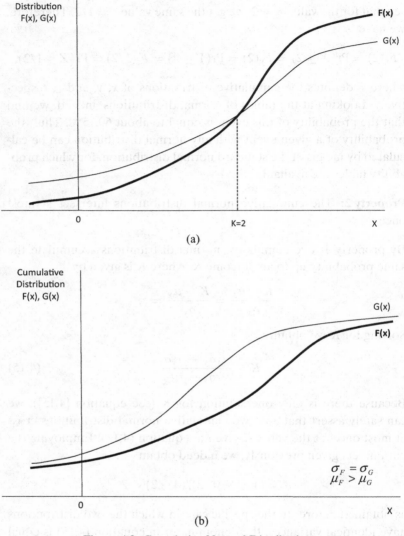

Figure 4.2. Cumulative Normal Distributions.

Property 3: The distribution with the higher variance is located above the distribution with the lower variance left of the intersection point, K.

Thus, for all values $k < K$, we have $F(k) < G(k)$, where F is the cumulative distribution with the smaller variance. Obviously, the opposite inequality holds for all values $k > K$, and equality holds at the intersection point, $k = K$ (see Figure 4.2a). Using these properties of the normal distribution, we show that the M-V rule is optimal as long as distributions of returns are normal and risk aversion is assumed.

Theorem 4.3: Let F and G denote two normal distributions.[11] Then:

a) If the variances of the two options under consideration are not identical, the M-V rule coincides with the SSD rule; hence, it is an optimal rule for all risk averters.

b) If the variances of the two distributions under consideration are identical, the M-V rule coincides with the FSD rule; hence, it is an optimal rule for all investors, risk averters and risk seekers alike.

Thus, dominance by M-V rule coincides with either FSD or SSD.[12]

Proof:

a) Suppose prospect F dominates prospect G by the M-V rule when the variances are unequal. Namely,

$$\mu_F \geq \mu_G \quad \text{and} \quad \sigma_F < \sigma_G. \tag{4.16}$$

The two normal distributions under consideration intersect once, at point K, where the cumulative probability of G is above the cumulative distribution of F, left of point K (see properties 2 and 3). The two cumulative distributions corresponding to this case are illustrated in Figure 4.3.

---

[11] The requirement of the normal distribution is actually too restrictive. It has been shown that the theorem holds also with elliptic distributions, which include the normal distributions as a specific case. For example, the theorem holds also for logistic distribution (see proof in Chapter 8), which also belongs to the elliptic family. For more details, see G. Chamberlain, "A Characterization of the Distributions That Imply Mean-Variance Utility Functions," *Econometrica*, 1983; and J. B. Berk, "Necessary Conditions for the CAPM," *Journal of Economic Theory*, 1997.

[12] The FSD rule is optimal for all preferences, with risk seeking and risk aversion alike. The SSD rule is optimal for risk-averse preferences. For definitions of FSD and SSD, see Chapter 3.

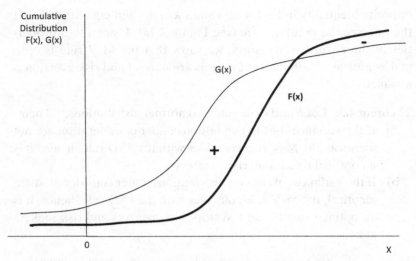

Figure 4.3. The Cumulative Normal Distributions

By equation (3.2″), given in Chapter 3 we have

$$\mu_F - \mu_G = \int_{-\infty}^{+\infty} [G(x) - F(x)]dx. \qquad (4.17)$$

Because by assumption of the theorem $\mu_F - \mu_G \geq 0$, the integral given on the right-hand side of equation (4.17) is non-negative. Graphically, it implies that the positive area denoted by " + " in Figure 4.3 is larger than (or equal to) the following negative area denoted by "−". There is only one intersection of the two normal distributions under consideration, which implies that for all values, $x < \infty$:[13]

$$\int_{-\infty}^{x} [G(x) - F(x)]dx > 0 \qquad (4.18)$$

Consequently, F dominates G by SSD (see Figure 4.3).

The opposite relation also holds: If F dominates G by SSD, we have dominance by the M-V rule as given by equation (4.16). To see this claim, recall that F dominating G by SSD implies that

$$\int_{-\infty}^{x} [G(x) - F(x)]dx \geq 0 \qquad (4.19)$$

---

[13] As for $x = \infty$, the integral given in eq. (4.16) is non-negative, by shifting to the left (i.e., for any value $x < \infty$, we reduce the negative area enclosed between the two distributions) (see Figure 4.3); hence, the integral given in eq. (4.17) is positive.

for all values x, so this inequality holds also for $x = \infty$, implying that by equation (4.17) $\mu_F \geq \mu_G$. Also, the dominance of F over G by SSD implies that G must be located above F, left of K; otherwise, the SSD condition is violated.[14] This implies that the variance of G must be greater than the variance of F. Thus, we also proved that equation (4.19) implies equation (4.16). To sum up, we can conclude: The M-V rule (as given by equation (4.16)) $\Leftrightarrow$ SSD (as given by equation (4.19)). In other words, the M-V rule (in the case of unequal variances) and the SSD rule coincide. Because the SSD rule is optimal for all risk averters, we actually proved that the M-V rule is also optimal, as long as risk aversion and normal distributions are assumed.

b) If the two variances are identical, the two distributions do not intersect and the distribution with the higher mean is located to the right of the distribution with the lower mean, as demonstrated in Figure 4.2b. We therefore have, in this case,

$$\mu_F > \mu_G, \sigma_F = \sigma_G \Leftrightarrow F \text{ dominates } G \text{ by the FSD rule.}$$

To sum up, if the distributions are normal, one can safely employ the M-V rule. The M-V rule with normal distribution is a case consistent with expected utility maximization corresponding to all risk averters (version (a) of the M-V rule) or a case consistent with expected utility corresponding to all unrestricted preferences (version (b) of the M-V rule).

Discussion

We have proved that the M-V rule is optimal when the return distributions are normal. The implication of this proof is that one can ignore all distributions' moments higher than the second one. However, this result is seemingly in contradiction to equation (4.4), showing that all distributions' moments are relevant for decision making and therefore one cannot rely solely on the mean and the variance of the return in the decision-making process. For example, take the logarithmic

---

[14] Recall that the distribution with the higher variance must be above the distribution with the lower variance, left of the intersection point of these two distributions.

preference to show that all derivatives are different from zero, implying that all moments are relevant in determining the expected utility.
This seemingly contradiction is resolved as follows:

i. With normal distributions, all odd moments are equal to zero
    because the distribution is symmetrical. Thus, even if investors
    like high positive skewness, in a comparison of two normal dis-
    tributions, this preference for skewness is irrelevant because for
    the two distributions under consideration, the skewness is equal
    to zero.

ii. However, with normal distributions, all even moments are pos-
    itive and affect expected utility, making one wonder how could
    the M-V rule be optimal; that is, how could only the mean and
    variance be relevant for decision making, when by equation
    (4.4), expected utility depends also on moments higher than
    the second one. This apparent contradiction is resolved once
    we recall that all even moments of the normal distribution are
    a function of the variance. We have the following mathematical
    relation between the variance and the other even moments:[15]

$$E(x - \mu)^{2k} = \frac{(2k)!}{2^k k!}(\sigma^2)^k, \quad \text{where } k = 1,2,3,\ldots$$

Note that on the left-hand side of the equation we have all the
even moments. For example, if $k = 1$, on the left-hand side we get
the variance. If $k = 2$, we get the kurtosis, and so on. Thus, all the
even moments are a function of the variance; namely, even by equation (4.4), expected utility depends only on the mean and variance:

$$EU(x) = f(\mu, \sigma^2)$$

Adding the assumption of risk aversion, we have that

$$\partial EU(x)\partial E(x) > 0 \quad \text{and} \quad \partial EU(x)/\sigma_x^2 < 0,$$

regardless of the fact that all even moments do not vanish. Thus, the
fact that all moments are a function of the variance explains why in the
normal case, one can make decisions solely by the mean and variance,
even though all even moments are not equal to zero.

---

[15] See M. Kendall and A. Stuart, *The Advanced Theory of Statistics*, Griffin, London,
1983.

4.7. THE MEAN-VARIANCE RULE AS AN APPROXIMATION TO EXPECTED UTILITY

So far, we have analyzed the conditions under which it is theoretically legitimate to employ the M-V rule. In this section, we analyze the cases where these theoretical conditions do not prevail, yet the M-V rule can still be employed in practice. In fact, in this section, we empirically analyze and answer the following two questions:

1. Suppose the distributions of returns are not normal (and not elliptical) and that the utility function is not quadratic. Would an astute selection from the M-V efficient set yield a portfolio with almost as great an expected utility as the maximum expected utility obtained with a direct maximization? If the answer to this question is positive for a wide class of risk-averse preferences, one can use the M-V rule without precise knowledge of the preference. Moreover, an investment manager can employ the M-V rule in portfolio selection, which can be useful for all his or her clients, despite their heterogeneous preferences, as long as risk aversion prevails.
2. Relying on the suggested quadratic approximation, $f(\mu, \sigma^2)$, is it guaranteed that an efficient M-V portfolio will be selected? If the answer is positive, one can focus on the M-V efficient set, as suggested by question 1. Otherwise, the M-V efficiency analysis may lose ground because inefficient portfolios may be optimal by the suggested quadratic approximation.

In this section, we first present the various M-V approximations to expected utility that have been suggested in the literature. Second, we analyze the relationship of the selected portfolio by the quadratic approximation to the M-V portfolios located on the efficient frontier. Finally, we demonstrate empirically the quality of the various M-V approximations to expected utility.

a) The Various Mean-Variance Quadratic Approximations

Several studies report that unless we have some extreme returns or pathological utility function, choosing a portfolio from the M-V efficient set yields almost the same expected utility as a direct maximization of expected utility. This suggests that with actual stock returns rather than hypothetical examples like those given here, the M-V rule can be employed in most cases, albeit not all cases, even when the classic theoretical justifications for the employment of the M-V rule do not prevail.

In studying the M-V approximation to expected utility, the basic question is whether there is some function f of the mean and variance such that

$$f(\mu, \sigma^2) \cong EU.$$

Although it is common in the literature to write the function as $f(\mu, \sigma^2)$, it is more precise to write this function, even for the same given data set, as $f(\mu, \sigma^2, U)$, because the selected approximation function depends also on the utility function with which expected utility is calculated.

One can analyze this approximation function theoretically: imposing some constraints on the preference or on the distributions of returns, one can study which constraints guarantee a relatively good approximation. However, as we demonstrate in the following section, the quality of the approximation is mainly an empirical rather than a theoretical question. The quality of the approximation may change from one data set to another. Moreover, even for a given data set, the quality of the approximation varies from one utility function to another.

Approximation of the utility function under consideration is central to Markowitz's[16] rationale for the employment of the M-V rule. As early as 1959, Markowitz suggested that if the range of the returns is not too wide, one can approximate the expected utility with some function of the mean and variance of return. Specifically, Markowitz suggests two possible quadratic approximations to expected utility. Ten years after publication of the book by Markowitz, Young and Trent[17] reported some empirical results corresponding to the approximations of $f(\mu, \sigma^2)$ to the logarithmic preference. They use annual and monthly data on 233 individual stocks and 4 synthetic portfolios

---

[16] H. M. Markowitz, *Portfolio Selection: Efficient Diversification of Investment*, Yale University Press, New Haven, 1970.

[17] W. E. Young and R. H. Trent, "Geometric Mean Approximation of Individual Securities and Portfolios Performance," *Journal of Financial and Quantitative Analysis*, 1969.

containing 4, 8, 16, and 32 stocks. Young and Trent report that for the logarithmic preference (which coincides with the maximization of the geometric mean), a simple function of the mean and variance provides an excellent approximation to expected utility. They conclude:

> Empirical evidence indicates that even though a number of monthly and annual distributions deviate significantly from normality, the approximation involving only the mean and variance produces quite accurate estimates of the geometric means of these distributions. (p. 179)

The best approximation is obtained for short horizon rates of returns, but Young and Trent report that for the logarithmic preference, monthly data reveal an excellent fit between the precise expected utility calculations and the M-V approximation, let alone returns corresponding to a shorter horizon.[18]

Although several studies[19] use different approaches to measure the deviation of the M-V rule's portfolio from the portfolio selected by the expected utility rule, we focus here on the study of Levy and Markowitz,[20] which was probably the first to analyze this approximation issue theoretically and empirically. In this section, we measure the quality of the approximation by the correlation between the ranking of investments by the M-V rule and the ranking by a direct expected

---

[18] Samuelson, and later Ohlson, analyze the conditions under which the mean and the variance are asymptotically sufficient for optimal decisions as the interval between portfolio revisions approaches zero. However, Young and Trent show that a monthly horizon is sufficient to obtain an excellent approximation. For more details, see Young and Trent, *op. cit.*, and P. A. Samuelson, "The Fundamental Approximation Theorem of Portfolio Analysis in Terms of Means, Variances and Higher Moments," *Review of Economic Studies*, 1970.

[19] See, for example, A. S. Dexter, J. N. Yu, and W. T. Ziemba, "Portfolio Selection in a Lognormal Market When the Investor Has a Power Utility Function: Computational Results." In M. A. H. Dempster (editor), *Stochastic Programming*, Academic Press, New York, 1980; L. M. Pully, "A General Mean-Variance Approximation to Expected Utility for Short Holding Periods," *Journal of Financial and Quantitative Analysis*, 1981; L. M. Pully, "Mean-Variance Approximation to Expected Logarithmic Utility," *Operation Research*, 1983; Y. Kroll, H. Levy, and H. M. Markowitz, "Mean-Variance versus Direct Utility Maximization," *Journal of Finance*, 1984; and L. H. Ederington, "Mean-Variance as an Approximation to Expected Utility Maximization," working paper, Washington University, St. Louis, 1986.

[20] H. Levy and H. Markowitz, "Approximating Expected Utility by a Function of the Mean and Variance," *American Economic Review*, 1979.

utility maximization. In Chapter 8, we extend this analysis and measure the financial loss in dollar terms from using the M-V rule rather than a direct expected utility maximization.

To justify employment of the M-V rule, it is common to expand the utility to a Taylor series and ignore moments greater than the second one to obtain that the approximated expected utility depends only on the means and variances. Expanding $U(x)$ about zero yields[21]

$$U(x) = U(0) + U'(0)x + .5U''(0)x^2 + \cdots \qquad (4.20)$$

Taking the expected value, we obtain

$$EU(x) \cong U(0) + U'(0)\mu + .5U''(0)(\mu^2 + \sigma^2), \qquad (4.20')$$

where, μ and σ^2 are the mean and the variance of x, respectively.

Similarly, expanding the utility to a Taylor series about the mean, μ, one obtains

$$U(x) = U(\mu) + U'(\mu)(x - \mu) + .5U''(\mu)(x - \mu)^2 + \cdots. \qquad (4.21)$$

and the expected utility can be approximated by

$$EU(x) \cong U(\mu) + .5U(\mu'')\sigma^2, \qquad (4.21')$$

where x is the return, namely $(1 +$ rate of return); similarly μ stands for $(1 +$ the mean rate of return).

Because the fit given in equation (4.21) is, in most cases, better than the fit given in equation (4.20), let us focus on this approximation. The precise fit of the quadratic approximation to the utility function is achieved at one point, where $\mu = x$. At this point, all terms but the first one on the right-hand side of equation (4.21) are equal to zero, and we have that the approximation exactly equals the precise utility. Graphically, it means that the utility function and the approximate quadratic coincide at this point.

Arrow and Pratt[22] object to the quadratic preference because as wealth changes, the quadratic preference reveals an increasing degree of absolute risk aversion. However, this criticism of the quadratic utility function does not apply to the quadratic approximation because

---

[21] Similar results are obtained when we expand the utility of the initial wealth plus x to a Taylor series. For simplicity, we ignore the initial wealth in the analyses in this section.

[22] See Arrow and Pratt, *op. cit.*

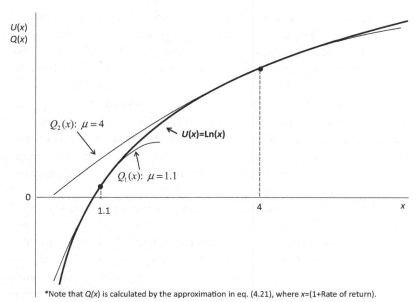

*Note that Q(x) is calculated by the approximation in eq. (4.21), where x=(1+Rate of return).

Figure 4.4. The Quadratic Approximation to $U(x) = \text{Ln}(x)$ for Two Prospects: One with a Mean of 1.1 and One with a Mean of 4, and $k = 0$*.

we have many quadratic approximations, each one to each level of wealth. Thus, the quadratic fit is "a custom-made fit" because it varies with the prospect under consideration as well as with the utility under consideration. Take, for example, two prospects with a mean return of, say, 10% and 300%. Then, for the same utility function, we have by equation (4.21), two fits, one for each prospect. Figure 4.4 demonstrates this case. We have a utility function U and two quadratic functions Q_1 and Q_2. As we see from the figure, $U = Q_1$ at value $\mu_1 = 10\%$, and $U = Q_2$ at value $\mu_2 = 300\%$, namely, at mean return of 1.1 and 4.0, respectively (we select such a large return for visual purposes because the two quadratic functions are apart). As we can see, when the prospect's mean return $(1 +$ mean rate of return) is 1.1, the fit is perfect with Q_1, and when the mean return is 4.0, the fit is perfect with another quadratic, Q_2. The same is true also with the quadratic approximation when the Taylor series is expanded about zero return: as wealth changes, we fit another quadratic corresponding to the new wealth level.[23]

---

[23] For more details and formal proof, see Levy and Markowitz, *op. cit.*

To find the quality of the suggested approximation, it is common to assume some specific utility function (e.g., logarithmic preference) and to use some empirical set of data to calculate the expected utility twice, once by calculating the expected utility directly (e.g., if preference is assumed to be logarithmic, by the expected value of the log return) and once by calculating the mean and the variance, and then employing either equation (4.20′) or (4.21′) (or other approximation methods; see the following discussion) to calculate the approximated expected utility. Some index based on the difference between the obtained results of these two calculations indicates the quality of the approximation.

Employing logarithmic preference and some empirical distributions, Markowitz[24] and Young and Trent[25] show that the approximation given in equation (4.21′) performed markedly better than the approximation given in equation (4.20′). However, note that because the utility function appears as a parameter in the approximation function (e.g., see equation [4.21]), it affects the quality of the approximation. This implies that for the same set of data, the approximation may prove to be excellent for one utility function and poor for another.

It is easy to see that both these approximations involve fitting a quadratic function to $U(x)$ about one value of x. Employing a similar idea, Levy and Markowitz suggest fitting the quadratic function to three judiciously chosen points on $U(x)$. Obviously, as we investigate the quality of the M-V approximation, it is suggested that these selected points be a function of the mean and variance. They suggest that the quadratic function passes through the following three points:

a) $[x = (\mu - k\sigma), U(\mu - k\sigma)]$
b) $[x = \mu, U(\mu)]$
c) $[(x = \mu + k\sigma), U(\mu + k\sigma)]$

where k, which is positive and is selected such that the best approximation is obtained (for a demonstration of the three points where the utility function and the quadratic function coincide, see Figure 4.7).

[24] H. M. Markowitz, *Portfolio Selection: Efficient Diversification of Investment*, Wiley, New York, 1959, Yale University Press, New Haven, 1970, Basil Blackwell 1991.
[25] W. E. Young and R. H. Trent, "Geometric Mean Approximation of Individual Securities and Portfolio Performance," *Journal of Financial and Quantitative Analysis*, 1969.

Of course, there is no one best value k because the selected value k depends on the data analyzed. The suggested quadratic function passing through these three points can be written in terms of deviations from the mean:

$$Q_k(x) = a_k + b_k(x - \mu) + c_k(x - \mu)^2, \qquad (4.22)$$

where the subscript k indicates that the various coefficients are a function of the selected value k. Taking the expected value yields

$$E(Q_k(x)) = a_k + c_k \sigma^2. \qquad (4.23)$$

Writing equation (4.22) corresponding to the three specific points given previously, we obtain for point a) where $x = (\mu - k\sigma)$:

$$U(\mu - k\sigma) = a_k + b_k((\mu - k\sigma) - \mu) + c_k((\mu - k\sigma) - \mu)^2$$
$$= a_k - b_k k\sigma + c_k k^2 \sigma^2.$$

Thus, the value of the quadratic function at point $\mu - k\sigma$ is, by construction, equal to $U(\mu - k\sigma)$.

By a similar calculation we get for point c):

$$U(\mu + k\sigma) = a_k + b_k k\sigma + c_k k^2 \sigma^2.$$

And for point b) we get:

$$U(\mu) = a_k \text{ (the other two terms are equal to zero).}$$

Using these three equations, we solve for the three parameters of the quadratic function, which passes through these three selected points. We have three equations and three unknowns. Simple algebra reveals that

$$a_k = U(\mu)$$
$$b_k = [U(\mu + k\sigma) - U(\mu - k\sigma)]/2k\sigma$$
$$c_k = [U(\mu + k\sigma) + U(\mu - k\sigma) - 2U(\mu)]/2k^2\sigma^2.$$

Substituting a_k and c_k in equation (4.23) yields

$$f_k[\mu, \sigma^2, U(x)] \equiv E(Q_k) = U(\mu) + [U(\mu + k\sigma)$$
$$+ U(\mu - k\sigma) - 2U(\mu)]/2k^2, \qquad (4.24)$$

where f_k (i.e., the function that determines the quadratic approximation, depending on the value k, on the parameters μ and σ as well as on the assumed utility function). It is worth noting that if $U'' < 0$, it is easy to see that the quadratic approximation given by equation (4.22) is also a risk-averse function as for all monotonic nondecreasing risk-averse U, $b_k > 0$, and $c_k < 0$ (see the previous definition of the coefficients in terms of U).[26]

b) Discussion: Mean-Variance Approximation and Mean-Variance Efficient Prospects[27]

By the Markowitz efficiency analysis, it is recommended that a portfolio from the M-V efficient set should be selected. It has also been suggested that the quadratic approximation, given in equation (4.24), should be employed to select the optimal portfolio. Are these two recommendations consistent? Is it possible that by maximizing equation (4.24), we end up with an M-V inefficient portfolio? We devote this section to analyzing these questions.

First, note that equation (4.24) measures the quadratic approximation of expected utility. However, unlike the commonly employed utility function, the approximation of the expected utility, $E(Q_k)$ is determined by parameters of the utility function itself, as well as on the mean and variance of the prospect under consideration (see equation (4.24)). Thus, by changing these parameters of the prospect under consideration, one does not shift from one point to another on a given utility function, but rather one shifts from one quadratic to another quadratic, as demonstrated in Figure 4.4. In such a case, one needs to verify that the prospect choice by the M-V approximation given by equation (4.24) does not end up with an inefficient M-V prospect. If an inefficient portfolio may be selected, this implies that one cannot confine the prospects choice only to the M-V efficient set because an inefficient M-V interior prospect may maximize the quadratic approximation. The good news, as we shall see, is that in the most general case, this scenario may occur with individual distinct prospects but not with diversified portfolios, which is the raison d'être for employment of the M-V rule. Furthermore, when one is willing to assume DARA,

---

[26] For every $k > 0$, $b_k > 0$ due to the monotonicity assumption. The coefficient $c_k < 0$ because for any concave function U, we have $U(\mu) - U(\mu - k\sigma) > U(\mu + k\sigma) - U(\mu)$.

[27] I would like to thank Moshe Levy for pointing out to me that the portfolio that maximizes the quadratic function may be M-V inefficient.

by employing equation (4.24), an M-V efficient portfolio will always be selected.

To explain this point further, suppose that an investor who is convinced that $E(Q_k)$ provides an excellent approximation to expected utility selects his or her investment by maximizing $E(Q_k)$ given by equation (4.24). Furthermore, suppose that the investor faces two distributions F and G, where $E_F(Q_k) > E_G(Q_k)$. Is it possible that $E_F < E_G$ and $\sigma_F > \sigma_G$? If such a situation is possible, the investor who selects the prospects by the highest $E(Q_k)$ (as recommended in the previous section) will select a portfolio that is inferior by the M-V rule. Alternatively, in such a case, the investor who selects a portfolio from the M-V efficient set (as recommended in this section) will not maximize $E(Q_k)$ because portfolio F, which maximizes $E(Q_k)$, is M-V inefficient and hence will not be considered at all by the investor because it is not in the efficient set.

We now show that in the most general case, when one is not willing to assume any assumption beyond that the utility is concave – indeed, when diversification between assets is not allowed – the preceding situation may occur, pointing out a drawback of the quadratic approximation. However, in the case that is more economically relevant, when diversification among various assets, as recommended by Markowitz, is allowed, such a situation is impossible: an M-V interior portfolio will never be selected, but a portfolio located on the M-V inefficient frontier (see segment (a), MVP in Figure 4.6) may be selected. Finally, when apart from the concavity assumption, DARA is also assumed, maximizing $E(Q_k)$ will always bring about an M-V efficient portfolio, a very satisfying result from the approximation methodology's point of view. Thus, in the most relevant case, maximization of the quadratic approximation cannot be achieved with an M-V inferior portfolio, and when DARA is assumed, the portfolio that maximizes equation (4.24) must be M-V efficient. In the analysis of this issue, we distinguish between the aforementioned cases as spelled out below.

c) A General Utility Function with No DARA Assumption

We shall split the analysis corresponding to this case into two cases, where in the one case diversification is not allowed and in the other case it is allowed.

1. Diversification is not allowed.

In this case, the quadratic approximation given by equation (4.24), indeed, may end up with a selection of an M-V inefficient prospect. Namely, it is possible that when one compares two prospects, F and G, and diversification between F and G is not allowed, $E_F(Q_k) > E_G(Q_k)$ generally does not guarantee that F dominates G by the M-V rule. In this case, selecting a portfolio by equation (4.24) may reveal that an M-V inefficient portfolio is selected, in contradiction to the recommendation of Markowitz, asserting that one should focus on the M-V efficient set of assets.

To show this claim, let us examine equation (4.24) carefully. By equation (4.24) we have

$$\partial E(Q_k)/\partial \sigma = [U'(\mu + k\sigma) - U'(\mu - k\sigma)]/2k < 0.$$

This term is negative because U' is declining by the assumption that the quadratic approximation is concave and $\mu + k\sigma > \mu - k\sigma$. Thus, the higher the variance, the lower the expected value of the quadratic approximation function, which is an encouraging result from the M-V analysis point of view. However, concerning the mean, it is possible that increasing the mean will induce a reduction in the expected approximation, which is a discouraging result from the M-V approximation perspective. Namely, the derivative (see equation (4.24))

$$\partial E(Q_k)/\partial \mu = U'(\mu) + [U'(\mu + k\sigma) + U'(\mu - k\sigma) - 2U'(\mu)]/2k^2$$

may be positive, zero, or negative. To see this claim, recall that the first term on the right-hand side is non-negative, but it may be close to zero; so the sign of the second term on the right-hand side may determine the sign of this derivative. Let us rewrite this term and investigate its possible sign. Ignoring k and the 2, which are positive, it can be rewritten as follows:

$$[U'(\mu + k\sigma) - U'(\mu)] - [U'(\mu) - U'(\mu - k\sigma)] \equiv A - B.$$

First note that as U' is declining, both A and B are negative. Because in the most general case we know only that the utility function is non-decreasing and concave, the derivative function may have several possible shapes. Figure 4.5 demonstrates two possible shapes, one with $A - B > 0$ and one with $A - B < 0$, revealing that the sign of this term cannot be determined unless some more restrictions are imposed

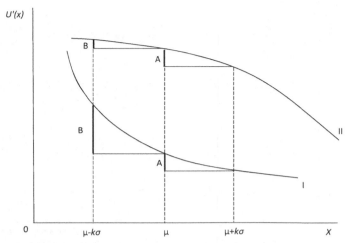

Figure 4.5. Utility Function with Various First Derivative, $U'(x)$.

on preference beyond the sign of the first two derivatives. However, because both A and B are negative, $A–B$ corresponding to case I in Figure 4.5 is positive and $A–B$ corresponding to case II is negative. (Looking at the length of the vertical line A and B is misleading because we are dealing with negative numbers.)

Note that both curves I and II, given in Figure 4.5, are consistent with the requirement that the utility under consideration is non-decreasing and concave because U' is positive and declining. However, recalling that both A and B are negative, we have the following possibilities:

$$\text{Case I}: A - B > 0 \Rightarrow \partial E(Q_k)/\partial \mu > 0 \qquad (4.25)$$

$$\text{Case II}: A - B < 0 \Rightarrow \partial E(Q_k)/\partial \mu < 0.$$

(This is possible but does not necessarily hold. It holds if $U'(\mu)$ is close to zero because this term is ignored here.)

Therefore, in case II, which is economically legitimate, we may end up with the quadratic approximation maximization with a portfolio that is M-V inefficient, because increasing the mean decreases the expected quadratic function given by equation (4.24). Decreasing the variance will increase $E(Q_k)$, but at a lower rate than the decrease due to the increase in the mean; hence, by the approximation, a M-V

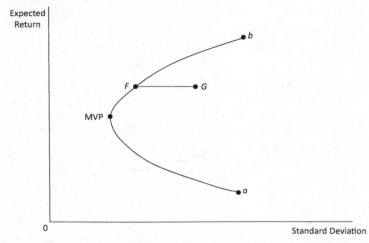

Figure 4.6. Dominance of Portfolio *F* over Portfolio *G* by the M-V Rule.

inefficient portfolio may be selected. In case I, the derivative is positive; hence, the prospect that maximizes equation (4.24) must be M-V efficient.

2. Diversification is allowed

The selection of an *interior* M-V portfolio by equation (4.24) is impossible, once one allows diversification. To see this, consider Figure 4.6. For any inefficient (interior) portfolio *G*, there is a portfolio *F* with an equal mean and smaller variance. *F* dominates *G* by the M-V rule (see Figure 4.6); but it is easy to show that also $E(Q_F) > E(Q_G)$ because the means are equal (hence, $\partial E(Q_k)/\partial \mu$ is irrelevant), and we proved that $\partial E(Q_k)/\partial \sigma < 0$.

Thus, when the investor considers two prospects with unequal means, the portfolio with the lower mean may reveal a higher expected value of the quadratic approximation given in equation (4.24), and hence may be selected, which is an undesired result. However, in the more relevant case, when one is allowed to create a diversified portfolio, the portfolio that maximizes the expected value of the quadratic approximation must be located on the M-V *frontier*. Therefore, one can safely ignore all the M-V *inferior* portfolios; they cannot maximize the expected quadratic function. Recalling that portfolio diversification is the raison d'être for Markowitz M-V analysis, the seeming drawback of the M-V quadratic approximation discussed previously loses ground. Yet, unless we add the DARA assumption, a portfolio located on the inefficient frontier segment a-MVP may be selected because for any portfolio on this segment, there is no other portfolio with an equal mean that dominates it by the M-V rule (see Figure 4.6).[28] Thus, the conclusion is that when diversification is allowed, one can safely select a portfolio located on the M-V frontier, but by the approximation method, the investor should not relegate segment a-MVP to the inefficient set.

d) A Risk-Averse Utility Function with DARA

So far, we have seen that employing the quadratic approximation may lead to the selection of a portfolio located on the M-V frontier but not necessarily on the M-V efficient set. As we shall see, when assuming DARA, the selection of a portfolio by the quadratic approximation guarantees that a portfolio located on the efficient M-V segment of the efficient frontier is selected. Assuming a preference with DARA is not a very strong assumption. Actually, the most commonly employed preferences in economics and finance are concave functions, which in addition reveal DARA. We show that when the DARA assumption is added, choosing a portfolio by the quadratic approximation will always result in a selection of an M-V efficient portfolio.

Let us show this claim by repeating the definition of DARA and its implications. With the following definition of the risk premium $\pi(w)$:

$$\pi(w) \cong -\frac{1}{\sigma^2}\frac{U''(w)}{U'(w)},$$

[28] We have proved that no interior portfolio can maximize the quadratic approximation. Yet a portfolio located on segment MVP-a of the frontier (see Figure 4.6) may maximize the quadratic approximation. However, recall that, in principle, a direct maximization of expected utility may also end up with an M-V inefficient portfolio and even with an interior portfolio (e.g., a portfolio with a relatively large skewness may be selected). As with the quadratic approximation, we have proved that no interior portfolio can maximize the expected value of the quadratic; it is suggested to construct the M-V efficient frontier, and to search on the whole frontier, which portfolio maximizes the quadratic approximation. The fact that no interior portfolio may maximize the quadratic technically allows us to search for that portfolio in a systematic manner, simply by moving on the M-V frontier. However, when DARA is assumed, one should search for the maximizing portfolio only on the efficient segment of the frontier.

DARA implies that[29]

$$\partial \pi(w)/\partial w = -\frac{1}{\sigma^2} \frac{U'(w)U'''(w) - [U''(w)]^2}{[U'(w)]^2} < 0.$$

This can occur only if $U'''(w) > 0$. Thus,[30]

$$\text{DARA} \Rightarrow \partial \pi(w)/\partial w < 0 \Rightarrow U'''(w) > 0.$$

It can easily be verified that in case I (see Figure 4.5), we have $U'''(w) > 0$ (because U'' is declining, when the changes are measured in absolute values, as wealth increases) and in case II the opposite holds. However, because both A and B are negative, in case I we have $A - B > 0$; therefore, $\partial E(Q_k)\partial \mu > 0$ (see equation [4.25]). In sum, we have the following relationship: $\partial E(Q_k)/\partial \sigma^2 < 0$, which holds for all concave functions, and $\partial E(Q_k)/\partial \mu > 0$, which holds for all concave DARA functions.

This result reveals the strength of the quadratic approximation as in the case of DARA, which virtually all economists accept; the quadratic approximation always results in the selection of a portfolio from the M-V efficient set. Let us summarize these results:

1. When diversification is not allowed and DARA is not assumed, maximization of equation (4.24) (i.e., employing the quadratic approximation) may reveal a choice of an M-V inefficient portfolio.

2. When diversification is allowed and DARA is not assumed, an *interior* portfolio will never be selected by maximization of equation (4.24), but a portfolio located on the inefficient segment of the frontier may be selected.

3. When risk aversion with DARA is assumed, choosing a portfolio by the quadratic approximation always leads to a choice from the M-V efficient set. Actually, it is sufficient to require that $U''' > 0$, and there is no need to require DARA. However, because DARA has an economic meaning, we formulate the requirement that guarantees a choice from the efficient set

---

[29] See K. J. Arrow, *Aspects of the Theory of Risk Bearing*, Markham Publishing Company, Chicago, 1971, and J. W. Pratt, "Risk Aversion in the Small and in the Large," *Econometrica*, 1964.

[30] Note that for the quadratic preference given by $U(x) = x + bx^2$ with $b < 0$, we have $\partial \pi/\partial x = \frac{1}{\sigma^2} \frac{4b^2}{(1+2bx)^2} > 0$, which is a major drawback of the quadratic utility function.

in terms of DARA. A word of caution is needed here: unless there is a perfect correlation between expected utility and the quadratic approximation, it is possible that by the expected utility maximization an interior M-V portfolio is selected (e.g., a portfolio with a very large positive skewness), despite the fact that by the quadratic approximation, an M-V efficient portfolio is selected. The gap between the expected utility of these two portfolios reflects the economic loss due to the employment of the quadratic approximation. As we see in Chapter 8, this loss is relatively very small and in some cases even negligible.

Because virtually all economists advocate that DARA must exist, and because most utility functions employed in economics and finance reveal DARA, the conclusion in point 3 seems to be the most relevant one: very positive results for the researchers who advocate employing equation (4.24).

Finally, note that when k approaches zero, it is easy to show that equation (4.24) turns out to be

$$\lim_{k \to 0} E(Q_K) = U(\mu) + .5U''(\mu)\sigma^2.$$

Hence, with $k = 0$, we have the simple proof that only M-V efficient portfolios will be selected by the quadratic approximation, because

$$\partial E(Q)/\partial \sigma^2 = .5U(\mu) < 0,$$

due to the risk-aversion assumption, and

$$\partial E(Q)/\partial \mu = U'(\mu) + .5U'''(\mu) > 0,$$

due to the monotonicity and the DARA assumption. Thus, with DARA, an M-V inefficient portfolio can never be selected by the quadratic approximation.

The most important result is that with DARA and with $E(Q_K)$, all investors select their portfolios from the M-V efficient set. This implies that the market portfolio must also be on the M-V frontier. This result is a key to the derivation of Black's zero beta model, discussed in Chapter 6. When the riskless asset is available by maximizing the approximation function, all investors (with no need to assume DARA) will select the same portfolio of risky assets; hence, the market portfolio must be again on the M-V frontier, an essential condition for the CAPM equilibrium to hold. Thus, if all investors maximize the

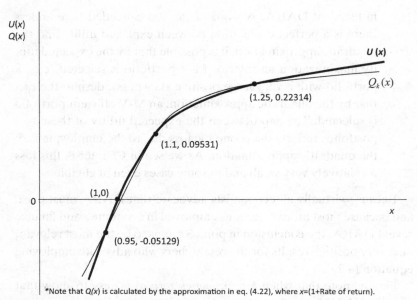

*Note that Q(x) is calculated by the approximation in eq. (4.22), where x=(1+Rate of return).

Figure 4.7. The Quadratic Approximation with Three-Point Fit: $U(x) = \ln(x)$, $\mu = 1.1$, $s = 0.15$, and $k = 1$.

quadratic approximation given by equation (4.24), with the usual market efficiency assumptions, the CAPM follows. This is a very strong result corresponding to the approximation of expected utility. Finally, without the results presented in this chapter, one needs to develop an algorithm to find the diversification strategy that maximizes equation (4.24). This is not a simple task because equation (4.24) depends on preferences. However, we show in this chapter that when diversification is allowed, one can avoid this effort because all investors select their portfolios from the M-V efficient set, for which an algorithm exists, an algorithm that does not depend on preferences.

e) The Quality of the Approximation

As with the one-point fit already discussed (see Figure 4.2) and also with the three-point fit, we have one approximation for each prospect, and no one approximation fits all prospects. Figure 4.7 illustrates the three-point fit approximation corresponding to a hypothetical prospect (of course, for another prospect, we get another function, which intersects with the utility function at three different points, which depend on the mean and the variance of the prospect). In drawing Figure 4.7, it is assumed that the preference is logarithmic, that the mean return is 1.1, the standard deviation is 0.15, and $k = 1$.

In this figure, the logarithmic function is drawn as a function of various hypothetical returns. However, the quadratic approximation Q_1 is calculated by employing equation (4.22), with the relevant parameters as defined already and for the mean and standard deviation of a specific prospect and for $k = 1$. The values obtained for U and Q with different levels of return are presented in Table 4.1. As we can see in Figure 4.7, the functions U and Q cross at three points. In this respect, we say that the quadratic fits the utility function under consideration at three points. Obviously, at these three points, the difference between the logarithmic function and the quadratic approximation, defined as $U(x) - Q(x)$, is equal to zero (see Table 4.1).

As mentioned, the quality of the approximation depends on the selected value k. For example, if we select $k = 1$, the term $U(\mu)$ cancels out and equation (4.24) reduces to

$$E(Q_1) = [U(\mu + \sigma) + U(\mu - \sigma)]/2.$$

With a little algebra, it can be shown that when $k \rightarrow 0$, we have

$$E(Q/k \rightarrow 0) = U(\mu) + .5U''(\mu)\sigma^2,$$

which is the approximation suggested by Markowitz.[31]

By analyzing the approximation with various values k, it has been found empirically that for the most widely employed preferences, the best approximation is obtained with a very small value k. Markowitz, who conducts a theoretical and empirical analysis aimed at analyzing the quality of the various approximations, realizes that the quality of the approximation cannot be based simply on the difference between $E(Q_k)$ and $EU(x)$, as the utility function is determined up to a positive linear transformation. Thus, the scale of the utility can be changed, and the difference between these two functions can be arbitrarily increased or decreased with a linear transformation. As a consequence, such a simple difference does not reflect the quality of the quadratic approximation. However, one can calculate the correlation between EU and EQ for various assets. The correlation is not

---

[31] See Markowitz, 1959, *op. cit.*

Table 4.1. *The Quadratic Approximation with Three-Point Fit:* $U(x) = Ln(x)$, $\mu = 1.1$, $\sigma = 0.1$, *and* $k = 1$. *See equation (4.24).*

R^*	$x = 1 + R$	$U(x)$	$Q(x)$	$U(x) - Q(x)$
− 0.70	0.30	− 1.20397	− 0.90348	− 0.30049
− 0.50	0.50	− 0.69315	− 0.60373	− 0.08942
− 0.30	0.70	− 0.35667	− 0.33735	− 0.01933
− 0.25	0.75	− 0.28768	− 0.27596	− 0.01172
− 0.20	0.80	− 0.22314	− 0.21667	− 0.00648
− 0.15	0.85	− 0.16252	− 0.15946	− 0.00306
− 0.10	0.90	− 0.10536	− 0.10433	− 0.00103
− 0.05	0.95	− 0.05129	− 0.05129	0.00000
0.00	1.00	0.00000	− 0.00034	0.00034
0.05	1.05	0.04879	0.04853	0.00026
0.10	1.10	0.09531	0.09531	0.00000
0.15	1.15	0.13976	0.14001	− 0.00024
0.20	1.20	0.18232	0.18262	− 0.00030
0.25	1.25	0.22314	0.22314	0.00000
0.30	1.30	0.26236	0.26158	0.00078
0.35	1.35	0.30010	0.29794	0.00217
0.40	1.40	0.33647	0.33221	0.00427
0.45	1.45	0.37156	0.36439	0.00718
0.50	1.50	0.40547	0.39449	0.01098
0.55	1.55	0.43825	0.42250	0.01576
0.60	1.60	0.47000	0.44842	0.02158
1.00	2.00	0.69315	0.58075	0.11240
1.50	2.50	0.91629	0.55846	0.35783
2.00	3.00	1.09861	0.32761	0.77100
2.50	3.50	1.25276	− 0.11179	1.36455
3.00	4.00	1.38629	− 0.75975	2.14604

* R = rate of return.

affected by a linear transformation, and hence it can serve as an index reflecting the quality of the approximation: A positive high correlation indicates a high-quality approximation and vice versa. Actually, if the correlation is (+1), one can safely employ the approximation because it leads to the same choice as the quadratic approximation. Markowitz suggests that the higher the correlation, the larger the chance that the investor will achieve almost maximum expected utility by relying solely on the means and variances of the various assets.

Table 4.2, taken from Levy and Markowitz, reports the correlation between the quadratic approximation and the direct expected utility

Table 4.2. *Correlation Between* EU(R) *and* f_k *(E, V, U($\bullet$))* *for Annual Returns of 149 Mutual Funds, 1958–67*

Utility Function		$k = 0.01$	0.10	0.60	1.00	2.00
$\log(1 + R)$		0.997	0.997	0.997	0.995	0.983
$(1 + R)^a$						
	$a = 0.1$	0.998	0.998	0.997	0.997	0.988
	$a = 0.3$	0.999	0.999	0.999	0.998	0.995
	$a = 0.5$	0.999	0.999	0.999	0.999	0.998
	$a = 0.7$	0.999	0.999	0.999	0.999	0.999
	$a = 0.9$	0.999	0.999	0.999	0.999	0.999
$-e^{-b(1 + R)}$						
	$b = 0.1$	0.999	0.999	0.999	0.999	0.999
	$b = 0.5$	0.999	0.999	0.999	0.999	0.999
	$b = 1.0$	0.997	0.997	0.997	0.996	0.995
	$b = 3.0$	0.949	0.949	0.941	0.924	0.817
	$b = 5.0$	0.855	0.855	0.852	0.837	0.738
	$b = 10.0$	0.447	0.449	0.503	0.522	0.458

Source: H. Levy and H. M. Markowitz, "Approximating Expected Utility by a Function of Mean and Variance," *American Economic Review*, 1979.

for 149 mutual funds covering a 10-year period for various utility functions and for various values k. Let us explain how the various values needed to compute the correlations have been calculated. First, the expected utility is calculated by using the ten annual returns (1 + rate of return) of each mutual fund, assigning an equal probability to each observation and assuming a given utility function, for example, the logarithmic function. Next, the mean return and the standard deviation are calculated. Selecting a value k and employing equation (4.24), the approximated expected utility $E(Q_k)$ is calculated. Having EU and EQ for each mutual fund, the correlation between these two vectors is calculated. These correlations are reported in Table 4.2.

A few conclusions can be drawn from this table:

i. In most cases, the correlation is very high. Actually, there is almost a perfect correlation between the two variables. Although not shown in the table, the mutual fund with the highest expected utility is also the optimal one by the quadratic approximation. So, with this specific data set, the encouraging result is that no loss is incurred by ignoring all the detailed distribution and focusing solely on the means and variances.

ii. Virtually in all cases, the lower the parameter k, the higher the correlation. Yet there are some exceptions. However, it is worth noting that the difference in the correlation coefficient does not change drastically for the values $0 \leq k \leq 1$.

iii. A poor performance (i.e., a relatively low correlation) is obtained for the exponential preference with a relatively high parameter b (e.g., $b = 10$). However, this result is technical, with not much economic relevance. The reason for the irrelevancy of such a preference is that it probably does not fit investors' behavior. For example, this preference with a parameter $b = 10$ reveals that the investor would prefer getting a prospect yielding a certain return of 10% rather than a prospect yielding zero or x with equal probabilities, regardless of the value of x. Thus, even if x is 1,000% with such a preference, the certain prospect yielding 10% is preferred. Therefore, the fact that a preference with such a high parameter b yields a poor performance (see Table 4.2) should not bother us because such a function probably does not fit the behavior of any investor.

One may wonder whether the approximation reveals such a good performance also with other assets, particularly individual assets, or whether it is unique for mutual funds that comprise many assets. Table 4.3 extends the analysis of Table 4.2 to other assets.

As shown in Table 4.3, the correlation is quite high also for individual stocks. Ignoring the high parameter b, the correlations are close to $(+1)$, particularly when monthly rates of returns are employed. The better performance with monthly rates of return relative to annual rates of return stems from the fact that with monthly returns, there are less-extreme observations. Indeed, Markowitz[32] has shown that the smaller the fluctuations in returns, the better the quadratic approximation. The third column of Table 4.3 presents the correlation for portfolios that are only slightly diversified (five or six stocks in each portfolio) when annual rates of returns are employed. The correlation increases substantially from the case of individual stocks. For example, for the logarithmic preference, the correlation increases from 0.880 to 0.998. The performance of the approximation with

[32] See Markowitz, *op. cit.*, 1991.

Table 4.3. *Correlation between* EU(R) *and* $f_{.01}$ (E, V, U(•)) *for Three Historical Distributions*

Utility Function		Annual Returns on 97 Stocks	Monthly Returns on 97 Stocks*	Random Portfolios of 5 or 6 Stocks*
$\log(1 + R)$		0.880	0.995	0.998
$(1 + R)^a$				
	a = 0.1	0.895	0.996	0.998
	a = 0.3	0.932	0.998	0.999
	a = 0.5	0.968	0.999	0.999
	a = 0.7	0.991	0.999	0.999
	a = 0.9	0.999	0.999	0.999
$-e^{-b(1 + R)}$				
	b = 0.1	0.999	0.999	0.999
	b = 0.5	0.961	0.999	0.999
	b = 1.0	0.850	0.997	0.998
	b = 3.0	0.850	0.976	0.958
	b = 5.0	0.863	0.961	0.919
	b = 10.0	0.659	0.899	0.768

* A sample of 100 stocks was randomly drawn from the CRSP (Center of Research in Security Prices, University of Chicago) tape, subject to the constraint that all had reported rates of return for the whole period 1948–68. Some mechanical problems reduced the usable sample size from 100 to 97.

Source: H. Levy and H. M. Markowitz, "Approximating Expected Utility by a Function of Mean and Variance," *American Economic Review*, 1979.

portfolios is better than the performance with individual assets for two reasons: with portfolios, less-extreme returns prevail (because the extreme returns of various assets tend to offset each other) than those with individual assets, and the portfolio returns are closer to a symmetrical distribution than the distribution of returns on individual assets. Having closer to symmetrical distribution implies that with portfolios, the impact of skewness on expected utility is relatively small, making the M-V quadratic approximation better with portfolios than with individual assets. Because the excellent approximation is achieved with relatively small portfolios containing five or six stocks, we conclude that "a little diversification goes a long way."

Finally, note that we employ quadratic approximation to measure expected utility. One may object to this approach because the quadratic utility function has some drawbacks, the major one being that it reveals an increasing degree of absolute risk aversion. The higher the wealth, the higher the premium one is willing to pay to get rid of a given small risk. Also, by this function, the greater one's wealth, the less one invests in the risky asset. However, this drawback of the quadratic utility function does not exist with the suggested quadratic approximation; the degree of risk aversion with the quadratic fit is identical to the degree of risk aversion of the utility function under consideration. Thus, if the utility function is, say, logarithmic, the quadratic fit will reveal the same risk aversion as the logarithmic preference.

Although the mathematical proof of this claim can be found in Levy and Markowitz,[33] the intuitive explanation for the claim is as follows: The approximation given in this chapter is different from the employment of $U(w)$, where U is quadratic and w stands for wealth. With the classic utility function, we employ the same function when wealth changes. Thus, the quadratic utility function depends solely on wealth. However, by the quadratic approximation discussed in this chapter, the quadratic function depends on the parameters of the prospect under consideration. Therefore, with two distributions with different parameters, a different quadratic is employed. Thus, the approximation given by equation (4.24) depends on μ and σ rather than on wealth, and hence it is fundamentally different from the classic quadratic utility function.

4.8. SUMMARY

M-V analysis, the CAPM, and particularly beta, which is an important component of the CAPM, are widely employed in academic research and by practitioners alike. However, there are ample examples showing that the popular M-V rule, which is the foundation of the CAPM (and beta), leads to paradoxical results. For example, we have shown in Chapter 3 that one may have two prospects such that one of the prospects has a higher expected utility than the other, despite having a lower mean and a higher variance. The reason for the higher expected utility of the M-V inferior prospect is that it has a large positive skewness, a feature desired by most investors. Moreover, one can

---

[33] See Levy and Markowitz, 1979, *op. cit.*

easily construct an example where there is no dominance by the M-V rule, yet one prospect dominates the other by FSD, a drawback of the M-V rule.

It is shown in this chapter that the M-V rule can be used in the following three scenarios:

a) The utility function is quadratic: in this case, the M-V rule is sufficient but not necessary. Thus, the M-V efficient set may be too large. As a result, we suggest two more rules that are stronger than the M-V rule.

b) Normal distribution in the face of risk aversion: In this case, the M-V rule is optimal and consistent with expected utility maximization. When the variances of the two prospects under consideration are unequal, the M-V rule coincides with the SSD rule. However, because the SSD rule is optimal for all risk averters, the M-V rule is also optimal. When the variances are equal, the M-V rule coincides with the FSD rule.

c) When neither normality, elliptic, nor quadratic preference prevails, one can employ the M-V rule as an approximation to expected utility. First, we have shown theoretically that with diversification and DARA preferences, the choice by the approximation will always be from the M-V efficient frontier. Second, even without diversification, unless the returns on the investment are too extreme (as characterizes the option market, for example), it is empirically shown that the ranking of the prospects by the suggested M-V approximation and the ranking of the prospects by the direct expected utility are highly correlated with a correlation coefficient that is close to 1. Thus, choosing a prospect from the M-V efficient set with a high probability maximizes also the expected utility, at least for some commonly employed preferences in economics and finance.

Finally, note that to calculate the quadratic approximation, one needs to know the utility function. Therefore, one may claim that the precise expected utility can be calculated, and there is no need to conduct an approximated calculation. Whereas this claim is valid in principle, it loses ground in practice: First, an investment consultant or a fund manager has many clients, each having a different unknown preference. Knowing that a portfolio can be selected by the M-V rule suggests a practical solution that may serve all investors. Second, even an individual investor may not know his or her preference, or at least cannot precisely specify it. Therefore, by selecting a prospect by the M-V rule, an "almost" optimal decision is made. Thus, knowing that the approximation is excellent for most relevant preferences releases the fund manager from the need to investigate the relevant precise preference.

Nevertheless, recall that the M-V analysis suggests only partial ordering; hence, the M-V approximation suggests that all risk averters by an astute selection from the efficient set will approximately maximize their expected utility. However, this approximation does not guide the investor about how to select the optimal portfolio from the M-V efficient set. In Chapter 5, we show that all investors select the same portfolio of risky assets as long as the riskless asset prevails. In such a case, the importance of the M-V approximation increases dramatically because when only risky assets are considered does the M-V rule provide a complete ordering.

5

The Capital Asset Pricing Model

5.1. INTRODUCTION

In the preceding chapters, we have discussed the theoretical foundations of the Mean-Variance (M-V) rule and analyzed the conditions under which one can safely employ this rule. We also demonstrated cases where the M-V rule is not allowed to be employed because it may yield paradoxical results. The analysis of the validity of the M-V analysis is of crucial importance because the M-V framework is the foundation of the Capital Asset Pricing Model (CAPM), to which we devote a substantial part of this book. Moreover, the CAPM assumes that investors make investment decisions by the M-V rule and is based on the M-V efficiency analysis. In this chapter, we assume that investors make their portfolio choices by the M-V rule and investigate the implication of the M-V portfolio selection framework to several issues, issues that pave the way to the development of the CAPM:

1. What is the optimal portfolio diversification strategy when only risky assets are available in the markets? Does the optimal choice vary across investors?
2. What is the optimal diversification strategy in risky assets when unlimited borrowing and lending at the risk-free asset prevail? Does it vary across investors?
3. Which economic factor determines how one should diversify between the risky asset and the riskless asset?
4. What is the risk index of an asset when only one risky asset is held in the portfolio?

5. What is the risk index of an individual asset when many other risky assets are held with the asset under consideration in the same portfolio? What is the risk index of the portfolio in such a case?
6. Employing the M-V rule and adding some additional assumptions regarding the efficiency of the market, what are the implied equilibrium prices of the various risky assets? What is the risk return equilibrium relation?

The answers to the first five questions facilitate the analysis corresponding to the sixth question, the one that constitutes the core of this chapter, where an equilibrium pricing model is derived, well known as the CAPM. This model was developed by Sharpe and Lintner, and it is mainly for this work that Sharpe won the Nobel Laureate in 1990.[1]

Answering these six questions is not an easy task, and to get a theoretical risk–return relation, some assumptions, apart from the one asserting that investors employ the M-V rule, are needed. In particular, determining meaningful equilibrium prices of risky assets, such that these theoretical equilibrium prices are substantially related to actual prices, is quite a challenge. The reason is that in practice, the modern securities market is a complex mechanism incorporating millions of investors and many decision variables. Therefore, probably no theoretical economic model can exhaustively describe how equilibrium prices are reached in such a complicated market. Therefore, to gain some meaningful insight to the market mechanism that determines equilibrium prices, some simplifying assumptions are required. Obviously, the more assumptions one is willing to assume, the simpler will be the obtained risk–return equilibrium asset pricing model. However, with many simplified assumptions, there is a risk that the derived equilibrium prices are "too theoretical" in the sense of being not related – or very weakly related to actual prices. Therefore, in choosing the employed set of assumptions, the researcher has to strive for a delicate balance between the need to obtain a simple (and understandable) model and the need to obtain a model with a meaningful descriptive power of actual pricing mechanism of risky assets.

---

[1] It is worth mentioning other papers, one unpublished and one that was published in 1966, that developed similar risk–return equilibrium relationships. See J. Treynor, "Towards a Theory of Market Value of Risky Assets," unpublished paper, 1962, and J. Mossin, "Equilibrium in a Capital Asset Market," *Econometrica*, 1966.

Relaxing the tension between the temptation to make more simplifying assumptions and the need to obtain a model that realistically explains market prices, market price changes, or investor's behavior is an art. The end result of each imposed set of assumptions is the emerged model whose quality (i.e., the economic value) should be carefully evaluated. In principle, a model that is applicable (i.e., not too complicated to be tested with actual data) would be considered the best model, even with a limited predictive power, unless one suggests an alternative model with a stronger predictive power. However, even this criterion is vague and not easy to employ: One model may have a larger predictability power than another with some set of assets, yet with another set of assets the opposite holds. Also, the ranking of the competing models by their quality may vary across various studied time periods and across countries.

Finally, the security market probably never reaches the predicted equilibrium. Even if all investors agree on the various parameters, as suggested by the CAPM, there are "noises" in the security market. In particular, liquidity traders induce price fluctuations and deviations from equilibrium. Also, firms issue stocks and risky bonds, inducing an increase in the supply of securities, and firms distribute cash dividends, inducing a decrease in the market value of the supply securities. Moreover, even technical errors may induce sharp fluctuations of equilibrium prices. For example, on Thursday, May 6, 2010, the Dow Jones index dropped by about 1,000 points (9.2 percent) in a matter of minutes and then recovered. It has been claimed that some human or mechanical errors caused these large fluctuations and the recovery that followed.

These noises stimulate continuous fluctuations in prices, suggesting that there is no equilibrium price, or if there is one, it is never reached! This would seem to vitiate the use of equilibrium models as a tool of explaining asset prices. In this context, recall the famous analogy drawn from dog racing, when the dogs go around the track chasing a mechanical rabbit. Suppose that in this rabbit–dog race, an equilibrium is reached if the dogs catch the rabbit, but when the dogs get close to the rabbit, an electrical power supply failure occurs. Hence, the equilibrium is never reached. The lesson from this analogy is that also in security markets, equilibrium may never be reached, but the knowledge that it may exist could explain price behavior toward this equilibrium, with fluctuations about it, exactly as knowledge of the existence of the rabbit is of paramount importance when attempting to explain the otherwise peculiar behavior of dogs.

In this chapter, we employ the set of assumptions that have been used by Sharpe and Lintner in the CAPM's derivation. In the next chapter (Chapter 6), we discuss some other models, most of which constitute an extension of the CAPM.

5.2. THE MEAN-VARIANCE EFFICIENT FRONTIER

In this section, we drive the M-V efficient frontier, which is the foundation of the CAPM. We start in the framework of Tobin, when there is one risky asset and cash – that is, the riskless asset. Then we turn to analyze Markowitz's n-risky asset case, and finally we derive the n-risky asset efficient frontier with a riskless asset. In all the following sections, apart from Section 5.4, it is assumed that the various parameters are given, and we analyze what should be the risk–return relationship for this given set of parameters, but we do not discuss how these parameters are determined. In Section 5.4, we discuss how prices and return parameters are determined simultaneously with market clearance, which is a necessary condition for reaching equilibrium prices.

a) The Mean-Variance Frontier with One Risky Asset and One Riskless Asset

In his 1958 article, Tobin[2] assumed that one risky asset (risky bond) and one riskless asset (cash) exist. In what follows, we extend Tobin's framework and assume that one risky asset (a bond or a stock) and one riskless asset that bears a positive riskless interest rate exist. We use the following notation:

R – The rate of return on the risky asset (a random variable)
w – The investment proportion in the riskless asset
μ – The mean of R
σ^2 – The variance of R
r – The riskless interest rate

[2] See J. Tobin, "Liquidity Preference as Behavior Towards Risk," *Review of Economic Studies*, 1958.

Mixing the risky asset and the riskless asset, the investor constructs a portfolio, whose return (a random variable), R_P, is given by

$$R_P = wr + (1 - w)R,$$

where the subscript p is a reminder that this is a return on a portfolio rather than an individual asset. The mean and standard deviation of the portfolio return are given by

$$\mu_P = wr + (1 - w)\mu \qquad (5.1)$$

and

$$\sigma_P = (1 - w)\sigma, \qquad (5.2)$$

respectively. Isolating w from equation (5.2) and substituting it in equation (5.1) yields

$$\mu_P = r + \frac{\mu - r}{\sigma}\sigma_P. \qquad (5.3)$$

This is the transformation line between risk and expected return. The *transformation line* is defined as the line providing the set of all available portfolios, obtained by mixing the risky asset with the riskless asset. The investor can choose any portfolio located on this line. Moreover, the higher the required mean return, μ_P, the higher the risk exposure, σ_P. As we shall see, the same linear risk–return principle is employed in deriving the CAPM.

Figure 5.1 illustrates the risk–return linear transformation line. The intercept of this line is at r and the slope of this line is $(\mu - r)/\sigma$, in accordance with equation (5.3). The selection of the optimal diversification between the risky asset and the riskless asset depends on the investor's taste (i.e., on the shape of the indifference curves). For example, if the tangency point of the indifference curve is at point a, the investor invests 100 percent of the invested capital in the risky asset with a mean of μ and standard deviation of σ. This investor neither borrows nor lends money at the riskless interest rate. The more "cautious investor" who fears risk exposure prefers to put some portion of his or her money in the riskless asset and hence selects portfolio b. Moreover, the very risk-averse investor may select point r, implying 100 percent investment in the riskless asset.

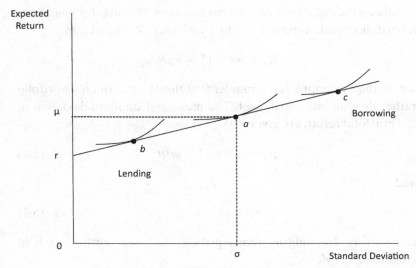

Figure 5.1. The Transformation Line: One Risky Asset and One Riskless Asset.

The other extreme case is related to an investor who is willing to take risk with the chance of getting a relatively high profit. This investor is represented by an indifference curve with a tangency at point c (see Figure 5.1). The explanation of the location left to point a is trivial; the investor puts some money in the riskless asset. Being located to the right of point a requires some additional explanation, however; the investor in this case levers his or her investment. Namely, for each dollar invested from the investor's equity, he or she borrows, say, another dollar and invests the $2 in the risky asset. In a good year, the return on the risky asset is higher than the riskless interest rate; hence, the leverage has a positive effect. For example, the investor makes, say, 10 percent on the $2 invested, and pays, say, 5 percent on the dollar borrowed, ending up with 15 percent return on the $1 invested from the investor's equity. However, this levered position is a two-edged sword because in a bad year the leverage cuts the profitability on the equity. For example, suppose that in a given year the rates of return on the risky asset is, say, −5 percent. Losing 5 percent on the invested $2 and paying 5 percent interest on the borrowed $1 leaves him or her with a loss of 15 percent on the $1 invested from the investor' equity. Recall that if the investor invested in the risky asset with no borrowing and no lending, this investor would have ended up with a loss of only 5 percent, and this loss is smaller than the loss with the levered investment.

This example demonstrates that investors may select different diversification strategies and that leverage makes the financial situation better in a good year and worse in a bad year. Because profit fluctuates more widely with leverage, we obtain a higher standard deviation on the levered portfolio relative to the unlevered one (compare points c and a in Figure 5.1).

To sum up, in the case of one risky and one riskless asset analysis, we can determine that the risk index of the risky asset is the variance of the rate of return on the risky asset, and the risk index of the portfolio is the variance of the rates of return on the portfolio. The asset allocation between the risky and the riskless assets is determined by the investor's taste – that is, by the indifference curves. Therefore, generally the diversification strategy varies across investors. Finally, note that the risk can be measured either by the variance or by the standard deviation; hence, we use these two measures of risk interchangeably.

b) The Mean-Variance Frontier with n-Risky Assets

In his pioneer 1952 article, Markowitz derived the M-V efficient set when the investors face n-risky assets. In this section, we present the M-V frontier analysis with n-risky assets, and in the next section, we add to these n-risky assets the riskless asset to obtain a straight line that is very similar in its structure to the one given in equation (5.3).

We employ the following notation:

R_i – The rate of return on the ith risky asset
$\mu_i = E(R_i)$ – The mean rate of return on the ith asset
$\sigma_i^2 = Var(R_i)$ – The variance of the return on the ith asset
$\sigma_{i,j} = Cov(R_i, R_j) = \rho_{i,j}\sigma_i\sigma_j$ – The covariance of the ith asset and
      the jth asset, where $\rho_{i,j}$ denotes the correlation coefficient.
w_i – The investment proportion in the ith asset with $\sum_{i=1}^{n} w_i = 1$.

The portfolio return, R_P, the portfolio mean return, μ_P, and the portfolio variance, σ_P^2, are given by

$$R_P = \sum_{i=1}^{n} w_i R_i, \qquad (5.4)$$

$$\mu_P = \sum_{i=1}^{n} w_i \mu_i, \qquad (5.5)$$

and

$$\sigma_P^2 = \sum_{i=1}^{n} \sum_{j=1}^{n} w_i w_j \sigma_{i,j} = \sum_{i=1}^{n} \sum_{j=1}^{n} w_i w_j \rho_{i,j} \sigma_i \sigma_j. \quad (5.6)$$

The portfolio variance can also be rewritten as

$$\sigma_P^2 = \sum_{i-1}^{n} w_i^2 \sigma_i^2 + \sum_{i=1}^{n} \sum_{j=1,j\neq i}^{n} w_i w_j \sigma_{i,j} \quad (5.6')$$

or as

$$\sigma_P^2 = \sum_{i=1}^{n} w_i^2 \sigma_i^2 + 2 \sum_{i=1}^{n} \sum_{j=1,j>i}^{n} w_i w_j \sigma_{i,j}. \quad (5.6'')$$

All these different forms of the portfolio variance are frequently used in the literature. Also, the last two equations can be rewritten in terms of $\rho_{i,j}$ rather than in terms of $\sigma_{i,j}$.

Using matrix algebra, the portfolio return (a random variable), the portfolio mean, and the portfolio variance are given by

$$R_P = \mathbf{w}'\mathbf{R}, \quad (5.7)$$

$$\mu_P = \mathbf{w}'\mathbf{\mu}, \quad (5.8)$$

$$\sigma_P^2 = \mathbf{w}'\mathbf{V}\mathbf{w}, \quad (5.9)$$

where the bold letters denote vectors and $\mathbf{V}$ denotes the variance–covariance matrix. In some cases, using matrix and vector formulations makes the presentation easier, and in some cases the use of matrix and vectors has its price, because it is less intuitive. Therefore, we will use the matrix algebra only when it makes the presentation easier with no loss of the economic intuition.

By the M-V analysis, one has to find a vector of investment weights, $\mathbf{w}$, that minimizes the portfolio variance for a given portfolio mean return or, alternatively, to find a vector of investment weights that maximizes the portfolio mean for a given portfolio variance. Thus, in finding the n-asset efficient frontier, we have to solve the following problem:

$$\underset{\mathbf{w}}{Min}\, \mathbf{w}'\mathbf{V}\mathbf{w} \quad (5.10)$$

subject to

$$\mu_P = \mathbf{w}'\mathbf{\mu}, \quad \mathbf{w}'\mathbf{1} = 1,$$

when the second constraint implies that the sum of all investment weights must be equal to 1 or 100 percent. Note that there is no constraint on the sign of the investment weight; hence, it can be negative, implying a short position in an asset.

For every given portfolio mean, we solve for the investment proportion that minimizes the portfolio variance. By changing the mean, μ_P, we derive all the points on the efficient frontier. The derivation of the M-V frontier and the corresponding investment proportions is commonly done by employing the Lagrange multiplier. One can write the following Lagrange function:

$$L = \mathbf{w}'\mathbf{V}\mathbf{w} + \lambda_1(\mu_P - \mathbf{w}'\boldsymbol{\mu}) + \lambda_2(1 - \mathbf{1}'\mathbf{w}). \tag{5.11}$$

By taking the derivative of L with respect to $\mathbf{w}$ and with respect to the two Lagrange multipliers and equating to zero, we obtain $n + 2$ equations with $n + 2$ unknowns; hence, in principle, the system is solvable. The output of such a solution is a vector of efficient investment weights (n variables as we have by assumption n-risky assets) and the value of the two Lagrange multipliers. However, if the matrix $\mathbf{V}$ is singular, it does not have an inverse matrix and the system is not solvable. This may occur when we have two risky assets that are perfectly correlated.

In the derivation of the CAPM, we employ some version of equation (5.11) when we also add the availability of riskless borrowing and lending. However, in practice, employing equation (5.11) with actual data usually reveals that virtually all portfolios located on the M-V frontier include short positions, and some of them are very large positions. Technically, it implies that the solution may include some negative investment weights $w_i < 0$. Because some institutional investors are not allowed by regulation to hold short positions and some investors willingly do not want to be in short position, one may add to equation (5.11) the constraint $\mathbf{w} \geq \mathbf{0}$. In such a case, the diversification strategy includes only positive or zero investment weights, and even if n is very large, the investor may end up with a portfolio that includes a very small number of assets, for example, ten assets, where all the other investment weights are equal to zero.

Figure 5.2 illustrates the M-V frontier with and without constraints on short selling. The various dots appearing in Figure 5.2 stand for the means and standard deviations of the individual n-risky assets. The

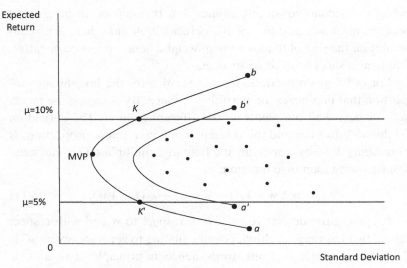

Figure 5.2. The Efficient Frontier: n-Risky Assets.

curve *ab* represents the M-V frontier when short selling is allowed, and the curve *a'b'* represents the M-V frontier when short selling is not allowed. The MVP is the minimum variance (or minimum standard deviation) portfolio. A few comments regarding the derivation technique of the M-V frontier are in order:

1. When we take the derivatives of equation (5.11), we also take the derivative with respect to λ_1 and equate it to zero:

$$\partial \lambda L / \partial \lambda_1 = 0 \Rightarrow \mu_p - \mathbf{w}'\boldsymbol{\mu} = 0 \Rightarrow \mu_P = \mathbf{w}'\boldsymbol{\mu}.$$

This constraint implies that the obtained solution to the portfolio's variance minimization must fulfill this constraint; therefore, we must end up with a portfolio with a given mean return that is predetermined. Figure 5.2 demonstrates the case where the portfolio mean return is predetermined to be 10 percent. Then all portfolios under consideration must yield a mean return of 10 percent. Graphically, this 10 percent constraint dictates that one should select a portfolio located on the horizontal straight line given in Figure 5.2. Taking the derivatives of the Lagrange function given in equation (5.11) with the 10 percent mean constraint, we obtain the portfolio with the minimum variance, provided the portfolio's mean return is 10 percent. This portfolio is denoted by point K in Figure 5.2.

Because one cannot find a portfolio with a 10 percent mean return and a lower variance than portfolio K, this portfolio, by construction, must be located on the M-V frontier. Repeating this procedure with another mean, say, 5 percent, we get another portfolio K', where, once again, portfolio K' by construction is located on the M-V frontier. Repeating this procedure for various portfolio means, we obtain the M-V frontier labeled by *ab* in Figure 5.2.

2. One can minimize the portfolio variance with no constraint on the portfolio's mean return. Namely, we solve the following problem:

$$\text{Min} \qquad \mathbf{w'Vw}$$
$$\text{Subject to:} \quad \mathbf{w'1} = 1$$

Because there is no constraint on the portfolio mean, we search for the portfolio with the minimum variance with the only imposed constraint asserting that the sum of all investment weight must be equal to 1. This portfolio is found by taking the derivative of equation (5.11) with respect to the n investment weights and with respect to λ_2, ending up with $n + 1$ equations and $n + 1$ unknowns, so the system is, in principle, solvable. Note that λ_1 is not included in this derivation (because we have no constraint on the portfolio's mean return); therefore, we have only $n + 1$ equations.

The portfolio obtained by the employment of this procedure is called the *minimum variance portfolio* (or MVP); see Figure 5.2. There is no other portfolio with a lower variance as long as 100 percent of the wealth under consideration is invested in risky assets. Thus, if an investor is considering an investment of, say, one million dollars in various assets, we denote this one million dollars by 100 percent (or simply 1), and we find the investment weights corresponding to the MVP, provided the one million dollars is all invested in the available risky assets – thus, the constraint that $\mathbf{w'1} = 1$ plays an important role in the M-V frontier derivation. Without this constraint, one can obtain a portfolio with a lower variance than the MVP by simply holding all the money in cash, resulting in a variance of zero.

From the preceding discussion, one thing is clear: in the derivation of the M-V frontier, one has first to decide how much he or she wishes to invest in risky assets. We call this amount 100 percent (or 1), and then one can proceed in deriving the M-V frontier. In the rest of the book, when analyzing portfolio diversification strategies, we always keep in mind that the analysis is for $1 of invested capital in risky assets, so the sum of all the investment weights must be equal to 1. The arbitrary selection of $1 does not affect the solution because the optimal solution to the portfolio diversification stemming from equation (5.11) is invariable in relation to the amount of money invested in the risky assets.

3. The M-V frontier is divided into two segments: section MVP-*a* is the inefficient segment, and segment MVP-*b* is the M-V efficient segment (see Figure 5.2). In consequence, being located on the M-V frontier does not guarantee M-V efficiency. The reason for the inefficiency of segment MVP-*a* is that for any portfolio located on this segment, there is a portfolio located vertically above it (located on the efficient segment MVP-*b*) that dominates it by the M-V rule: it has the same variance and higher mean than the inferior portfolio has.

4. With no constraint, the M-V frontier is a hyperbola.[3] The efficient set with the short-selling constraint, which is not a hyperbola, is located to the right of the curve with no such constraint. See Figure *a'b'*, which is located right of curve *ab*. This result stems from the well-known fact that the more constraints one imposes on the optimization problem given by equation (5.11), for a given portfolio mean, the higher the variance of the achieved portfolio.

c) The Mean-Variance Frontier with *n*-Risky Assets and the Riskless Asset

The final step before turning to the CAPM's proof is the analysis of the M-V efficient frontier with *n*-risky assets and the riskless asset. In essence, it is a natural extension of previous discussions because it

[3] See A. D. Roy, "Safety-First and the Holding of Assets," *Econometrica*, 1952, and R. C. Merton, "An Analytical Derivation of the Efficient Portfolio," *Journal of Financial and Quantitative Analysis*, 1972.

combines the results of sections a) and b) discussed previously. The return on such a portfolio is R_P, given by

$$R_P = \sum_{i=1}^{n} w_i R_i + \left(1 - \sum_{i=1}^{n} w_i\right) r, \qquad (5.12)$$

where r denotes the riskless interest rate and all the other notations are defined as before. We distinguish between three possible situations:

1. $\sum_{i=1}^{n} w_i = 1$, a case where the investor neither borrows nor lends money at the riskless interest rate. In this case, 100 percent of the invested capital is invested in the risky assets.
2. $\sum_{i=1}^{n} w_i < 1$, a case where the investor allocates some proportion of his or her invested capital to the riskless asset. Hence, less than 100 percent is invested in the risky assets.
3. $\sum_{i=1}^{n} w_i > 1$, a case where the investor borrows at the riskless asset and invests his or her own money as well as the borrowed money in the risky assets. Thus, more than 100 percent of the investor's capital is invested in the risky assets.

Taking the expected value and the variance of the portfolio return given in equation (5.12) yields

$$\mu_P = \sum_{i=1}^{n} w_i \mu_i + \left(1 - \sum_{i=1}^{n} w_i\right) r \qquad (5.13)$$

and

$$\sigma_P^2 = \sum_{i=1}^{n} \sum_{j=1}^{n} w_i w_j \sigma_{i,j}. \qquad (5.14)$$

Note that the portfolio variance formula is not affected by the existence of the riskless asset (compare equations (5.14) and (5.6)). However, although the formula is unchanged by the introduction of the riskless asset, the magnitude of the variance may be affected as the investment weights are affected. For example, suppose that the investor diversifies \$1 in the n-risky assets and obtains a portfolio with a variance of, say, 10. Now let us see how the magnitude of the portfolio variance may change with the introduction of the riskless asset. Suppose that the investor borrows \$1 and invests \$2 in the same portfolio and in the same proportions in the various risky assets. In this case, the portfolio variance increases to 40.[4] Similarly, by investing some proportion of the capital in the riskless asset, the variance decreases. Thus, the portfolio's variance changes with the introduction of the riskless asset, although the variance formula is unchanged.

In section a) we have seen that a mix of any risky portfolio with the riskless asset creates infinite possible diversification strategies between these two assets, where all possible portfolios are located on the straight line in the mean standard deviation space, connecting the risk-free asset and the risky portfolio (see equation (5.3)). In section b) we demonstrate how the M-V efficient frontier is created based on n-risky assets. The next step is to integrate the results of sections a) and b); exactly as we derived equation (5.3), we can mix any point taken from the M-V n-assets frontier and create a transformation line where the investor can select her optimal portfolio from all possible portfolios located on this line. Actually, one can create many transformation lines, although all lines but one, the tangency line, are inefficient.

Figure 5.3 demonstrates the M-V frontier corresponding to n-risky assets when the possibility to borrow and lend money at the riskless asset is allowed. Curve a-MVP-b is exactly like the one given in Figure 5.2. It represents the efficient frontier composed of n available risky assets. By the same mathematical procedure employed to derive equation (5.3), one can create many transformation lines like line A and line B given in Figure 5.3. However, line B, although feasible, is inefficient because for any portfolio located on line B, there is a portfolio located on line A that dominates it by the M-V rule. Take, for example, portfolio K. Then portfolio K' dominates it because it has the same standard deviation and a higher mean return. Similarly, portfolio K'' also dominates portfolio K because it has the same mean return as portfolio K but a smaller standard deviation. Actually, all portfolios located between point K'' and point K' dominate portfolio K by the M-V rule. By the same argument, one can show that for any point, like point K, located on line B there is at least one portfolio located on line A, which dominates it, so selecting a portfolio located on line B constitutes an inefficient diversification strategy.

---

[4] As each of the investment weights is multiplied by 2, the variance of the portfolio increases by four times the previous variance when no leverage is employed.

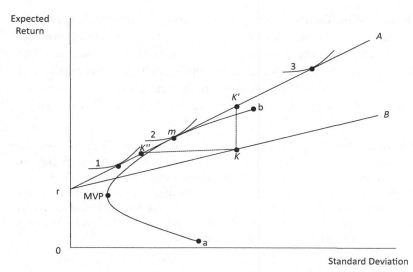

Figure 5.3. The Efficient Frontier: *n*-Risky Assets with Borrowing and Lending.

The preceding argument leads to the conclusion that a transformation line dominates by the M-V rule all transformation lines located below it. Therefore, there is only one line from which investors should select their portfolios: the highest feasible line, which is the tangency line, line *A* in our graphical example (see Figure 5.3). Under homogeneous beliefs, all investors hold the same tangent portfolio; hence, by market clearance reasoning, this portfolio must be the market portfolio. Therefore, we conclude that when all investors hold the same tangent portfolio, in equilibrium, it must be the market portfolio, with market weights identical to the weights in the tangency portfolio.

As discussed, portfolio *m* as the tangency portfolio is the one employed to obtain the highest transformation line. Investors with indifference curves labeled by 1 will invest a portion of their money in portfolio *m* and a portion in the riskless asset. An investor with indifference curve, labeled by 2, allocates 100 percent of his or her investment to the risky assets. Finally, an investor whose indifference curve is labeled by 3 borrows money and invests his or her money as well as the borrowed money in portfolio *m*. The important conclusion from the preceding discussion is that we have the same investment diversification strategy in the risky assets regardless of preference: all investors mix portfolio m, the tangency portfolio, with the riskless asset. The fact that various investors have various indifference curves does not affect the diversification mix in the risky assets. This property is well known in the literature as the *separation theorem*, as follows:

Separation Theorem: Assuming homogeneous expectations, the optimal investment selection procedure can be separated into two stages. In stage a), investors select their portfolios of risky assets. In this stage, all investors select the same portfolio of risky assets regardless of their preferences. All investors select portfolio m (see Figure 5.3). In stage b), investors make a decision on the mix of portfolio m and the riskless asset. In this stage, the choice depends on preferences, as demonstrated in Figure 5.3.

Example: Suppose that the tangency portfolio, portfolio m, is composed of three stocks, stocks A, B, and C, with proportions of 1/4, 1/4, and 1/2, respectively. An investor who neither borrows nor lends, and whose invested capital is, say, $10,000 purchases portfolio m, hence invests $2,500 (which is 1/4 times $10,000) in stock A, $2,500 in stock B, and $5,000 in stock C. Suppose that another investor with an invested capital of $10,000 decides to invest $5,000 in the riskless asset and only $5,000 in the risky tangency portfolio, portfolio m. This investor will invest $1,250 (which is 1/4 times $5,000) in stock A, $1,250 in stock B, and $2,500 in stock C. Now suppose that a third investor, who has $10,000 of invested capital, decides to borrow an additional $10,000 and invest the available $20,000 in the risky portfolio, portfolio m. This investor will invest $5,000 in stock A (which is 1/4 times $20,000), $5,000 in stock B, and $10,000 in stock C. Note that all three investors hold the same proportions of risky assets, regardless of whether they invest only in the risky asset or whether they also invest in the riskless asset. This example illustrates the separation theorem: All investors invest in the same portfolio of risky asset regardless of the amount of money invested and regardless of the dollar amount invested. The size of the investment and the borrowing-lending policy has no effect on the choice of the proportions of the risky assets in the portfolio. Because the selection of portfolio m is not affected by the dollar amount of the invested capital, it is common to assume $1 of invested capital, which gives investment weights in percents. This separation theorem is a fundamental ingredient needed for the derivation of the CAPM.

Finally, like in equation (5.3), in the next equation, we can drive the transformation line with portfolio m and the riskless asset to obtain the well-known Capital Market Line (CML):

$$\mu_P = r + \frac{\mu_m - r}{\sigma_m}\sigma_p. \tag{5.15}$$

Comparing equations (5.3) and (5.15) reveals one important difference: in equation (5.3), we have some asset whose mean and variance are given by (μ, σ^2), whereas in equation (5.13), we connect the riskless asset in a straight line with a specific portfolio, the *tangency portfolio*, whose parameters are (μ_m, σ_m^2). All portfolios located on one of the straight lines, described either by equation (5.3) or by equation (5.15), whose parameters (μ_P, σ_P^2), are attainable by mixing the riskless asset with a risky asset, where the risky asset can be an individual asset or a portfolio. However, of all the attainable transformation lines, there is only one efficient line, the line with the highest slope.

As can be seen from equation (5.15), in this case, the risk of the held portfolio, like in the one risky asset case, is measured by the standard deviation (or variance) of the return on this portfolio. Also, like in the one risky asset case, the optimal diversification strategy depends on the indifference curves and therefore varies across investors. However, there is one crucial difference between the one risky asset case and the n-risky assets case: Whereas in the one risky asset case, the individual asset variance is the risk index, in the n-assets case, the individual asset variance is not its measure of risk. It is a rather more complicated risk measure that is hidden in the portfolio variance. As we see in the next section, it is a risk index called *beta*, which is much different from the variance.

So far, we have defined portfolio m as the tangency portfolio. Later in this chapter, we will see that under some additional assumption, this portfolio is in fact the *market portfolio*, namely, a portfolio that includes all available risky assets in the market exactly according to their market value weight. When the *tangency portfolio m* is equal to the *market portfolio*, the straight line given by equation (5.15) is called the CML. We turn now to derive the CAPM.

5.3. THE DERIVATION OF THE CAPITAL ASSET PRICING MODEL

In this section, we derive the CAPM by two methodos as suggested by Sharpe[5] and Lintner.[6] These two methods employ different approaches and were published in 1964 and 1965, respectively.

The CAPM provides a linear relation between the mean return on an individual security (or a portfolio) and the risk of this security, when the risk is measured by *beta*, which is the slope of the regression line, where in this regression, the dependent variable is the rate of rerun on security i and the explanatory variable is the rate of return on the market portfolio. Given a set of parameters regarding the means, variances, and covariances, Sharpe and Lintner prove that under a set of assumptions, the following relationship holds:

$$\mu_i = r + (\mu_m - r)\beta_i,$$

where

μ_i = The mean return on security i, denoted also by $E(R_i)$

μ_m = The mean return on the market portfolio, composed of all available risky assets in the market, denoted also by $E(R_m)$

r = The riskless interest rate

$\beta_i = Cov(R_i, R_m)/\sigma_m^2$, and R_i and R_m are the rates of returns (random variables) on security i and on the market portfolio, respectively

As we see in the next section, to guarantee equilibrium, the market should clear out, and the market clearance and the various parameters are determined simultaneously. However, in the meantime, we assume that the various parameters are given with no discussion of how they are determined.

Before we prove this linear risk–expected return relation and discuss the economic meaning of beta as the risk index, let us spell out the set of assumptions one needs to make to obtain this equilibrium model. The following assumptions are needed for the CAPM to hold:

[5] W. F. Sharpe, "Capital Asset Prices: A Theory of Market Equilibrium," *Journal of Finance*, 1964.

[6] J. Lintner, "Security Prices, Risk and the Maximal Gain from Diversification," *Journal of Finance*, 1965.

1. Investors are risk averse.
2. Investors select their investment by the M-V rule (see Chapter 4 for the conditions under which the M-V rule is optimal).
3. Perfect capital market: This assumption contains the following elements:
    a. The market comprises many buyers and sellers of risky securities, none of whose transactions are large enough to affect the prices of these securities.
    b. No transaction costs, no capital or income taxes.
    c. Perfect divisibility: Even with a relatively small invested capital, the investor can purchase as many securities as he or she wishes.
    d. All investors have the same information on the relevant securities, and this information provided to them is costless.
4. All investors who are exposed to the same costless information also have homogeneous expectations regarding the mean returns, variances, and the various correlations. Homogeneous expectations do not follow immediately from the fact that all investors have the same information because, generally investors, based on the same information, may form different expectations regarding the various parameters. Therefore, we need to add this specific assumption.
5. The risk-free interest rate is an exogenous variable.

This is a very demanding set of assumptions. However, after the publication of the CAPM, some important articles have been published relaxing several of these assumptions. Generally, the obtained result is that the more assumptions are relaxed, the more complicated, less intuitive, and less applicable is the obtained risk–rerun equilibrium relation. In this chapter, we discuss the classic CAPM, which is derived under this set of assumptions; the next chapter (Chapter 6) is devoted to some extensions of the CAPM.

a) Sharpe's Capital Asset Pricing Model Derivation

Given the set of equilibrium parameters corresponding to the various available assets, Figure 5.4 illustrates the M-V frontier, as well as the straight line, which tangents the M-V frontier at point *m* (we discuss in

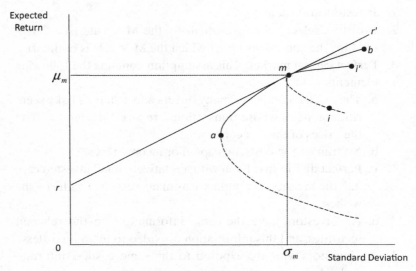

Figure 5.4. The Efficient Frontier.

the subsequent section how these parameters are determined in equilibrium).The segment *ab* is the M-V efficient set, and portfolio *m* is the tangency portfolio. Line *rr'* is the tangency line, where *r* stands for the riskless interest rate. Given the *n*-available risky assets and the riskless interest rate, one can take the derivatives of equation (5.11), given previously, to solve for this frontier. Because the minimization of the Lagrange function (see equation (5.11)) is done with the riskless interest rate, the solutions to the equations, after taking the relevant derivatives and equating them to zero, are the investment weights corresponding to all portfolios located on line *rr'*. One unique portfolio, which is of crucial importance to the CAPM derivation, located on this line is the portfolio with $\sum_i^n w_i = 1$; namely, a portfolio with no borrowing and no lending, portfolio *m* (see Figure 5.4). Actually, this is the only portfolio located on the efficient frontier *rr'*, which is composed solely from risky assets.

Having the efficient frontier *ab*, and the tangency line *rr'*, Sharpe investigates the interior frontier created by mixing portfolio *m* with a single interior security, say, security *i* (see Figure 5.4). The obtained frontier from such a mix is denoted by the curve *ii'*. If 100 percent of the capital is invested in security *i*, we obtain point *i* on this frontier. If 100 percent of the capital is invested in portfolio *m*, point *m* is obtained. Because *ab* is the frontier created by all available assets, curve *ii'* is by definition an interior frontier, and thus it cannot cross curve *ab*. But because curve *ii'* has a point on curve *ab* (point *m*), there must be a tangency point of the curves *ii'* and *ab* at point *m*. However, at point *m*, there is another important tangency point; it is the tangency point of the M-V frontier of risky assets, curve *ab*, and the straight line *rr'*. Sharpe uses the property that at point *m*, by construction, the two tangency points discussed previously are equal to derive the CAPM, as we elaborate in the following.

The rate of return on a portfolio composed of portfolio *m* and security *i* is given by

$$R_P = w_i R_i + (1 - w_i) R_m, \qquad (5.16)$$

where

w_i = The proportion invested in security *i*
$1 - w_i$ = The proportion invested in portfolio *m*
R_i = The rate of return on security *i*
R_m = The rate of return on portfolio *m*

By changing the investment proportion w_i, we get various portfolios located on curve *ii'*. Note that for all portfolios located on segment *im*, the two assets are in long positions, whereas the segment *mi'* corresponds to portfolios with short position in security *i*, and a long position in portfolio *m*.

Because the slope of line *rr'* is equal to $(\mu_m - r)/\sigma_m$, we get at point *m* the following relation:

$$\frac{\mu_m - r}{\sigma_m} = \text{Slope of curve } ii' \text{at point } m. \qquad (5.17)$$

Equation (5.17) is the main equation needed to prove the CAPM by Sharpe's approach. Once equation (5.17) is understood, technically one needs only to find these two derivatives, equate them, and the CAPM follows. Thus, only a number of technical steps remain to derive the CAPM from equation (5.17).

Using equation (5.16), we can calculate the expected return and the variance of the portfolios composed of asset *i* and *m* as follows:

$$\mu_P = w_i \mu_i + (1 - w_i) \mu_m$$

and

$$\sigma_P^2 = w_i^2 \sigma_i^2 + (1 - w_i)^2 \sigma_m^2 + 2w_i(1 - w_i)\sigma_{i,m},$$

where (μ_P, σ_P^2) are the mean return and the variance of the created portfolio, (μ_i, σ_i^2) are the parameters of security i, and (μ_m, σ_m^2) are the parameters of portfolio m, where $\sigma_{i,m}$ stands for the covariance of the return on security i and the return on portfolio m.

Taking the derivative with respect to w_i of the preceding two equations yields

$$\partial \mu_P / \partial w_i = \mu_i - \mu_m \tag{5.18}$$

and

$$\partial \sigma_P / \partial w_i = \frac{1}{2\sigma_P}\left[2w_i\sigma_i^2 - 2(1 - w_i)\sigma_m^2 + 2\sigma_{im} - 4w_i\sigma_{im}\right]. \tag{5.19}$$

Because we are looking at the value of the derivatives at point m, and because at this point $w_i = 0$ and $\sigma_P = \sigma_m$, equation (5.19) at this point is reduced to

$$\partial \sigma_P / \partial w_i = \left(\sigma_{im} - \sigma_m^2\right) / \sigma_m. \tag{5.20}$$

Let us turn back to equation (5.18): by the chain rule, we have

$$\partial \mu_P / w_i = (\partial \mu_P / \partial \sigma_P)(\partial \sigma_P / \partial w_i),$$

which can be written also as

$$\partial \mu_P / \partial \sigma_P = (\partial \mu_P / \partial w_i)/(\partial \sigma_P / \partial w_i). \tag{5.21}$$

The left-hand side of equation (5.21) is the slope of the derivative at point m. But at this point, the slope is equal to the slope of the line rr'. Using the equality of the two slopes and equations (5.18) and (5.19) yields

$$\frac{\mu_m - r}{\sigma_m} = \frac{(\mu_i - \mu_m)\sigma_m}{\sigma_{im} - \sigma_m^2}.$$

Cross-multiplying, we obtain the linear relation,

$$\mu_i = r + (\mu_m - r)\sigma_{im}/\sigma_m^2.$$

But because

$$\sigma_{im}/\sigma_m^2 = Cov(R_i, R_m)/\sigma_m^2 = \beta_i{}^7,$$

we finally obtain the linear relation between the mean return of security i and the risk of security i given by beta, well known as the CAPM:

$$\mu_i = r + (\mu_m - r)\beta_i. \tag{5.22}$$

Because this equation can be derived for all securities like asset i, it holds for all risky assets. Note that asset i can be an individual asset or a portfolio, as the whole proof of Sharpe can be done by selecting some M-V interior portfolio rather than an individual asset. Finally, it is common to write the CAPM equation also in the following form:

$$E(R_i) = r + [E(R_m) - r]\beta_i \quad \text{for } i = 1, 2, \dots n,$$

where E denotes the expected value.

b) Lintner's Capital Asset Pricing Model Derivation

Lintner employs a completely different approach to derive the CAPM. Having n-risky assets and the riskless asset, Lintner seeks the investment proportions in all risky assets that maximize the slope of the transformation line, line rA in Figure 5.3. Thus, the problem that Lintner solves is

$$\max_{w}(\tan \alpha) = \max \frac{ER_P - r}{\sigma_p}, \tag{5.23}$$

subject to

$$\sum_i^n w_i = 1,$$

where ER_P (which is equal to μ_P in Sharpe's formulation; however, we switch to this notation because it is commonly employed in Lintner's model) and σ_p are the portfolio mean and variance as defined by equations (5.5) and (5.6), respectively, and α is the slope of the line rA given in Figure 5.3. By taking the derivative with respect to each w_i (recall that the portfolio mean and variance are written in

---

[7] Beta is the slope of the regression line of R_{it} on R_{mt}.

terms of w_i) and equating the result to zero, Lintner obtains n equations with n unknowns; hence, the system is, in principle, solvable. After some algebraic manipulations, the risk–return linear equation (5.22) is obtained. Thus, by maximizing the slope of the transformation line, Lintner finds the investment proportions corresponding to line rA given in Figure 5.3 – namely, the investment weights corresponding to portfolio m given in Figure 5.3.

We formulate here a similar problem to the one employed by Lintner. The suggested formulation has the advantage of shedding light on the economic interpretation of some other variables, particularly on the market price of risk. First, we consider portfolios composed of n-risky assets and the riskless asset. Define the Lagrange function L as follows:

$$L = \sigma_P + \lambda \left[ER_P - \sum_{i=1}^{n} w_i\, ER_i - (1 - \sum_{i}^{n} w_i)r \right],$$

where

$$\sigma_P = \left[\sum_{i=1}^{n} w_i^2 \sigma_i^2 + 2 \sum_{j=1}^{n} \sum_{j=1, j>i}^{n} w_i w_j \sigma_{i,j} \right]^{1/2},$$

$$ER_P = \sum_{i=1}^{n} w_i\, ER_i + \left(1 - \sum_{i=1}^{n} w_i\right) r$$

and λ is a Lagrange multiplier.

Note that the portfolio mean return corresponds to the investment in the n risky asset and the investment in the riskless asset. The term $(1 - \sum_{i=1}^{n} w_i)$ stands for the proportion of borrowing or lending. Minimizing the portfolio standard deviation for a given portfolio mean return is tantamount to maximization of the slope of the transformation line as suggested by Lintner. Thus, the formulation suggested here achieves the same goal of maximizing the slope of the transformation line.

Taking the derivative of L with respect to the Lagrange multiplier, λ, yields

$$\partial L/\partial \lambda = 0 \Rightarrow ER_P = \sum_{i=1}^{n} w_i\, ER_i + \left(1 - \sum_{i=1}^{n} w_i\right) r.$$

Therefore, this constraint guarantees that we solve for a portfolio with a minimum standard deviation for a given preset portfolio mean return. Taking the derivative of L with respect to each value w_i and equating to zero induces n equations with n unknowns, which are the investment weights in the *n*-risky assets that minimize the portfolio standard deviation. The resulting $n + 1$ equations are the following:

$$\partial L/\partial w_1 = (1/2\sigma_P)\left[2w_1\sigma_1^2 + 2\sum_{j=2}^{n} w_j\sigma_{1,j}\right] - \lambda(ER_1 - r) = 0.$$

$$\partial L/\partial w_2 = (1/2\sigma_P)\left[2w_2\sigma_2^2 + 2\sum_{j=1,i\neq2}^{n} w_j\sigma_{2,j}\right] - \lambda(ER_2 - r) = 0.$$

$$\vdots \qquad \vdots \qquad \vdots \qquad \vdots$$

$$\partial L/\partial w_i = (1/2\sigma_P)\left[2w_i\sigma_i^2 + 2\sum_{j=1,j\neq i}^{n} w_j\sigma_{i,j}\right] - \lambda(ER_i - r) = 0.$$

$$\vdots \qquad \vdots \qquad \vdots \qquad \vdots$$

$$\partial L/\partial w_n = (1/2\sigma_P)\left[2w_n\sigma_n^2 + 2\sum_{j=1}^{n-1} w_j\sigma_{n,j}\right] - \lambda(ER_n - r) = 0.$$

$$(5.24)$$

and the last equation is given by

$$\partial L/\partial \lambda = ER_P - \sum_{i=1}^{n} w_i\, ER_i - \left(1 - \sum_{i=1}^{n} w_i\right)r = 0.$$

This set of equations holds for any *efficient* portfolio P, whose expected return is fixed at ER_P, and in particular for portfolio m whose expected return is ER_m and is also M-V efficient. Thus, we can also rewrite equation (5.24) with portfolio m rather than with portfolio P. With portfolio m, the typical equation corresponding to asset i will be

$$\partial L/\partial w_i = (1/2\sigma_m)\left[2w_i\sigma_i^2 + 2\sum_{j=1,j\neq i}^{n} w_j\sigma_{ij}\right] - \lambda(ER_i - r) = 0.$$

$$(5.24')$$

Dividing the left-hand side of all terms in equation (5.24) by 2, and multiplying the first equation by w_1, the second equation by w_2, etc. ... and summing over all the *n* equations yields[8]

$$\sigma_P = \lambda\left(\sum_{i=1}^{n} w_i\, ER_i - \sum_{i=1}^{n} w_i r\right).$$

Adding and subtracting r from the right-hand side of this equation, we can rewrite it as

$$\sigma_P = \lambda\left[\sum_{i=1}^{n} w_i\, ER_i + \left(1 - \sum_{i=1}^{n} w_i\right)r - r\right].$$

---

[8] Note that summing all terms inside the square brackets, after multiplying by w_i and dividing by 2, we get $\sum_i^n w_i^2\sigma_i^2 + \sum_i^n \sum_{j=1,j\neq i}^{n} w_i w_j\sigma_{ij} = \sigma_P^2$. After reducing by σ_P, we obtain on the left-hand side of the equation σ_P.

Hence,

$$1/\lambda = \frac{ER_P - r}{\sigma_P}.$$

The last equation holds for all M-V efficient portfolios, suggesting that it also holds for the efficient portfolio with no riskless asset, portfolio m (see Figure 5.24′). Thus,

$$1/\lambda = \frac{ER_m - r}{\sigma_m}. \tag{5.25}$$

The reciprocal of the Lagrange multiplier is the slope of the highest attainable transformation line. It measures the price of unit of risk: alternatively, it measures the required risk premium per one unit of standard deviation at the optimum.

We turn now to determine the equilibrium risk–return relation. Let us take one equation from equation (5.24), say the ith equation. More precisely, let us take the equation corresponding to portfolio m, which is also efficient; that is, equation (5.24′). It can be rewritten as follows:

$$ER_i = r + \frac{1}{\lambda\sigma_m}\left[w_i\sigma_i^2 + \sum_{j=1, j\neq i}^{n} w_j\sigma_{i,j}\right]. \tag{5.24″}$$

The last equation can be rewritten as follows:

$$ER_i = r + \frac{1}{\lambda}(\partial\sigma_m/\partial w_i). \tag{5.24‴}$$

Namely, the expected rate of return on security i is equal to the riskless interest rate plus a premium, where the risk premium is equal to the price of risk times the marginal contribution of security i to the risk of the held portfolio at the optimum.

Substituting for λ in equation (5.24″) (by employing equation [5.25]) yields

$$ER_i = r + \frac{ER_m - r}{\sigma_m^2}\left[w_i\sigma_i^2 + \sum_{j=1, j\neq i}^{n} w_j\sigma_{i,j}\right].$$

Recalling that the term in the square brackets in equation (5.24″) is equal to the covariance between the rate of return of security i and the market portfolio,[9] we get

$$ER_i = r + \frac{ER_m - r}{\sigma_m^2}Cov(R_i, R_m).$$

[9] $Cov(R_i, R_m) = Cov(R_i, \sum_i^n w_i R_i) = w_i\sigma_i^2 + \sum_{j=1, j\neq i}^{n} w_j\sigma_{ij}.$

Employing the definition of beta[10] we finally obtain

$$ER_i = r + (ER_m - r)\beta_i,$$

which is identical to the linear risk–return relation derived by Sharpe. This linear risk–return relation can also be rewritten in the following commonly employed form:

$$\mu_i = r + (\mu_m - r)\beta_i.$$

This linear relation, derived both by Sharpe and Lintner, in fact describes what is well known as the Security Market Line (SML), where all available assets are included and beta is the relevant measure of risk. In other words, facing two securities with the same beta, we expect to get the same expected return on these two securities.

c) Discussion

The CML and SML have some important implications regarding the risk measure of assets and the risk premium. Because Sharpe and Lintner arrive at the same CAPM formula, the implication discussed as follows relates to both.

1. The SML, the CML, and the Risk Measure

To analyze the SML and CML, let us first write side by side these two important equations, which are related to the CAPM. The CML corresponds only to efficient portfolios, and the SML corresponds to individual securities, efficient portfolios, and inefficient portfolios alike. The two formulas are as follows:

$$\text{CML: } \mu_P = r + \frac{\mu_m - r}{\sigma_m}\sigma_P \qquad (5.26)$$

$$\text{SML: } \mu_i = r + (\mu_m - r)\beta_i. \qquad (5.27)$$

Equation (5.26) holds only for M-V efficient portfolios. In other words, every risk-averse investor who invests by the M-V rule will invest in the highest tangency portfolio, portfolio m, and the riskless asset. By doing so, the investor maximizes his or her expected utility

---

[10] In the regression of the return of security i on the return on the market portfolio, beta is the slope of this regression line given by $Cov(R_i, R_m)/\sigma_m^2$. See also Section 5.3.

because the highest indifference curve is achieved. Every investor may choose a different combination of the pairs (μ_P, σ_P) according to his or her taste. Thus, although all investors invest in the same risky portfolio, portfolio m, they differ with respect to the diversification between the risky portfolio and the riskless asset.

From the CML equation, it is transparent that the risk of the efficient portfolio is measured by the variance or by the standard deviation of the held portfolio. However, from the formula of the SML, it is equally clear that the risk measure of an asset, an individual security or a portfolio alike, is beta. Finally, although the end result of the CAPM is the SML formula, it cannot be achieved without the separation theorem, which is based on optimal investment diversification policy as advocated by the superiority of the CML over any other transformation line. For this reason, the CML is needed to derive the SML. The SML, which is the core equation of the CAPM, does not correspond only to efficient portfolios but also to all available assets in the market.

Figure 5.5 illustrates the SML and the CML Figure 5.5a provides the CML and Figure 5.5b provides the SML. The CML corresponds to all efficient portfolios and the SML corresponds to all available assets. Because portfolio m is efficient, it appears on both lines. Indeed, as we shall see in the following section, for efficient portfolios, the SML and CML lines can be used to predict the expected rate of return corresponding to efficient portfolios.

2. Beta and Risk Premium

As we shall see, in equilibrium, the tangency portfolio, portfolio m, must be also the market portfolio, which is composed of all available risky assets, where the proportion of asset i in portfolio m is equal to its relative weight in the market.

The beta of each asset measures its risk, provided the asset is held in the tangency portfolio, portfolio m. The higher the beta, the higher the equilibrium expected return on the asset. Namely, the higher the beta of a specific asset under consideration, the higher the required risk premium from this asset. For example, suppose that a firm with a beta equal to 1, as a result of changes in macroeconomic reasons, is suddenly exposed to higher risk; hence, beta increases. The increase in risk can be also a decision variable of the firm's management. For example, the firm may decide to increase leverage, which, in turn,

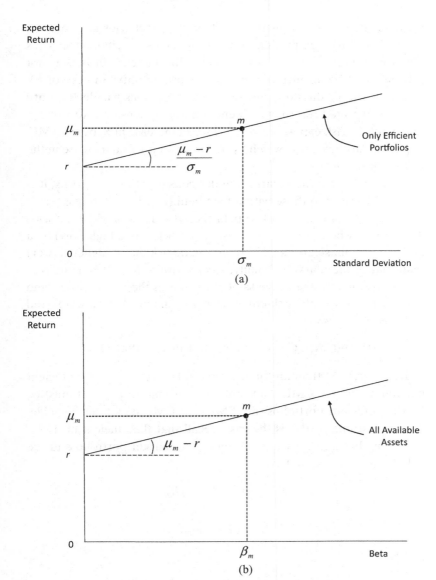

Figure 5.5. The Capital Market Line (CML) and the Security Market Line (SML).

increases beta. With an increase in beta, two scenarios are possible: a) the firm's average profitability also increases, which compensates investors for the increase in beta; or b) the increase in beta is not accompanied by an increase in average profitability. In case of b), investors will sell the stock, and the price of the stock will decline until the new expected return is high enough to compensate investors for the increased risk exposure. In any case, an increase in β, by the SML, implies an increase in μ, which by definition implies an increase in the risk premium, $\mu - r$.

Note that when the securities under consideration are stocks, it is common to refer to those with a high beta (i.e., $\beta > 1$) as aggressive stocks and to those with a low beta (i.e., $\beta < 1$) as defensive stocks. This is so as when an investor invests in a stock with a high (low) beta and exposes himself or herself to systematic risk that is higher (lower) than that of the markets. Finally, stocks with a $\beta = 1$, implying that they move on average in the same direction as the market does, and hence have systematic risk equal to that of the markets, are referred to as *neutral stocks*.

3.   CML and SML Corresponding to Efficient Portfolios

Because the SML holds for all assets and therefore also for efficient portfolios, and the CML holds only for efficient portfolio, it must be that for efficient portfolios, the SML and CML equations coincide. To see that indeed this is the case, recall that the efficient portfolio is nothing but a linear combination of the market portfolio and the riskless asset. Thus, we have

$$R_P = \alpha r + (1 - \alpha) R_m$$

$$\sigma_P = (1 - \alpha)\sigma_m,$$

and because

$$\beta_m = Cov(R_m, R_m)/\sigma_m^2 = \sigma_m^2/\sigma_m^2 = 1,$$

we finally have[11]

$$\beta_P = (1 - \alpha)\beta_m = 1 - \alpha.$$

[11] $\beta_P = Cov[\alpha r + (1 - \alpha) R_m, R_m]/\sigma_m^2 = (1 - \alpha)Cov(R_m, R_m)/\sigma_m^2 = (1 - \alpha)\beta_m = 1 - \alpha.$

Write the SML for the specific case of an efficient portfolio:

$$\mu_P = r + (\mu_m - r)\beta_p.$$

Substituting for β_P yields

$$\mu_P = r + (\mu_m - r)(1 - \alpha),$$

but because $(1 - \alpha) = \sigma_P/\sigma_m$, substituting this term in the preceding equation, we finally obtain that the SML of efficient portfolios coincides with its CML:

$$\mu_P = r + \frac{\mu_m - r}{\sigma_m}\sigma_P = r + (\mu_m - r)\beta_P.$$

We stress that this identity of the SML and CML is intact only for efficient portfolios.

4. Systematic and Nonsystematic Risk

In a portfolio context, the variance of the individual asset plays a minor role in determining its risk. To see this, recall that by the SML, β_i is the only parameter related directly to security i. So, theoretically, the variance of security i plays a minor role in determining the risk premium. This implies that in a portfolio setting, the individual's asset variance does not measure risk. We say that it plays a minor role in measuring risk and not completely no role at all, as the variance is a component, albeit a small one, of beta. However, as it is only one element of many other covariances that determine beta (see equation 5.6″), its role in a large market with many securities is negligible.

The variance of security i can be decomposed to the component that affects asset pricing and to the component that does not. Regressing the rate of return of security i on the rate of return on the market portfolio, we have

$$R_{it} = \alpha_i + \beta_i R_{mt} + e_{it},$$

where e_{it} is the regression residual and β_i is the same beta included in the SML formula. Taking the variance of both sides of the previous equation yields

$$\sigma_i^2 = \beta_i^2 \sigma_m^2 + \sigma_{e_i}^2$$

(the variance of the intercept, which is a constant, is equal to zero and the covariance between R and e is by construction equal to zero).

Because only beta and the variance of the market portfolio appear in the SML formula, we see that the variance of the individual asset affects asset pricing only via beta. The variance of the residual, which is the other component of the variance of security i, has no effect on asset pricing.

Having a large portfolio, it is commonly claimed that by having an efficient diversification the residual variance σ_e^2 is "washed out," because the error terms of the various securities included in the tangency portfolio tend to cancel each other. However, even efficient diversification cannot wash out the market portfolio variance, which reflects the macroeconomic factors, particularly cycles in the whole economy. Whereas the explanation corresponding to the macroeconomic fluctuations, which cannot vanish even in a well-diversified portfolio, is intact, the explanation regarding the residual variance, being "washed out" in a large and well-diversified portfolio is not complete. To see this claim, suppose that there are only three securities in the market. All the proofs and the resulting SML are intact in this small capital market also. Thus, the residual variance plays no role in price determination even in this small market, where the error terms certainly do not cancel each other. The explanation for why beta, and not the variance, determines the risk premium is that beta measures the marginal contribution of security i to the held portfolio risk at the optimum; hence, it is the appropriate risk index (see equation [5.24$'''$]).

Two names appear in the literature for the preceding two components of the variance. The names that are self-explanatory of these two components of the variance of security i are as follows:

$\beta_i^2 \sigma_m^2$ – Systematic risk, or nondiversifiable risk
σ_e^2 – Nonsystematic risk, or diversifiable risk

5. The Price of a Unit of Risk and Risk Premium

Taking the ith equation from equation (5.24), and recalling that portfolio m is also an efficient portfolio, we substitute it for portfolio m to obtain that at the optimum, for each asset i, the following must hold:

$$\frac{1}{\lambda} \frac{\partial \sigma_m}{\partial w_i} = ER_i - r.$$

Namely, the required risk premium, $ER - r$ is equal to the price of unit of risk, $\frac{1}{\lambda}$ times the marginal contribution of the security to the market portfolio risk at the optimum, measured by $\partial \sigma_m / \partial w_i$ (see also equation [5.24''']).

5.4. EQUILIBRIUM IN THE STOCK MARKET

So far, we have discussed the optimal diversification strategy for a given set of parameters. We show that for this given set of parameters, all M-V investors diversify between the riskless asset and the tangency portfolio, which we denote by portfolio m. Investing in the tangency portfolio maximizes the investor's expected utility. Because all investors invest in the same portfolio of risky asset, we obtain the Separation Theorem, which in turn leads to the SML. However, all these results are obtained so long as a given set of parameters on which all investors agree exists. But how are these parameters determined? Do they change over time? And, if so, what causes these changes? Is the set of parameters under consideration consistent with or in contradiction to market equilibrium? With the given set of parameters, do we have market clearance? This section is devoted to these issues.

As usual in economics, we advocate also in the CAPM that the set of parameters is determined by the supply and demand for the risky assets and a market clearance is a necessary condition for equilibrium. Before we analyze the equilibrium in the stock market, let us define some basic aggregate relationships. Although the CAPM corresponds to all risky assets, in this section, for simplicity and without loss of generality, we refer to the risky assets as *stocks*.

Because of the Separation Theorem, the following must hold:

$$w_i S_0 = V_{i0} \quad \text{or} \quad w_i = V_{i0}/S_0, \quad (5.28)$$

where

$S_0 =$ Total capital invested in all risky assets by all investors at time 0

$V_{i0} =$ The market value of the shares of stock i, outstanding in the base period 0

$w_i =$ The optimal proportion of stock i in the tangency portfolio, portfolio m (see Figure 5.4). We emphasize that w_i is not an arbitrary investment proportion, but rather it is the proportion corresponding to portfolio m, the tangency portfolio. For simplicity, we do not add a superstar to this notation to emphasize that it is the optimal investment weight. Because we consider only the investment in the risky assets, owing to the Separation Theorem, the proportions w_i/w_j for all pairs (i,j) are identical across all investors independent of their invested capital.

Having n-risky assets (namely, n firms that issued stocks), the total supply of stocks in the market must be equal to the total invested capital (i.e., to the total demand). This equilibrium market clearance condition can be written as follows:

$$S_0 = T_0 = \sum_{i=1}^{n} V_{i0}, \tag{5.29}$$

where T_0 stands for the current market value of all shares – that is, the size of the market. The subscript zero emphasizes that this is the market values at time zero, which, as we shall see later, is the equilibrium market value of all shares.

Because we analyze here the total invested capital in stocks, we must also have the following constraints:

$$\sum_{i=1}^{n} w_i = \frac{\sum_{i=1}^{n} V_{i0}}{T_0} = 1.$$

The Sharpe-Lintner CAPM is a one-period model: investors invest at time $t = 0$ and the firms liquidate their assets at time $t = 1$. The value of firm i at period 1 is unknown, and therefore it is a random variable given by $\tilde{V}_{i1}$ with an expected value of $E(\tilde{V}_{i1}) = V_{i1}$. By the homogeneous expectation assumption of the CAPM, all inventors agree on the distribution of the end of period value of all firms; hence, they also agree on the *expected* end of period value $V_{i1.}$. The expected rate of return on the investment in security i is given by

$$ER_i = \frac{V_{i1} - V_{i0}}{V_{i0}}. \tag{5.30}$$

Equation (5.30) is a key equation to understanding the CAPM equilibrium process. Because all investors agree on the end of period value V_{i1}, by determining the equilibrium stock price, V_{i0} is determined; consequently, the expected rate of return is determined. Thus,

based on the information on the distributions of all V_{i1} $(i = 1, 2, \ldots n)$ –
particularly on the variances, expected values, and the covariance corresponding to these variables – the investors construct their optimal
portfolios; and by the demand and supply to each stock, the equilibrium values V_{io} are determined (for $i = 1, 2, \ldots n$), which by equation
(5.30) simultaneously determines the expected rates of returns on the
various assets ER_i $(i = 1, 2, \ldots n)$, values that determine the SML.
Thus, the market is in equilibrium, when all investors invest in the
tangency portfolio, and the parameters needed to calculate this tangency portfolio are determined by investors such that market clearance exists.

We now turn to the economic interpretation of the equilibrium values and the aggregate market price of risk. We need to add some
notations:

$\tilde{\sigma}_i^2 = $ The variance of the aggregate value of security i
$\tilde{\sigma}_{i,j} = $ The covariance between the aggregate values of firm i and
  firm j
$\sigma_i^2 = $ The variance per one dollar investment in security i
$\sigma_{i,j} = $ The covariance per \$1 investment in securities i and j

All these parameters are determined by the distribution of the end-
of-period values of the various firms.

Having equilibrium values V_{i0}, we have the following statistical
relationships:

$$\sigma_i^2 = \tilde{\sigma}_i^2 / V_{i0}^2 \quad \text{and} \quad \sigma_{ij} = \tilde{\sigma}_{i,j} / V_{i0} V_{j0}, \tag{5.31}$$

where, by dividing by the values of the firms, we shift from dollar terms to percentage terms. We employ these relationships in the
derivation of equilibrium in terms of aggregate values.

Take the ith equation from equation (5.24′) and rewrite it (after
reducing by 2, and selecting portfolio m as the efficient portfolio) as
follows:

$$\lambda(ER_i - r) = \frac{1}{\sigma_m} \left[w_i \sigma_i^2 + \sum_{j=1.j\neq i}^{n} w_j \sigma_{i,j} \right].$$

Employing equation (5.30), equation (5.31), and the fact that in equilibrium $w_i = V_{i0}/S_0 = V_{i0}/T_0$ yields

$$\lambda \left[\frac{V_{i1} - V_{i0}}{V_{i0}} - r \right] = \frac{1}{\sigma_m} \left[\frac{V_{i0}}{T_0} \frac{\tilde{\sigma}_i^2}{(V_{i0}^2)} + \sum_{j=1, j \neq i}^{n} \frac{V_{j0}}{T_0} \frac{\tilde{\sigma}_{i,j}}{V_{i0} V_{j0}} \right].$$

Multiplying both sides by V_{i0} and canceling some terms yields

$$\lambda \left[V_{i1} - (1+r)V_{i0} \right] = \frac{1}{T_0 \sigma_m} \left[\tilde{\sigma}_i^2 + \sum_{j=1, j \neq i}^{n} \tilde{\sigma}_{i,j} \right].$$

Dividing both sides by λ and recalling that $1/\lambda = \frac{ER_m - r}{\sigma_m}$ yields the following equilibrium equation:

$$V_{i1} - (1+r)V_{i0} = \frac{ER_m - r}{\sigma_m} \frac{1}{T_0} \left[\tilde{\sigma}_i^2 + \sum_{j=1, j \neq i}^{n} \tilde{\sigma}_{i,j} \right].$$

This is the equilibrium equation stipulating the aggregate equilibrium value of the equity of each firm. All investors have homogeneous expectation on the variances and covariance of the aggregate future values $\tilde{\sigma}_i^2$ and $\tilde{\sigma}_{i,j}$ as well as on the end-of-period aggregate expected value V_{i1}. Having these expectations, the equilibrium values V_{i0} for $i = 1, 2, \ldots n$ are simultaneously determined. But, once the expected future value and the equilibrium current values are also determined, ER_i is technically determined. Should the value V_{i0} deviate from the equilibrium value given in the previous formula, the prices of the various securities will adjust, and all the parameters will change until equilibrium is restored.

Using the preceding equation, one can isolate the equilibrium value of the equity of firm I as follows:

$$V_{i0} = \left[V_{i1} - \frac{ER_m - r}{\sigma_m^2} \frac{1}{T_0} \left(\tilde{\sigma}_i^2 + \sum_{j=1, j \neq i}^{n} \tilde{\sigma}_{i,j} \right) \right] / (1+r).$$

Multiplying and dividing by T_0 finally yields

$$V_{i0} = \left[V_{i1} - \frac{T_0 ER_m - T_0 r}{T_0^2 \sigma_m^2} (\tilde{\sigma}_i^2 + \sum_{j=1, j \neq i}^{n} \tilde{\sigma}_{i,j}) \right] / (1+r). \quad (5.32)$$

This equilibrium equation has a very interesting interpretation: the equilibrium aggregate value of security i is equal to the present value of the *certainty equivalent* of the future cash, flows to the investors. It is given by the future expected value V_{i1} less the risk premium, discounted at the riskless interest rate.

However, an elaboration is called for on the risk premium. The risk of security i is measured by its contribution of this security to the risk of the aggregate portfolio. It is given by the aggregate variance of security i and all its aggregate covariances with the other securities (see inner brackets). When we multiply this risk by the market price of risk, we obtain the required risk premium. The market price of risk is given by

$$\gamma \equiv \frac{T_0 E R_m - T_0 r}{T_0^2 \sigma_m^2},$$

which is equal to the aggregate expected return less the aggregate return should all the money be invested in the riskless interest rate; namely, the aggregate risk premium, divided by the aggregate market risk. Note that if σ_m^2 is the variance per one invested dollar, then the aggregate variance, when T_0 is invested in the capital market, is $T_0^2 \sigma_m^2$.

Because T_0 stands for the equilibrium market value of all traded risky assets, the price of one unit of risk, stated in terms of the variance (rather than the standard deviation), decreases with the market size. This result stems from the fact that we have T_0^2 in the denominator of the preceding term and only T_0 in the numerator.

Finally, the equilibrium risk–return relation can also be stated in terms of the share price. Equation (5.32) can be rewritten as follows:

$$N_i P_{io} = \left[N_i P_{i1} - \gamma \left(N_i^2 \sigma_i^2 + \sum_{j=1, j\neq i}^{n} N_i N_j \sigma_{ij} \right) \right] / (1 + r), \quad (5.33)$$

where γ is the price of a unit of risk, $N_i P_{io} = V_{io}$, $N_{i1} P_{i1} = V_{i1}$ (where P_{i1} is the expected price of stock i in period 1), and the variance and covariance in equation (5.32) are stated in per-share terms; hence, $N_i^2 \sigma_i^2$ is, for example, the variance of the total value of firm i, given in equation (5.32). Dividing by N_i yields the equilibrium price of stock i,

$$P_{io} = \left[P_{i1} - \gamma \left(N_i \sigma_i^2 + \sum_{j=1, j\neq i}^{n} N_j \sigma_{ij} \right) \right] / (1 + r). \quad (5.34)$$

5.5. SUMMARY

Assuming that investors are risk averse and choose their portfolios by the M-V rule, we analyze the M-V efficient sets under various scenarios. We reach the following conclusions:

1. When investors face only one risky asset and one riskless asset, they all face a transformation line connecting the riskless interest rate and the expected return on the risky asset. Each investor chooses the optimum diversification between these two assets according to his or her preference. Of course, the selected portfolio maximizes the individual investor's expected utility. In this framework, even if investors do not agree on the expected return and the risk of the risky asset, they all still diversify between these two assets. However, the unique feature of this case is that it provides the investors a transformation line, on which they can move by changing the asset allocation investment strategy. The more the investors move to the right on this transformation line, the more is invested in the risky asset, implying that the investor expects a higher rate of return but also is exposed to higher risk. This simple result paves the way to the derivation of the CML and, in turn, the SML (see conclusions that follow).

2. When the investor faces n-risky assets and the risk-free asset, he or she is free to connect any asset or any combination of risky assets with the riskless asset. Each such selection creates a transformation line exactly as obtained with the one risky asset case. The goal of the investor is to obtain the highest expected return for a given risk, which is tantamount to selecting the transformation line with the largest angle. By selecting this highest transformation line, the investor reaches the highest possible indifference curve and hence maximizes expected utility.

3. With homogeneous expectations, all investors will invest in the same portfolio of risky asset, the one with the highest transformation line. After selecting the optimal risky portfolio, each investor can move on the transformation line by mixing the optimal risk portfolio with the riskless asset. This two-stage investment process is well known as the Separation Theorem. The transformation line with the highest slope, from which all

investors select the optimal portfolio of risky asset, is called the CML. The risk of the selected portfolio is measured by the portfolio variance (or standard deviation).

4. If one adds to the M-V and homogeneous expectation assumptions several assumptions asserting mainly that there is a perfect and efficient market, the CAPM of Sharpe and Lintner is derived. According to this model, all assets, individual securities, and portfolios – efficient and inefficient – are located on the SML, a line relating the expected return on each asset to its risk, when the risk is measured by beta, rather than by the variance. Thus, although the variance measures the risk of the efficient portfolio held, beta measures the risk of each individual asset when it is held in an efficient portfolio. In short, beta measures the contribution of each asset held in the portfolio to the portfolio risk.

5. This linear SML relation does not guarantee equilibrium in the capital market because it is derived under the assumption that the various parameters are given. However, in equilibrium, the market should clear. Adding the market clearance condition, for given homogenous beliefs about the distribution of the future value of each security (which is a random variable), the current equilibrium stock prices, beta, and the mean returns are determined simultaneously. If the market is not cleared, prices will adjust and readjust until it is cleared. Once the market is cleared, we have the SML with parameters that are consistent with equilibrium. Determining the equilibrium prices in this setting is called the CAPM.

In this chapter, we derive the CAPM under some assumptions, where some of them (e.g., no taxes or homogeneous expectations) are clearly not realistic assumptions. In the next chapter, we relax some of these assumptions and provide some extensions to the CAPM. In the subsequent chapters, we examine the validity of the CAPM empirically. It is possible that even if the assumptions are unrealistic, investors behave "as if" these assumptions hold.

6

Extensions of the Capital Asset Pricing Model

6.1. INTRODUCTION

Although this book is devoted mainly to the classic Capital Asset Pricing Model (CAPM) and its relation to behavioral economics, it is worthwhile to discuss briefly the other related risk–return models, particularly the various extensions of the CAPM.

The Sharpe–Lintner CAPM was derived under a set of assumptions, some of which are very restrictive and some of which are in sharp contradiction to what one observes in practice. There are two basic courses one can take to handle these restrictive and unrealistic assumptions. The first course relies on the *positive economics* approach suggested by Milton Friedman,[1] asserting that in some models, although the underlying assumptions clearly do not hold in practice, it is still justifiable to use these models as long as investors behave "as if" these assumptions hold. The procedure to examine whether investors behave as if the assumptions are intact is done by examining the empirical fit of the data to the estimates predicted by the model under scrutiny. If there is a good fit between the theoretical estimates of the model and the observed data, then the theoretical model can be safely used despite the unrealistic assumptions made to derive it.

The second course is a theoretical one rather than an empirical one. By this approach, one relaxes one or more of the unrealistic assumptions that underline the CAPM and derives another theoretical model

---

[1] M. Friedman, "The Methodology of Positive Economics," in *Essays in Positive Economics*, Chicago and London, University of Chicago Press, 1953.

that is a spinoff of the CAPM. For example, one can relax the assumption asserting that unlimited borrowing and lending are available and derive the Zero Beta Model (ZBM), which is a generalization of the CAPM to the case where the riskless asset does not exist. Similarly, the CAPM assumes no fixed transaction costs per asset held, allowing the investor to diversify his or her portfolio such that all available assets in the market are included in the optimal held portfolio. By adding fixed transaction costs per asset held to the model – that is, relaxing an unrealistic assumption – a similar yet a probably more accurate risk–return model is developed. However, this new model is also more complicated and, thus, very hard to test empirically. The fixed transaction costs in this model can be out-of-pocket direct costs or indirect costs that relate to the time and effort the investor allocates to studying and following the financial statements and the changes in prices corresponding to each asset held.

In addition to these two basic courses, another course that can be taken to handle the CAPM's unrealistic underlying assumptions is to suggest another asset-pricing model that relies on a completely different set of assumptions – for example, the Arbitrage Pricing Theory (APT) model, under which the CAPM emerges as one of the possible equilibrium solutions. In such cases, one has to evaluate the restrictions imposed by the set of assumptions corresponding to the various competing models.

These courses may lead to the creation of related models, or extensions of the classic CAPM, on which we focus in this chapter. Later, we shall see in Chapters 9, 10, and 11 that the CAPM is intact also within the Cumulative Prospect Theory (CPT) framework. Some of the extensions of the CAPM are also intact under CPT, but some of the extensions that assume that preference must be strictly concave are not. Also, to have coexistence of the CAPM and CPT, in most cases, the normality of the distribution of returns assumption is needed (see Chapter 11). Yet, normality should not be precise. The financial costs of assuming normality when the distribution of returns is not actually normal is discussed in Chapter 8. Finally, not all risk-return models require normality. Most notable is the APT, which is intact even without normality. Moreover, the APT is valid also within CPT.

We now turn to consider briefly a few extensions of the CAPM and a few alternative models, where the common feature of these models is that they yield some risk–return relation.

6.2. THE ZERO BETA MODEL

In 1972, Fisher Black[2] suggested an equilibrium risk–return model under which the assumption of the existence of riskless borrowing and lending is relaxed. This is an important extension of the CAPM because, in practice, the following facts cast doubt on the existence of riskless borrowing and lending:

a) Generally, at a given interest rate, one can deposit as much money as one wishes, but the amount one can borrow is limited.

b) The borrowing interest rate is generally higher than the lending interest rate; hence, assuming unlimited borrowing and lending at the same interest rate is unrealistic.

c) Even if borrowing and lending at the same riskless interest rate is possible, the inflation rate is uncertain; thus, the real interest rate is not riskless anymore. In this case, an asset that is riskless in nominal terms is risky in real terms and is therefore not characterized by a zero variance as the CAPM assumes.

Black suggests solving the following problem:

$$Minimize\ \sigma_P^2 = \sum_{i=1}^{n} x_i^2 \sigma_i^2 + \sum_{i=1}^{n} \sum_{j=1, j \neq i}^{n} x_i x_j \sigma_{ij},$$

subject to

$$\sum_{i=1}^{n} x_i = 1 \quad \text{and} \quad \sum_{i=1}^{n} x_i \mu_i = \mu_m,$$

where x_i is the investment proportion in the ith asset, n denotes the number of risky assets, and the other parameters are as defined in Chapter 5. As can be seen from this formulation, the riskless asset does not exist.

---

[2] F. Black, "Capital Market Equilibrium with Restricted Borrowing," *Journal of Business*, 1972.

Using a similar technique to the one employed to derive the CAPM (see Chapter 5), Black derives the following equilibrium risk–return formula:

$$\mu_i = \mu_z + (\mu_m - \mu_z)\beta_i, \qquad (6.1)$$

where μ_i, μ_m stands for the mean return on the ith asset and on the market portfolio, respectively, and β_i is the beta of the ith asset. However, unlike the CAPM, asset z or, to be more precise, portfolio z, needs special attention. This portfolio has a zero beta with portfolio m (i.e., it is a zero beta portfolio) – hence the name Zero Beta Model. Thus, we have

$$\beta_i = Cov(R_i, R_m)/\sigma_m^2 \quad \text{and} \quad \beta_z = Cov(R_z, R_m)/\sigma_m^2 = 0,$$

where R_i, R_z, and R_m are the rates of return on asset i, on portfolio z, and on the market portfolio, respectively.

The mathematical proof of the zero beta equilibrium risk–return relation given by equation (6.1), which is very similar to the proof of the CAPM given in Chapter 5, can be found in the 1972 article by Black as well as in many finance textbooks. However, we would like to elaborate in this chapter on the meaning of a zero beta portfolio and the implication of this model to the Separation Theorem. We will show that the zero beta Separation Theorem is somewhat different than the Separation Theorem corresponding to the CAPM.

Figure 6.1 illustrates the Mean-Variance (M-V) efficient frontier where the efficient set given by the segment MVP-b and the inefficient segment of the frontier is given by MVP-a. We also add to this figure line zz' that we will refer to later in this section.

Consider the market portfolio, portfolio m, and the line that is tangent to this point with an intercept μ_z. Because there is no riskless asset, the investor selects a portfolio according to his or her taste, namely, by the tangency point of the individual investor's indifference curve with the efficient set curve. For example, an investor with an indifference curve I_1 will select the optimal portfolio m_1, whereas an investor with an indifference curve I_2 will select the optimal portfolio m_2. Thus, unlike the CAPM, not all investors hold the same combination of risky assets. Moreover, each investor has her zero beta portfolio, depending on the selected optimal portfolio of risky assets.

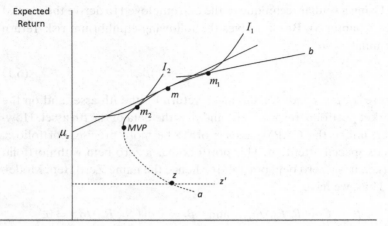

Figure 6.1. The Zero Beta Portfolio Corresponding to Portfolio m.

Figure 6.2 demonstrates this property with the two portfolios given in Figure 6.1. The investor who holds portfolio m_1 has a zero beta portfolio corresponding to this portfolio given by the tangency line to this point on the efficient frontier; hence, μ_{z_1} is the mean return on this zero beta portfolio. Similarly, an investor who holds optimal portfolio

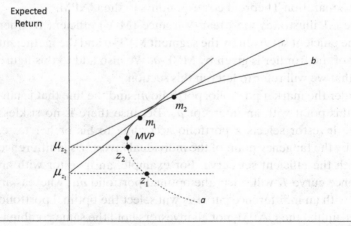

Figure 6.2. The Zero Beta Portfolios Corresponding to Two Efficient Portfolios.

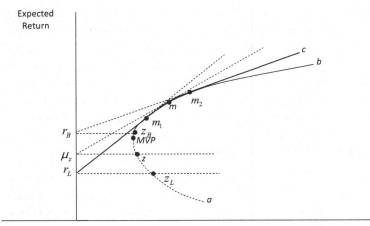

Figure 6.3. The Zero Beta Portfolios with a Borrowing Interest Rate Higher Than the Lending Interest Rate.

m_2 will have a zero beta portfolio with a mean μ_{z_2}. The zero beta portfolio is the portfolio with the minimum variance for a given expected return. These are portfolios z_1 and z_2 corresponding to portfolios m_1 and m_2, respectively.

The procedure for graphically finding a zero beta portfolio is as follows: For a given set of parameters, first derive the efficient frontier in the mean–standard deviation space. Then select any portfolio located on this frontier. Draw the tangency line to the selected point, and find the intercept of this line with the vertical axes; this is the mean return on the zero beta portfolios. Finally, draw a horizontal line parallel to the horizontal axis starting from the mean return on the zero beta portfolio. At the intersection point of this horizontal line with the frontier, we find the zero beta portfolio. In terms of Figure 6.2, these steps imply, for example, moving from point m_1 to point μ_{z_1} and then moving horizontally from point μ_{z_1} to point z_1, which is the zero beta portfolio corresponding to the efficient portfolio m_1. Because this process can start with any efficient portfolio, there is an infinite number of zero beta portfolios, each corresponding to the selected efficient portfolio.

If there is a riskless asset but with a borrowing rate that is higher than the lending rate, we obtain an efficient set given by $r_L m_1 m_2 c$ (Figure 6.3). This is a very realistic situation because with the absence of inflation, there are in practice two interest rates: the borrowing rate and the lending rate. In this case, for investors whose tangency point of the indifference curve with the frontier is on line $r_L m_1$, the zero beta portfolio will be z_L. For investors with a tangency point on line $m_2 b$, the zero beta portfolio is z_B. Finally, for a tangency point in the segment $m_1 m_2$, the zero beta portfolio depends on the location of the tangency point. For example, for the tangency point at point m, the zero beta portfolio is portfolio z (see Figure 6.3).

The ZBM has the following properties:

a) All assets located on line $\mu_z\, z'$ have the same mean return (see Figure 6.1). Portfolio z is the one with the minimum variance for this constant mean. By the equilibrium equation (6.1), for each asset we have

$$\mu_i = \mu_z + (\mu_m - \mu_z)\beta_i.$$

Therefore, for all portfolios located on line $\mu_z z'$ in Figure 6.1 (as $\mu_i = \mu_z$), we have

$$\mu_z = \mu_z + (\mu_m - \mu_z)\beta_z,$$

and hence, mathematically, we must have $\beta_z = 0$. Therefore, all portfolios located on this horizontal line have zero betas, and portfolio z is the zero beta portfolio with the *minimum* variance. Of course, in this specific case, beta is calculated with returns on portfolios z and m (see Figure 6.1).

b) Investors hold different efficient portfolios composed of different mixes of risky assets, reflecting their taste regarding return and risk (see Figure 6.1). This is in contrast to the CAPM, under which all investors hold the same mix of risky assets.

c) Roll[3] has shown that any M-V efficient portfolio can be created by some mixture of two other efficient portfolios. Thus, one can take portfolios z and m given in Figure 6.1 and, by mixing them with various proportions, any point of the frontier can be achieved. Therefore, we have a two-fund Separation Theorem in the following sense: in the first step all investors can choose

---

[3] R. Roll, "A Critique of the Asset Pricing Theory's Tests: Part I: On Past and Potential Testability of Theory," *Journal of Financial Economics*, 1977.

two portfolios, say z and m. This step may be common to all investors. In the second step, each investor will find the desired mix of these two portfolios, ending with the point on the frontier that is optimal from the specific investor's point of view. This is similar to, yet different from, the CAPM Separation Theorem. Let us explain. Under the CAPM, all investors first select portfolio m and the riskless asset, and then they diversify between these two assets; with the ZBM, each investor can arbitrarily select the two portfolios to create the desired mix of assets. Thus, in both cases, we have two portfolios with which the optimal mix is created, but with the ZBM, these two portfolios may change from one investor to another.

d) For any efficient portfolio located on the efficient segment of the frontier, there is a zero beta portfolio located on the inefficient segment of the frontier. Thus, the zero beta portfolios are M-V inefficient. Therefore, the mean rate of return on asset i can be written as

$$\mu_i = \mu_{z_i} + (\mu_{m_i} - \mu_{z_i})\beta_{z_i},$$

where the portfolio m_i is an efficient portfolio and portfolio z_i is the corresponding zero beta portfolio. However, because the mean of asset i can be rewritten also with the market portfolio, we can write it as in equation (6.1); hence, this version of the CAPM holds when the zero beta portfolio plays the role of the riskless interest rate in the CAPM.

Finally, although under the CAPM all investors select their optimal portfolio from the straight line, the capital market line (CML), under the ZBM, the optimal portfolio is selected from the efficient frontier, namely, curve *MVP-b* (see Figure 6.1).

In Chapter 11, we contrast the CAPM with CPT and show that the CAPM and CPT can coexist. The same conclusion is intact for the ZBM and CPT. Although this issue is discussed later in the book, it is sufficient to mention here that this important extension of the CAPM is also valid in CPT framework. With normal distributions of returns and in the absence of the riskless asset, all CPT investors select their portfolios from curve MVP-b; hence, the zero beta equilibrium model is intact also with CPT.

6.3. THE SEGMENTED CAPITAL ASSET PRICING MODEL

One of the CAPM assumptions is that there is a perfect divisibility; specifically, even investors with a relatively small investment sum can invest in a very large number of stocks – actually, in all available risky assets in the market. In practice, there are transaction costs, which traditionally decrease, percentage wise, with the size of the investment. Furthermore, generally, there are fixed and variable costs involved with investing in each asset that is included in the portfolio. The fixed costs can be direct out-of-pocket money paid or indirect costs related to the time one allocates to follow the financial statements and to keep records of all the available information corresponding to the asset held. In such a case, investors will tend to hold a relatively small number of risky assets in the portfolio, in contradiction to the CAPM's assumption asserting that all available assets must be held in the optimal portfolio of each investor. *Fixed* (per asset held, independent of the amount of money invested in the asset) and *variable* (proportional to the amount of money invested) transaction costs are the theme of Levy's[4] segmented CAPM, which is a generalization of the CAPM. By this model, it may be optimal to hold a small number of assets in the optimal portfolio.

Merton[5] suggests another motivation for the segmented CAPM: Investors in various professions tend to invest in stocks that are related to their field of expertise. For example, computer scientists invest in information technology, or IT, stocks because they feel they have more knowledge about these stocks than about other stocks. Similarly, physicians tend to hold stocks of medical firms, and the same principle is intact for other professions. Therefore, under this principle, investors limit themselves to some type of firms, ending up with a relatively small number of assets in their portfolio.

Regardless of the reasons that justify holding a relatively small number of assets in the portfolio, empirical evidence indeed shows that the held portfolio is extremely small, sharply contradicting the

---

[4] H. Levy, "Equilibrium in an Imperfect Market: A Constraint on the Number of Securities in the Portfolio," *American Economic Review*, 1978.

[5] R. C. Merton, "A Simple Model of Capital Market Equilibrium with Incomplete Information," *Journal of Finance*, 1987.

CAPM. Blume, Crockett, and Friend[6] report that individuals held highly undiversified portfolios. Their sample, which includes 17,056 individual tax forms, reveals that 34.1 percent of the individuals held only one stock, 50 percent held no more than two stocks, and only 10.7 percent held more than ten stocks in their portfolios. Although only firms that pay cash dividends are included in this sample, it is obvious from these findings that the investors typically hold a relatively small number of assets in their portfolios. Blume and Friend[7] report that the average number of assets in the portfolios included in their survey was 3.41. Because the aforementioned studies are from several decades ago, one may think that because of decrease in transaction costs over time, individuals nowadays will include more stocks in their portfolios. The facts show that this is not the case. Barber and Odean,[8] who studied the portfolios of 78,000 sample households, corresponding to six years ending in December 1997, report that the households held on average only four stocks, with an average worth of $47,000. Because the sample distribution of the investment is positively skewed, as expected, the medians were smaller: 2.6 stocks in the median portfolio with a median worth of $16,000. Thus, the reduction in transaction costs over the last few decades did not change the tendency of investors to hold only a small number of assets in their portfolios.

These findings lend support to the hypothesis that following the prices and other information corresponding to the stocks one includes in the portfolio is very time consuming, and it is almost impossible to follow a large number of stocks, which explains why there is no increase in the number of stocks held over time in response to the reduction in transaction costs. An alternative explanation for the small number of stocks in the held portfolios is that investors feel that they have the knowledge regarding the future stocks winners and hence focus only on these stocks. This explanation is in line with Merton's explanation for the observed segmented market. A support to the view asserting that transaction costs are not the main

---

[6] M. E. Blume, J. Crockett, and I. Friend, "Stock Ownership in the United States: Characteristics and Trends," *Survey of Current Business*, 1974.

[7] M. E. Blume and I. Friend, "The Asset Structure of Individual Portfolios and Some Implication to Utility Functions," *Journal of Finance*, 1975.

[8] B. M. Barber and T. Odean, "Boys Will Be Boys: Gender, Overconfidence, and Common Stock Investment," *Quarterly Journal of Economics*, 2001.

explanation for the observed small portfolios is provided by Levy.[9] In his reported experiment, subjects were required to select a portfolio out of twenty available risky assets. Despite the fact that no transaction costs were involved at all, the portfolios included on average only 4.9 stocks and the corresponding median was 3.2.

Thus, empirical and experimental findings clearly reveal that the number of assets that are held on average in the portfolio is very small, whereas by the CAPM, several thousands of assets should be held in the optimal portfolio. The consequence of the small number of assets held in the portfolio is that the variance explains cross-section returns and, in some empirical tests, the explanatory power of the variance is even larger than the explanatory power of beta.

Because the observed investment behavior deviates substantially from what is assumed by the CAPM, an analysis of this deviation on the equilibrium risk–return relation is called for. In this section, we fill this void. We present an extension of the CAPM suggested by Levy and Merton. Both models yield almost identical results, providing a generalization of the CAPM. It is a generalization, because when one includes zero fixed costs, the segmented model collapses to the classic CAPM. Hereafter, we call the model presented in this section the segmented CAPM, or the GCAPM (for Generalized CAPM).

By the GCAPM, there are K investors in the market, and the kth investor invests T_k in n_k risky assets when $n_k \leq N$, where N stands for all available risky assets in the market. Assuming risk aversion and normality, each investor decides simultaneously on the number of assets held in his or her optimal portfolio as well as on the optimal diversification. With this respect, the common M-V efficiency analysis is applied, but this time with a limited number of assets rather than with all assets, as done in the CAPM derivation. Figure 6.4 presents several efficient sets corresponding to various investors, as well as the market efficient set, which is composed of all available assets.

Investors holding two assets in their portfolios will derive the efficient set with these two assets and have their "little CAPM" with two assets where line rm_2 is their "little CML." Similarly, investors who hold three assets in their portfolio will have the little CML given by

---

[9] H. Levy, "Risk and Return: An Experimental Analysis," *International Economic Review*, 1997.

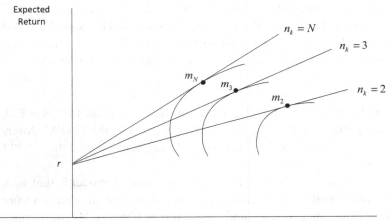

Figure 6.4. Several Efficient Sets with Assets ($k = 2, 3, N$).

rm_3. By the same token, we may have many more little CMLs. Finally, with all available assets, we have the common CML given by rm_N, where N stands for all available risky assets.

Thus, having n_K assets that the kth investor selects, he or she may consider this as the universe of assets and employ the portfolio's variance minimization for a given portfolio mean return to derive the little CAPM that is relevant to all investors who invest in these subgroups of assets. Having the little CAPM for each group of investors, one can aggregate all these little CAPMs to obtain the following segmented CAPM equilibrium model:

$$\mu_i = r + \frac{\sum_K T_K(\mu_K - r)}{\sum_K T_K}\beta_{iK}, \tag{6.2}$$

where

μ_i is the equilibrium mean return on the ith risky asset.

μ_K is the mean return on the optimal unlevered portfolio of the kth investor.

T_K is the invested wealth of the kth investor in risky assets.

β_{iK} is the beta calculated with the rates of return of the ith asset and with rates of return corresponding to the optimal portfolio of the kth investor. Namely,

$$\beta_{iK} = Cov(R_i, R_K)/\sigma_{R_K}^2.$$

Note that in equation (6.2), the risk of the ith asset is a weighted average of the beta calculated with various portfolios. This model is called the GCAPM because when all investors hold the same market portfolio $\mu_K = \mu_m$ for all inventors K, and equation (6.2) reduces to

$$\mu_i = r + (\mu_m - r)\beta_i,$$

as we have $\beta_{iK} = \beta_i$ and $\sum_K T_K$ is canceled out. Thus, the GCAPM, or the segmented CAPM, as expected, reduces to the CAPM. Alternatively, we have in this case only one segment; hence, the CAPM follows.

The important result of the segmented market model is that with a normal distribution, all investors select their optimal portfolio from their "little efficient sets" and, as we see in Chapter 11, this implies that the GCAPM is intact also under CPT. The reason is that with normal distributions, all CPT investors with a limited number of assets in their portfolios also select their optimal portfolios from this little M-V efficient set, exactly as M-V's inventors do.

6.4. MERTON'S INTERTEMPORAL CAPITAL ASSET PRICING MODEL

Merton suggests another equilibrium model that, under some assumptions, yields the same risk–return linear relation as advocated by the CAPM but is stated in terms of instantaneous parameters rather than discrete parameters. Although this model collapses to the CAPM under some assumptions, it should not be considered strictly as an extension of the CAPM because Merton's model is based on the concept of finding the optimal consumption over time.

The Intertemporal Capital Asset Pricing Model (ICAPM) is a model that assumes that investors act to maximize the expected utility of their lifetime consumption. Given this objective function, the demand function for risky assets and the equilibrium prices are derived. This model allows a nonstable opportunity set; hence, the risk–return equilibrium relation depends on the uncertain changes in future investment opportunities. Thus, unlike the CAPM, which is a discrete one-period model, the ICAPM is a continuous-consumption investment model that allows the future efficient set, at any given time, to be uncertain.

Merton assumes a perfect market, implying that all assets have limited liability, there are no transaction costs, assets are perfectly divisible, there is a very large number of investors, all investors trade at the market price, the capital market is always in equilibrium, short sales are allowed, and the borrowing interest rate is equal to the lending interest rate. These are the standard assumptions of a perfect market, assumptions needed also for the derivation of the discrete CAPM. However, for the ICAPM, one needs to make one more critical assumption: trading in assets takes place continuously in time. This last assumption makes the no-transaction-costs assumption also very critical to the ICAPM. Although the no-transaction-costs assumption is made also in the derivation of the discrete CAPM, this assumption is not critical to the CAPM. First, variable transaction costs, given as a percentage of the investment amount in each asset, can be easily incorporated into the CAPM, and even fixed transaction costs per asset held can be incorporated, resulting in the general (or segmented) market CAPM (GCAPM), which is a spinoff of the CAPM (as discussed in the previous section). With the ICAPM, imposing even a very small and reasonable transaction cost is impossible. The reason is that the continuous trading will wipe out all profits, and the expected rate of return on the risky asset will be negative net of transaction costs, an unacceptable result.

The expected rate of return, α, and the variance of each asset, σ^2, which are assumed to exist, are given by

$$\alpha \equiv E_t[(P(t+h) - P(t))/P(t)]/h$$

and

$$\sigma^2 \equiv E_t[([P(t+h) - P(t)]/P(t) - \alpha h)^2]/h,$$

where E_t is the conditional expectation operator. As h approaches zero, α is the instantaneous expected return and σ^2 is the instantaneous variance. Apart from having a continuous time model with portfolio revisions, at every instant of time, the preceding definitions have a unique feature: these parameters are not constant over time but are conditional on the state of the economy. Thus, at any given time t, a different set of parameters is possible.

By the ICAPM, the instantaneous return on the risky asset i is given by the Itó processes given by

$$dP_i/P_i = \alpha_i dt + \sigma_i dz_i,$$

where dz_i is a Gaussian random variable. At any time t, the parameters α_i, σ_i^2, and ρ_{ij} determine the investment opportunity set, where ρ_{ij} is the instantaneous correlation between the returns on assets i and j.

Assuming that there are n distinct risky assets and a riskless asset, Merton derives the optimum lifetime optimal consumption and the equilibrium asset price. The assumed riskless asset is instantaneous in the sense that at each instant of time, the investor knows with certainty what he or she can earn over the next instant. Thus, at time t, the riskless interest rate $r(t)$ for the next instant is known with certainty, but the future riskless interest rates are uncertain.

Having this return-generating process, Merton assumes that the kth consumer acts to maximize the following function:

$$\max E_0 \left[\int_O^{T_K} U^K[c^K(s), s]ds + B^K[W^K(T^K), T^K] \right], \quad (6.3)$$

where E_0 is the conditional expectation operator, which is conditional on the current value of the investor's wealth, W^K, the state variables of the investment opportunity set, and T^K, which is the distribution of his or her age of death. The instantaneous consumption is given by $c^k(t)$. The consumer acts to maximize the expected value of the strictly concave utility function, U^K, and B^K is a strictly concave utility of terminal wealth (bequest).

By maximizing the expected value of the lifetime consumption, the demand for risky assets is obtained. However, an equation that is analogous to the CAPM is obtained only when one adds the assumption that the investment opportunity set is constant over time (i.e., the various instantaneous parameters are constant over time). With the constant opportunity set, Merton derives the equilibrium equation:

$$\alpha_i = r + (\alpha_m - r)\beta_i, \quad (6.4)$$

where, α_i and α_m are the instantaneous expected return on the ith asset and on the market portfolio, respectively; r is the instantaneous riskless interest rate; and β_i is the beta measured with the instantaneous rates of returns. Equation (6.4) is the continuous analogues equation of the Sharpe-Lintner discrete CAPM.

Unlike the previous extensions of the CAPM, Merton's continuous equilibrium model is in contradiction to the behavioral model suggested by PT. The reason is that the lifetime consumption model of Merton assumes that consumers act to maximize equation (6.3) when the utility is strictly concave. In addition, in the continuous model, the distribution of returns at any finite time is lognormal rather than normal, as required to prove the CAPM. The mathematical results depend on this assumption. However, by PT, the preference is S-shaped (see Chapters 9, 10, and 11) and includes a risk-seeking segment, in contradiction to the necessary risk-aversion assumption made by Merton.

Breeden[10] further develops the Merton ICAPM in various directions. He also suggests continuous time analysis when the investor's preference for consumption plays a central role in deriving equilibrium prices. His intertemporal pricing model states that the equilibrium expected excess return on a risky asset should be proportional to its covariance of the returns with changes in the aggregate real consumption. Thus, instead of the common Sharpe-Lintner beta, he suggests that what determines prices is the *consumption beta*. Several empirical studies examine the validity of the consumption beta model. Although we do not elaborate on these models here, we do refer interested readers to the articles relevant to this chapter (e.g., see footnote 10).

6.5. THE HETEROGENEOUS BELIEFS CAPITAL ASSET PRICING MODEL

The various versions of the CAPM discussed so far explicitly assume homogeneous expectations regarding the various parameters: the means, the variances, and the various correlations. In practice, it is hard to believe that all investors share the same expectations. One may be tempted to believe that the segmented CAPM takes

---

[10] D. T. Breeden, "An Intertemporal Asset Pricing Model with Stochastic Consumption and Investment Opportunities," *Journal of Financial Economics*, 1979.

into account the possible heterogeneous expectations because by this model, the portfolio composition varies across investors. This belief is false because with heterogeneous expectation, it is expected that despite the differences in beliefs across investors, all will hold many assets in their portfolios, whereas under the segmented market regimen, only a small number of assets is held in the portfolio. Moreover, in the segmented market model, it is assumed that investors have identical beliefs, which induces another difference between the segmented market model and the heterogeneous model. Therefore, the heterogeneous expectation setting needs special attention.

Under heterogeneous expectations, investors face a different subjective M-V efficient set and, hence, hold different portfolios. Thus, the two-fund Separation Theorem that characterizes the CAPM does not hold. To the best of our knowledge, Lintner[11] was first to suggest an equilibrium model with heterogeneous expectations. The heterogeneous expectations can be formulated in various ways. Williams,[12] for example, assumes that investors continuously process information from the observed returns, update their subjective beliefs, and revise their portfolios accordingly. Although Williams suggests a complicated model, over time, as the investors accumulate more information, their beliefs converge, and therefore their portfolios converge to the market portfolio. Hence, all investors end up holding the same mix of risky assets.

DeMarzo and Skiadas[13] assume that the investors' heterogeneous beliefs arise from heterogeneous private information they possess. They show that the security market line (SML) also holds perfectly with heterogeneous expectations. Admati[14] analyzes the equilibrium relation with heterogeneous expectations with normal distributions

---

[11] We follow here the proof as given in J. Lintner, "Security Prices, Risk and Maximal Gains from Diversification," *Journal of Finance*, 1965. See also J. Lintner, "The Aggregation of Inventors Diverse Judgment and Preferences in Purely Competitive Markets," *Journal of Financial and Quantitative Analysis*, 1969.

[12] J. T. Williams, "Capital Asset Prices with Heterogeneous Beliefs," *Journal of Financial Economics*, 1977.

[13] P. DeMarzo and C. Skiadas, "Aggregation, Determinacy, and Informational Efficiency for a Class of Economics with Asymmetric Information," *Journal of Economic Theory*, 1998.

[14] A. Admati, "A Noisy Rational Expectation for Multi-Asset Securities Markets," *Econometrica*, 1985.

and constant absolute risk-aversion preferences. These two models assume that prices are fully revealing or partially revealing, which is employed in the investment decision making. The final result of these two models implies that the CAPM is intact or that a model that is very similar to the CAPM is intact.

In line of Biais, Bossaerts, and Spatt,[15] who assume that the heterogeneous beliefs may be a result of heterogeneous private information, or a result of different interpretation of the same information, Levy, Levy, and Benita[16] develop an equilibrium model with unbiased heterogeneous beliefs. They prove that in a large market with $K \Rightarrow \infty$ investors and an infinite number of risky assets $n \Rightarrow \infty$, the CAPM holds precisely, even if prices are not informative. However, when the number of assets and number of investors is finite but sufficiently large, the CAPM is almost intact despite the fact that investors hold portfolios located below the CML and despite the fact that the two-fund Separation Theorem characterizing the CAPM does not hold.

We will not elaborate on the various heterogeneous models but rather focus on one of them, the one suggested by Lintner. We derive and discuss the equilibrium model with heterogeneous expectations as suggested by him as early as 1969. However, before turning to do so, recall that if the CAPM is intact or almost intact also with heterogeneous expectations, this implies that the CAPM is robust. Moreover, as we see in Chapter 11, the CAPM is intact also under CPT; hence, the heterogeneous CAPM, which converges to the CAPM, is also intact under CPT, as long as normality exists.

By rearranging equation (5.34) given in Chapter 5, we have

$$P_{i1} - (1+r)P_{i0} = \gamma \left[N_i \sigma_i^2 + \sum_{j=1, j \neq i}^n N_j \sigma_{ij} \right].$$

Now suppose that there are heterogeneous expectations. The kth investor will be in equilibrium if the following holds:

$$P_{i1(k)} - (1+r)P_{i0} = \gamma_k \left[N_{i(k)} \sigma_{i(k)}^2 + \sum_{j=1, j \neq i}^n N_{j(k)} \sigma_{ij(k)} \right] \equiv \gamma_k \theta_k.$$

[15] B. Biais, P. Bossaerts, and C. Spatt, "Equilibrium Asset Pricing Under Heterogeneous Information," EFA 2004 Maastricht Meetings Paper No. 5083, 13th Annual Utah Winter Finance Conference; AFA 2003, Washington, DC, meetings.
[16] H. Levy, M. Levy, and G. Benita," Capital Asset Pricing with Heterogeneous Beliefs," *Journal of Business*, 2006.

Note that P_{io} is identical for all investors because it is the equilibrium price. However, $P_{i1(k)}$, which is the end of period value, is subjective and depends on the heterogeneous beliefs – hence, the index k, which denotes the kth investor. We also define the term in the square brackets by θ_k. Because each investor may have different estimates of the various parameters, he or she faces a different subjective efficient frontier. Therefore, the optimal number of shares held in the optimal portfolio varies across investors. If the preceding equation holds, the kth investor is in equilibrium. Also, the price of unit of risk is subjective because it depends on the portfolio held. Define

$$\gamma_k \equiv A_k / B_k,$$

where A_k denotes the aggregate excess dollar return of the portfolio held by the kth investor and B_k denotes the end-of-period variance of the value of the portfolio held. Using these definitions, we have

$$B_k[P_{i1(k)} - (1 + r)P_{io}] = A_k\theta_k.$$

Summing the last equation across all investors k yields

$$\sum_k B_k P_{i1(k)} - (1 + r)P_0 \sum_k B_k = \sum_k A_k\theta_k.$$

Hence,

$$(1 + r)P_{i0} = \frac{\sum_k B_k P_{i1(k)}}{\sum_k B_k} - \gamma \frac{\sum_k A_k\theta_k}{\sum_k B_k}$$

because

$$\frac{\sum_k A_k\theta_k}{\sum_k B_k} = \frac{\sum_k A_k}{\sum_k B_k} \frac{\sum_k A_k\theta_k}{\sum_k A_k} = \gamma \frac{\sum_k A_k\theta_k}{\sum_k A_k},$$

where γ is the total excess return across all investors divided by the variance of aggregate end-of-period value of all assets held. Therefore, the equilibrium market price of the ith stock with heterogeneous expectations is given by

$$P_{i0} = \left[\frac{\sum_k B_k P_{i1(k)}}{\sum_k B_k} - \gamma \frac{\sum_k A_k\theta_k}{\sum_k A_k} \right] / (1 + r). \tag{6.5}$$

This equilibrium equation is very similar to the equilibrium equation with homogeneous expectations: γ is the same in the two frameworks, and the difference is that the end-of-period price and the risk of each share are in the heterogeneous case a weighted average of the various investors' estimates. It is easy to verify that if the expectations are homogeneous, the heterogeneous equilibrium equation collapses to the CAPM equilibrium, equation (5.34); see Chapter 5.

6.6. THE CONDITIONAL CAPITAL ASSET PRICING MODEL

Despite the argument that with *ex-ante* parameters the CAPM cannot be rejected (see Chapter 7), some empirical anomalies still exist, such as those observed in the cross-section return tests. In particular, the CAPM has difficulties in explaining why over several decades, adjusted for risk, small firms outperform large firms, a phenomenon well known as the *size effect*, implying that an abnormal return is recorded for small firms. In Chapter 7 we show that a substantial portion of this abnormal profit can be explained by the fact that in the statistical tests, short-horizon holding periods are employed, whereas the actual investment horizon is much longer, approximately one year. Yet some portion of the abnormal small-firm return still exists, which is still considered to be a market anomaly. Similarly, it has been observed that firms with relatively high book-to-market (B/M) ratios tend to outperform those with low B/M ratios, known as the *value premium*. Another anomaly is associated with "momentum" – which are stocks with high prior returns during the past year on average that continue to outperform those with low prior returns.

The CAPM discussed in Chapter 5 is called the static, or the stable, CAPM because beta and the risk premium are assumed to be constant. It is also called the unconditional CAPM, as conditional information plays no role in determining equilibrium prices of risky assets. The conditional CAPM is an extension of the CAPM, an extension that takes into account the flow of information that may affect beta, the risk premium as well as the relationship between these two variables. One of the goals of the conditional CAPM is to employ the available current information in order to explain the CAPM's anomalies and to improve the predicted future returns that are obtained with the static CAPM. If the conditional CAPM is successful in out-of-sample tests, then an investment in practice may also yield a higher *ex-ante* Sharpe ratio by employing the conditional CAPM.

Suppose that at the beginning of the year there is a flow of information – for example, IBM increases its cash dividends; Xerox issues bonds and thus increases its leverage; bad macroeconomic data have been released; and so forth. Although such information is not taken into account in the static CAPM, the conditional CAPM may use this information to predict the risk–return tradeoff for the coming year.

Time-varying risk premium is also very important because it may change in various ways, particularly with various magnitudes in response to changes in business cycles. It is well known that firms with different types of business are affected differently in recession time. Specifically, during a recession, leverage causes equity beta to increase, which in turn may create an anomaly with the CAPM but not with the conditional CAPM, which takes such possible changes in beta into account.

By the conditional CAPM, we have the following relationship:

$$R_{i,t} - r = \alpha_{i,t} + \beta_{i,t}(R_{m,t} - r) + \varepsilon_{i,t}, \tag{6.6}$$

where all the parameters are as defined in the CAPM with the exception that all parameters are as estimated at time t. Because the available information may change with time, so do these estimates. Thus, beta may also change, implying that it is not constant over time. Namely, when time elapses, more information is available, and beta is estimated conditional on the available information. By this model, beta at time t is given by

$$\beta_{i,t} = Cov(R_{i,t}, R_{m,t})/Var(R_{m,t}).$$

But, as economic information at time t, denoted by I_t, is available, the conditional beta can be rewritten as

$$\beta_{i,t} = Cov(R_{i,t}, R_{m,t}/I_t)/Var(R_{m,t}/I_t).$$

Equation (6.6) describes the theoretical relation between risk and return as suggested by the conditional model. We turn to describe the equation that empirically estimates equation (6.6). It is common in the literature to denote all available information at time t by I_{t-1} and the corresponding beta at time t by β_{t-1}; therefore, the excess return on the ith asset at time t is estimated as follows:

$$R_{i,t} - r = \gamma_{0,t-1} + \gamma_{1,t-1} \beta_{i,t-1} + \varepsilon_{i,t}, \qquad (6.7)$$

where $\gamma_{0,t-1}$ is the intercept as estimated based on all the available information and $\gamma_{1,t-1}$ is the estimate of the risk premium. If the CAPM is intact, we expect the intercept not to be significantly different from zero. Taking the expectation of both sides of the last equation, and recalling that the expected value of the error term is zero, we obtain

$$E(R_{i,t}) - r = E(\gamma_{0,t-1}) + E[(\gamma_{1,t-1})(\beta_{i,t-1})].$$

Using the rule $Cov(x, y) = E(xy) - E(x)E(y)$, the conditional CAPM can be rewritten as

$$E(R_{i,t}) - r = E(\gamma_{0,t-1}) + E(\gamma_{1,t-1})E(\beta_{i,t-1}) + Cov(\gamma_{i,t-1}, \beta_{i,t-1}).$$

Thus, unlike with the unconditional CAPM, with the conditional CAPM we also have the last term, which measures the covariance of beta with the risk premium. For example, it is possible that during various phases of the economic cycle, the risk premium changes and the betas of different firms change with the risk premium in different ways. Specifically, during recessions, the hypothesis is that the risk premium is relatively high, and leveraged firms face a tougher economic situation; hence, the beta of levered firms tends to increase in a recession with the risk premium, inducing a positive covariance of these two variables.

Finally, note that if the covariance is equal to zero and the intercept is also zero, the preceding equation coincides with the static CAPM (where the various expected values are equal to the CAPM's parameters). In this respect, the conditional CAPM can be considered an extension of the CAPM. Of course, the motivation for this extension is to explain some empirical anomalies obtained with the static CAPM and to be better able to predict future returns on risky assets.

The empirical tests of the conditional CAPM reveal inconclusive results regarding the goodness of fit to the empirical data and the existing market anomalies. This should not come as a surprise, however, because there are several ways to estimate the conditional parameters and various ways to include the relevant information in the statistical data. In fact, the conditional CAPM is an ad hoc attempt to find statistical methods to explain market anomalies and to predict future prices better. The risk of data mining with this method is also substantial.

In accordance with the main theme of this book, it has been shown that with conditional parameters of the ICAPM, the market portfolio may be located on the M-V efficient frontier at every time period, yet with the multiperiod unconditional parameters, the market portfolio is interior to the M-V efficient frontier. This is in line of our claim that the CAPM is intact with *ex-ante* parameters but not with *ex-post* parameters, as the conditional model estimates the *ex-ante* parameters better.[17]

Numerous studies have attempted to test the CAPM with time-varying parameters, relying on the hypothesis that risk premium, beta, and alpha change with macroeconomic cycles and that the correlations between these variables also change over time. Taking these time variation parameters into account may yield a better explanation of the cross-section returns on stocks on the one hand and may lay ground to a better investment strategy on the other hand.

Studying a universe of 3,123 stocks covering the period 1972–2003, Avramov and Chordia[18] show that returns are predictable (out-of-sample analysis) by the dividend yield, the term spread, the default spread, and the treasury-bill yield. The outperforming investment strategies hold small-cap, growth, and momentum stocks. However, these strategies are not constant over time. In recession periods,

---

[17] See L. P. Hansen and S. F. Richard, "The Role of Conditioning Information in Deducing Testable Restrictions Implied by Dynamic Asset Pricing Models," *Journal of the Econometric Society*, 1987. See also M. C. Jensen, "The Performance of Mutual Funds in the Period 1945–1964," *Journal of Finance*, 1968; P. H. Dybvig and S. A. Ross, "Differential Information and Performance Measurement Using a Security Market Line," *Journal of Finance*, 1985; and R. Jagannathan and Z. Wang, "The Conditional CAPM and the Cross-Section of Expected Returns," *Journal of Finance*, 1996. For testing the conditional ICAPM, see G. Bekaert and R. Harvey, "Time-Varying World Market Integration," *Journal of Finance*, 1995. For testing cross-section returns across the world market, see W. E. Ferson and C. R. Harvey, "The Risk and Predictability of International Equity Returns," *Review of Financial Studies*, 1993. See also J. Lewellen and S. Nagal, "The Conditional CAPM Does Not Explain Asset-Pricing Anomalies," *Journal of Financial Economics*, 2006, who test whether the conditional CAPM can explain cross-section variation in returns.

[18] D. Avramov and T. Chordia, "Pricing Stock Returns," *Journal of Finance*, 2006.

by the recommended strategy, less is invested in momentum stocks and more is invested in small-cap stocks. Using this strategy, which relies on conditional estimates of the various variables, they show that the out-of-sample Sharpe ratio is substantially higher than the Sharpe ratio of the stable CAPM investment strategy as well as some other strategies recommended in the financial literature. Obviously, in an efficient market, when these suggested methods become well known, practitioners use them, and the extra-abnormal profit implied by the suggested strategy vanishes, as occurs with some other well-known anomalies – for example, the weekday abnormal effects (see Schwert[19]).

How is the discussion of the conditional CAPM related to behavioral economics? As we see in Chapter 11, when the distribution of returns is normal, the CAPM holds also with CPT. The conditional CAPM is related to the empirical tests of the validity of the CAPM, not to the CAPM's validity under CPT. Regarding the empirical validity of the CAPM, employing the conditional CAPM can only improve the goodness of fit. This is because if the CAPM empirically does not hold with stable parameters, it may hold each year with time-varying parameters. The conditional CAPM is one more way to rescue the CAPM from empirical test results, asserting that the time-varying parameters are better estimates of the *ex-ante* CAPM parameters. If this is not the case, and the various parameters do not change with the flow of information, the conditional CAPM collapses to the stable CAPM. In sum, if the conditional CAPM is intact, with normal distributions, it is intact also under CPT, as explained in detail in Chapter 11.

6.7. ROSS'S ARBITRAGE PRICING THEORY

Ross[20] suggests another asset-pricing model, which is based on a different set of assumptions than that which underlines the CAPM.

---

[19] G. W. Schwert, "Anomalies and Market Efficiency," in G. M. Constantindes, M. Harris, and R. Stulz, *Handbook of the Economics of Finance*, 2003.

[20] S. A. Ross, "Mutual Fund Separation in Financial Theory," *Journal of Economic Theory*, 1978, and S. A. Ross, "The Arbitrage Theory of Capital Asset Pricing Theory," *Econometrica*, 1976.

Moreover, his model is general and the CAPM is obtained as a specific case of the APT.

To derive the APT, Ross assumes neither risk aversion nor normality of returns. However, he makes the following assumptions:

1. The returns are generated by some specific process.
2. Investors hold a portfolio composed of a very large number of assets, some of which must be in a short position and some in a long position.
3. All the proceeds from the short sales are transferred to the investor. These proceeds are used to buy stocks, which are in long position.

Comparing the CAPM and the APT, there is some difference regarding the short-sell assumption. Even though under the CAPM (with homogeneous expectations) short selling is possible, in equilibrium investors do not use this option because all investors hold the same market portfolio; namely, they are all in long positions in all assets. If deviations from the CAPM equilibrium occur, investors may take a short position in some stocks, or they may reduce the positive investment proportion until equilibrium is restored. By the APT, if deviations from equilibrium occur, an arbitrage profit is available. However, in this case, to avoid an arbitrage profit, short selling is not only allowed, it *must* be used. The reason is that one creates a zero-investment portfolio, and thus one must be in a short position in some assets to finance using the proceeds for the long positions.

By the APT, it is assumed that the return-generating processes are given by

$$R_i = ER_i + \beta_i[I - E(I)] + e_i, \qquad (6.8)$$

where R_i is the rate of return on security i ($i = 1, 2, 3 \ldots \ldots \ldots n$, when we have n risky assets):

I is the value of the factor generating the security returns, whose mean is $E(I)$.

β_i is the coefficient measuring the effect of changes in factor I on the rate of return R_i.

e_i is a random deviation (noise).

Like in the CAPM, the factor I is common to all securities; hence, a subscript i is not assigned to this variable. This common factor may be the gross national product (GNP); the percentage of employed people in the population; the index of exports; or any other macro-economic variable that is shared by all securities. It can even be the Standard and Poor's index or the index of the market portfolio, which includes all traded assets in the market. Using the market portfolio as the return-generating factor is a specific case where, as we shall see subsequently, the APT collapses to the CAPM.

The main idea of the APT is that the investor can create a portfolio whose beta with the factor I is zero and that requires a zero net investment. This portfolio is the zero beta portfolio, which is similar in this respect to the zero beta portfolio discussed in Section 6.2. Thus, Ross shows that it is possible to create a portfolio R_P with the following properties:

a) $R_P = \sum_{i=1}^{n} x_i R_i$
b) $\beta_P = \sum_{i=1}^{n} x_i \beta_i = 0$
c) $\sum_{i=1}^{n} x_i = 0,$

where x_i $(i = 1, 2, \ldots n)$ is not any arbitrary investment proportion but rather a specific investment proportion that provides a zero beta and a zero net investment portfolio. There is no constraint on the sign of this variable. Thus, with, say, three securities, we may have that $x_1 = -100$, $x_2 = +50$ and $x_3 = +50$, and hence the sum of these three variables is zero, implying the notion of a zero net investment portfolio. Of course, the proceeds from the short sale are used to finance the long positions in the other two securities. Condition b) stipulates that the constructed portfolio has a zero beta with the return-generating factor. Generally, on a portfolio with a zero beta, one can expect to earn the riskless interest rate in equilibrium. However, for this particular portfolio, the net investment is zero; therefore, a zero return is expected on this portfolio; otherwise, a money machine is created.

The proof that such a zero beta, zero net investment portfolio exists can be found in Ross, so we discuss now the implication of such a portfolio to equilibrium asset pricing and the relation of APT to the CAPM. Multiplying equation (6.5) by x_i, yields

$$x_i R_i = x_i ER_i + x_i \beta_i [I - E(I)] + x_i e_i.$$

Summing overall assets i to obtain the portfolio rate of return,

$$R_P \equiv \sum_{i=1}^{n} x_i R_i = \sum_{i=1}^{n} x_i E R_i$$
$$+ [I - E(I)] \sum_{i=1}^{n} x_i \beta_i + \sum_{i=1}^{n} x_i e_i. \qquad (6.9)$$

Because this is a zero beta portfolio, we obtain

$$R_P = E R_P. \qquad (6.10)$$

Let us explain equation (6.10). First, by definition, $\sum_{i=1}^{n} x_i E R_i = E R_P$. Second, because by construction we have a zero beta portfolio, we have that $\sum_{i=1}^{n} x_i \beta_i = 0$. Finally, the last term on the right-hand side of equation (6.9) is approximately equal to zero. Formally, $\sum_{i=1}^{n} x_i e_i \approx 0$. The explanation for this assertion is that with a very large portfolio composed of many assets, the error terms tend to cancel each other; hence, their sum is equal to zero. Thus, equation (6.10) asserts that the seemingly random variable, the rate of return on the zero beta portfolios, is not random because it is equal to the mean rate of return on the zero beta portfolio, and this mean is obviously a constant number. This mean rate of return on the zero beta portfolios has a zero variance.

The rate of return on this portfolio must be equal to zero; otherwise, an arbitrage opportunity is available. For example, suppose this portfolio yields a constant return, say, $R_P = 1\%$. This means that a portfolio with a zero investment creates a certain profit with zero risk (because it is a certain income). Investors can duplicate such a portfolio many times, say, n times, and create a certain profit of \$$n$. Making n very large, an infinite arbitrage profit is possible. Hence, prices will change until in equilibrium the arbitrage profit vanishes. Thus, in equilibrium, we must have

$$R_P = E R_P = 0$$

Using the following three conditions that characterize the zero beta portfolio, we obtain

$$\sum_{i=1}^{n} x_i = 0, \sum_{i=1}^{n} x_i \beta_i = 0 \quad \text{and} \quad R_P = \sum_{i=1}^{n} x_i R_i = 0.$$

Ross shows with little algebra that the following must hold:

$$ER_i = ER_Z + (EI - ER_Z)\beta_i, \qquad (6.11)$$

where $ER_P = ER_Z$ is the zero beta portfolio and I is the return generating factor. This model can be extended to several factors generating the rate of return, producing the following equilibrium equation:

$$ER_i = ER_Z + \beta_{i1}(I_1 - EI_1) + \beta_{i2}(I_2 - EI_2)$$
$$+ \cdots \beta_{in}(I_n - EI_n)$$

Of course, an important empirical question corresponds to the relevant economic factors that generate returns. Several studies analyze this issue empirically. The most comprehensive empirical study identifying these factors is the one published in 1986 by Chen, Roll, and Ross.[21]

The most interesting result from our point of view is the one given by equation (6.10), because it provides the CAPM as a special case of the APT model. To see this, assume that the return-generating factor is the market portfolio index. Then equation (6.10) can be rewritten as

$$ER_i = ER_Z + (ER_m - ER_Z)\beta_i,$$

which is the zero beta CAPM.

Because we devote this book to the integration of finance theory with behavioral economics, we next ask whether the APT–CAPM is valid under PT. As we see in Chapter 11, the answer to this question is positive: arbitrage implies First-degree Stochastic Dominance (FSD), and we show in Chapter 11 that FSD is not violated by CPT's decision weights. Therefore, the APT is also valid in the CPT framework. CPT also advocates that risk seeking does not prevail in the whole range of outcomes and, because the arbitrage argument is not restricted to risk-averse preferences, the APT–CAPM holds also for risk-seeking preferences.

---

[21] See N. F. Chen, R. Roll, and S. A. Ross, "Economic Forces and Stock Market," *Journal of Business*, 1986.

6.8. SUMMARY

The CAPM is one of the pillars of modern finance. It is therefore no wonder that the CAPM is a subject of numerous empirical and theoretical studies. In this chapter, we briefly study some of the theoretical extensions of the CAPM. Some of the models are not exactly extensions of the CAPM but are rather suggested substitute models to the CAPM. Yet all these models have one common feature that is similar to the CAPM: they establish a risk–return relation, when risk is measured in a portfolio context.

The closest model to the CAPM is the zero beta model, which simply assumes that the riskless asset does not exist and implies that in equilibrium, the zero beta portfolio return takes the role of the riskless interest rate.

The general (or segmented) CAPM, or GCAPM, assumes that only a small number of assets are held (as observed in practice), and thus the risk measure is some weighted average of the betas of all small portfolios held by the various segments in the market. If the barriers (e.g., fixed transaction costs or limited information) to holding a large portfolio are relaxed, the general (or segmented) CAPM collapses to the CAPM – hence the name GCAPM.

The heterogeneous CAPM assumes that investors have different beliefs and therefore face different efficient sets. The linear risk–return relation induced by this model is similar to the CAPM, with the exception that the relevant beta is a weighted average of all individual betas, calculated with the various portfolios held.

The ICAPM is a more general model than the CAPM; it assumes maximization of the utility of lifetime consumption. Although this model does not require the investment opportunity to be stable over time, when the stability constraint is imposed, a continuous risk–return equation is obtained, which is analogous to the discrete Sharpe-Lintner CAPM. The consumption CAPM also assumes maximization of expected utility of consumption, suggesting that the measure of risk is the beta of the rate of return with the aggregate consumption.

The conditional CAPM is an extension of the CAPM to the case of unstable parameters over time. It is particularly important for the empirical tests of the risk–return linear relation as well as for establishing a practical investment strategy. Facing various anomalies, the conditional CAPM asserts that in each period, the parameters of the CAPM vary depending on the available information at a certain instant of time.

Finally, the APT is a different model that relies on a specific linear return-generating process. The end result is a multifactor model, where the expected return of each security depends on the n-betas related to the n-factors. However, when one factor is employed, and this factor is equal to the market portfolio, the APT collapses to the stable CAPM, although a different set of assumptions underline these two models.

In Chapter 11, we discuss the CAPM in a behavioral and hence in some cases an irrational setting. Specifically, we contrast the CAPM with the CPT. We show that the CAPM and most of its extensions, albeit not all of them, and the CPT can coexist, which is quite an encouraging result.

7

The Capital Asset Pricing Model Cannot Be Rejected

Empirical and Experimental Evidence

7.1. INTRODUCTION

One can evaluate the validity of the Capital Asset Pricing Model (CAPM, also called the SLB model for Sharpe, Lintner, and Black, whose contribution, development of the equilibrium risk–return relation, is discussed in detail in Chapter 5) by two alternative methods: (1) by examining the assumptions needed to the CAPM, and (2) by its empirical explanatory power. A short glimpse at the assumptions made to derive the CAPM is sufficient to raise skepticism regarding the model's validity. Thus, examining the CAPM's assumptions reveals a discouraging result because most of these assumptions do not hold in practice and therefore can barely be justified.

Let us demonstrate this claim with only two of these assumptions. In the CAPM derivation, it is assumed that investors select their optimal portfolio by the M-V criterion. This assumption can be theoretically justified when the distribution of returns are jointly "normal" (although there is some generalization of the Mean-Variance [M-V] rule to all elliptic distributions, without loss of generality, we explain the main idea given here with normal distributions). Theoretically, rates of returns can never be precisely normal because prices are bounded from below (i.e., the stock price can be zero but not negative). Another assumption that is employed in the derivation of the CAPM is the one that assumes no transaction cost and perfect investment divisibility; this assumption implies that even an individual investor with a relatively small amount of money to be invested can fully diversify and buy all available risky assets. This is, of course, an

186

unrealistic assumption because in practice, transaction costs constitute a barrier to the number of assets one can purchase. By the same token, one can criticize the other assumptions that are employed in the derivation of the CAPM. Hence, with this theoretical approach, the CAPM would be rejected because most assumptions needed to derive it do not hold in practice.

The other approach to evaluate the validity of the CAPM is the *positive economics* approach suggested by Friedman.[1] By this approach, what is relevant to the validity and usefulness of a model is its explanatory power. If investors behave "as if" all the CAPM assumptions hold, the CAPM would have an explanatory power for asset prices. Thus, by this approach, what is relevant for the CAPM evaluation is its empirical validity rather than the validity of the assumptions that have been made to derive the model under consideration. Let us demonstrate this positive economics approach with a few examples.

Suppose that a theoretical argument and empirical evidence that refute the normality assumption exist. However, in practice, the distributions of returns are approximately normal; thus, the financial loss resulting from assuming normality is negligible (see Chapter 8). In this case, investors may make investment decisions "as if" normality exists, although it does not. Hence, the CAPM may approximately hold even though the return distributions are not precisely normal. Similarly, one may argue that the unrealistic perfect divisibility assumption is also not crucial because investors can diversify by holding mutual funds and exchange traded funds (ETFs); hence, almost perfect divisibility is achieved even with a relatively small investment.

Yet investors who hold a small number of assets that are not mutual funds contradict the CAPM because all available assets should be included in the portfolio. However, one may argue that by holding four or five stocks rather than the whole market portfolio, most of the benefit from diversification is achieved and the CAPM would be empirically approximately intact even in this little diversification case. Moreover, if the CAPM does not approximately hold, another spinoff of the CAPM, the general CAPM (or GCAPM), is intact when a small

---

[1] See M. Friedman, "The Methodology of Positive Economics," in *Essays in Positive Economics*, Chicago University Press, Chicago and London, 1953.

number of assets is included in the various optimal portfolios and the risk index is a weighted average of the various betas calculated with the various small portfolios. In a similar way, one can defend by the "as if" argument each of the assumptions that is employed in the derivation of the CAPM.

By the positive economics approach, there is only one ultimate test: Does the CAPM explain prices of risky assets? If the answer is positive, the need to make unrealistic assumptions to derive the CAPM is irrelevant. Indeed, most theoretical models in economics are judged by their explanatory power rather than by the assumptions needed to derive them. Obviously, because the returns are random variables, one does not expect to obtain a perfect empirical fit of the sample data to the theoretical model. By the positive economic approach, a model is considered to be the best model if it has substantial explanatory power and if there is no other model with better explanatory power. In this chapter, we adopt the positive economics approach and discuss the empirical tests of the CAPM, emphasizing its explanatory power.

As discussed in previous chapters, the CAPM asserts that the mean rate of return of each risky asset is related linearly to its beta. Because there are many risky assets traded in the market, the next natural step by the positive economics approach is to test the risk–return relation implied by the CAPM empirically. Because the true parameters are unknown, one needs first to estimate the expected rate of return on each asset and the corresponding beta by using the sample data. Although there are many methods to estimate these parameters, it is common to use the sample average return and the sample beta of each asset as the estimate of the corresponding unknown parameters. If the CAPM is *ex-ante* valid, one would expect to get a positive and significant relationship between the sample average return and the sample beta. Also, one would expect a relatively high and significant correlation between these two variables.

The number of studies that empirically test the CAPM is enormous; thus, we discuss in this chapter only a few of them. Indeed, after the publication of Sharpe–Lintner CAPMs (in 1964 and 1965, respectively), numerous papers empirically have tested various aspects of the CAPM, with data taken from various countries and with data covering various periods and subperiods, with different proxies for the market portfolio (needed to calculate beta) and with different sets of risky assets.

Early empirical tests support the CAPM, at least partially. In most early tests, a positive and significant relationship between average return and beta has been found, which supports beta as a risk index. Of course, the documented coefficient of correlation is substantially below 1, indicating possible deviation from the perfect CAPM model, measurement errors, and wrong identification of the market portfolio. However, the coefficients of the various regressions that test the CAPM significantly deviate from what is expected by this model. Moreover, other variables not included in the CAPM have explanatory power of the variation in the mean return across assets, serving as evidence that beta does not capture all risk factors.

Despite these deviations from the model, the enthusiasm of having a simple and elegant risk–return model with an empirical positive relationship between mean return and beta is expressed in virtually all textbooks in finance, which typically devote a large portion to the CAPM and its applications to various issues in finance. Indeed, the CAPM has turned out to be one of the pillars of finance and economics of uncertainty and asset pricing.

Although the CAPM has become one of the most important topics being taught in virtually all business schools, some researchers have started to raise doubt about the validity of the CAPM. Also, more recent empirical tests show no relationship between average return and beta, casting doubt on the validity of the CAPM and also raising questions regarding the finance curriculum, which heavily relies on CAPM.

However, there is one important drawback characterizing most empirical studies that reject the CAPM: Whereas the fact that the sample average return is a random variable, which may deviate from the true mean return, that is taken into account in the various (*second-pass* regression) significance tests, the fact that beta is also a random variable and does not necessarily represent the *ex-ante* beta is generally not taken into account. However, researchers did not overlook this issue, and some attempts have been made to measure the effect of this difference between *ex-post* and *ex-ante* beta on the regression coefficients, which are evaluated in estimating the CAPM. Indeed, Sharpe argues that the fact that *ex-ante* betas are not employed in the statistical test of the CAPM invalidates the empirical rejection of the CAPM. Regarding the CAPM and the equilibrium model, he asserts that the model "Concern(s) future, as opposed to historical, investment returns."[2] Recent studies of the CAPM incorporate this view of Sharpe. Indeed, recent research revealing that the CAPM cannot be rejected relies on the fact that once *ex-ante* parameters, particularly *ex-ante* beta, are considered, there is no evidence that justifies the rejection of the CAPM.

We show in this chapter that the first wave of empirical studies reveal some empirical support for the CAPM. The second wave of empirical studies strongly rejects the CAPM. To complete the "seesaw" view regarding the CAPM, in the second part of this chapter, we discuss the third wave – albeit this wave is much smaller than the previous two waves – of empirical studies that supports the CAPM. In the last part of this chapter, we join the enthusiasm of the early years and show that the CAPM cannot be rejected and that it is too early to change the curriculum of finance departments. To be more specific, we show in this chapter, in line with Sharpe's argument, that the CAPM cannot be rejected with *ex-ante* parameters, although it is rejected with *ex-post* and irrelevant parameters. The difference between *ex-post* parameters and *ex-ante* parameters (mainly regarding factors that affect beta), not taken into account by the common empirical studies, is the main explanation for the change in the conclusion regarding the model: the CAPM cannot be empirically rejected. Of course, the CAPM has its drawbacks, but it is still the best available model, and there is no reason to replace it before a better model – with a larger explanatory power – is suggested.

We start this chapter with a review of early studies (starting in the 1960s) supporting the CAPM (at least partially); continue to the early 1990s studies, some of which strongly reject the CAPM; and then discuss some other studies, some of which are quite recent (i.e., published in the twenty-first century), showing that the CAPM cannot be rejected. The results defending the CAPM draw heavily on the empirical articles by H. Levy[3] and M. Levy and R. Roll,[4] as well as on some experimental studies.

---

[2] See *Raleigh News Observer*, February, 23, 1992.
[3] See H. Levy, "A Test of the CAPM via a Confidence Level Approach," *The Journal of Portfolio Management*, 1981.
[4] See M. Levy and R. Roll, "The Market Portfolio May Be Mean/Variance Efficient After All," *Review of Financial Studies*, 2010.

7.2. THE EARLY TESTS OF THE CAPITAL ASSET PRICING MODEL: PARTIAL SUPPORT FOR THE CAPM

Lintner was a pioneer in testing the CAPM. He suggests the following two-stage procedure for testing the CAPM, also known as *first-pass* and *second-pass* regressions, or the *time-series* and the *cross-section* regressions. Because this two-stage procedure has become the norm procedure in the early testing of the CAPM, let us elaborate on this procedure and then report the empirical results of the early studies that test the model.

(i) The First-Pass Regression (Time-Series Regression)

Suppose that one faces N securities, and for each security, the annual rate of return is calculated for T years. The annual rate of return on some market portfolio proxy, for example, the Standard and Poor's (S&P) 500 stock index, for these T years is also available. Using these data, one runs the following *time-series* regression:

$$R_{it} = a_i + b_i R_{mt} + e_{it}, \tag{7.1}$$

where R_{it} and R_{mt} stand for the rate of return on the *ith* security ($i = 1, 2, \ldots N$) in year t ($t = 1, 2, \ldots T$) and on the market portfolio, respectively. The values a_i and b_i are the estimates of the regression intercept and the slope of the regression line corresponding to asset i. b_i is the estimate of beta of the *ith* asset and the term e_{it}, the residual, has a mean value of zero by construction. Thus, if we have N securities, we run this regression N times, each time with different security; hence, we obtain N estimates of beta, b_i. These N beta estimates are the basic input employed in testing the CAPM by the *second-pass* regression, described as follows.

(ii) The Second-Pass Regression (Cross-Section Regression)

The input for the *second-pass* regression is the N values of the beta estimates and the N sample average rates of return corresponding to the N risky assets. Thus, we have N pairs of ($\bar{R}_i$, b_i), where each pair corresponds to one asset. In the second-pass regression, we have only one regression, called the *cross-section* regression of the following form:

$$\bar{R}_i = a_1 + a_2 b_i + \varepsilon_i, \tag{7.2}$$

where $\bar{R}_i$ and b_i are the average rate of return and beta estimate, respectively, taken from the first-pass regression; ε_i is the error term; and a_1 and a_2 are the second-pass regression intercept and slope, respectively. Note that although in the first-pass regression we have N regressions, in the second-pass regression, we have only one cross-section regression.

The first-pass regression is employed to obtain the estimates of the various betas, and the second-pass regression is employed to test the validity of the CAPM directly. To see this, let us rewrite the CAPM equation as follows:

$$\mu_i = r + (\mu_m - r)\beta_i. \tag{7.2'}$$

As can be seen, equations (7.2) and (7.2′) have very similar structure. If the CAPM holds perfectly with the empirical data, we expect to obtain that

$$a_1 = r \quad \text{and} \quad a_2 = \mu_m - r.$$

Obviously, such ideal results never hold empirically. At best, one expects to find that a_1 is not significantly different from r and that a_2 is not significantly different from $\mu_m - r$, and the correlation in equation (7.2) is reasonably high, implying that betas *explain* – albeit not perfectly – the variation in the mean returns across assets. Having this explanation of the CAPM's testing procedure employed in the earlier studies, we turn now to the empirical results. Because there are numerous studies that test the CAPM, we cannot cover them all here. However, reviewing some of the most influential and highly cited empirical studies is sufficient to reveal the flavor of the early studies and their implication regarding the validity of the CAPM.

a) The Study by Lintner

As early as 1965, Lintner[5] tested the CAPM, which was established in 1964 by Sharpe and in 1965 by Lintner himself. Lintner employs

[5] J. Lintner, "Security Prices and Risk: The Theory of Comparative Analysis of AT&T and Leading Industrials," paper presented at the Conference on the Economics of Public Utilities, Chicago, 1965.

the first-pass and second- pass regressions as explained already. In his sample, there are 301 stocks with annual rates of return corresponding to the period 1954–1963. After estimating the mean annual return of each security and the corresponding beta, he runs the following second-pass regression:

$$\bar{R}_i = a_1 + a_2 b_i + a_3 S_{e_i}^2 + \varepsilon_i, \tag{7.3}$$

where the coefficient a_1 is the intercept, and the coefficients a_2 and a_3 stand for the marginal effect of beta and the residual variance ($S_{e_i}^2$) on the average return of the *ith* asset. The residual variance is the variance of the residuals, e_i, given in regression (7.1). Obviously, if one strictly wishes to test the CAPM, $S_{e_i}^2$ should not be included in the regression. However, Lintner has observed that the residual variance significantly explains the variation in mean returns; hence, he also included this variable as an explanatory variable.

If the CAPM holds, we expect the following results: a_1 should not be significantly different from the risk-free interest rate, a_2 should not be significantly different from the risk premium $\mu_m - r$, and a_3 should not be significantly different from zero. Moreover, the correlation should be substantial and significantly higher than zero. However, to get some, albeit not complete, empirical support to the CAPM, we expect at least a positive relationship between $\bar{R}$ and b; namely, beta is also a measure of risk (i.e., the higher beta, or its estimate b, the higher the average return). Of course, the higher the correlation between the average return and beta, the better beta serves as a measure of risk.

Lintner obtains the following results:

$$\bar{R}_i = 0.108 + 0.063b + 0.237 S_{ei}^2$$
$$\phantom{\bar{R}_i = 0.108 + } (0.009) \quad (0.035)$$
$$\phantom{\bar{R}_i = 0.108 + } t = 6.9 \quad t = 7.8 \tag{7.4}$$

with a multiple correlation of $\rho = 0.541$. Note that in parentheses the standard deviation of the various estimates are given and below them the corresponding *t*-values. From these results, the following conclusions can be drawn:

1. The encouraging result that supports beta as a measure of risk (albeit not the only risk measure) is that there is a positive and a significant relationship between mean return and the estimate

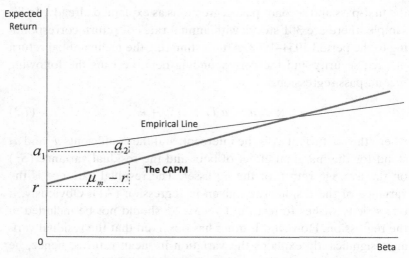

Figure 7.1. The Capital Asset Pricing Model and the Empirical Line.

of beta; the higher b_i, the higher, on average, the average rate of return of the asset under consideration.

2. In the period covered in this study, the risk premium (i.e., the difference between the rate of return on the market portfolio and the risk-free interest rate) was 16.5 percent. However, Lintner obtains a much lower estimate for this value – only 6.3 percent.

3. The coefficient a_1, which is an estimate of the risk-free interest rate, is 10.8 percent, which is much higher than the risk-free interest rate prevailing in this period.

4. Finally, the coefficient a_3 is positive and significant, whereas according to the CAPM, it should not be significantly different from zero. Thus, the empirical results support the hypothesis that the residual variance also serves as a measure of risk.

Figure 7.1 illustrates the typical deviation between the CAPM and the empirical results as obtained by Lintner, as well as by other researchers.

As can be seen, a_1 is larger than the interest rate and a_2 is smaller than what is expected by the CAPM. Hence, the empirical line is flatter than the theoretical line. Thus, the encouraging result is that there is a positive and a significant relation between the sample beta and the

Table 7.1. *The Second-Pass Regressions, 1954–1963: Miller and Scholes' Study*

$\bar{R}_i =$	a_1	$+$	a_2	$+$	$a_3 S_{ei}^2$	ρ^2
	0.122		0.071			0.19
	(0.007)		(0.006)			
	$t = 18.6$		$t = 12.34$			
	0.163				0.393	0.28
	(0.004)				(0.025)	
	$t = 46.1$				$t = 15.74$	
	0.127		0.042		0.310	0.33
	(0.006)		(0.006)		(0.026)	
	$t = 21.31$		$t = 7.40$		$t = 11.76$	

Source: M. Miller and M. Scholes, "Rates of Return in Relation to Risk: A Reexamination of Some Recent Studies," in M. Jensen (editor), *Studies in the Theory of Capital Markets*, Praeger, New York, 1972.

average return. The discouraging results are that the coefficients are significantly different from what is expected by the CAPM.

b) The Study by Miller and Scholes

Miller and Scholes[6] replicate and extend Lintner's study by employing a larger sample and by analyzing some possible reasons for the observed biases in the results. Covering the same period as Lintner has, they obtain in the second-pass regression the results reported in Table 7.1.

As can be seen from Table 7.1, the results are very similar to those obtained by Lintner. When both b_i and the residual variance are included as explanatory variables, both are positive and highly significant. They find that $\rho^2 = 0.19$, with beta alone as an explanatory variable, implies that there are some other variables not included in the CAPM that explain variation in the average return across assets. It is interesting to note that the residual variance by itself explains 28 percent of the variation in mean returns. Thus, if one has to choose only one variable, b_i or the residual variance, $S_{e_i}^2$, the latter, has a larger

---

[6] M. Miller and M. Scholes, "Rates of Return in Relation to Risk: A Reexamination of Some Recent Studies," in M. Jensen (editor), *Studies in the Theory of Capital Markets*, Praeger, New York, 1972.

explanatory power. Finally, if both the residual variance and the estimate of beta are employed as explanatory variables, both are positive and significant with $\rho^2 = 0.33$.

Miller and Scholes analyze the impact of various statistical measurement errors on the results obtained in the empirical test of the CAPM. In particular, they focus on the fact that b_i is an estimate of β; but, in the second-pass regression, it is implicitly assumed that b_i is equal to β. Conducting some statistical analysis, they conclude that indeed the second-pass regression results are biased. They show that the coefficient of b_i is downward biased, and if one corrects for this bias, the second-pass regression would be less flat than the one obtained by Lintner. In other words, correcting for this possible bias, the empirical results become closer to what is expected by the CAPM. As we see later in this chapter, with an appropriate correction in β estimates, indeed, the CAPM cannot be rejected.

c) The Study by Black, Jensen, and Scholes

Black, Jensen, and Scholes[7] (BJ&S) test the CAPM with monthly data covering the period 1926–1966. To minimize the errors involved in estimating beta, they group all stocks into ten portfolios, where 10 percent of the stocks with the highest beta form the first portfolio, 10 percent of the stocks with the second highest beta form the second portfolio, and so on. By employing a beta of a portfolio composed of many stocks in the regression, the measurement errors of each individual asset may cancel out or at least diminish. In short, the purpose of this grouping technique is to reduce measurement errors of beta, which is estimated by the first-pass regression. It is worth mentioning that this issue also bothers Miller and Scholes (see previous discussion), who try to account for possible biases in estimating beta. As mentioned, we shall see a more general treatment of the difference between b_i and β_i, which leads us to conclude that the CAPM cannot be empirically rejected.

BJ&S test the CAPM and the zero beta model (ZBM) of Black by time-series as well as cross-section technique. Because they cover a

---

[7] F. Black, M. C. Jensen, and M. Scholes, "The Capital Asset Pricing Model: Some Empirical Tests," in M. C. Jensen (editor), *Studies in the Theory of Capital Markets*, Praeger, New York, 1972.

very long period, they study also whether the results are stable across various subperiods. Whereas they report that the results vary across the various subperiods, for the whole period studied by them, 1926–1966, they find a linear relationship between average rerun of the ten portfolios and the corresponding betas. However, although they find in the cross-section regression that the average return is strongly related to beta, there are some systematic deviations from the CAPM predicted results. Moreover, unlike the previous studies, they find that beta almost completely explains the variation of the mean returns because the coefficient of determination in their study is almost perfect with $\rho^2 = .98$. However, as mentioned, this does not imply a strict support of the CAPM because the intercept and the slope of the regression line are significantly different from what is predicted by the CAPM.

They also run a time-series test of the CAPM, where the excess return of portfolio j is regressed against the excess return on the market portfolio. Because we deal with access return, the CAPM predicts that the regression intercept of all portfolios will not be significantly different from zero. Table 7.2, taken from BJ&S, reports their results.

As we can see from Table 7.2, the intercept is mostly insignificantly different from zero, which is in line with the CAPM. However, as we can also see, the change in the intercept is not random, and it is negative for portfolios 1–5 (when 1 stands for the riskiest portfolio and 10 stands for the portfolio with the lowest risk) and positive for portfolios 6–10. This systematic change in the intercept is evidence against the CAPM. Thus, the time-series test of the CAPM yields ambiguous results. Having systematic deviation of the intercept from what is expected, BJ&S reject the CAPM despite the high explanatory power of beta. They conclude:

The evidence presented in Section II indicate that excess return on asset is not strictly proportional to its β, and we believe that this evidence ... is sufficiently strong to warrant rejection of the traditional form of the model. (BJ&S, p. 82)

Thus, these reported results support beta as a measure of risk but reject the strict CAPM. One possible explanation for the deviation from the strict CAPM is that riskless borrowing and lending may not be available; hence, the ZBM of Black (also called the two-factor model) may fit the empirical results better. (Another possible explanation, not discussed by BJ&S, is that the monthly betas are biased,

Table 7.2. Summary of Statistics for Time-Series Tests, Entire Period (January 1931–December 1965)*

Item†	Portfolio No.										$\bar{R}_m$
	1	2	3	4	5	6	7	8	9	10	
$\hat{\beta}$	1.5614	1.3838	1.2483	1.1625	1.0572	0.9229	0.8531	0.7534	0.6291	0.4992	1.0000
$\hat{\alpha} \bullet 10^2$	-0.0829	-0.1938	-0.0649	-0.0167	-0.0543	0.0593	0.0462	0.0812	0.1968	0.2012	
$t(\hat{\alpha})$	-0.4274	-1.9935	-0.7597	-0.2468	-0.8869	0.7878	0.7050	1.1837	2.3126	1.8684	
$r(\bar{R}, \bar{R}_M)$	0.9625	0.9875	0.9882	0.9914	0.9915	0.9833	0.9851	0.9793	0.9560	0.8981	
$r(\tilde{e}_t, \tilde{e}_{t-1})$	0.0549	-0.0638	0.0366	0.0073	-0.0708	-0.1248	0.1294	0.1041	0.0444	0.0092	
$\sigma(\tilde{e})$	0.0393	0.0197	0.0173	0.0137	0.0124	0.0152	0.0133	0.0139	0.0172	0.0218	
$\bar{R}$	0.0213	0.0177	0.0171	0.0163	0.0145	0.0137	0.0126	0.0115	0.0109	0.0091	0.0142
σ	0.1445	0.1248	0.1126	0.1045	0.0950	0.0836	0.0772	0.0685	0.0586	0.0495	0.0891

* Sample Size for Each Regression = 420.

† $\bar{R}_m$ = Average monthly excess return, σ = standard deviation of the monthly excess returns, r = correlation coefficient.

Source: F. Black, M. C. Jensen, and M. Scholes, "The Capital Asset Pricing Model: Some Empirical Tests," in M. C. Jensen (editor), Studies in the Theory of Capital Markets, Praeger, New York, 1972.

and it is possible that the systematic biases in the intercepts would vanish with betas estimated with annual rates of returns; see forthcoming discussion.) Indeed, BJ&S advocate that the empirical results suggest:

The evidence indicates the existence of a linear relation between risk and return and is therefore consistent with a form of the two-factor model. (BJ&S, p. 82)

Thus, although the CAPM with a riskless asset is rejected, the ZBM, which is an extension of the CAPM, is not. To summarize the findings of this study, beta strongly explains variation in returns, but the excess return on the various portfolios indicates that the strict CAPM has no empirical support and some modification in the CAPM is called for. BJ&S suggest that the zero beta model of Black may fit the empirical results better.

However, one word of caution is called for before we reach any ultimate conclusion regarding beta as a measure of risk and the linear relationship obtained between beta and returns: The CAPM is a model of individual assets as well as portfolios pricing. If one rejects the CAPM with portfolios, then the CAPM is rejected. However, if one does not reject the CAPM with portfolios, it does not imply that individual assets are also well priced by the CAPM. Indeed, it is possible that the CAPM is appropriate for large portfolios but not for individual assets. Thus, it is possible that the dramatic increase in the coefficient of determination in the BJ&S study compared with previous empirical studies is due to a reduction in the measurement errors of beta. However, one needs to recall that whereas the previous empirical studies test the CAPM directly, the study by BJ&S tests the CAPM only for portfolios, which are a subgroup of all assets; therefore, less general conclusions can be drawn from these empirical results.

d) The Study by Fama and MacBeth

Fama and MacBeth[8] employ a slightly different technique to study empirically the validity of the CAPM. They form twenty portfolios, and for each portfolio they estimate its beta. The betas are measured

---

[8] E. Fama and J. D. MacBeth, "Tests of the Multi-Period Two-Parameter Model," *Journal of Political Economy*, 1974.

by the first-pass regression. Having these betas, they run for each month a cross-section regression of the following form:

$$R_{it} = a_{1t} + a_{2t}b_i + a_{3t}b_i^2 + a_{4t}S_{ei}^2 + \varepsilon_{it}, \tag{7.5}$$

where R_{it} is the rate of return on portfolio i in month t, b_i stands for the estimate of beta, and the other symbols denote the other variables as defined in other studies. However, note that this cross-section regression is conducted separately for each month; thus, for each regression we have different parameter estimates and hence have to add the subscript t to emphasize this fact and that the coefficient of each regression is a_{it}. The test given by equation (7.5) is not limited to the strict CAPM's test because it also tests whether b^2 and the residual variance also explain variation across portfolios returns.

The next step suggested by this technique of the CAPM testing is to calculate for each coefficient the average value across all months and to employ the t-test to examine whether this average is significantly different from zero.

Fama and MacBeth report that the average value of a_2 is positive and significantly different from zero (hence, beta and average return are positively correlated), whereas a_3 and a_4 are not significantly different from zero. Thus, b^2 and particularly the residual variance do not explain the variation in returns, which is in contrast to previous studies. Therefore, this study supports the CAPM, indicating that a linear relationship between mean return and beta prevails as predicted by this model. Yet recall that this study also employs portfolios rather than individual assets; therefore, it has the advantage of minimizing the measurement errors in beta and the disadvantage of not testing asset pricing of individual assets. Thus, in the case of supporting the CAPM, one cannot generalize it to individual risky assets.

e) The Role of Beta and the Variance as Explanatory Variables

The fact that in some studies the residual variance plays an important role in explaining the variation of mean returns across assets is in contradiction to the classic CAPM but not to the GCAPM of Levy[9] and

---

[9] H. Levy, "Equilibrium in an Imperfect Market: A Constraint on the Number of Securities in the Portfolio," *American Economic Review*, 1978.

Table 7.3. *Second-Pass Regressions with Annual Data, 1948–1968: Levy's Study*

$\bar{R}_i =$	a_1	+	$a_2\hat{\beta}_i$	+	$a_3\hat{S}^2_{e_i}$	+	$a_4\hat{\sigma}^2_i$	ρ^2
	0.109		0.037					0.21
	(0.009)		(0.008)					
	$t = 12.0$		$t = 5.1$					
	0.122						0.219	0.38
	(0.005)						(0.029)	
	$t = 22.9$						$t = 7.7$	
	0.126				0.248			0.32
	(0.005)				(0.036)			
	$t = 23.4$				$t = 6.8$			
	0.117		0.008				0.197	0.38
	(0.008)		(0.009)				(0.038)	
	$t = 14.2$		$t = 0.9$				$t = 5.2$	
	0.106		0.024		0.201			0.39
	(0.008)		(0.007)		(0.038)			
	$t = 13.2$		$t = 3.3$		$t = 5.3$			

Source: H. Levy, "Equilibrium in an Imperfect Market: A Constraint on the Number of Securities in the Portfolio," *American Economic Review*, 1978.

Merton.[10] By the GCAPM, for various reasons, most investors hold portfolios that contain a relatively small number of assets. Therefore, the explanatory power of each individual asset's variance becomes relatively large. For example, if only three stocks are held in the portfolio, it is natural that the assets' variance or the residual variance will play an important role in explaining asset pricing.

Motivated by this argument, Levy conducts the first-pass and second-pass regressions with a sample of 101 stocks covering the period 1948–1968. The regression results corresponding to annual rates of returns with various explanatory variables are reported in Table 7.3.

The positive result from the CAPM's point of view is that when only the sample beta is employed as an explanatory variable, as advocated by the CAPM, the obtained beta coefficient is positive and significant: the higher the beta, the higher the mean return. The coefficient of determination is 0.21. However, the discouraging result from the CAPM's point of view is that when the variance of each stock

---

[10] See R. Merton, "A Simple Model of Capital Market Equilibrium with Incomplete Information," *Journal of Finance*, 1987.

serves as a risk measure rather than beta, an even better fit is obtained, with a coefficient of determination of 0.38. When beta and the variance are included together as explanatory variables, the coefficient of determination remains 0.38. The even more striking result is that the coefficient of beta becomes insignificant with a t-value of 0.9.

There are two not mutually exclusive explanations for these results: First, because people hold only a small number of assets in their portfolio, the variance plays a more important role in explaining variation in average returns than beta does. However, because investors commonly hold more than one asset, the variance of the asset itself does not capture the whole risk of the asset; hence, beta is also an important measure of risk. Another technical explanation is that beta and the variance are correlated with a coefficient of determination of 0.43. So, to some extent, these two variables can serve as a proxy for each other. The interpretation of the results is further complicated by the fact that a substantial portion of investors holds large portfolios in the form of mutual funds and ETFs; therefore, for these investors, beta should play a more significant role than the individual asset variance. Thus, the risk measure is neither the variance nor beta but some mix of the two parameters.

To summarize, from these early studies' empirical results we can conclude that generally there is a positive significant relationship between average returns and beta. Thus, there is empirical evidence that beta is a measure of risk, albeit not a perfect one. However, because this relationship is far from being perfect, it leads us to conclude that there are also other variables that measure risk, that there are measurement errors in estimating beta, or both. Alternatively, it is possible that the sample estimates of betas differ in some systematic manner from the *ex-ante* betas, which induce the unsatisfactory results from the viewpoint of CAPM's advocates.

7.3. THE SECOND CYCLE OF TESTS: MAINLY REJECTION OF THE CAPM

A second cycle of research adds new evidence against the CAPM, which has become very well known in the literature as the small firm effect (SFE). Basically, it has been found empirically that small firms (known also by the name *small caps*) with relatively small market value tend to earn on average more than large firms (known by the name *large caps*) after accounting for risk as measured by beta. Next, it has been found that the market-to-book-value ratio is also a major factor in explaining variation in mean returns across assets. Moreover, in one study, when beta alone serves as the explanatory variable, in contrast to virtually all previous studies, it turns out to be insignificant. These findings strongly reject the CAPM, which asserts that beta and only beta should determine variation in the mean return. In this section, we discuss these deviations from the CAPM, which constitute the main empirical evidence against the CAPM.

a) The Small Firm Effect

Some market anomalies that contradict the CAPM were published before 1981, and two major studies were published in 1981 in the same journal and in the same issue. These two studies document the size effect, or what is better known as the SFE; the return on stocks of firms with relatively small market value (small-cap stocks) is above what is predicted by the CAPM, and the opposite holds with regard to large firms (large-cap stocks). However, because the abnormal profit that is recorded with small firms is relatively large compared with the little negative abnormal return corresponding to large firms, it is common in the literature to call this effect the SFE. Obviously, if there are systematic abnormal returns in the market, it is evidence against the validity of the CAPM.

Banz[11] examines the relationship between the return on stocks, their corresponding beta, and their corresponding relative market size. Thus, in addition to the CAPM's mean return–beta linear relationship, he adds the relative market size of the firm as an explanatory variable of returns. Using monthly returns during the period 1926–1975 of all stocks listed in the New York Stock Exchange, he finds a negative relationship between size and return after accounting for beta. Namely, stocks of relatively small firms gain an abnormal return that is not explained by the CAPM. Dividing the whole period

---

[11] R. W. Banz, "The Relationship Between Return and Market Value of Common Stocks," *Journal of Financial Economics*, 1981.

studied into subperiods, Banz obtains the following results regarding the coefficient of the size variable in the regression when return is the dependent variable and beta and size serve as explanatory variables:

Period	Market-Size Coefficient	*t*-value
1936–1975	–0.00052	–2.92
1936–1955	–0.00043	–2.12
1956–1975	–0.00062	–2.09
1936–1945	–0.00075	–2.32
1946–1955	–0.00015	–0.65
1956–1965	–0.00039	–1.27
1966–1975	–0.00080	–1.55

Source: Taken from Table 1 of the paper, see footnote 11.

As can be seen from the table *t*-values, the market size coefficient is always negative, and in four of the seven subperiods, it is also significant. From this evidence, Banz concludes that the smaller the firm, the higher, on average, the mean return; thus, the beta of the CAPM does not capture the whole risk.

Although these reported results are very strong, we would like to mention at this point that monthly rates of return are employed in this study, and if investors invest for a longer horizon (e.g., one year), the SFE may vanish or at least be substantially reduced the SFE results are not invariant to the assumed holding period. We discuss this issue in detail later in this chapter.

In the same issue of the *Journal of Financial Economics* in which Banz published his article, another article was published by Reinganum,[12] which also analyzes the SFE. He analyzes empirically the various anomalies that contradict the CAPM. In particular, he finds that portfolios that are classified either by price/earning ratio (P/E) or by size yield returns that are inconsistent with the CAPM, leading him to conclude that either the CAPM is misclassified or that the market is inefficient.

[12] M. R. Reinganum, "Misspecification of Capital Asset Pricing; Empirical Anomalies Based on Earnings' Yield and Market Values," *Journal of Financial Economics*, 1981.

The P/E anomaly, which was discovered by Basu,[13] reveals that after accounting for beta, the lower the P/E, the larger the abnormal return. In addition, the lower the market size of the firm, the higher the abnormal return, consistent with Banz. However, it seems that P/E and size measure the same missing economic variable, because when both are included in the regression as explanatory variables, the size effect almost completely accounts for the P/E effect. In other words, after controlling for size, the P/E ratio seems to induce only a negligible anomaly. Indeed, Reignanum argues that the size and P/E are probably associated with some missing factors, and these missing factors are closely related to the firm's size.

These two studies have two things in common that are relevant for the rest of this chapter's analysis: First, there is an SFE or size anomaly, where the smaller the size of the firm, the higher the abnormal return. Second, both studies employ short horizon rates of return to estimate the beta of the various stocks (or portfolios). These horizons of one day or one month are clearly shorter than the average actual investment horizon, which is about one year, or even longer. This fact has strong implication to the CAPM's empirical tests and, as we shall see later in this chapter, the abnormal return drastically shrinks when beta is estimated with rates of return corresponding to longer and more relevant investment horizons.

b) The Three-Factor Model of Fama and French

Probably the paper that is most critical about the validity of the CAPM is the highly cited paper published by Fama and French in 1992.[14] Employing monthly rates of return, they run regressions that are similar in structure to those of Fama and MacBeth. They regress the rates of return on various combinations of explanatory variables. Table 7.4 provides their main empirical results.

The explanatory variables are β, ME (which is the market value of equity; namely, the size variable), B/E (which is the book value

---

[13] S. Basu, "Investment Performance of Common Stocks in Relation to their Price-Earning Ratios: A Test of the Efficient Market Hypothesis," *Journal of Finance*, 1977.

[14] E. F. Fama and K. R. French, "The Cross-Section of Expected Stock Returns," *Journal of Finance*, 1992.

Table 7.4. *Average Slopes (t-Statistics) from Month-by-Month Regression of Stock Returns on β, Size, Book-to-Market Equity, Leverage, and E/P: July 1963–December 1990*

B	Ln(ME)	Ln(BE/ME)	Ln(A/ME)	Ln(A/BE)	E/P Dummy	E(+)/P
0.15						
(0.46)						
	-0.15					
	(-2.58)					
-0.37	-0.17					
(-1.21)	(-3.41)					
		0.50				
		(5.71)				
			0.50	-0.57		
			(5.69)	(-5.34)		
					0.57	4.72
					(2.28)	(4.57)
	-0.11	0.35				
	(-1.99)	(4.44)				
	-0.11		0.35	-0.50		
	(-2.06)		(4.32)	(-4.56)		
	-0.16				0.06	2.99
	(-3.06)				(0.38)	(3.04)
	-0.13	0.33			-0.14	0.87
	(-2.47)	(4.46)			(-0.90)	(1.23)
	-0.13		0.32	-0.46	-0.08	1.15
	(-2.47)		(4.28)	(-4.45)	(-0.56)	(1.57)

[*] ME, market equity; BE, book equity; A, book value of total assets; EP, earnings per share divided by stock price; E(+), positive earnings.

Source: E. F. Fama and K. R. French, "The Cross-Section of Expected Stock Returns," *Journal of Finance*, 1992.

relative to the market value of equity), A/ME (which is the ratio of the book value of the assets to the market value of equity), A/BE (which is the asset value divided by the book value of equity), and E/P, which is the ratio of earning to price. This last variable is treated as follows: If earnings are positive, then $(E+)/P$ is the ratio of total earnings to total market value of equity and the dummy variable E/P is zero. If earnings are negative, $(E+)/P$ is equal to 0, and the dummy variable is 1. Thus, with this variable, E stands for earnings and P for the stock price and the variable $(E+)/P$ stands for the E/P ratio only when earnings are positive.

The strongest evidence of this study against the CAPM is that β alone does not explain variation in returns: the estimate of beta's coefficient is only 0.15 with a t-value of only 0.46 (see Table 7.4). Thus, this coefficient is not significantly different from zero. This is in contrast to the early study by Fama and MacBeth, which shows that beta is meaningful in explaining returns. The explanation suggested by the authors for this difference in the results corresponding to these two studies, particularly the difference in the role that beta plays in explaining reruns, is that the results in these two studies correspond to two different time periods: in the Fama-French study, beta plays no economic role in explaining returns for the period 1963–1990, whereas for the earlier period studied by Fama and MacBeth, beta does play a significant role.

In contrast to the negligible and insignificant role that beta plays in explaining returns, Fama and French show that the size effect (ME) is highly significant with a t-value of –2.58. Specifically, the smaller the firm size, the higher the return. The E/P dummy variable as well as the $(E+)/P$ ratio are significant when these two variables are the only explanatory variables. However, when one adds size or book to market values as explanatory variables, the price-earnings variables become insignificant.

Thus, the conclusion of Fama and French is that size and book to market value are the crucial variables that explain returns. In another article, Fama and French[15] suggest the Three-Factor Model, where beta, size, and book to market ratio are employed as the factors that explain variation in the stock returns. Basically, they claim that these three variables capture the main explanation for return variability across assets. Both of these studies by Fama and French present evidence against the CAPM because they show that beta has little or no explanatory power.

c) The Study of Gibbons, Ross, and Shanken: A Multivariate Test of Alphas

Gibbons, Ross, and Shanken[16] (GR&S) suggest a statistical procedure for testing the CAPM in a multivariate framework. Like BJ&S, they

[15] F. Fama and K. R. French, "Common Risk Factors in the Return on Stocks and Bonds," *Journal of Financial Economics*, 1993.

[16] M. Gibbons, S. Ross, and J. Shanken, "A Test of the Efficiency of the Market Portfolio," *Econometrica*, 1989.

focus on the component of the excess return measured by α, where if this value is significantly different from zero, the CAPM is rejected. Whereas GR&S study the significance of each alpha separately, GJ&S suggest a multivariate test that examines the significance of the vector of the alphas for a given market proxy portfolio under consideration. Thus, for any given portfolio, they test whether it is *ex-ante* M-V efficient.

Having N assets and T monthly rates of returns, they run a linear regression by which the alpha and beta of each asset is estimated. Having these estimates of alphas, the null hypothesis they test is

$$H_0 : a_{ip} = 0 \quad \text{for all} \quad i = 1, 2, \ldots, N$$

where i stands for the *ith* asset in the portfolio denoted by p. The suggested test is very similar in its structure to the one of BJ&S with two main differences: First, in the regression, BJ&S employ the market portfolio, whereas GR&S test whether any given portfolio is efficient. Second, and even more important, whereas BJ&S report for each regression the univariate estimates of alpha and the corresponding t-value, GR&S conduct a multivariate test of all alphas simultaneously.

GR&S suggest the following statistic, which is stated in terms of the well-known Sharpe ratio:

$$W = \left[\frac{\sqrt{1 + \hat{\theta}^{*2}}}{\sqrt{1 + \hat{\theta}_p^2}} \right]^2 - 1 = \psi^2 - 1, \qquad (7.6)$$

where $\hat{\theta}^*$ is the maximum *ex-post* Sharpe ratio; that is, the maximum *ex-post* mean excess return per unit of standard deviation, and $\hat{\theta}_p$ is the relevant Sharpe ratio of the portfolio under consideration. Thus, the W statistic is actually some function of the *ex-post* Sharpe ratio of the highest tangency portfolio and the *ex-post* Sharpe ratio of the portfolio under consideration. W has an F distribution, and the null hypothesis is rejected when the two Sharpe measures have a relatively large difference between them. Obviously, when the portfolio under consideration is also *ex-post* M-V efficient, $W = 0$ and the null hypothesis cannot be rejected.

With the multivariate test, GR&S reach inconclusive results because with one set of data the CAPM is rejected and with another set it is not. When they choose the Center of Research Security Prices (CRSP) Equally Weighted Index as the portfolio under consideration, they conclude:

> Our multivariate test confirms the conclusion reached by BJS for their overall time in that the *ex-ante* efficiency of the CRSP [data provided by the CRSP at the University of Chicago] Equally Weighted Index cannot be rejected: equivalently, if this index is taken as the true market portfolio, then the Sharpe-Lintner version of the CAPM cannot be rejected. (GR&S, p. 1129)

However, when for a given proxy for the market portfolio they consider twelve industries as twelve possible risky assets and employ the same *W* statistics, they reach an opposite conclusion:

> The multivariate F statistics rejects the hypothesis of ex-ante efficiency at about one percent significance level. (GR&S, p. 1137)

In summary, the empirical studies discussed here are inconclusive: In some cases, the CAPM is rejected and, in some cases, the empirical results conform to the CAPM. Specifically, the results are very sensitive to the market proxy portfolios selected for testing the CAPM, as well as to the sample period selected to test the model.

7.4. ROLL'S CRITIQUE OF THE EMPIRICAL TESTS

The empirical tests discussed in the preceding are based on various forms of regressions that test whether there is a linear relationship between risk and mean return. In a breakthrough article, Roll[17] shows that if the proxy to the market portfolio used to estimate beta in the first-pass regression is M-V efficient, then in the second-pass regression, one should get a perfect linear line between the sample mean rate of return and the sample beta. Moreover, this perfect linear relationship is tautological: it neither proves nor disproves the CAPM theory. To see this claim, suppose that one takes, say, ten stocks, rather than all available stocks in the market, and derives with these ten stocks the M-V frontier. Then, if one takes any portfolio from this efficient frontier to serve as the market portfolio employed to calculate beta, then a perfect linear relationship is obtained in the second-pass

---

[17] R. Roll, "A Critique of the Asset Theory's Pricing Tests: Part I: On Past and Potential Testability of the Theory," *Journal of Financial Economics*, 1977.

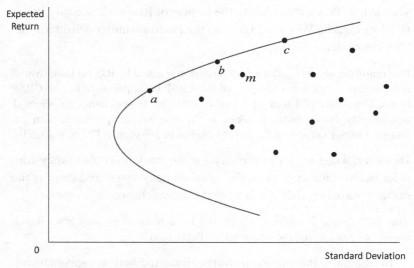

Figure 7.2. The Efficient Portfolio and the Market Portfolio.

regression as a technical result. Because we deal in this example with only ten stocks, it does not prove that the CAPM holds despite the perfect linear relationship. Also, the obtained linear relationship does not depend on investors' preferences or on the normality assumption of the distribution of rates of returns. Furthermore, this linear relationship is obtained with any efficient portfolio, even if it includes short sales positions. Obviously, such a portfolio does not conform to the CAPM.

Figure 7.2 illustrates Roll's main claim: Suppose that one selects at random only, say, ten stocks (see dots in Figure 7.2) out of the N stocks available in the market. These ten stocks are employed to derive the M-V efficient frontier. Roll claims that if one takes efficient portfolios (e.g., a, b, or c) or, for that matter, any portfolio located on the efficient frontier, and uses it to calculate the beta of each of the ten assets under consideration, then in the second-pass regression, a perfect fit is obtained, although the intercept of this line varies with the selected portfolio. Obviously, if one takes all available assets and derives the frontier, and if the market portfolio, which is employed in calculating betas, is located inside the frontier (see portfolio m), the perfect linear fit between mean return and beta, as predicted by the CAPM, cannot hold.

Thus, Roll claims that the only legitimate test of the CAPM is that testing whether the market portfolio is M-V efficient. If it is efficient, the linear risk–return follows as a technical result. Moreover, with an efficient portfolio, the relationship as predicted by the CAPM will follow technically, and there is no need to conduct all the regression analyses employed in the various studies discussed previously. It is interesting to note that the equivalence between the linear relationship between mean return and beta in the sample and the market portfolio efficiency was also realized by both Fama[18] and Ross.[19]

Although Roll employs matrix algebra to prove his claim, one can get an easy one-page proof that is similar to Lintner's proof of the CAPM. All one has to do is replace in the Lagrange function (see Section 5.3*b* in Chapter 5) the variance σ_i^2 by the sample variance $S^2_{i,}$ replace the mean μ_i by the sample mean $\bar{R}_i$ and replace the covariance $\sigma_{i,j}$ by the sample covariance $S_{i,j}$. Then, with any sample-efficient portfolio, the SML is obtained, but this time with sample estimates of the various parameters. To avoid repetition, we will not prove this claim here. However, the proof's steps are identical to those employed in the CAPM derivation.[20] Therefore, we obtain by Roll's argument that

$$\bar{R}_i = r + (\bar{R}_p - r)b_i, \qquad (7.7)$$

where b_i is the sample beta of the *ith* asset, as long as an efficient portfolio is employed to estimate beta.

Thus, with sample data exactly like that with the population parameters, with the portfolio variance minimization for a given portfolio average return, we derive a sample M-V efficient portfolio. Hence, by Roll we get as a technical result that there is a linear relationship between sample average return and sample beta, exactly as obtained in the CAPM with population mean return and population beta, as long as beta is calculated with respect to any efficient sample portfolio.

[18] E. Fama, *Foundation of Finance*, Basic Books, New York, 1976.
[19] S. Ross, "The Capital Asset Pricing Model (CAPM), Short Sales Restrictions and Related Issues," *Journal of Finance*, 1977.
[20] For a proof along these lines, see H. Levy and M. Sarnat, *Portfolio and Investment Selection: Theory and Practice*, Prentice-Hall, New York, 1983.

7.5. SHORT POSITIONS EVERYWHERE ON THE FRONTIER: ALLEGEDLY PROVIDES EVIDENCE AGAINST THE CAPITAL ASSET PRICING MODEL

If the empirical results of the CAPM tests precisely fit to the Sharpe–Lintner's CAPM, the market portfolio should be at the tangent point. Thus, the following should simultaneously hold:

1. The market portfolio must be located on the M-V efficient frontier.
2. The slope of the tangency line to the efficient frontier should be equal to the observed risk premium.
3. The intercept of this line should be equal to the riskless interest rate.
4. The investment proportions in the tangency portfolio must be all positive and equal to the market portfolio proportions; otherwise, with homogeneous expectation, the market is not cleared out.

We discuss in this section points 1 and 4. Generally, we cannot empirically include all available assets in the regression analysis; therefore, some proxy to the market portfolio (e.g., the S&P 500 Index) is employed empirically as the market portfolio. It is documented that in almost any empirical derivation of the CAPM, the portfolios located on the efficient frontier are composed of negative as well as positive investment proportions; hence, the S&P portfolio (or, for that matter, any market portfolio), which is, by definition, composed of only positive investment proportions, must be interior to the frontier, violating the preceding points 1) and 4). Therefore, the fact that negative investment proportions prevail almost everywhere on the frontier, by Roll's argument, is evidence against the CAPM.

H. Levy,[21] as early as 1983, has shown empirically that with a random sample of five stocks in all portfolios on the M-V frontier, there is one asset in short position. When the number of total assets grows to ten, four assets appear in short position; and with fifteen

---

[21] H. Levy, "The Capital Asset Pricing Model: Theory and Empiricism," *The Economic Journal*, 1983.

assets, seven or eight are in short position. Moreover, as the number of assets increases, the short positions are about 50 percent of all assets under consideration. Levy claims that the relatively high correlations between returns of the various assets make it impossible to find positive portfolios (i.e., portfolios with all positive weights) on the M-V efficient frontier. Because the market portfolio is composed of a very large number of assets, short positions are everywhere, and therefore the market portfolio or its proxy cannot be M-V efficient; hence, the CAPM is rejected. (Recall that Roll, Ross, and Fama correctly claim that the efficiency of the market portfolio and the exact linear relationship between mean return and beta are equivalent.)

Green[22] analyzed the conditions that guarantee the existence of a positive portfolio on the frontier, and Green and Hollifield[23] computed the global minimum variance portfolio for different sets of ten assets. They find that of the ninety different sets of assets examined, eighty-nine sets include short positions; hence, it is very unlikely to find a positive portfolio on the efficient frontier.

M. Levy[24] conducted some calculations regarding the probability of finding a positive portfolio on the M-V frontier. He shows that this probability approaches zero as the number of assets grows and asserts as follows:

This means that if we sample 100,000,000 different sets of 50 stocks every second and calculate the tangency portfolio for each set it will take us about 10^{14} years before we find a positive portfolio – much longer than the age of the universe. (M. Levy, p. 7)

Thus, all these theoretical arguments and empirical evidence strongly claim that the M-V efficient frontier does not contain a positive portfolio; hence, the market portfolio must be interior to the frontier, which by Roll, Ross, and Fama implies that the Sharpe–Lintner CAPM is rejected.

[22] R. C. Green, "Positively Weighted Portfolios on the Minimum Variance Frontier," *Journal of Finance*, 1986.

[23] R. C. Green and B. Hollifield, "When Will All Mean-Variance Efficient Portfolios Be Well Diversified?," *Journal of Finance*, 1992.

[24] M. Levy, "Positive Optimal Portfolios Are All Around," *Working Paper*, Hebrew University, 2009.

7.6. THE CAPITAL ASSET PRICING MODEL CANNOT BE REJECTED ON EMPIRICAL GROUND AFTER ALL

All these empirical tests at best reveal a partial support of the Sharpe–Lintner CAPM. In most studies, the sample beta and the sample average return are positively associated; hence, beta can serve, albeit not solely, as a measure of risk. Yet there are other variables with relatively high explanatory power, and the regression coefficients are almost always significantly different from what is predicted by the CAPM. The strongest empirical study refuting the CAPM is probably the one by Fama and French revealing no significant association between return and beta, casting doubt on the suitability of beta as a measure of risk.

In evaluating the empirical studies, one should recall that the CAPM is stated with *ex-ante* parameters, whereas the empirical studies employ the *ex-post* estimates of these parameters. The statistical significance tests allegedly should account for the differences between the actual parameters and their corresponding estimates; however, we show below that the statistical tests do not account for all the differences between *ex-post* and *ex-ante* values; therefore, based on the preceding commonly employed statistical procedure, we cannot reject the CAPM. Let us elaborate.

By the CAPM, we have the following linear relationship:

$$\mu_i = r + (\mu_m - r)\beta_i, \tag{7.7}$$

whereas by the second-pass regression, which is designed to test the CAPM, we have

$$\bar{R}_i = a_1 + a_2 b_i + \varepsilon_i. \tag{7.8}$$

Of course, we do not have the *ex-ante* parameters and therefore we conduct statistical significance tests to account for the random difference between $\bar{R}_i$ and μ_i and between $\mu_m - r$ and $\bar{R}_m - r$. However, in the second-pass regression, which tests the CAPM, it is implicitly or explicitly assumed that b_i, which is estimated from the first-pass regression, is the correct beta and, hence, is equal to β_i. Of course, any deviation between b and the true beta can bias the results and induce a rejection of the CAPM when actually the CAPM cannot be rejected.

Virtually all researchers who tested the CAPM are aware of this problem. Moreover, some of them try to incorporate into the beta estimation procedure some measurement errors. Thus, they try to correct the second-pass regression such that it will not be vulnerable to such measurement errors. There are several methods to account for possible differences between b and β. However, with the commonly employed methods for correction of the possible measurement errors, the CAPM is still rejected or at best has only a partial support.

We shall now show that with several new and not commonly employed methods, some of which have been only recently published, the CAPM cannot be rejected. Namely, with *ex-ante* β, the CAPM is alive and well. We discuss in the following the CAPM test with these methods for correction for beta estimation.

a) Confidence Interval of the β Approach

Suppose that for each sample value b_i there is a confidence interval (CI), say $(L_1 - L_2)_i$, such that we can say that the true β_i is located with a certain probability within this interval. Given a vector of b denoted by **b**, one can build a joint, say, 95% CI such that all β_i will each be simultaneously located in the corresponding interval $(L_1 - L_2)_i$ (to be statistically more precise, the probability is 95 percent that the CIs, which are the random variables, will jointly cover the parameters). If with this *ex-ante* β_i, which can be changed within the relevant CIs, the CAPM cannot be rejected, we can safely say that with a probability of 95 percent, the CAPM cannot be rejected. Indeed, as early as 1981, Levy[25] employed this approach to account for the fact that b_i ($i = 1,2,\dots N$), which is employed in the second-pass regression, is not the *ex-ante* β_i.

For simplicity, assume that $\bar{R}_i = \mu_i$ ($i = 1,2\dots N$) and $\bar{R}_m = \mu_m$; hence, there are no errors with these variables. However, with N risky assets, the vector $b = (b_1, b_2,\dots b_n)$ is estimated by the first-pass regression and, hence, for every random sample, we get another vector b. For example, as illustrated in Figure 7.3, suppose that $N = 2$, namely, that we have only two stocks. Furthermore,

---

[25] H. Levy, "A Test of the CAPM via Confidence Level Approach," *The Journal of Portfolio Management*, 1981.

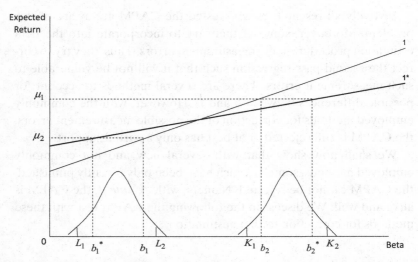

Figure 7.3. Confidence Interval of Beta and the Capital Asset Pricing Model.

suppose that with one sample, we may get the values b_1 and b_2, and with another sample we may get estimates b_1^* and b_2^*. Therefore, with these two samples, we would get regression lines 1 and 1^*, respectively; see Figure 7.3. Because with some reasonable probability, the true beta of the first stock can be anywhere within the CI range (L_1, L_2), and the true beta of the second stock can be anywhere in the CI range (K_1, K_2), we may get many regression lines when the probability to get a certain specific line is zero.

Thus, one may construct a CI to the vector of the true betas and ask whether there is a legitimate beta vector located well within the joint CI that is consistent with the CAPM. Suppose we allow each beta to be located anywhere within m standard deviations around its estimate b_i. Then we have

$$P_r \left\{ \bigcap_{i=1}^{N} (b_i - mS_{bi}) \le \beta_i \le b_i + mS_{bi} \right\} = 0.95. \qquad (7.9)$$

Thus, we require that the true beta of all stocks will be simultaneously in the range of m standard deviations to each side of b_i, where S_{bi} is the standard deviation of b_i. A simple calculation reveals that for, say $N = 110$ stocks (which is the sample size of Levy), m, which satisfies equation (7.9), is equal to 3.3. Of course, if one changes the joint confidence probability from 0.95 to another number, m will also change.

Levy employed this confidence level approach with a sample of 110 stocks covering the period 1941–1975. For this period, the average rate of return on the market portfolio was 16.4 percent. Then the value of the market line is estimated to be

$$\mu_i = r + (.164 - r)\beta_i,$$

where the parameters μ_i and β_i are unknown.

Thus, we have a line with a slope of $(0.164-r)$ and an intercept of r. Suppose that this is the true CAPM line. Then we take each b_i and shift it as close as possible to this line so long as we do not violate the CI bounds. In our specific example, with 95 percent joint CI, we can shift each b_i up to 3.3 standard deviations to each side. Having this new vector, denoted by $\mathbf{b}^*$, we can run a regression of $\bar{R}_i$ on $\mathbf{b}_i^*$. In this new regression, $\mathbf{b}$ is assumed to be the true beta vector, and we test whether the CAPM is intact with this CI approach.

Table 7.5, taken from Levy's study, provides the results for different assumed r values (hence, for different assumed theoretical lines). As we can see, we have three null hypotheses, $H_0^{(a)}$, $H_0^{(b)}$, and $H_0^{(c)}$, corresponding to riskless interest rate of 3, 4, and 5 percent, respectively. In all cases, the rate of return on the market portfolio is 16.4 percent. Table 7.5 reveals that with unadjusted beta, the CAPM is rejected because a_0 is significantly higher than the assumed interest rate, a_1 is significantly lower than (16.4 percent $- r$), and the correlation is relatively small. However, with the relevant and commonly used 95 percent CI ($m = 3.3$ standard deviations), the coefficients a_1 and a_2 are not significantly different from the market line parameters and the correlation is very high – hence, an almost perfect fit between the sample line and the theoretical line is obtained and therefore the CAPM cannot be rejected.

To summarize, the CI approach, when the fact that the true betas differ from the sample beta is accounted for, the CAPM cannot be rejected, and this is true for various relevant assumed riskless interest rates. Yet recall that we assert, unlike previous empirical studies, that the CAPM cannot be rejected, but we do not prove that it is correct. It is possible to have other theoretical asset-pricing models that also cannot be rejected.

Table 7.5. Second-Pass Regression: $\bar{R}_i = a_1 + a_2 b_i + e_i$: Confidence Level Approach: 1941–1975*

Parameters of the Null Hypothesis	Coefficients	Unadjusted Data	m = 1	m = 2	m = 3	m = 3.3
$H_0^{(a)}$	ρ^2	0.219	0.510	0.728	0.903	0.933
r = 0.03	a_1	0.118	0.072	0.050	0.032	0.029
		(0.010)	(0.010)	(0.007)	(0.004)	(0.004)
	a_2	0.064	0.108	0.122	0.135	0.136
$\bar{R}_m - r = 0.134$		(0.010)	(0.010)	(0.007)	(0.004)	(0.004)
$H_0^{(b)}$	ρ^2	0.219	0.519	0.734	0.901	0.923
r = 0.04	a_1	0.118	0.074	0.055	0.041	0.038
		(0.010)	(0.009)	(0.007)	(0.004)	(0.004)
	a_2	0.064	0.106	0.116	0.126	0.128
$\bar{R}_m - r = 0.124$		(0.010)	(0.010)	(0.007)	(0.004)	(0.004)
$H_0^{(c)}$	ρ^2	0.219	0.527	0.739	0.898	0.918
r = 0.05	a_1	0.118	0.076	0.062	0.049	0.048
		(0.010)	(0.009)	(0.006)	(0.004)	(0.004)
	a_2	0.064	0.104	0.110	0.118	0.118
$\bar{R}_m - r = 0.114$		(0.011)	(0.009)	(0.006)	(0.006)	(0.003)

* Standard deviations are in parentheses.

Source: H. Levy, "A Test of the CAPM via Confidence Level Approach," Journal of Portfolio Management, 1981.

b) A Positive Portfolio Exists with *Ex-Ante* Means

As argued previously, the fact that in almost all empirical studies the efficient set does not include any positive portfolio is evidence against the validity of the CAPM. In a recent study, M. Levy claims that although the chance to have a positive portfolio is close to zero, he also argues that there is always a positive portfolio "close by."[26]

Like the errors in beta discussed already, here the focus is on the difference between the sample average rate of return employed in deriving the M-V efficient frontier and the true unknown expected rates of return that should be employed. Suppose that μ_i^* and μ_i^{sam} stand for the true unknown mean of asset i, which guarantees a positive portfolio, and the sample mean, respectively. If $\mu_i = \mu_i^*$ for all assets under consideration, a positive portfolio is obtained. However, if these values are not identical, it is suggested to change the sample mean until a positive portfolio is obtained. Of course, if only small changes are required, the argument against the CAPM loses ground, because these little changes are statistically allowed.

Given a sample covariance matrix C, M. Levy suggests solving the following problem:

$$\text{Minimize D } (\mu^{sam}, \mu)$$
$$\text{Subject to: } \mathbf{x} = (C^{-1})\mu/[1'(C)^{-1}\mu] > 0 \qquad (7.11)$$

where $\mathbf{x}$ is the vector of investment proportions in the selected portfolio, μ^{sam} is the vector of the sample means and μ is the vector of the mean returns of the N assets, which, if it is included in the efficient set derivation, guarantees a positive portfolio $\mathbf{x} > 0$. There are many vectors of the means μ that guarantee that a positive portfolio is obtained. However, we are looking for that vector that minimizes the required changes in the sample means. Thus, D is a distance function that minimizes the distance between the sample mean vector and the selected vector of means, which guarantees a positive portfolio $\mathbf{x} > 0$. The function D is given by

$$D(\mu^{sam}, \mu) = \left\{ \frac{1}{N} \sum_i^N (\mu_i - \mu_i^{sam})^2 \right\}^{1/2}. \qquad (7.12)$$

---

[26] See M. Levy, *op. cit.*

Table 7.6. *A Sample Tangency Portfolio and the Closest Positive Portfolio**

Stock No.	μ^{sam}	X^{sam}	μ	X	$\mu - \mu^{sam}$	t-value
1	0.0146	0.3819	0.0134	0.2851	−0.0012	−0.1123
2	0.0104	0.1217	0.0102	0.1198	−0.0002	−0.0167
3	0.0005	−0.2024	0.0041	0.0000†	0.0036	0.5191
4	0.0105	0.2332	0.0093	0.1883	−0.0012	−0.1572
5	0.0038	−0.0122	0.0042	0.0189	0.0004	0.0383
6	0.0098	0.6185	0.0077	0.3878	−0.0021	−0.3194
7	0.0015	−0.1911	0.0052	0.0000†	0.0037	0.4864
8	0.0065	−0.0086	0.0068	0.0000†	0.0003	0.0411
9	0.0058	0.0301	0.0052	0.0000†	−0.0006	−0.0733
10	0.0044	0.0290	0.0047	0.0000†	0.0003	0.0487

* The table provides sample means μ^{sam} and the corresponding investment proportions X^{sam}; the new means μ, which minimizes the function D; the corresponding investment proportions, X; the required changes $\mu - \mu^{sam}$; and the t-values of the differences between μ^{sam} and μ.
† The solution satisfies the strict inequality $x^* > 0$. These portfolio weights are too small to be recorded with the five-digit precision of the table, but they are all strictly positive.
Source: M. Levy, "Positive Portfolios Are All Around," *Working Paper*, Hebrew University of Jerusalem, 2009.

Suppose that D is minimized and a vector of means μ is obtained. How far is the distance between the vector of the sample means μ^{sam} and the vector and the means μ? Is this difference within a range that is statistically allowed?

Levy shows that indeed only small changes, which are statistically allowed, in the means guarantee a positive portfolio. Table 7.6 reports the efficient set derivation with ten stocks.

The first two columns provide the sample means and the sample investment proportions. As can be seen, four of the ten assets are in short position. The next two columns report the vector μ solved by equation (7.11) and the new investment proportions, all of which are positive, as is required by this equation. The last two columns report the needed changes in the means and the t-values. As can be seen, very small changes in the means are required to guarantee a positive portfolio, changes that are statistically allowed (see the relatively small t-values). Calculating the joint probability for the changes reported in the table, Levy concludes that using *ex-ante* possible parameters

μ, which are statistically legitimate, rather than the sample means, a positive portfolio exists; hence, the CAPM cannot be rejected simply because all portfolios on the sample frontier include negative investment weights. The intriguing question is why, empirically, we do not find these positive portfolios. Why do none of the empirical studies find a sample vector similar to μ such that a positive portfolio is empirically obtained? The answer to these questions is given by Levy as follows:[27]

Thus parameter sets leading to positive portfolios are somewhat similar to rational numbers: if a point in parameter space is chosen at random it almost surely leads to an optimal portfolio with negative weights (an irrational number on the number line). On the other hand, one can always find a point in parameter space very close by that will yield a positive optimal portfolio (a close by rational number). (M. Levy, p. 13)

Thus, there is an infinite number of M-V efficient positive portfolios consistent with the sample parameters, but the chance of obtaining one of them empirically is very close to zero, explaining the observed empirical findings revealing efficient portfolios that contain only portfolios with some short positions.

c) Reverse Engineering: The Approach of M. Levy and R. Roll

In a breakthrough study, M. Levy and R. Roll[28] (L&R) employ a "reverse-engineering" technique to test whether the CAPM is rejected with *ex-ante* parameters. This optimization problem is similar in spirit to Sharpe's (2007) "reverse-optimization" problem, an approach that was first used in an innovative article by Best and Grauer (1985).[29] By the method suggested by L&R, a proxy to the market portfolio is selected, and a set of parameters is found such that this proxy is M-V efficient. Obviously, this method is supportive of the CAPM or to the ZBM only if these selected parameters,

---

[27] See M. Levy, *op. cit.*
[28] See M. Levy and R. Roll, *op. cit.*
[29] See Best, M. J., and R. R. Grauer, 1985, "Capital Asset Pricing Compatible with Observed Market Value Weights, *Journal of Finance*, 40, 85–103, 1985, and W. F. Sharpe, "Expected Utility Asset Allocation," *Financial Analysts Journal* 63, 18–30, 2007.

which guarantee that the market portfolio proxy is M-V efficient, are close, in statistical significance terms, to the sample estimates of these parameters.

Levy and Roll's main claim is that because the sample parameters are random variables and the *ex-ante* parameters are unknown, one should consider a statistically legitimate difference between the two sets of parameters (the sample estimates and the suggested new set of parameters) in examining whether the market portfolio proxy (e.g., the S&P 500 Index) is located on the M-V efficient frontier.

Whereas in the standard approach one starts with the sample parameters and then derives the M-V efficient portfolios implied by these parameters, in the L&R's "reverse engineering" approach, one starts with a given market portfolio proxy and requires that the parameters are such that this proxy is M-V efficient. There are many parameters sets ensuring this efficiency, but L&R look for the set that is as close as possible to the sample parameter set.

Although possible differences in means, variances, and covariances should be considered, for simplicity, L&R assume that correlation in the sample and in the population is identical; hence, they focus only on the differences in the means and variances. Obviously, for given correlations, changes in variances imply changes in covariances.

They establish the following distance D function as follows:

$$D[(\mu, \sigma), (\mu, \sigma)^{sam}]$$

$$= \left\{ \alpha \frac{1}{N} \sum_{i}^{N} \left(\frac{\mu_i - \mu_i^{sam}}{\sigma_i^{sam}} \right)^2 + (1 - \alpha) \frac{1}{N} \sum_{i}^{N} \left(\frac{\sigma_i - \sigma_i^{sam}}{\sigma^{sam}} \right)^2 \right\}^{0.5}$$

The goal is to find a vector μ and a vector σ such that for given sample means and variances, the function D is minimized and that with these adjusted parameters, the market portfolio proxy is M-V efficient. Taking a sample of 100 large stocks and using their value-weighted portfolio as the market proxy, they find that with the sample parameters, this proxy is inefficient; actually, it is deep inside the efficient frontier (see point m in Figure 7.4). However, by changing the parameters, a new frontier is established such that the proxy to the market portfolio is M-V efficient.

In Figure 7.4, AB is the M-V frontier with the sample parameters and $A'B'$ is the frontier with the adjusted parameters. The two

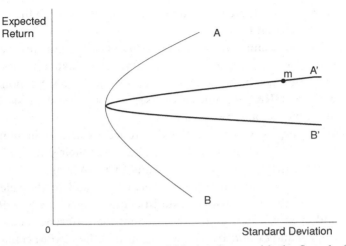

Figure 7.4. The Efficient Frontier and Market Proxy with the Sample (AB) and the Adjusted (A′B′) Return Parameters. *Source:* M. Levy and R. Roll, "The Market Portfolio May Be Mean-Variance Efficient After All," *Review of Financial Studies*, 2010.

frontiers are quite different. However, the astonishing result is that only little changes in the parameters are required to achieve frontier A′B′, changes that are allowed with a reasonable significance level.

Thus, employing the distance function D, L&R find a set of parameters that is not statistically significantly different from the sample set of parameters (with each parameter conducting a separate test as well as with a joint test), yielding an *ex-ante* efficient set, namely, set A′B′ in Figure 7.4, such that the proxy to the market portfolio is located on the *ex-ante* frontier. Therefore, the CAPM cannot be rejected with these *ex-ante* parameters.

How can these results be reconciled with those of Gibbons, Ross, and Shanken (GR&S) discussed in Section 7.3c? Indeed, L&R discuss the differences between these two studies. Here is the summary of the differences and similarities of these two studies:

1. First, recall that GR&S reject the CAPM when the twelve industries' portfolios are selected as the assets from which one constructs the M-V efficient set, but they cannot reject the CAPM when the equally weighted CRSP portfolio is employed as the proxy to the market portfolio. Thus, with one market

proxy choice, there is a complete agreement between the results of GR&S and L&R.

2. With the sample where a disagreement in the conclusion prevails, the simple explanation is that L&R take into account the difference between *ex-post* and *ex-ante* beta's components, whereas GR&S do not. Of course, in any statistical tests, such difference should be taken into account.

3. However, even without the difference explained in point 2, L&R repeat the study of GR&S and, using their statistical procedure, they show that the results of GR&S are very sensitive to the assumed riskless interest rate and to the selected time period. Even with the statistical test suggested by GR&S, and even without taking into account the differences between *ex-post* and *ex-ante* betas, L&R show that the CAPM cannot be rejected for a wide range of relevant riskless interest-rate values as well as for other sample periods.

To summarize the comparison of these two studies, GR&S reveal mixed results regarding the CAPM rejection; even in the one case where they reject the CAPM, it cannot be rejected for another selected period and for another relevant riskless interest rate, let alone for other legitimate *ex-ante* parameters. Thus, even using the statistical test of GR&S, the results of their study are quite in agreement with the results of L&R, asserting that the CAPM cannot be rejected.

d) The Small Firm Effect and the Investment Horizon

The CAPM assumes that all investors face the same set of parameters; namely, all investors face the same end of the investment period distributions of return. There are two crucial questions in this respect:

1. What is the relevant or typical investment holding period?
2. What biases may emerge in the empirical testing of the CAPM if one employs rates of return corresponding to a shorter or a longer holding period than the actual holding period?

The answers to these two questions are crucial because of the prevailing difference between the actual holding period and the assumed holding period in empirical research: the typical investment holding period is larger than a year, whereas most empirical studies that test the CAPM, including the SFE studies, rely on monthly rates of return.

The relevant investment horizon for CAPM testing is the planned investment horizon. As a result of transaction costs, it is obvious that this investment horizon cannot be very short. Indeed, it is found empirically to be about one year and in some studies even longer. Atkins and Dyl[30] document the median holding period of investors in the NASDQ and the New York Stock Exchange to be between two to about five years with a tendency to decline over time. Yet, in the period that SFE has been discovered (1981) and reaffirmed (1992), the median investment horizon is reported to be well greater than one year.

Naes and Ødegaard[31] conducted a detailed investigation of the holding period of individual investors in the Oslo Stock Exchange during 1992–2003. Figure 7.5 reports their results. As we can see from this figure, the median holding period is about one year.

Benartzi and Thaler[32] provide compelling argument that the investment horizon is about a year, and Barber and Odean[33] document that the investors, turnover on average is 80 percent of their portfolio annually.

Taking all this empirical evidence into account, it is obvious that the planned investment horizon is closer to one year rather than to one month or one week. Because virtually all SFE studies employ monthly data and some studies even employ shorter horizon rates of return, we turn now to investigate the effect of assuming a relatively short investment horizon on the SFE phenomenon.

For simplicity of the discussion, suppose that the SFE studies are conducted with monthly rates of returns and the investment horizon is one year. However, the same analysis is valid for any other short and long horizons, when the holding period is longer than the assumed horizon in the empirical SFE studies. We use herein the

---

[30] A. B. Atkins and E. A. Dyl, "Transaction Costs and the Holding Periods for Common Stocks," *Journal of Finance*, 1997.

[31] R. Naes and B. A. Ødegaard, "The Link Between Investor Holding Period and Liquidity," *Working Paper*, 2007.

[32] S. Benartzi and R. Thaler, "Myopic Loss Aversion and the Equity Risk Premium Puzzle," *Quarterly Journal of Economics*, 1995.

[33] B. Barber and T. Odean, "Trading Hazardous to Your Wealth: The Common Stock Investment Performance of Individual Investors," *Journal of Finance*, 1999.

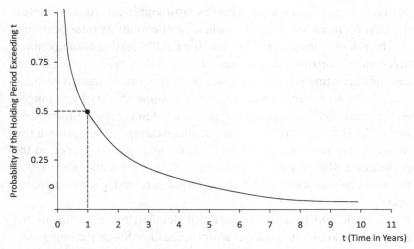

Figure 7.5. Distribution of the Holding Period. *Source:* R. Naes and B. A. Ødegaard, "The Link Between Investor Holding Period and Liquidity," *Working Paper*, 2007.

terms monthly and annual horizons or one-period and n-period horizon interchangeably, when the short horizon refers to the horizon employed in the empirical studies and the long horizon refers to the actual holding period.

Denote the monthly return by R_t (i.e., it is $1 +$ rate of return). Then the longer n period return is given by R, where

$$R = R_1 R_2 \ldots\ldots\ldots R_n.$$

Because R is a product rather than the sum of the monthly returns, the various parameters and, particularly beta, may be systematically biased by the fact that the investor's typical horizon is longer than the one employed in the SFE studies. In contrast, if returns would be additive, one could employ any arbitrary investment horizon without affecting the results systematically, as long as the returns are identically and independently distributed over time (*i.i.d.*). Obviously, if returns are dependent over time, the assumed investment horizon trivially affects the results. However, as we shall see, even when returns are *i.i.d.*, the various CAPM parameters are affected in some systematic way by the assumed investment horizon because the end-of-period return is a product rather than the sum of the short-term returns.

Some empirical studies employ the Log returns, which mathematically creates additivity of the end-of-period Log returns. Because this is a common technique, let us start with the additive return, which, in our view, is an incorrect way to measure the end-of-period return. With an additive assumption, the end-of-period return on a given stock is

$$R = R_1 + R_2 + \ldots\ldots\ldots R_n$$

and on the market portfolio it is

$$R_m = R_{m1} + R_{m2} + \ldots\ldots\ldots R_{mn}$$

when n is the number of periods and m indicates the market portfolio.

The n period holding return beta is given by, β_n, where

$$\beta_n = Cov(R_1 + R_2 + \ldots R_n, R_{m1} + R_{m2}$$
$$+ \ldots R_{mn})/Var(R_{m1} + R_{m2} \ldots + R_{mn}).$$

Assuming *i.i.d*, we obtain

$$\beta_n = nCov(R_1, R_m)/n\sigma_m^2 = \beta_1 \qquad (7.13)$$

where n stands for the number of short periods (e.g., each period is one month), β_n and β_1 stand for the n-period and one-period beta (which is the same for each single period), and R_1 and R_m stand for the one-period return on the stock and on the market portfolio, respectively. By the additivity property of returns, we also have for the expected return on the stock, on the market portfolio, and on the riskless asset, the following relationship between the n-period returns and the one-period returns:

$$\mu_n = n\mu, \mu_{nm} = n\mu_m, r_n = nr,$$

where μ_n and μ stand for the n-period and one-period mean return on the stock under consideration, μ_{nm} and μ_m stand for the n-period mean return and the one-period return on the market portfolio, and r_n and r stand for the n-period and one-period riskless interest rate. Therefore, if the n-period CAPM is intact, we have

$$n\mu_i = nr + (n\mu_m - nr)\beta_{ni}$$

and, after reducing by n and recalling that in the additive case $\beta_{ni} = \beta_i$ (see equation [7.13]), we determine that the CAPM also holds for each one-period, namely,

$$\mu_i = r + (\mu_m - r)\beta_i.$$

By the same token, if the CAPM holds for the one-period horizon, it holds for any longer horizon as long as returns are *i.i.d.*, and the end-of-period return is the sum rather than the product of the short-period returns. Thus, by assuming additivity, the CAPM as well as beta are invariant to the assumed investment horizon; hence, SFE biases are not expected as a result of the employment of various investment horizons.

Tempted by this additivity property, some researchers work with the *Log* of end-of-period returns. Indeed,

$$Log(R) = Log(R_1 R_2 \ldots \ldots \ldots R_n)$$
$$= Log\, R_1 + Log\, R_2 \ldots \ldots Log\, R_n$$

and $Log\, R_m$ can be written in a similar way, creating the additivity property with *Log* returns. Although employing the *Log* function reduces dramatically the difficult issues corresponding to the comparison of the one-period and n-period CAPM, there is no economic justification to use the *Log return* because the utility function is defined in terms of the end-of-period accumulated wealth, not in terms of *Log wealth*, and the end-of-period distribution of return is defined on the product of the short-term returns rather than on the sum of the short-term *Log returns*. Therefore, generally, one cannot employ the *Log returns* of the terminal wealth; hence, the additivity of returns does not prevail.

Being convinced that, in practice, the holding period realized return is the product of the short-period returns, we turn now to the analysis of the effect of the assumed investment period the CAPM and on SFE, when the n-period return is a product of the short one-period returns.

As early as 1972, Levy[34] showed theoretically that the Sharpe ratio of various portfolios changes with the horizon in some systematic way. Namely, even if the Sharpe ratio of all assets is constant for some

---

[34] H. Levy, "Portfolio Performance and the Investment Horizon," *Management Science*, 1972.

holding period (as required by the CAPM), it is not constant for any other assumed holding period. Thus, the CAPM is not invariant to the assumed investment horizon and because the changes in the Sharpe ratio that accompany the changes in the horizon are systematic, it indicates but does not prove that the SFE may be due to the employment of a relatively short horizon in the empirical SFE studies.

Levhari and Levy[35] studied, theoretically and empirically, the effect of the assumed investment horizon on beta and on the CAPM. They report that aggressive stocks tend to be even more aggressive as the horizon increases and defensive stocks become more defensive when the horizon increases. Neutral stocks, with beta equal to 1, are not affected by the employed horizon, which remains equal to 1 for all assumed horizons.

Handa, Kothari, and Wesley[36] document that the theoretical results of Levhari and Levy are empirically valid. Table 7.7 reveals the empirical finding on the relation of beta, the firm size, and the assumed investment horizon.

The table presents twenty portfolios where MV1 is 5 percent of the smallest firms and MV20 contains the 5 percent that are the largest firms. As expected, the smallest firms have relatively large beta, which decreases as the size increases. However, the most interesting finding is the confirmation of theoretical findings of Levhari and Levy: as the horizon increases, say, from one week to one year, the beta of aggressive stocks (small firms) increases, but the beta of defensive stocks (large firms) tends to decrease. This finding has a strong implication to the SFE studies. First, recall that small firms typically have relatively large betas, generally larger than 1. If the actual horizon is about one year and studies of SFE employ monthly data in calculating the abnormal return, they take into account a much smaller beta than the actual beta; hence, an artificial SFE may emerge. For example, with the smallest firm portfolio, beta is equal to 1.41 with monthly data. However, with annual data, beta is equal to 1.66. Therefore, with monthly data, the measured risk is smaller and, hence, an abnormal return may be recorded. This abnormal return may be irrelevant for

---

[35] D. Levhari and H. Levy, "The Capital Asset Pricing Model and the Investment Horizon," *Review of Economics and Statistics*, 1977.

[36] P. Handa, S. P. Kothari and C. Wesley, "The Relation Between the Return Intervals and Betas: Implication to the Size Effect," *Journal of Financial Economics*, 1993.

Table 7.7. *Mean Portfolio Beta with Returns Measured over Different Horizons**

Portfolio	Year	Six Months	Four Months	Three Months	Two Months	Month	Week	Day
MV1	1.66	1.60	1.57	1.51	1.53	1.41	1.18	0.99
MV2	1.38	1.41	1.42	1.37	1.33	1.27	1.13	1.02
MV3	1.31	1.31	1.35	1.32	1.29	1.23	1.12	1.04
MV4	1.18	1.20	1.21	1.21	1.17	1.18	1.13	1.08
MV5	1.16	1.19	1.17	1.16	1.17	1.14	1.11	1.08
MV6	1.22	1.14	1.15	1.12	1.11	1.11	1.10	1.10
MV7	1.10	1.11	1.11	1.08	1.08	1.08	1.10	1.09
MV8	1.10	1.09	1.07	1.06	1.05	1.04	1.10	1.10
MV9	1.04	1.01	1.02	1.03	1.01	1.03	1.08	1.09
MV10	0.94	0.98	0.97	0.99	0.99	1.00	1.05	1.05
MV11	1.00	0.97	0.96	0.99	0.99	0.99	1.02	1.03
MV12	0.97	0.94	0.93	0.94	0.94	0.96	0.96	0.98
MV13	0.88	0.88	0.88	0.88	0.89	0.92	0.95	0.96
MV14	0.87	0.87	0.88	0.88	0.88	0.91	0.93	0.97
MV15	0.83	0.86	0.85	0.86	0.87	0.88	0.91	0.95
MV16	0.79	0.79	0.79	0.81	0.82	0.85	0.90	0.93
MV17	0.72	0.73	0.74	0.77	0.80	0.81	0.87	0.90
MV18	0.70	0.73	0.71	0.77	0.77	0.79	0.85	0.90
MV19	0.59	0.62	0.63	0.66	0.68	0.71	0.79	0.86
MV20	0.56	0.58	0.58	0.61	0.63	0.67	0.78	0.90

* The 20 portfolios are ranked by size. MV1 is the portfolio of smallest stocks and MV20 is the portfolio of largest stocks. For each portfolio, β is measured for different horizons. Note that the small stock portfolio has the highest β, the large stock portfolio has the lowest β, and β decreases almost monotonically with size. As the investment horizon shortens, generally large βs decrease, small βs increase, and βs close to 1 remain almost unchanged.

Source: P. Handa, S. P. Kothari, and C. Weoley, "The Relation Between the Return Intervals and Betas: Implication to the Size Effect," *Journal of Financial Economics*, 1993.

annual holding period's investors because the risk they face is much larger and the abnormal return may vanish with the relevant annual beta. At this point, two comments are called for:

1. With additive returns, this could not happen because beta is invariant to the assumed investment horizon. Table 7.7 indicates that the fact that the end-of-period return is a product rather than the sum of the one-period return has a nonnegligible effect on beta.
2. The fact that beta changes systematically with the investment horizon is not sufficient for the explanation for the SFE bias

because the other parameters also change in a nonadditive way; therefore, a more complicated analysis is required to examine the combined effect of the horizon on the SFE.

The combined analysis of the various effects of the assumed horizon on the SFE phenomenon was conducted by Levy and Levy,[37] whose main theoretical results are as follows: If the CAPM perfectly holds for n period horizon, say, one year, then for a shorter horizon, say, one month, we expect to find SFE. Thus, if researchers would employ annual data, no SFE is predicted because the CAPM holds. However, with monthly data, SFE is expected by the CAPM. Their main formal claim is given by Theorem 1 of their paper, which is stated as follows:

Theorem: Suppose the CAPM holds for n-period horizon; that is, the n-period Treynor[38] index $\frac{\mu_j^n - r^n}{\beta_{nj}}$ is constant across all stock. Then, for one-period horizon, the Treynor Index is a monotonically increasing function of β, that is, $\frac{\partial}{\partial \beta}\left(\frac{\mu-r}{\beta}\right) > 0$. Namely, for aggressive stocks, abnormal returns are predicted with one-period returns. Given that aggressive stocks are typically small-firm stocks, this means that for the one-period horizon, the SFE prevails.

Thus, it is proved mathematically that with a short horizon (e.g., one month), an SFE is expected. What is left is to measure this effect empirically and to estimate the magnitude of the horizon-induced SFE.

Levy and Levy analyzed the effect of the assumed investment horizon when the returns are independent over time as well as when serial correlation exists. The results are very similar in the two cases, and incorporating serial correlation (which empirically exists) even enhances the results. Figure 7.6 is drawn with actual annual returns and interest-rate figures and with actual observed serial correlation corresponding to the S&P 500 Index. It is assumed that the CAPM perfectly holds with annual data. Then the implied monthly mean return and monthly beta are theoretically calculated for each portfolio, when portfolios are sorted by size. The portfolios marked by ▲ denote the points for the ten portfolios under consideration, where

---

[37] M. Levy and H. Levy, "The Small Firm Effect: A Financial Mirage?," *Journal of Portfolio Management*, 2011.

[38] J. L. Treynor, "How to Rate Management Investment Funds," *Harvard Business Review*, 1965.

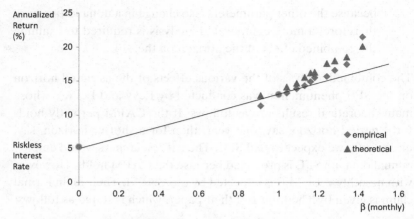

Figure 7.6. The Empirical and Theoretical Small Firm Effect. *Sources:* Ibbotson Associates, *Stocks, Bonds, Bills and Inflation, 2007 Yearbook*, Ibbotson Associates, Chicago; and M. Levy and H. Levy, "The Small Firm Effect: Financial Mirage?," *Journal of Portfolio Management*, 2011.

the small stock portfolios generally have a higher beta. It is important to emphasize that these portfolios' parameters are calculated by the mathematical formulas as advocated by Levy and Levy. As can be seen, the small stock portfolios are mathematically predicted to be located above the CAPM line; hence, with monthly data, the SFE is mathematically predicted. Ignoring the mathematical relation between short and long horizon parameters, one can calculate the portfolios' monthly mean return and beta based solely on empirical data rather than on the mathematical formulas, which can be employed to calculate the monthly parameters from the annual parameters. These portfolios are denoted by diamonds in Figure 7.6. It is interesting that the SFE calculated with the mathematical formulas suggested by Levy and Levy is very similar to the actual SFE reported by Ibbotson,[39] which relies purely on actual data.

To summarize, if the CAPM holds with annual data, it is expected to have an SFE with monthly or any shorter data. The same is true even if the CAPM does not precisely hold with annual data: even if the CAPM does not hold and SFE does not exist with annual data, it emerges with monthly or any other shorter data.

---

[39] See Ibbotson Associates, *Stocks, Bonds, Bills and Inflation, 2007 Yearbook*, Ibbotson Associates, Chicago.

Thus, for investors with an annual holding period, there is no SFE with annual data, and there is a SFE effect with monthly data, but this does not represent abnormal profit because the investors who invest for a one-year holding period face beta that is much different from the monthly irrelevant beta. Can investors with monthly horizon benefit from the SFE? Not really, because if the CAPM holds for annual horizon, it does not hold for monthly horizon; therefore, the CAPM and beta are irrelevant for a short holding period and the measured excess return is economically irrelevant. Furthermore, with transaction costs, investing for a very short horizon may yield, on average, a negative rate of return; therefore, to begin, investors will not have a short investment horizon. Having these results, it seems that the SFE is like a financial mirage of cool water in the desert – it looks tempting, but once you get closer and try to drink, it vanishes.

7.7. EXPERIMENTAL STUDIES OF THE CAPITAL ASSET PRICING MARKET

In all the empirical tests of the CAPM discussed here so far, one does not know the *ex-ante* parameters, but an attempt is made to account for the differences between the sample *ex-post* and population *ex-ante* parameters. In the attempts to account for the differences between *ex-ante* and *ex-post* betas (or some beta components), various statistical tools are employed. A completely different approach is to employ experiments of asset pricing where the subjects simultaneously determine the equilibrium prices and the *ex-ante* parameters. In this respect, the experimental studies have an edge over the empirical studies, which can never employ the precise *ex-ante* parameters. To the best of our knowledge, the first experimental testing of the equilibrium model with *ex-ante* parameters was conducted by Levy.[40] The experiment involved a substantial monetary payoff, which increases the reliability of the obtained results. Let us elaborate on this technique.

The CAPM's experimental testing of Levy is quite extensive and contains ten trading rounds where the investment results and market

---

[40] H. Levy, "Risk and Return: An Experimental Analysis," *International Economic Review*, 1997.

prices are reported to the subjects at the end of each trading round. In a nutshell, this experiment has the following structure: The subjects observe the current price of twenty risky assets, and they have information on the riskless interest rate at which they can borrow and lend money. In the last trading round, which is relevant for testing the CAPM, every subject has wealth and a portfolio of stock he or she selected in the previous trading round. The subjects send the central computer the investor's demand and supply function for each asset (e.g., at price of \$10, buy me 100 stocks; at price of \$9, buy me 200 stocks, and so forth). Similarly, at a higher price, he or she may send sell orders (supply function for the stock). Having the aggregate supply and demand functions, the computer determines the equilibrium price for each of the twenty assets when the equilibrium price clears the market.

Thus, at the beginning of the last trading round, equilibrium prices are determined, and at the end of this round, all firms liquidate their assets, which are transferred to the stockholders. The end-of-period liquidation values are normally distributed, with parameters known to the subjects. As the equilibrium price of the stock of each firm is determined by the aggregate supply and demand for the stock, the current equilibrium value of each firm, denoted by V_i^*, is also determined. Given the end-of-period distribution of each firm, the subjects determine the equilibrium value of each firm; hence, they determine simultaneously all parameters, including the *ex-ante* mean return and beta. To see this, recall that

$$\mu_i = \frac{V_{i9}}{V_i^*} E(1 + \tilde{R}_i) = \frac{E(\tilde{V}_{i10})}{V_i^*}$$

where V_{i9} is the observed liquidation value of form i at the end of the ninth trading round, E stands for expected value operator, and $\tilde{R}_i$ is a random variable standing for the next period rate of return. Also note that $V_{i9} E(1 + \tilde{R}) = E(\tilde{V}_{i10})$, which is the liquidation value at the end of the tenth round. Hence, determining the current market value (i.e., at the beginning of the last trading round) of the firm by the aggregate demand and supply function (V_i^*), and observing (reported to the subjects) the current balance-sheet value of the firm's assets (all held in traded assets whose market value can be easily calculated), V_{i9}, we determine also the mean of the stock of the ith firm given by

Table 7.8. *The Explanatory Variable of the Variation in Mean Returns**

β^*	β	σ	σ^2	S_{ei}^2	Adjusted ρ^2
4.850					0.71
(6.49)					
	0.065				0.70
	(6.33)				
		0.719			0.43
		(3.63)			
			3.0002		0.40
			(3.40)		
	0.060			0.237	0.73
	(5.63)			(1.30)	
4.495				0.252	0.74
(5.86)				(1.43)	
4.032		0.255			0.75
(4.43)		(1.408)			
3.103	0.013	0.242			0.75
(1.03)	(0.32)	(1.33)			
3.005	0.025				0.72
(0.98)	(0.62)				

* The *t*-values are shown in parentheses.
Source: H. Levy, "Risk and Return: An Experimental Analysis," *International Economic Review*, 1997.

μ_i. By a similar argument, determination of the equilibrium value of each firm, together with the information on the statistical distribution of the firm's liquidation values and covariances between them (also known to the subjects), will determine the *ex-ante* variance of each stock, the covariances and, hence, the *ex-ante* beta of each stock. Thus, in this experiment, the end-of-period distribution of the firms' values are known and by their demand–supply functions, the subjects determine simultaneously the current equilibrium values, which dictate the expected rate of return, variance, and beta of each stock.

Because the experiment provides data on the wealth of as well as on the portfolio held by each subject at the beginning of the last trading period, one can test the CAPM as well as the GCAPM, but this time with *ex-ante* parameters, which, according to Sharpe, is the only legitimate way to test the CAPM. Table 7.8 provides the regression results across the twenty stocks available in the market in this experiment with *ex-ante* parameters.

First, note that β^* and β stand for the GCAPM and the CAPM risk measures, respectively. As can be seen from the table, these two risk measure coefficients are positive and highly significant, which is in contrast to the empirical studies that reject the CAPM with *ex-post* parameters. Moreover, unlike most empirical studies with *ex-ante* parameters, the ρ^2 is very high, about 70 percent in both cases. The variance coefficient is also significant, but it has a much lower explanatory power than beta does. Moreover, when the standard deviation and one of the betas are included in the regression, only beta turns to be significant. The residual variance is not significant when it is included with beta as an explanatory variable. Finally, when both the CAPM beta and the GCAPM beta are included together as explanatory variables, both are insignificant as a result of the multiculinearity because these two betas are highly correlated.

To summarize, experimental studies allow us to design an experiment such that the equilibrium model is tested with *ex-ante* parameters. We find strong support for beta as a measure of risk, and the coefficient of determination is very high. These results conform to the recent studies that do not reject the CAPM when one accounts for the difference between *ex-post* and *ex-ante* betas or other parameters that composed the betas.

In 2002, Bossaerts and Plott[41] published an experimental study testing the validity of the CAPM. They conducted a total of seven experiments and examined the convergence toward the CAPM of the subjects' portfolios. Three securities provide dividends in the next period, and the paid dividend is random, because it depends on the state of nature. In each period, the traders were endowed with units of two of the three assets as well as with cash. To examine whether the CAPM has experimental support, they compare the Sharpe ratio of the market portfolio and the actual maximum Sharpe ratio. If the difference between these two ratios is zero, this means that the traders select their portfolios such that the Sharpe ratio is maximized. They conclude:

Specific to this paper, CAPM principles appear at work even when markets are thin. The experimental evidence contrasts with field research (see e.g., Fama and French, 1992), which suggests that the latter may well be hampered

---

[41] P. Bossaerts and C. Plott, "The CAPM in Thin Experimental Financial Markets," *Journal of Economic Dynamics & Control*, 2002.

by the complexity of the environment which is beyond the researcher's control but about which the researcher necessarily has to make assumptions.... Most of these aspects are tightly controlled in experimental setting. (p. 1110)

Thus, like Levy, Bosseaerts and Plott also point out that the empirical studies have drawbacks that can be eliminated in experimental studies. Having this advantage of the experimental studies, they find that subjects gradually move up in M-V space, thus converging to the CAPM equilibrium.

These two experimental studies, although much different in their structure, come to the same conclusion: The evidence supports the CAPM, which is in sharp contrast to empirical studies that rely on *ex-post* parameters, revealing that beta has no explanatory power.

7.8. SUMMARY

One can evaluate the validity of the CAPM either by examining the validity of the assumptions made to derive it or by a positive economics approach, asserting that if the model can explain asset pricing and there is no other model with better explanatory power, then we accept the model, even if the assumptions needed to derive it are unrealistic. This chapter is devoted to the positive economics approach; that is, we discuss the empirical tests of the CAPM.

The first empirical test of the CAPM was conducted by Lintner himself. He finds that mean return and beta are positively related and that the coefficient of beta is significant. This provides some support for the CAPM. However, he also reports that other factors, for example, the residual variance, have a relatively strong explanatory power of return variation across assets, which contradicts the CAPM. Most subsequent empirical studies reveal a positive relation between mean return and beta, yet there are some deviations from what is expected by the CAPM; for example, the intercept of the regression line is much larger than the riskless interest rate.

The studies with the strongest evidence against the CAPM are the SFE studies and the study published by Fama and French in 1992. Sharpe, the father of the CAPM, responded to these negative results by saying that they use *ex-post* parameters, whereas the CAPM is stated with *ex-ante* parameters and, hence, the empirical evidence cannot constitute evidence against the CAPM.

We show in this chapter that, indeed, the CAPM cannot be rejected for the following reasons:

1. Beta employed in the CAPM tests is taken from the first-pass regression and is assumed to be the true beta. If one adds a confidence interval to these sample betas, the CAPM cannot be rejected.

2. The fact that short positions appear almost everywhere on the M-V efficient frontier, and the market portfolio must be positive, does not contradict the CAPM, because with little changes in the assets means, which are well within the statistical error bounds, many positive portfolios appear on the efficient frontier.

3. With small changes to the parameters, to reflect the differences between *ex-post* and *ex-ante* parameters, the market portfolio is located on the M-V efficient frontier. Hence, the fact that the market portfolio is found to be interior to the frontier is not evidence against the CAPM.

4. Employing experimental studies with *ex-ante* parameters reveals a strong, almost linear relation between mean return and beta with a coefficient of determination of about 70 percent; hence, the CAPM cannot be rejected.

5. Finally, the SFE is evidence against the CAPM. Here, the defense for the CAPM comes from a different angle: investors typically invest for about one year, and the SFE is documented with monthly data. This introduces a systematic horizon bias. If the CAPM perfectly holds with annual data, the CAPM actually *predicts* that the SFE will emerge with monthly data. However, for the one-year horizon investors, the monthly SFE has no economic value; for the short-horizon investors, the SFE is irrelevant because the CAPM for short horizon does not hold and beta is meaningless. Furthermore, with transaction costs, it is not economically worthwhile to have a short planned investment horizon.

Thus, the CAPM cannot be empirically rejected with *ex-ante* parameters. This, of course, does not mean that this is the best model for asset pricing because it is possible that other potential models also cannot be rejected. In such a case, the best model among the competitive theoretical models will be selected by its explanatory power measured with *ex-ante* parameters.

8

Theoretical and Empirical Criticism of the Mean-Variance Rule

8.1. INTRODUCTION

We have seen in Chapter 4 that the Mean-Variance (M-V) rule can justifiably be employed under investment decision settings, in three distinct cases: 1) when the utility function is quadratic, 2) when distributions of return are normal in the face of risk aversion, and 3) when the variance of rates of return is not too large. The assumption under quadratic preferences is generally not accepted because this function has some well-known drawbacks, which have been discussed in detail in Chapter 4. Employing the M-V rule as an approximation to expected utility, although generally providing an excellent approximation, may raise some objections because the quality of the approximation depends on the data set involved: it may provide an excellent fit in one case and not such a good fit in another case. Therefore, the most compelling theoretical argument for the employment of the M-V rule is the case when the distributions of returns are normal in the face of risk aversion. Although the M-V rule is optimal for all distributions that belong to the elliptic family (discussed later in this chapter), we focus first on the normal distribution because most traditional empirical goodness-of-fit tests are for normality.

The crucial question raised in the normal case is whether it is reasonable to assume that price changes or returns are normally distributed. We devote a substantial portion of this chapter to the statistical validity of the normality assumption and the economic consequences to the investor who employs the M-V rule when the distributions of return significantly deviate from normality. We employ various approaches to analyze the normality assumption and the induced economic loss when distributions are not normal, but investors make investment decisions "as if" the distributions are normal. Of course, the closer the empirical distribution to the normal distribution, the smaller the expected loss induced by the employment of the M-V rule.

In this chapter, we first investigate theoretically whether the normal distribution follows when we assume that stock price changes follow a pattern that is similar to a cumulative series of random numbers, a process well known as a *random walk*. We suggest some rationale for the random-walk process and compare the normal distribution, which follows one possible price-generating process, to the Paretian distribution, which follows another possible price-generating process. We then analyze the similarities and differences of these two theoretical distributions.

Second, we shift to purely statistical testing procedures, aiming to test the validity of the normality hypothesis with empirical data on rates of return, covering various assets and various time periods. We do not confine ourselves to the empirical test of the normal distribution: we also examine empirically whether there is another theoretical distribution that fits the empirical data better than the normal distribution. Having some empirical distributions of return, we try to fit the best theoretical distribution to each of the existing empirical data sets. The commonly employed procedure is to assume some theoretical distribution (e.g., normal distribution, log-normal distribution) and use some standard statistical test to check whether the null hypothesis asserting that the empirical observations are drawn from the theoretical distribution under consideration is rejected.

The empirical tests may reveal various results, which may help us to divide all resulting cases into two groups: 1) cases where assuming normality (or assuming the distribution is elliptic) is reasonable, and 2) cases where doing so can be misleading. For example, it is possible that for rates of return corresponding to relatively short investment horizons (e.g., one week, one month), the normal distribution cannot be rejected, but for relatively long horizon rates of return (e.g., investment holding period of one year or longer), the normal distribution hypothesis is rejected. Similarly, we may find that the normality hypothesis regarding the distributions of the rates of return on individual securities is rejected, whereas the normality hypothesis regarding distributions corresponding to portfolios of assets (e.g., mutual funds) is not rejected. The implication of such possible results would be that the M-V can be safely employed in some cases but not in all cases.

Finally, we ask the following question, which is practically oriented: What is the financial loss that results from the employment of the M-V rule in cases where the null hypothesis asserting that the distributions of rate of return are normal is rejected? One can measure this loss by several methods. For example, one can establish some index that measures the expected utility loss induced by making investment choices by the M-V rule, when the distributions are actually not normal. Another method that provides some indication of the economic loss, as we have seen in Chapter 4, is by measuring the correlation of the ranking of the various risky assets by expected utility and by the M-V rule, knowing that the M-V rule provides only an approximation to the precise expected utility. With this approach, if the correlation is +1, there is no loss. However, it is hard to evaluate the economic loss if the correlation is less than perfect. We concluded in Chapter 4 that the higher the correlation between the ranking of the prospect by expected utility and the ranking by the M-V rule, the better the M-V approximation. Yet, by this approach, having a correlation of say, 0.95, does not provide an estimate of the potential economic loss as a result of the employment of the M-V rule in cases where the distributions of rates of return are not normal.

In this chapter, we discuss another approach to evaluate the economic consequences of the normality assumption: we measure the financial loss involved when one employs the M-V rule when the distributions are actually not normal. To be more specific, suppose that one statistically rejects the normality hypothesis. Then we suggest the following procedure to measure the financial loss when the M-V rule is employed in such a case: For a given empirical distribution of rates of return on various individual assets (e.g., stocks), we first find the optimal diversified portfolio, which maximizes the expected utility. Having this portfolio, we measure the expected utility corresponding to the selected portfolio. Having the optimal selected portfolio and the corresponding expected utility, we can calculate the certainty equivalent of this portfolio. Suppose that the certainty equivalent is, say, $10,000. In the second step, we select the best portfolio by the M-V rule (the method for selecting the M-V rule is explained in detail to follow), and we calculate the expected utility corresponding to this portfolio. Using the same utility function as before, we calculate the certainty equivalent of this M-V portfolio. Suppose the certainty equivalent is, say, $9,995. Then we assert that loss resulting from the employment of the M-V rule, when normality is rejected, is $5. Of course, to get some meaningful conclusion, one needs to repeat this procedure for various most commonly employed preferences as well as for various sets of data. We expect that the larger the deviation from normality, the larger the financial loss would be. However, it may be that the normality is statistically rejected yet the economic loss is negligible, say, $2 per $10,000 of investment. In such a case, we can conclude that although normality is statistically rejected, the M-V rule can be practically employed. Finally, when the distribution is precisely normal, the financial loss is, by definition, equal to zero.

Although most of this chapter is devoted to the statistical validity of the normal distribution and to the induced economic loss involved when one uses the M-V rule when normality does not prevail, we also devote a section to some objections to the M-V rule, even in the case where normality precisely prevails. Thus, even if the financial loss is zero, there is some objection to the employment of the M-V rule in certain cases. Accounting for these rather intuitive objections to the M-V rule, we show that even if these objections are accepted, the M-V rule is still intact, and although some portion of the M-V efficient set may be considered inefficient, the M-V rule and the Capital Asset Pricing Model (CAPM) can still be safely employed.

8.2. DISTRIBUTION OF RETURNS: THEORETICAL APPROACH

There are two basic approaches to analyze the shape of the distribution of returns on risky assets. The first one is theoretical and the other one, which is a more prominent one, is empirical. This section is devoted to the theoretical approach, and the next section is devoted to the empirical approach.

By the theoretical approach, one makes some assumptions on the price-generating process and studies mathematically the implied theoretical distribution of returns. The common assumption made in deriving the distribution of returns is that the future path of the price level of the stock (and, for that matter, of any other asset) behaves like a path of a series of cumulated random numbers – hence the term *random-walk theory*. If, indeed, the random-walk theory describes well the price path of a security, we have the followings implications:

1. The series of past price changes have no memory and hence cannot be used to predict future prices. This is similar to the observed results of tossing a fair coin: the series of past results are of no value in predicting the result of the next toss.
2. Investment strategies that are commonly employed by chartists and are based on past price changes have no economic value, exactly as the series of random numbers cannot be used to predict the result of the next draw from the random number table.
3. If price changes follow random walk, we say that successive price changes are identical, independently distributed random variables, commonly denoted by *i.i.d.*

Although the random-walk hypothesis can be tested empirically, it is interesting to spell out the economic and statistical reasoning for such a model of price-changes behavior. As early as 1900, Bachelier,[1] and later on some other researchers, suggested some rationale for the random-walk model. The explanation is as follows: The price of an asset is affected by new information flowing into the market, as well as by noise regarding the true value of the asset. The noise may include psychological and other factors that vary from one individual investor to another. Both the new economic information and the noise flowing into the market affect the demand and supply for the asset in a random way. If the new successive bits of information flowing into the market are independent over time and the noise is also independent – and

[1] See L. J. B. A. Bachelier, *Le Jeu, la chance, et le hazard*, E. Flammarion, Paris, 1914, chaps. xviii–xix.

hence random – then the successive price changes that are determined by the new information and the noise arriving to the market will also be independent over time.[2]

By the central-limit theorem, a sum of identically and independent random variables, each with the same mean and variance, at the limit (when the number of random variables is very large) is distributed normally as long as both the mean and the variance of the random variables are finite. When the variance is infinite, the sum has Paretian characteristics.

Bachelier suggests that price changes that are given by[3]

$$\Delta P = P(t + T) - P(t), \qquad (8.1)$$

where $\Delta P =$ price change over time interval and $P(t + T)$ and $P(t) =$ asset price in time $(t + T)$ and t, respectively.

This price change is a result of many random and independent transactions taking place in the period under consideration. Because by assumption the variance is finite, by the central-limit theorem, the price change for any time interval is Gaussian, or normal.

In sum, normality is obtained under the assumption that during any given time interval (e.g., one day), the number of independent trans-actions is very large. In such a case, the price change over this given time interval is a sum of very large independent and identical random variables, implying by the central-limit theorem that the price changes follow the normal distribution as long as the variance is finite.

Although price change, as suggested by equation (8.1), leading to the normal distribution, nowadays is well known as the "Brownian motion," there is ample empirical evidence that the normal distribution does not appropriately describe changes in stock prices. This dis-crepancy between the normal distribution suggested by Bachelier and

---

[2] The psychological factors may be not random and, hence, may induce a short-term deviation from normality. However, the timing of the psychological factor effect may be random. For example, major aviation crashes create a bad mood and a negative sentiment, affecting the market far beyond the direct and indirect economic loss due to the crash. However, the timing of such crashes and, hence, their effect on the mar-ket, is random. For more details, see G. Kaplanski and H. Levy, "Sentiment and Stock Prices: The Case of Aviation Disasters," *Journal of Financial Economics*, 2009.

[3] See also M. F. M. Osborne, "Brownian Motion in the Stock Market," *Operation Research*, 1959.

empirical evidence has led Mandelbrot[4] to suggest another theoretical and a more general model to describe price changes of assets. His model is broad enough to cover the finite as well as the infinite variance cases. He suggests that the difference in the natural logarithm of stock prices is distributed normally. Namely,

$$L(t, T) = \log_e P(t + T) - \log_e P(t) \qquad (8.2)$$

is a random variable, which distributes normally for every selected time interval T. He further suggests that the distribution of returns is stable Paretian, allowing an infinite variance, when the normal distribution is a special case of this wide family of distributions. This Paretian distribution is defined by the log of its characteristic function as follows:

$$\log f(t) = \log E(e^{i\mu t} |t|^\alpha [1 + i\beta(t/|t|)w(t, \alpha)],$$

where $i = \sqrt{-1}$, μ is a random variable, and the value $w(t, \alpha)$ is given by

$$w(t, \alpha) = \tan \frac{\pi \alpha}{2} \text{ if } \alpha \neq 1, \quad \text{and} \quad \frac{2}{\pi} \log |t| \text{ if } \alpha = 1.$$

The Paretian distribution has four parameters: the location parameter, δ; the scale parameter, γ; the skewness parameter, β; and the characteristic exponent, α, which measures the height of the function in the extreme tails. When $\beta = 0$, the distribution is symmetric. The range of α is $0 < \alpha \leq 2$, and when $\alpha = 2$, the distribution is normal and, of course, symmetric, and the variance is finite (otherwise, the variance is infinite).

Thus, the crucial parameter is α, which measures the probability or the height of the distribution in the extreme tails and, in addition, indicates whether the distribution under consideration is normal. When $\alpha < 2$, a distribution with fatter extreme tails than those of the normal distribution is obtained (i.e., the Paretian distribution). Indeed, to test for normality, it is common to test whether this parameter is equal to 2. The distribution is called *stable* because as it is stable under additions. Namely, if one sums two Paretian random variables, the sum is also Paretian.

---

[4] B. Mandelbrot, "The Variation of Certain Speculative Prices," *Journal of Business*, 1963.

When $\alpha < 2$, theoretically, the M-V rule is invalid because the distribution is not normal, and the only question one should be worried about is concerning the magnitude of the economic loss incurred when the M-V rule is employed. However, we stress that when $\alpha = 2$, the distribution of the log change of price is normal, and it is justifiable to employ the M-V with *log returns* but not with *returns*. The reason is that by the preceding generating process, the log returns, and not the returns, distribute normally. Nonetheless, because expected utility is defined on wealth and not on log of wealth, theoretically, one cannot use the M-V rule even when $\alpha = 2$. Let us elaborate.

Using the process given by equation (8.2), we have for an investor who invests W_0 in the stock, a terminal wealth given by W_T, when the investment is for time interval T. Suppose that during this time interval, there are n independent transactions and each transaction induces a new price and, hence, produces a return corresponding to the previous period. Assume that these transactions are random and thus create returns that are *i.i.d.*, an assumption needed to apply the central-limit theorem. The terminal wealth of the investor would be

$$W_T = W_0 \left(\frac{P_1}{P_0} \frac{P_2}{P_1} \cdots\cdots\cdots \frac{P_n}{P_{n-1}} \right).$$

Taking the natural logarithm of the terminal value yields

$$\ln W_T = \ln W_0 + \sum\nolimits_{i=1}^n \ln \frac{P_i}{P_{i-1}} = \ln W_0 + \sum\nolimits_{i=1}^n (\ln P_i - \ln P_{i-1}).$$

Because by assumption there are many transactions in each time interval (n is very large), the second term on the right-hand side is composed of a very large number of identical independent random variables. Therefore, by the central-limit theorem, the distribution of log W_T has a Paretian distribution; and if the parameter $\alpha = 2$, then $\ln W_T$ is normally distributed.

We claim here that even in the case of normality, there is no justification to employ the M-V rule because the utility function is defined on terminal wealth, not on the logarithm of the wealth. Thus, by the expected utility paradigm, the investor should maximize

$$EU(W_T) = \int U(W_T) f(W_T) d(W_T)$$

and not

$$EU(\ln W_T) = \int (U(\ln W_T) f(\ln W_T) d(\ln W_T).$$

Because in expected utility framework, the wealth, not the log wealth, is relevant for decision making, we should consider the implication of the suggested price-generating process given on the distribution of W_T, not on the distribution of $\ln W_T$.[5] Indeed, the distribution of the terminal wealth, W_T, is log normal rather than normal, with the following parameters:

$$EW_T = e^{\mu + 1/2\sigma^2}$$

$$VarW_T = e^{2\mu + \sigma^2}(e^{\sigma^2} - 1)$$

where μ and σ are the mean and standard deviation of $\ln W_T$. As can be seen from these formulas, the log normal distribution also depends only on the mean and variance, but these two parameters are dependent and the distribution is not symmetric. Also, the log normal distribution is not stable – namely, not invariant to additions – and, hence, a sum of two log-normal variables does not distribute log normally. All these differences between the normal and the log-normal distributions account for the fact that the M-V rule is not an optimal investment rule in the log-normal case. This finding is important because, as we shall see, for a relatively long investment horizon, the empirical distribution tends to fit the log-normal distribution well. Thus, we claim that in such situations, the M-V rule is not optimal.

The log-normal distribution emerging as a result of a very large number of independent transactions is not new and is also employed in other economic models. For example, in the option model of Black and Scholes[6] and in the continuous-time CAPM of Merton,[7] it is

---

[5] When the utility function is logarithmic, then one should maximize the expected utility of $\ln W_T$. However, even in this case, the value that should be maximized is given by $\int (\ln W_T) f(W_T) dW_T$. Note that $f(W_T)$ and note that $f(\ln W_T)$ determines the expected utility. It is worth noting that if the preference is logarithmic, by maximizing the geometric mean, one achieves expected utility maximization. For more details, see H. A. Latané, "Criteria for Choice among Risky Ventures," *Journal of Political Economy*, 1959; and H. M. Markowitz," Investment for the Long Run: New Evidence for an Old Rule," *Journal of Finance*, 1976.

[6] F. Black and M. Scholes, "The Pricing of Options and Corporate Liabilities," *Journal of Political Economy*, 1973.

[7] R. C. Merton, "Intertemporal Capital Asset Pricing Model," *Econometrica*, 1973.

assumed that a very large number of transactions – and, therefore, the terminal wealth, which is the product rather than the sum of all the rates of returns – is log-normally distributed. Thus, the implication of this result is that even with $\alpha = 2$, the distribution of the terminal wealth is not normal; hence, theoretically, one cannot employ the M-V rule even in this case.[8]

In summary, we have several possible theoretical distributions, all of which share one thing in common: it is assumed that there is a very large number of identical independent random transactions, and hence the central-limit theorem can be employed to derive the theoretical distribution. The three distributions that have been discussed in this section are the following:

a) The process suggested by Bachelier[9] given by equation (8.1), implying a normal distribution of returns. The normal distribution in this case is induced by the fact that prices rather than log prices are employed by Bachelier.

b) The process suggested by Mandelbrot suggesting that the relevant theoretical distribution is the Paretian distribution. In this model, changes of log prices rather than prices are employed. In this case, the normal distribution (of the log differences) is a special case when $\alpha = 2$.

c) When we have a Paretian distribution with $\alpha = 2$, the logarithm of terminal wealth is distributed normally. This implies that the terminal wealth, which is the relevant economic variable, is distributed log-normally.

For cases b) and c), the M-V rule is not optimal and may lead to an economic loss. In case a), as we already have shown, the M-V rule is optimal.

---

[8] The optimal rule for log-normal random variables is as follows: F dominates G for all risk averters if and only if

$$E_F(x) \geq E_G(x) \quad \text{and} \quad E_F(x)/\sigma_F(x) \leq E_G(x)/\sigma_G(x)$$

and there is at least one strict inequality, when x stands for return and not log-return. For more details, see H. Levy, "Stochastic Dominance Among Log-Normal Prospects," *International Economic Review*, 1973.

[9] See L. J. B. A. Bachelier, *Le Jeu, la chance, et le hazard*, E. Flammarion, Paris, 1914, chaps. xviii–xix.

Which theoretical distribution best fits the empirical rates of return? Normal? Log normal? Alternatively, it is possible that another distribution (e.g., the logistic distribution) fits the empirical data best. In the next section, we examine empirically which theoretical distribution best fits the empirical distribution. In particular, we examine whether the normal distribution hypothesis is rejected. Then, we examine the economic loss induced by the employment of the M-V rule with empirical rates of return, which are not normally distributed.

8.3. THE EMPIRICAL DISTRIBUTION OF RETURN: THE PARETIAN VERSUS THE NORMAL DISTRIBUTION

So far, we have discussed the possible theoretical distribution of asset prices. However, which distribution is most appropriate for investment decision making is an empirical rather than a theoretical question. In this section, we first report on the early statistical tests of the normality of returns, and then we conduct a "horse race" between various theoretical distributions, analyzing which distribution best fits the observed data. As we shall see, the best fit may change with the type of data and particularly with the holding-period returns. It may be, for example, that with monthly returns, one theoretical distribution best fits the data, and with annual rates of return another distribution best fits the data.

The empirical distribution of price changes usually differs considerably from the normal distribution. Although we frequently observe symmetrical empirical distributions, it is also generally too "peaked" relative to the sampling from the normal distribution. Figure 8.1 demonstrates the histogram of changes in the monthly price of wool during the years 1890–1937. From this histogram, which covers a very large number of observations, we conclude the following:

1. The empirical histogram, like the normal distribution, also seems to be "bell" shaped.
2. The height of the empirical histogram in the center is substantially higher than the height of the normal distribution in the center. Therefore, we say that the empirical distribution is too "peaked."

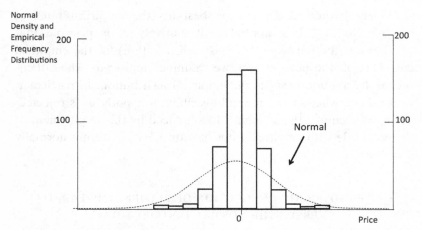

Figure 8.1. Monthly Price Difference of Wool, 1890–1937. *Source:* Gerhard Tintner, *The Variate Difference Method*, Bloomington, IN, 1940. Note that this is an approximated figure.

3. Although not seen in Figure 8.1, generally, the tails of the distribution of price changes are extraordinarily long, and it has been reported that the sample variance varies in an erratic way and, hence, does not seem to tend to any limit. This fact is consistent with the Paretian distribution, which does not have a finite variance, and is inconsistent with the normal distribution, which has a finite variance.

In an article that covers a wide spectrum of the price-generating process of thirty stocks that compose the Dow Johns Index, Fama[10] examined the distribution of returns. He finds empirical evidence supporting the hypothesis that the stock market may conform with the independence assumption of the random walk, which is needed for the central-limit theorem, which, in turn, is essential in the derivation of the theoretical distribution of stock-price changes. Like in previous studies,[11] Fama finds some degree of leptokurtosis (fat tails) in

[10] E. F. Fama, "The Behavior of Market Prices," *Journal of Business*, 1965.

[11] See S. S. Alexander, "Price Movements in Speculative Markets: Trends of Random Walks," *Industrial Management Review* II, 1961, pp. 7–26. P. H. Cootner, "Stock Prices: Random vs. Systematic Changes," *Industrial Management Review* III, 1962, pp. 25–45. M. G. Kendall, "The Analysis of Economic Time-Series," *Journal of the Royal Statistical Society* (Ser. A), XCVI, 1953, pp. 11–25. A. Moore, "A Statistical Analysis of Common Stock Process," unpublished Ph.D. dissertation, Graduate

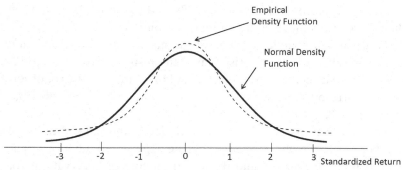

Figure 8.2. The Empirical Versus the Normal Distribution. *Source:* E. F. Fama, "The Behavior of Stock Market Prices," *Journal of Business*, 1965, pp. 34–105. Note that this figure is an approximation of Figure 1 (p. 49).

the distribution of each of the thirty individual stocks he studied. The existence of leptokurtosis means that there are too many observations in the neighborhood of the mean of the empirical distribution and too many observations out in the tails of the empirical distribution relative to the normal distribution. Thus, the empirical distributions of the thirty stocks studied by Fama are more peaked in the center and have longer tails compared with what would be predicted by normal distributions.

Fama provides detailed tables demonstrating the differences between the empirical and the normal distributions, and Figure 8.2, which is similar to the one presented in Fama's article, summarizes the data in the most transparent way.

The dashed curve represents the empirical distribution and the solid curve denotes the normal density function. Fama reports that within half a standard deviation of the mean, the curve of the empirical density is above the curve of the normal density function. In this range there are, on average, for the thirty stocks studied, about 8.4 percent more observations relative to what is expected by normal distribution. The empirical and the normal distributions cut twice. Of particular interest is the intersection taking place about 1.5 to 2 standard deviations from the mean. In these tails, the empirical distribution is above the normal distribution, implying that there are

School of Business, University of Chicago, 1962. B. Mandelbrot, "The Variation of Certain Speculative Prices," *Journal of Business*, 1963.

too many more observations in the tails of the empirical distribution than there are in those of the normal distribution.

To get a better understanding of the magnitude of the deviation from normality and the consistency of the results across the various stocks, Fama calculated the expected and the actual number of observations corresponding to various intervals of the tails of the distributions. Table 8.1 provides the results.

Table 8.1 reports, for each stock included in the sample, the total number of sample observations (N^*), the expected number of observations under normality, and the actual number of observations for various intervals corresponding to the left tail of the distribution. For example, for Allied Chemical, there are altogether 1,223 observations. For the range of three or more standard deviations left and right from the center ($>3S$), the expected number of observations under normality is 3.3; empirically, it has been found that there are sixteen observations in this range. The impressive results reported in this table is that beyond three standard deviations there should be, on average, by the normality assumption three or four observations per stock, whereas the actual number of observations is six to twenty-three, depending on the stock under consideration. The expected number of observations four standard deviations or more of the mean is about 0.10; but in all stocks except one, there is one or more observations in this range. An extreme difference characterizes AT&T: in this range, the expected number of observations for AT&T is 0.08, but the actual number of observations is nine – quite a big difference.

Comparing only the normal and the Paretian distributions, Figures 8.1, and 8.2, as well as Table 8.1, seem to provide strong evidence supporting the Paretian distribution because the Paretian distribution has "fat tails." It is possible that another distribution fits the data better. However, if one compares only these two distributions, there is visual support to the Paretian distribution in the sense that empirically there are more observations in the center and the tails of the distribution relative to what is expected by the normal distribution. Of course, visual and intuitive support is insufficient, and one needs to conduct a statistical test to figure out if, indeed, the normal distribution is rejected.

Table 8.1. *Analysis of Extreme Tail Areas in Terms of Number of Observations Rather Than Relative Frequencies*

Stock	N*	Interval							
		>2 S		>3 S		>4 S		>5 S	
		Expected No.	Actual No.	Expected No.	Actual No.	Expected No.	Actual No.	Expected No.	Actual No.
Allied Chemical	1,223	55.5	55	3.3	16	0.08	4	0.0007	2
Alcoa	1,190	54.1	69	3.2	7	0.07	0	0.0007	0
American Can	1,219	55.5	62	3.3	19	0.08	6	0.0007	3
AT&T	1,219	55.5	51	3.3	17	0.08	9	0.0007	6
American Tobacco	1,283	58.4	69	3.5	20	0.08	7	0.0008	4
Anaconda	1,193	54.3	57	3.2	8	0.08	1	0.0007	0
Bethlehem Steel	1,200	54.6	62	3.2	15	0.08	4	0.0007	1
Chrysler	1,692	77.0	87	4.6	16	0.11	4	0.0010	1
Du Pont	1,243	56.6	66	3.4	8	0.08	3	0.0007	1
Eastman Kodak	1,238	56.3	66	3.3	13	0.08	2	0.0007	2
General Electric	1,693	77.0	97	4.6	22	0.11	5	0.0010	1
General Foods	1,408	64.1	75	3.8	22	0.09	3	0.0008	1
General Motors	1,446	65.8	62	3.9	13	0.09	6	0.0001	3
Goodyear	1,162	52.9	57	3.1	10	0.07	4	0.0007	2
International Harvester	1,200	54.6	63	3.2	15	0.08	4	0.0007	1
International Nickel	1,243	56.5	73	3.4	16	0.08	6	0.0007	0
International Paper	1,447	65.8	82	3.9	19	0.09	5	0.0009	0
Johns Manville	1,205	54.8	62	3.2	11	0.08	3	0.0007	1
Owens Illinois	1,237	56.3	66	3.3	20	0.08	3	0.0007	1

(continued)

Table 8.1 (continued)

Stock	N*	Interval							
		>2S		>3S		>4S		>5S	
		Expected No.	Actual No.	Expected No.	Actual No.	Expected No.	Actual No.	Expected No.	Actual No.
Procter & Gamble	1,447	65.8	90	3.9	20	0.09	6	0.0009	2
Sears	1,236	56.2	63	3.3	21	0.08	8	0.0007	5
Standard Oil (CA)	1,693	77.0	95	4.6	14	0.11	5	0.0010	1
Standard Oil (NJ)	1,156	52.5	51	3.1	12	0.07	3	0.0007	2
Swift & Co.	1,446	65.8	86	3.9	18	0.09	4	0.0009	0
Texaco	1,159	52.7	56	3.1	14	0.07	2	0.0007	0
Union Carbide	1,118	50.9	67	3.0	6	0.07	1	0.0007	0
United Aircraft	1,200	54.6	60	3.2	11	0.08	3	0.0007	1
U.S. Steel	1,200	54.6	59	3.2	8	0.08	1	0.0007	0
Westinghouse	1,448	65.9	72	3.9	14	0.09	3	0.0009	2
Woolworth	1,445	65.7	78	3.9	23	0.09	5	0.0009	2
Totals		1,787.4	2,058	105.8	448	2.51	120	0.0233	45

*Total sample size.

Source: E. F. Fama, "The Behavior of Stock Market Prices," Journal of Business, 1965, pp. 34–105.

One way to handle the deviations from normality is to treat some of the observations as "outliers." However, this approach is misleading for two reasons: First, there are too many outliers, which, by definition of the term, cannot be treated as outliers. Second, because this leptokurtosis appears in many empirical studies that cover various time periods and prices of various assets, it probably conforms with the price-generating process as suggested by Mandelbrot (or by similar distributions) and hence cannot be ignored or treated as outliers.

Fama conducted a statistical test aiming to examine whether the normal or the Paretian distribution fits the data better corresponding to the 30 Dow Jones stocks. He employed several methods to estimate the parameter α of the Paretian distribution. Recall that such a test is actually a test of normality of the log-returns, because if α is not significantly different from 2, the normality cannot be rejected. Fama summarizes the results of the various test as follows:

In sum, the results of section III and IV seem to indicate that the daily changes in log price of stocks of large mature companies follow stable Paretian distribution with characteristic exponent close to 2, but nevertheless less than 2. In other words, the Mandelbrot hypothesis seems to fit the data better than the Gaussian hypothesis. (Fama, 1965, p. 68)

8.4. A HORSE RACE BETWEEN VARIOUS RELEVANT DISTRIBUTIONS: THE CHARACTERISTICS OF THE VARIOUS DISTRIBUTIONS AND THE METHODOLOGY

Traditionally, the M-V rule is considered to be optimal when the distributions of returns are normal. However, Ross, Chamberlin, Owen and Rabinovitch, and Berk[12] have shown that the M-V rule is consistent with expected utility maximization for a family of distributions, where the normal distribution is one of the members of this family. For example, the M-V rule is optimal and the CAPM is intact for the

---

[12] See S. A. Ross, "Mutual Funds Separation in Financial Theory – The Separating Distributions," *Journal of Economic Theory*, 1978; R. Owen and R. Rabinovitch, "On the Class of Elliptical Distributions and their Applications to the Theory of Portfolio Choice," *Journal of Finance*, 1983; G. Chamberlain, "Characterization of the Distributions that Imply Mean-Variance Utility Functions," *Journal of Economic Theory*, 1983; and J. B. Berk, "Necessary Conditions for the CAPM," *Journal of Economic Theory*, 1997.

elliptical family of distributions, where the normal, logistic, and many other distributions, which fulfill some restrictions, belong to this family. Thus, normality is not necessary for employment of the M-V rule, and one can safely employ the M-V rule when selecting between random variables whose distribution is elliptic. We mention the logistic distribution because in many cases, as shown subsequently, it fits best the empirical data.

Studying the theoretical distribution that fits best the empirical rates of return is a popular research field with numerous articles published on this issue. As the various studies cover different sets of data and different time periods, it is not surprising that we have inconclusive results. The reason is that one theoretical distribution may fit the data best when daily rates of return are considered and another distribution fits the data best with, say, annual rates of return. We mention here a few of these studies, and then we provide comparative results where many distributions are considered with different sets of data.

As discussed in the previous section, Fama, who studied the distributions of the stocks included in the Dow Jones Index, concludes that the distributions are not normal. However, he does not study a wide class of distributions but rather focuses on the Paretian distribution, concluding that with the Paretian framework $\alpha < 2$, normality is rejected. Thus, if the Paretian distribution is accepted as the best-fit distribution, the implied result is that the second moment, the variance, is infinite.

Officer[13] concludes that the empirical evidence rejects normality as well as the Paretian distribution. Specifically, the empirical evidence indicates that the observed distributions, as shown before, have a higher peak and fatter tails than what is predicted by the normal distribution. However, the variance is finite, which is in contradiction to what is expected by the Paretian distribution.

About two decades after publication of the study of Officer, Gray and French[14] studied the daily returns on the S&P Index, covering the

---

[13] R. R. Officer, "The Distribution of Stock Return," *Journal of the American Statistical Association*, 1972.

[14] B. Gray and D. French, "Empirical Comparisons of Distributional Models for Stocks Index Returns," *Journal of Business*, 1990.

period 1979–1987. They examined the goodness of fit of several theoretical distributions: the normal, the logistic, the Student's t distribution, and the exponential distribution. With daily return on the S&P Index, the main conclusion is that the normal distribution is strongly rejected. The best fit is found to be with the exponential distribution. Several other distributions also provide a relatively good fit.

Zhou[15] also rejects the normality. He finds that assuming normality, the M-V efficiency of an index of stocks, which serves as a proxy to the market portfolio, is rejected. However, with an elliptical distribution, the M-V efficiency of this proxy cannot be rejected. Indeed, as we see herein, the logistic distribution has two important features: it belongs to the elliptical family of distributions (for which the M-V rule is optimal), and it best fits the empirical distributions in many cases. Thus, it is not surprising that the M-V efficiency of the market portfolio cannot be rejected with elliptical distributions (for more details regarding the logistic distribution, particularly its fit to empirical data, see the following).

So far, virtually all studies agree that the empirical distribution has fatter tails than the normal distribution has. However, some studies claim that the typical distribution is characterized also by a positive "skewness." Although one can prove mathematically that under *i.i.d.*, for a relatively long investment horizon, the distribution must be positively skewed (because the distribution tends to be log normal), Harvey and Siddique[16] show empirically that positive skewness exists in the market – a skewness that is an important factor in asset pricing. Harvey et al.[17] show that the skewed normal distribution best fits the weekly rates of return, where this distribution allows, on the one hand, having a positive skewness and, on the other hand, allows having fat tails, as has been found in most empirical studies.[18]

[15] G. Zhou, "Asset Pricing Under Alternative Distributions," *Journal of Finance*, 1993.
[16] C. R. Harvey and A. Siddique, "Conditional Skewness in Asset Pricing," *Journal of Finance*, 2000.
[17] C. R. Harvey, J. C. Liechty, M. Liechty, and P. Muller, "Portfolio Selection with High Moments," *Working Paper*, Duke University, 2002.
[18] Having relatively fat tails has a very important implication to risk management and value at risk calculation. For a very thorough analysis of this issue, see S. M. Focardi and F. J. Fabozzi, "Fat Tails, Scaling, and Stable Laws: A Critical Look at Modeling External Events in Financial Phenomena," *Journal of Risk Finance*, 2003.

Thus, the main conclusion from these studies is that normality is rejected in favor of a distribution that is more peaked and has heavier tails, but there is disagreement regarding the shape of the best-fit distribution and whether or not it has a positive skewness. The disagreement is not surprising because it is expected that different theoretical distributions will best fit different sets of data. In particular, two main factors should influence the best-fit distribution: (1) the assumed investment horizon, and (2) whether the asset under consideration is an individual stock or a portfolio of stocks (e.g., the S&P 500 or the D-J Index).

Levy and Duchin[19] conducted a comprehensive study in which the best theoretical fit to the empirical data is examined by a horse race of eleven distributions, most of them covered in the studies already mentioned. They report the best theoretical fit to various empirical distributions, where these distributions differ in the assumed investment horizon and correspond to individual stocks as well as to a portfolio of stocks. One set of data employed in their study corresponds to five portfolios with monthly rates of return covering the period 1926–2001. The five portfolios include common stocks, small stocks, long-term corporate bonds, long-term government bonds, and Treasury bills, as reported by Ibbotson Associates.[20] The other set of data corresponds to individual stocks: the empirical distributions of the thirty stocks composing the D-J Index are examined with daily, weekly, and monthly rates of return. Thus, the variety of assets and the variety of assumed investment horizons provide many cases; one distribution may best fit one set of data and another distribution may best fit another set of data. For example, if, say, the normal distribution best fits the distribution of daily rates of return and the log-normal distribution best fits the distribution of monthly rates of return, the normal distribution would be relevant for investors who revise their investment on a daily basis, whereas the log-normal distribution would be relevant for investors with a planned holding period of one month. Thus, the analysis of distributions with various assumed investment holding periods is of crucial practical importance.

[19] H. Levy and R. Duchin, "Asset Return Distribution and the Investment Horizon," *Journal of Portfolio Management*, 2004.

[20] Ibbotson Associates, *Stocks, Bonds, Bills, and Inflation: 2001 Yearbook*, Ibbotson Associates, Inc., Chicago, 2002.

Table 8.2. *The Eleven Distributions Covered in the Empirical Study*

Domain	
Normal	$-\infty \le x \le +\infty$
Beta	$0 \le x \le 1$
Exponential	$0 \le x \le +\infty$
Extreme Value	$-\infty \le x \le +\infty$
Gamma	$0 \le x \le +\infty$
Logistic	$-\infty \le x \le +\infty$
Lognormal	$0 \le x \le +\infty$
Student's t	$-\infty \le x \le +\infty$
Skewed Normal	$-\infty \le x \le +\infty$
Stable Paretian	The Stable Paretian distribution has 4 parameters that affect the domain and skewness
Weibull	$0 \le x \le +\infty$

Source: O. E. Bamdorff Nielsen, T. Mikosch, and S. I. Resnick, *Levy Process-Theory and Application*, Springer-Verlag, New York, 2001.

Table 8.2 provides the eleven distributions participating in the goodness-of-fit horse race and some properties of these distributions. Table 8.3 provides the domain of these distributions.

The eleven distributions are very different in their shape, particularly in their domain. Some distributions are defined only on the positive domain, whereas others are defined on both the negative as well as the positive domain. Therefore, in testing for goodness of fit, the distributions of returns are examined, namely, the distributions of $1 +$ rate of return.[21]

Before reporting the results, let us explain how the distribution of the best fit is selected and how the statistical significance tests have been conducted. For each empirical distribution and for each theoretical distribution, the Kolmogorov-Smirnov (K-S) value D is calculated, where

$$D = \underset{1 \le i \le N}{Max} \left| F(Y_i) - \frac{n_i}{N} \right| \qquad (8.3)$$

---

[21] In this chapter, we examine the whole empirical distributions of returns. However, some studies examine only the distributions of large fluctuations in returns. For example, it has been found that large fluctuations fit the Power Laws distributions well; see X. Gabaix, P. Goplkrishnan, and V. Plerou, "A Theory of Power-Law Distributions in Financial Market Fluctuations," *Nature*, 2003.

Table 8.3. *Theoretical Distribution Functions: Descriptions*

	Density Function	Parameters	Mean	Variance	Skewness
Normal	$f(x) = \dfrac{1}{\sqrt{2\pi}\sigma} e^{-\frac{1}{2}\left(\frac{x-\mu}{\sigma}\right)^2}$	μ Location σ scale $\sigma > 0$	μ	σ^2	0
Exponential	$f(x) = \dfrac{e^{-x/\beta}}{\beta}$	β scale $\beta > 0$	β	β^2	2
Extreme Value	$f(x) = \dfrac{1}{b}\left(\dfrac{1}{e^{\frac{x-a}{b}+\exp\frac{a-x}{b}}}\right)$	a Location b scale $b > 0$	$a + .577b$	$\dfrac{\pi^2 b^2}{6}$	1.139
Gamma	$f(x) = \dfrac{1}{\beta\Gamma(\alpha)}\left(\dfrac{x}{\beta}\right)^{\alpha-1} e^{-x/\beta}$	α Location β scale $\beta > 0$	$\beta\alpha$	$\beta^2\alpha$	$\dfrac{2}{\sqrt{\alpha}}$
Logistic	$f(x) = \dfrac{\sec h^2\left(\frac{1}{2}\cdot\frac{(x-a)}{S}\right)}{4S}$	α Location S scale $S > 1$	α	$\dfrac{\pi^2 S^2}{3}$	0
Log normal	$f(x) = \dfrac{1}{x\sqrt{2\pi}\sigma} e^{-\frac{1}{2}\left(\frac{\ln x - \mu}{\sigma}\right)^2}$	$\mu > 0\ \sigma > 0$	$e^{\mu+\frac{\sigma^2}{2}}$	$e^{2\mu}e^{\sigma^2}\left(e^{\sigma^2}-1\right)$	$(w+2)\sqrt{w-1}\ \ w=\sigma^2$

Source: H. Levy and R. Duchin, "Asset Return Distributions and the Investment Horizon," *Journal of Portfolio Management*, 2004, pp. 47–62.

where F is the cumulative distribution of the distribution under consideration; Y_i is the ith observation, when all the observations are ordered by increasing values; n_i is the number of observations in the sample with values less or equal to Y_i, where $1 \le i \le N$; and N is the number of observations in the empirical study. Thus, F is the theoretical cumulative distribution, and $\frac{n_i}{N}$ is the empirical cumulative distribution. Although there are several ways to measure the difference between the theoretical and the empirical distributions, Levy and Duchin rely on the statistic D: The smaller the distance D, the better the obtained fit, according to this criterion, between the theoretical and the empirical distribution.

For example, suppose we have an empirical distribution that consists of 100 observations and we wish to calculate the value D for the normal distribution. In the first step, we calculate the sample mean and variance and use these two values as estimates of the parameters of the normal distribution. Then, for each sample value, we use the normal distribution to calculate the theoretical cumulative probability up to this value, as well as the cumulative empirical probability (given by $\frac{n_i}{N}$), and the highest difference as measured at all point Y_i is denoted by D. If there is a perfect fit between the two distributions, the value D is equal to zero and, of course, the theoretical distribution under consideration cannot be rejected. If the sample value D is larger than some critical value, the theoretical distribution is rejected because there is a large and an unexplained difference between the two cumulative distributions.

8.5. SHORT INVESTMENT HORIZON AND THE LOGISTIC DISTRIBUTION

In the analysis that follows, we distinguish between an investment horizon up to one year and an investment horizon longer than one year. Such a distinction is important because there is ample evidence that the typical investment horizon is about one year, and it may be a little shorter than one year. The division to a horizon longer and shorter than one year is also important in the hindsight of the results: up to a one-year horizon, the logistic distribution, generally, is the dominant one; hence, a longer section is devoted to the analysis and the discussion of this distribution. We first present the results and then discuss the properties of the logistic distribution and its implication to the validity of the M-V analysis and the CAPM.

a) The Empirical Result for the Relatively Short Horizon

The results corresponding to the Dow Jones thirty stocks that compose the index are reported in Table 8.4. We calculate for each stock the value D, and in the table we report only the theoretical distributions that best fit the empirical distribution, namely, the theoretical distributions with the smallest value D.

In this table, one asterisk denotes that the theoretical distribution cannot be rejected at 1 percent significance level, two asterisks denote that the theoretical distribution cannot be rejected at 5 percent significance level, and three asterisks denote that the theoretical distribution cannot be rejected even at 10 percent significance level. Finally, no asterisk denotes that the theoretical distribution is rejected at a significant level less than 1 percent. Thus, the larger the number of asterisks, the better the fit of the theoretical distribution to the empirical distribution. For example, if a given distribution cannot be rejected at 10 percent significant level, it will not be rejected at any significant level less than 10 percent.

The amazing result reported in this table is the strong dominance of the logistic distribution. For daily returns, the logistic distribution is the best fit for twenty-six of the thirty stocks, as well as for the D-J Index (a portfolio of thirty stocks). For weekly returns, it is the best fit for all thirty stocks, as well as for the index. For monthly returns, it is the best fit for twenty-six of the thirty individual distributions, as well as for the index. With the monthly returns, the normal distribution is the best fit for only two stocks. With the daily and weekly returns, the normal distribution does not serve as the best fit for any of the distributions. Thus, these initial findings are not encouraging: The normal distribution, which is traditionally needed to derive the M-V analysis, does not fit the empirical data well; hence, the traditional theoretical argument for the M-V rule (and the CAPM) seemingly loses ground. As we shall see in the following, this is not the case because the M-V rule is also optimal for the logistic distribution; in addition, the M-V rule can be employed as an excellent approximation to expected utility with a negligible financial loss.

Table 8.4. *Theoretical Distribution According to K-S Test for
Dow Jones Stocks*

Ticker Symbol	Daily	Weekly	Monthly
3M	Logistic[*]	Logistic[**]	Logistic[***]
AA	Logistic	Logistic[**]	Logistic[***]
AXP	Logistic[***]	Logistic[*]	Logistic
BA	Logistic[***]	Logistic[***]	Logistic[***]
C	Logistic[**]	Logistic[***]	Logistic[***]
CAT	Logistic[*]	Logistic[***]	Logistic[***]
DD	Levy	Logistic[**]	Normal[***]
DIS	Logistic[*]	Logistic[***]	Logistic[***]
EK	Levy	Logistic[*]	Logistic[***]
GE	Logistic[**]	Logistic[***]	Logistic[***]
GM	Logistic[*]	Logistic[***]	Logistic[*]
HD	Logistic[***]	Logistic[***]	Normal[***]
HON	Logistic	Logistic[*]	Logistic[***]
HPQ	Logistic	Logistic[***]	Logistic[***]
IBM	Logistic[*]	Logistic[**]	Gamma[***]
INTC	Logistic[***]	Logistic[***]	Logistic[***]
IP	Logistic[**]	Logistic[***]	Logistic[***]
JNJ	Logistic[***]	Logistic[***]	Beta[***]
JPM	Logistic[*]	Logistic[***]	Logistic[*]
KO	Logistic[**]	Logistic	Logistic[***]
MCD	Logistic[*]	Logistic[***]	Beta[***]
MO	Logistic	Logistic[**]	Logistic[***]
MRK	Levy	Logistic[***]	Logistic[***]
MSFT	Logistic[**]	Logistic[***]	Logistic[***]
PG	Logistic[*]	Logistic[***]	Logistic[***]
SBC	Logistic[*]	Logistic[***]	Logistic[***]
T	Levy	Logistic	Logistic[***]
UTX	Logistic[***]	Logistic[*]	Lognormal[***]
WMT	Logistic[***]	Logistic[***]	Logistic
XDM	Logistic[***]	Logistic[***]	Logistic[***]
Industrial Index	Logistic[**]	Logistic[***]	Logistic[***]

[*],[**],[***] imply that the null hypothesis cannot be rejected at the 1%, 5%, and 10% levels. No asterisk means the result is rejected at 1%. Thus, the more asterisks, the better the goodness of fit. Treasury bill returns are given in real values instead of nominal values because they do not converge to any theoretical distribution when examined in nominal values.

The critical values of the Kolmogorov-Smirnov goodness of fit test for the Levy distribution are not available.

Source: H. Levy and R. Duchin, "Asset Return Distributions and the Investment Horizon," *Journal of Portfolio Management*, 2004, pp. 47–62.

Table 8.5. *Theoretical Distribution According to Kolmogorov-Smirnov Test for Ibbotson Data*

Month(s)	Common Stock	Small Stock	LT Corporate Bonds	LT Government Bonds	Treasury Bills
1	Logistic***	Logistic***	Logistic	Logistic	Logistic
2	Logistic***	Logistic***	Logistic	Logistic*	Logistic*
3	Logistic***	Logistic***	Logistic*	Logistic*	Logistic**
4	Logistic***	Logistic***	Logistic***	Logistic***	Logistic*
5	Logistic***	Logistic***	Logistic***	Logistic***	Logistic**
6	Logistic***	Logistic***	Logistic***	Logistic***	Logistic***
7	Logistic***	Logistic***	Logistic***	Logistic***	Logistic***
8	Logistic***	Logistic***	Logistic***	Logistic***	Logistic***
9	Logistic***	Logistic***	Logistic***	Extreme Value***	Logistic***
10	Beta***	Logistic***	Logistic***	Extreme Value***	Logistic***
11	Logistic***	Logistic***	Logistic***	Extreme Value***	Logistic***
12	Weibull***	Logistic***	Extreme Value***	Extreme Value***	Logistic***

*,**,*** imply that the null hypothesis cannot be rejected at the 1%, 5%, and 10% levels. No asterisk means the result is rejected at 1%. Thus, the more asterisks, the better the goodness of fit. Treasury bill returns are given in real values instead of nominal values because they do not converge to any theoretical distribution when examined in nominal values.
Source: H. Levy and R. Duchin, "Asset Return Distributions and the Investment Horizon," *Journal of Portfolio Management*, 2004, pp. 47–62.

Looking at the number of asterisks assigned to the logistic distribution, we see many cases of three asterisks, implying that the logistic distribution cannot be rejected at 10 percent, let alone in the more commonly employed significant levels of 5 or 1 percent. This phenomenon is particularly profound for monthly returns, where we have three asterisks in twenty-six of the thirty stocks, as well as for the index itself.

So far, we have reported on returns corresponding to relatively short investment horizons of less than one month. We turn now to report the goodness of fit for investment horizons of one month or longer. The data are taken from Ibbotson Associates corresponding to five portfolios of assets. Hence, in comparison to the previous data, we have two more dimensions to analyze: namely, longer investment horizons, and portfolios rather than individual assets. Table 8.5 reports the results.

The interesting result is that with portfolios, like with individual assets, for monthly rates of returns, the logistic distribution is the best fit for all five portfolios. Actually, up to the eight-month investment horizon, the logistic distribution dominates the other ten theoretical distributions for all five portfolios under consideration. For horizons larger than eight months, some other distribution better fits the data. However, the seemingly most discouraging result is that the normal distribution does not appear at all in Table 8.5.

As we see in Table 8.4, and even more intensively in Table 8.5, the best distributions that fit the results are not invariant to the assumed investment horizon. Therefore, the analysis of the validity of the M-V rule is also not invariant to the selected investment horizon. Furthermore, a few more questions arise:

- Can one test the CAPM and employ the M-V analysis for any arbitrary investment horizon?
- Do the various parameters needed for portfolio investment decisions, particularly the correlations, also vary with the assumed investment horizon? If the answer is positive, different optimal portfolios exist for various investment horizons.
- Does the best-fit distribution change with the assumed investment horizon?
- Is the M-V rule optimal for the logistic distribution, which fits best the data for relatively short investment horizons?
- Finally, if the investment horizon is a crucial factor, what is the typical investment horizon?

We address these questions in the next section.

b) The Horizon Effect on Various Parameters

First we explain what we mean by the term *investment horizon*. In all empirical tests, we generally employ the assets' return. Suppose we have detailed data covering a period of ten years, and we wish to employ M-V analysis to find the optimal portfolio. Should we employ the ten annual observations? Maybe we would be better off by employing 120 monthly observations or maybe many more weekly or daily observations. We emphasize that in all cases we use the same data set, but in each alternative, we divide the set into different subsets.

We will see in the following that most empirical results are not invariant to the assumed investment horizon. Thus, one cannot select the investment horizon arbitrarily, and it is therefore important to identify the typical investment horizon or the investment horizon of the specific investor with whom we are dealing. In particular, the theoretical distribution that fits the data best, constituting the subject of this chapter, may vary with the assumed investment horizon.

As shown in Table 8.5, despite the dominance of the logistic distribution, the goodness of fit varies with the assumed investment horizon. This phenomenon, which is enhanced even once we move to a longer horizon than one year (Table 8.7), is not surprising because the various parameters that determine the shape of the distribution – and are important to investment diversification – are not invariant to the employed investment horizon.

In particular, the results of the M-V investment optimization (i.e., finding the optimal portfolio composition) and testing for the CAPM validity are not invariant to the assumed investment period, well known as the *investment horizon*. Because the annual rate of return is a *product* of, say, the monthly returns rather than the *sum* of the twelve monthly rates of return, the variance and beta of each asset may be affected in a nonlinear manner by the length of the investment horizon. To the best of our knowledge, Tobin[22] was the first to compare the one-period and multiperiod M-V analysis. He shows the following nonlinear mathematical relationship:

$$1 + R_n = (1 + R)^n$$

$$1 + \mu_n = (1 + \mu)^n$$

$$\sigma_n^2 = [\sigma^2 + (1 + \mu)^2]^n - (1 + \mu)^{2n}.$$

Where the subscript n is added, we refer to n-period parameter; otherwise, it is the one-period parameter. As we can see, for example, the annual variance is not simply twelve times the monthly variance; rather, it changes in a complex way with the investment horizon, and the higher the mean, the higher the variance.

---

[22] J. Tobin, "The Theory of Portfolio Selection," in F. Y. Hahn and F. P. Berchling (editors), *The Theory of Interest Rates*, MacMillan, London, 1965.

Beta and other parameters that are important economic variables affecting the optimal investment decisions are also not invariant to the employed investment horizon. Levy,[23] Levhari and Levy,[24] and Handa, Kothari, and Wasley[25] show that the various parameters needed for investment portfolio analysis are very sensitive to the assumed investment horizon. The fact that the parameters are not invariant to the assumed investment horizon has been proved mathematically, even when returns are independent and identically distributed, and it is showed empirically, even when deviations from this assumption may take place. Table 8.6 illustrates the importance of the assumed investment horizon on beta.

As we can see, the changes in beta induced by changes in the assumed investment horizon are not random, but rather they are systematic. For example, the beta of aggressive stocks increases from 0.99 with daily rates of returns to 1.66 when calculated with annual rates of returns (see MV1 in Table 8.6). The opposite holds for defensive stocks: beta decreases from 0.90 with daily rates of return to 0.56 with annual rates of returns (see MV20 in Table 8.6). It is worth noting that the betas reported in this table are calculated for the same period. However, this period is sliced into different time intervals when calculating the returns, varying from daily to annual rates of returns.

Like beta changes in Table 8.6, the variance and the mean also change in some systematic manner with changes in the assumed investment horizon. Moreover, the correlations, which are so essential in determining the M-V efficient frontier, particularly the composition of the tangency portfolio (see Chapter 5), vary in some systematic manner with an increase in the investment horizon. Actually, Levy and Shwartz[26] have shown that when the investment horizon increases, all the correlations diminish, eventually approaching zero. This result is crucial to portfolio selection because diversification relies on these correlations. The findings corresponding to the

---

[23] H. Levy, "Portfolio Performance and the Investment Horizon," *Management Science*, 1972.

[24] D. Levhari and H. Levy, "The Capital Asset Pricing Model and the Investment Horizon," *Review of Economic and Statistics*, 1977.

[25] P. Handa, S. P. Kothari, and C. Wasley, "The Relation between the Return Interval and Betas: Implication for the Size Effect," *Journal of Financial Economics*, 1989.

[26] H. Levy and G. Schwarz, "Correlations and the Time Interval Over Which the Variables Are Measured," *Journal of Econometrics*, 1997.

Table 8.6. *Mean Portfolio Beta with Returns Measured over Different Horizons*

Portfolio	Year	Six Months	Four Months	Three Months	Two Months	Month	Week	Day
				Mean Portfolio Beta				
MV1	1.66	1.60	1.57	1.51	1.53	1.41	1.18	0.99
MV2	1.38	1.41	1.42	1.37	1.33	1.27	1.13	1.02
MV3	1.31	1.31	1.35	1.32	1.29	1.23	1.12	1.04
MV4	1.18	1.20	1.21	1.21	1.17	1.18	1.13	1.08
MV5	1.16	1.19	1.17	1.16	1.17	1.14	1.11	1.08
MV6	1.22	1.14	1.15	1.12	1.11	1.11	1.10	1.10
MV7	1.10	1.11	1.11	1.08	1.08	1.08	1.10	1.09
MV8	1.10	1.09	1.07	1.06	1.05	1.04	1.10	1.10
MV9	1.04	1.01	1.02	1.03	1.01	1.03	1.08	1.09
MV10	0.94	0.98	0.97	0.99	0.99	1.00	1.05	1.05
MV11	1.00	0.97	0.96	0.99	0.99	0.99	1.02	1.03
MV12	0.97	0.94	0.93	0.94	0.94	0.96	0.96	0.98
MV13	0.88	0.88	0.88	0.88	0.89	0.92	0.95	0.96
MV14	0.87	0.87	0.88	0.88	0.88	0.91	0.93	0.97
MV15	0.83	0.86	0.85	0.86	0.87	0.88	0.91	0.95
MV16	0.79	0.79	0.79	0.81	0.82	0.85	0.90	0.93
MV17	0.72	0.73	0.74	0.77	0.80	0.81	0.87	0.90
MV18	0.70	0.73	0.71	0.77	0.77	0.79	0.85	0.90
MV19	0.59	0.62	0.63	0.66	0.68	0.71	0.79	0.86
MV20	0.56	0.58	0.58	0.61	0.63	0.67	0.78	0.90

Source: This table is reproduced from Handa, Kothari, and Wasley (1989). The 20 portfolios are ranked by size. MV1 is the portfolio of smallest stocks, and MV20 is the portfolio of largest stocks. For each portfolio, β is measured for different horizons. Note that the small stock portfolio has the highest β, the large stock portfolio has the lowest β, and β decreases almost monotonically with size. As the investment horizon shortens, generally large βs decrease, small βs increase, and βs close to 1 remain almost unchanged.

correlations and the investment horizon are summarized in the following theorem.

Theorem 8.1: Let ρ_n be the correlation coefficient of X_n and Y_n.. As n approaches infinity, $lim\ \rho_n = 0$, except when $Y = kX$ for some positive k, in which case $\rho_n = 1$ for all n.

In this theorem, X_n and Y_n stand for the accumulated return for n periods, which, according to our previous definition, is given by $(1 + R)^n$.

What is the implication of these findings to goodness-of-fit tests? What is the implication to the investigation of whether normality prevails and, therefore, to the validity of the M-V rule and the CAPM? The clear implication emerging from Table 8.6, as well as from the preceding theoretical analysis showing the relationship between the one-period and the multiperiod parameters, is that the various parameters change with the assumed investment horizon. Hence, stating the relevant investment horizon is crucial for decision making.

The main message from the preceding statement is very clear: Because the return for any period is a product rather than the sum of the shorter intervals returns, this may affect all the parameters in a peculiar way. By the same token, the distribution of returns also changes with the assumed time interval. For example, if X_1 and X_2 stand for the return in periods 1 and 2, the return for the two periods is $X_1 X_2$. If the return on each period is normally distributed, the return corresponding to the two-period investment horizon is not normal anymore. Hence, theoretically and empirically, we expect the distribution to change with the assumed investment horizon. Therefore, there is no meaning to test for normality in general because one should rather test for normality or, for that matter, for any other distribution, for a given horizon; generally, there is no one distribution that best fits the returns for all possible investment horizons.

If, indeed, the results of the goodness-of-fit tests vary with the assumed investment horizon, the next question is: What is the relevant investment horizon? Unfortunately, here we can provide only a vague answer because the investment horizon varies across investors. Naes and Ødegaard[27] conduct detailed research on the holding period of all investors in the Oslo Stock Exchange during 1992–2003 and show that the median holding period is about one year. Figure 8.3 provides the distribution of the holding period as it emerges from their study.

Benartzi and Thaler[28] argue that inventors tend to evaluate their investments every ten to twelve months. Thus, the planned investment horizon is less than one year. Odean[29] shows that investors turn over on average 80 percent of their portfolio annually. Thus, the evidence

---

[27] R. Naes and B. A. Ødegaard, "Liquidity and Asset Pricing: Evidence on the Role of Investor Holding Period," *EFA Athens Meeting Paper*, 2009.

[28] S. Benartzi and R. Thaler, "Myopic Loss Aversion and Equity Risk Premium Puzzle," *The Quarterly Journal of Economics*, 1995.

[29] T. Odean, "Do Investors Trade Too Much?" *American Economic Review*, 1999.

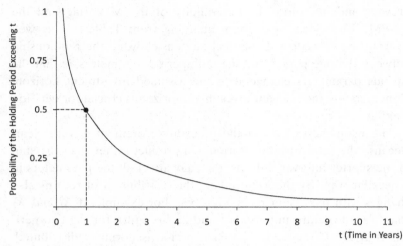

Figure 8.3. Distribution of the Holding Period. *Source:* R. Naes and B. A. Ødegaard, "Liquidity and Asset Pricing: Evidence in the Role of Investor Holding Period," EFA, 2009.

suggests that for a large segment of investors, the investment horizon is less than one year. Moreover, in recent years, the transaction costs have tended to decline. Because transaction costs are a barrier to portfolio turnover decisions, we speculate that the investment horizon has become even shorter than ten to twelve months in recent years.

From the preceding discussion, we conclude that when testing for normality and goodness of fit, it is expected to find different results for different assumed investment horizons. Indeed, we will show in the following section that when an investment horizon longer than one year is considered, drastically different results are obtained. Yet, because there is evidence that about 50 percent of the investors have an investment horizon of less than one year (and this horizon tends to decline in recent years), and because the logistic distribution is the dominating distribution in the goodness-of-fit test for horizons shorter than a year, we next turn to investigate the implication of these findings to the M-V analysis. Later, we investigate the best-fit distribution for those investors with a very long investment horizon.

c) The Logistic Distribution: The M-V Rule Is Optimal

The logistic distribution best fits the empirical distribution for a relatively short investment horizon. In addition, there is evidence that the

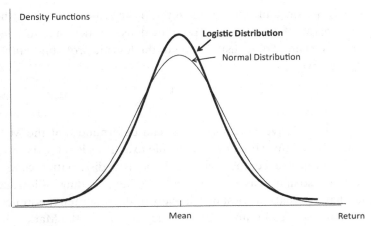

Figure 8.4. The Logistic and the Normal Distributions with an Equal Mean and Variance.

typical investment horizon is relatively short in the domain when the logistic distribution is superior.

Because the logistic distribution generally reveals the best approximation for an investment horizon of less than a year for all types of assets, it is worthwhile to analyze the logistic distribution in more detail, showing the difference between this distribution and the normal distribution, and analyzing whether the M-V rule is allowed to be employed when the distribution is logistic. Figure 8.4 demonstrates on one graph the logistic and the normal distribution where the two distributions have the same mean and the same variance. As can be seen, the logistic distribution is symmetrical like the normal distribution, it is more peaked than the normal distribution, and it has heavier tails. Thus, it resembles the stable Paretian distribution with one important distinction: the Paretian distribution does not have a finite variance, whereas the logistic distribution does have a finite variance.

Because the logistic distribution fits best the empirical distribution in most cases, it is natural to check whether the M-V rule is optimal when a logistic rather than a normal distribution is assumed. The logistic distribution, like the normal distribution, has two parameters: 1) the location parameter, the mean; and 2) the scale parameter, the variance. The logistic distribution has the following parameters:

Mean denoted by μ

Variance denoted by $\dfrac{\pi^2}{3}s^2$.

Because $\frac{\pi^2}{3}$ is constant, the parameter s is the scale parameter: the larger this parameter, the more spread the density function of this distribution. The cumulative distribution of the logistic probability function is given by

$$F(x) = \frac{1}{1 + e^{-\frac{(x-\mu)}{s}}}.$$

Using this cumulative distribution, we can determine that the M-V rule is an optimal investment decision rule exactly as it is for the normal distribution. Hence, the fact that the logistic distribution cannot be rejected in so many cases, as presented in the preceding tables, and the fact that it reveals the best fit relatively to the other ten theoretical distributions covered in this study provide support for the Markowitz M-V analysis and for the CAPM from rather a surprising angle. The optimality of the M-V rule for the logistic distributions is given in the following theorem.

Theorem 8.2: Suppose a risk-averse investor faces two logistic distributions, whose cumulative distributions are $F(x)$ and $G(x)$, respectively. Then F dominates G by the M-V rule if and only if the expected utility of F is larger than the expected utility of G for all risk-averse utility functions. Namely,

$$E_F(x) \geq E_G(x) \quad \text{and} \quad \sigma_F(x) \leq \sigma_G(x) \iff E_F U(x) \geq E_G U(x)$$

for all nondecreasing concave preferences. To avoid trivial cases, we require at least one strict inequality on both sides of this equation.

Proof: For simplicity of the proof, we assume that the mean of F is strictly larger than the mean of G and that the variance of F is strictly smaller than the variance of G. (A similar proof is intact when there is only one strict inequality.)

First note that two cumulative logistic distributions cross at most once, and the intersection point is given by the value x_0, which fulfills the following condition:

$$\frac{x_0 - \mu_1}{s_1} = \frac{x_0 - \mu_2}{s_2},$$

where (μ_1, s_1) and (μ_2, s_2) are the parameters of the two logistic distributions we compare. As with the normal distribution, the logistic

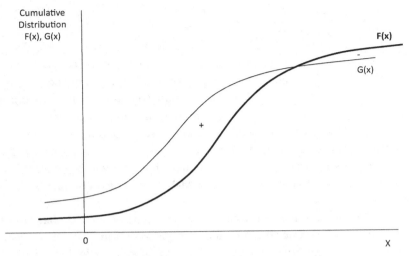

Figure 8.5. The Logistic Cumulative Distributions.

cumulative distribution with the higher variance has a thicker left tail, and because the distributions cross at most once, *F* and *G* are as illustrated in Figure 8.5.

We claim that the negative area enclosed between these two distributions is smaller, in absolute value, than the positive area enclosed between these two distributions (see Figure 8.5). The reason is that, as we saw in Chapter 3, the following holds for any two distributions under comparison and, hence, also holds for the two logistic distributions:

$$\mu_F - \mu_G = \int_{-\infty}^{+\infty} [G(x) - F(x)]dx \qquad (8.4)$$

(see equation (3.2) in Chapter 3). Because the two distributions cross only once, and by assumption $\mu_F > \mu_G$, then by equation (8.4), the (+) area given in Figure 8.5 is larger, in absolute value, than the (–) area, implying that for any value *x*, the following must hold:

$$\int_{-\infty}^{x} [G(t) - F(t)]dt \geq 0 \quad \text{for all } x. \qquad (8.5)$$

However, the last inequality implies that *F* dominates *G* by the Second-degree stochastic dominance (SSD; see Chapter 3); hence, every risk averter would prefer F over G. Therefore, $E_F U(x) \geq E_G U(x)$ for all risk-averse utility functions.

The other side of the proof is very similar: The two logistic distributions intersect at most once, and if every risk averter prefers F over G, we have SSD; hence, equation (8.5) holds. This equation implies that the mean of F is larger than (or equal to) the mean of G. In addition, equation (8.5) implies that left to the intersection point, F must be below G, and therefore F must have a smaller variance. Hence, the SSD dominance implies that the relationship of the two logistic distributions must be like those shown in Figure 8.5, implying that F dominates G by the M-V rule, which completes the proof.

Finally, two comments are called for: First, the proof is similar also when there is only one strict inequality in the M-V criterion. Hence, as in the normal case, the M-V rule is an optimal rule for logistic distributions in the face of risk aversion. Second, if the variances of the two logistic distributions are equal, as in the normal case, the two logistic distributions do not intersect, and the one with the higher mean is completely located below the one with the lower mean. In such a case, F dominates G by FSD, let alone by SSD.

In summary, we have three important results:

1. The logistic distribution is more peaked and has fatter tails compared with the normal distribution, conforming with empirical data.
2. The logistic distribution reveals the best fit to empirical distributions in most cases when the investment horizon is less than one year.
3. The M-V rule is an optimal decision rule for the logistic distribution.

These are very promising results because the logistic distribution, which fits the empirical data nicely, can substitute the normal distribution, which is empirically rejected. Thus, it seems that the M-V analysis and the CAPM can be employed with logistic distributions. However, there is one drawback of this distribution compared with the normal distribution: a sum of two logistic random variables does not distribute according to the logistic distribution. However, this sum has an elliptic distribution for which the M-V rule is optimal and the

CAPM holds. We elaborate on the logistic distribution later in this chapter.

8.6. GOODNESS OF FIT: INVESTMENT HORIZON LONGER THAN ONE YEAR

We have seen that the investment horizon has a profound effect on the various parameters as well as on the goodness-of-fit empirical tests and results. Although up to an investment horizon of one year it seems that the logistic distribution is the dominating one, we have a first indication that its dominance loses ground as we reach a one-year horizon (see the relatively longer horizons in Table 8.5). In this section, we investigate empirically the theoretical distribution with the best fit for a relatively long investment horizon, longer than one year.

Because there are not enough long periods to study the distribution of relatively long investment horizons (e.g., a four-year investment horizon), "bootstrapping" is employed when the investment horizon is lengthened. Ten thousand observations are drawn from the monthly rates of returns covering the period 1926–2001, taken from Ibbotson Associates. The observations are drawn separately from the distribution of five securities: 1) stocks, 2) small stocks, 3) long-term government bonds, 4) long-term corporate bonds, and 5) Treasury bills. Suppose we investigate the monthly return distribution. Then we draw one observation, write down the result, and return it to the population. Repeating this procedure ten thousand times, we obtained the monthly distribution. Suppose now that we wish to estimate the annual return distribution. In this case, we draw twelve observations without replacement and calculate the annual rate of return as follows: $(1 + R_{12}) = \pi_{i=1}^{12}(1 + R_i)$, where R_i is the monthly rate of return corresponding to month 1, and R_{12} is the first annual rate of return we write down. Then we return these twelve observations to the population and repeat this procedure ten thousand times to obtain the distribution corresponding to an annual investment horizon. By the same method, we estimate the distribution of returns corresponding to various investment horizons. Table 8.7 reports the results.

This table reveals, once again, that for a relatively short investment horizon, the logistic distribution is the dominating one. Yet the

Table 8.7. *Best Theoretical Distribution According to Kolmogorov-Smirnov for Simulation-Generated Data Based on Ibbotson Data*

Month(s)	Common Stock	Small Stock	LT Corporate Bonds	LT Government Bonds	Treasury Bills
1	Logistic	Logistic	Logistic	Logistic	Logistic
2	Logistic	Logistic	Logistic	Logistic	Logistic
3	Logistic**	Logistic	Logistic	Logistic**	Logistic
4	Logistic**	Logistic	Logistic	Logistic**	Logistic
5	Logistic***	Logistic	Logistic*	Logistic**	Logistic
6	Logistic***	Logistic	Logistic**	Gamma*	Gamma*
7	Logistic***	Logistic	Logistic**	Logistic*	Gamma***
8	Logistic**	Logistic	Logistic**	Gamma	Gamma***
9	Logistic	Lognormal	Logistic**	Gamma*	Gamma*
10	Logistic*	Lognormal	Gamma*	Logistic*	Gamma*
11	Logistic	Lognormal	Logistic*	Gamma*	Gamma***
12	Gamma*	Extreme Value	Gamma*	Gamma***	Gamma*
13	Gamma	Lognormal	Gamma*	Gamma***	Gamma*
14	Lognormal*	Lognormal*	Gamma***	Gamma***	Gamma***
15	Gamma	Extreme Value**	Gamma**	Gamma*	Gamma*
16	Gamma*	Extreme Value***	Gamma***	Gamma***	Gamma**
17	Gamma	Extreme Value**	Gamma***	Gamma***	Gamma*
18	Lognormal*	Extreme Value***	Gamma*	Gamma***	Gamma*
19	Gamma*	Extreme Value***	Gamma***	Gamma***	Gamma*
20	Lognormal*	Extreme Value**	Gamma**	Gamma***	Gamma*
21	Lognormal*	Extreme Value***	Gamma***	Gamma***	Gamma**
22	Gamma*	Extreme Value***	Gamma***	Gamma***	Gamma**
23	Lognormal	Lognormal*	Gamma**	Gamma*	Gamma*
24	Lognormal***	Extreme Value***	Gamma***	Gamma***	Gamma**
25	Lognormal*	Extreme Value***	Gamma***	Gamma**	Gamma**

26	Gamma***	Extreme Value***	Gamma**	Gamma*	Gamma*
27	Gamma*	Extreme Value***	Gamma**	Gamma**	Gamma*
28	Lognormal**	Extreme Value*	Gamma*	Gamma**	Gamma*
29	Gamma***	Lognormal***	Gamma***	Gamma***	Gamma**
30	Lognormal**	Lognormal*	Gamma***	Gamma*	Gamma**
31	Lognormal**	Lognormal***	Gamma**	Gamma***	Gamma**
32	Lognormal**	Lognormal***	Gamma***	Gamma***	Gamma*
33	Lognormal***	Lognormal***	Gamma***	Gamma***	Gamma*
34	Extreme Value***	Lognormal***	Gamma**	Gamma**	Gamma*
35	Lognormal***	Lognormal***	Gamma***	Gamma*	Gamma**
36	Lognormal***	Lognormal***	Gamma***	Gamma***	Gamma**
37	Extreme Value***	Lognormal***	Gamma***	Gamma**	Gamma**
38	Lognormal***	Lognormal***	Gamma***	Gamma***	Gamma*
39	Extreme Value***	Lognormal***	Gamma***	Gamma***	Gamma*
40	Extreme Value***	Lognormal***	Gamma***	Gamma***	Gamma*
41	Extreme Value***	Lognormal***	Gamma***	Gamma***	Gamma**
42	Extreme Value***	Lognormal***	Gamma***	Gamma***	Gamma*
43	Extreme Value***	Lognormal**	Gamma***	Gamma***	Gamma*
44	Extreme Value***	Lognormal***	Gamma***	Gamma***	Gamma*
45	Extreme Value***	Lognormal***	Gamma***	Gamma***	Gamma***
46	Extreme Value***	Lognormal***	Gamma***	Gamma***	Gamma***
47	Extreme Value***	Lognormal***	Gamma***	Gamma***	Gamma**
48	Extreme Value***	Lognormal***	Gamma***	Gamma***	Gamma**

*, **, *** imply that H_0 cannot be rejected at the 1%, 5%, and 10% levels. No asterisk means the result is rejected at 1%. Thus, the more asterisks, the better the goodness of fit.

Source: H. Levy and R. Duchin, "Asset Return Distributions and the Investment Horizon," *Journal of Portfolio Management*, 2004, pp. 47–62.

277

result is not as strong in favor of the logistic distribution as reported in Table 8.5. The main possible explanation for the difference in the strength of the logistic distribution in the two cases is that whereas in Table 8.7, by construction, the returns are independent over time, this is not the case in the result reported in Table 8.5. Hence, serial correlation may affect the intensity of the results. Yet, in practice, a complete independence probably does not exist; therefore, the strong results in favor of the logistic distribution for relatively short investment horizons, as reported in Table 8.5, are more relevant.

Another phenomenon is that the logistic distribution completely disappears from Table 8.7 for relatively long horizons. The "extreme," the "gamma," and the "log-normal" distributions fit the data best. There is something in common to all these three distributions: they are all positively skewed. Thus, even if the monthly distributions are symmetric, the multiperiod distributions tend to be positively skewed. This explains why the symmetrical distribution best fits short investment horizons, not the long investment horizons, as the empirical distributions are positively skewed. These results are not surprising because it can be proved theoretically that if the one-period distribution of returns is symmetric (e.g., normal), the multiperiod distribution of returns is not normal and actually is positively skewed. The longer the multiperiod horizon, the more skewness is built, and for an infinitely large horizon, the log-normal distribution, which is positively skewed, is obtained. Thus, positive skewness is generated with an increase in the investment horizon, even if the one-period distribution is symmetric (e.g., normal or logistic). Figure 8.6 demonstrates the goodness of fit of the empirical annual returns on the small stock portfolio to three theoretical distributions. The log-normal and the extreme distributions fit the empirical distribution very nicely, whereas the fit of the logistic distribution is relatively poor. Thus, there is almost a perfect fit between the theoretical and the positively skewed distribution and the empirical distribution, whereas the symmetrical distribution is not doing so well. Actually, any symmetrical distribution would not fit the data well. These results are even more extreme as we compare distributions of return corresponding to an investment horizon of more than one year.

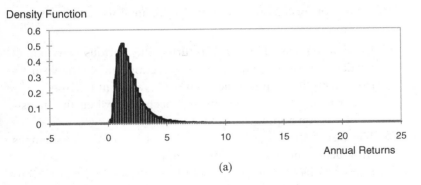

(a)

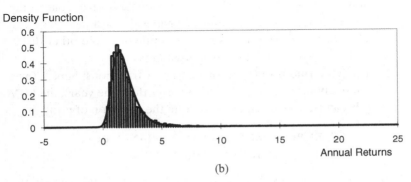

(b)

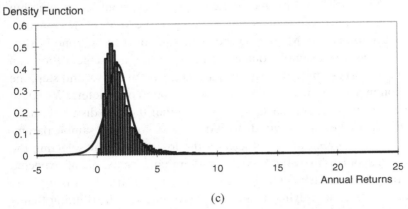

(c)

Figure 8.6. Ibbotson Small Stocks Simulated Annual Returns: Empirical Versus Theoretical PDFs. (a) Empirical versus log normal PDFs. (b) Empirical versus extreme value PDFs. (c) Empirical versus logistic PDFs.

The main conclusions from the preceding analysis can be summarized as follows:

1. Even if one assumes *i.i.d.* returns, the various parameters needed for investment portfolio selection and for measuring risk are not invariant to the assumed investment horizon.
2. In particular, all correlations approach zero when the investment horizon approaches infinity.
3. The distribution that best fits the empirical data also changes with the assumed investment horizon.
4. For a relatively short investment horizon, the logistic distribution reveals the best fit, whereas for a longer horizon, one of the positively skewed distributions provides the best fit.
5. The normal distribution is rejected in favor of the other distributions (log-normal, extreme, or gamma).
6. The M-V rule is optimal for logistic distributions; hence, for a relatively short horizon (a little shorter than one year), the M-V rule can be safely employed despite the rejection of normality.

8.7. EMPLOYING THE MEAN-VARIANCE RULE: THE ECONOMIC LOSS

Because the normal distribution is strongly rejected and because the logistic distribution fits nicely the empirical distribution in some but not in all cases, it is obvious that investing by the M-V rule may involve an economic loss. Measuring the economic loss can be done in various ways. For example, one can employ in the first stage a Bayesian analysis to estimate the various parameters.[30] In the second step, the economic loss is measured with these estimated parameters. We adopt here a different approach: it is assumed that the past distributions of return are the true *ex-ante* distributions; therefore, past sample parameters are correct, and we focus on the loss induced by selecting the optimal portfolio by the M-V rule rather than by maximizing expected utility. Thus, it is assumed that the empirical distribution is the true distribution; so, relying on any other (parametric) distribution that is different from the empirical distribution results in a loss. Of course, to be able to measure the economic loss, one needs to assume some utility function.

---

[30] S. Kandel and R. F. Stambaugh, "On the Predictability of Stock Returns: An Asset-Allocation Perspective," *Journal of Finance*, 1996.

We now demonstrate the magnitude of the economic loss when the constant relative risk aversion (CRRA) utility function of the following form is assumed:

$$U(W) = \frac{W^{1-\gamma}}{1-\gamma},$$

where the wealth $W > 0$ and the risk-aversion parameter $\gamma > 0$. The parameter γ is changed to reflect different degrees of risk aversion. Because other commonly employed preferences reveal very similar results, we focus here on the results corresponding to this preference.

Suppose one faces n assets and for each asset there are T rates of return (e.g., $n = 30$) for the thirty stocks composing the D-J Index, and $T = 10$, reflecting the fact that for each assets we have, say, ten annual rates of returns. Then we employ the following stages to measure the economic loss:

1. Find the optimal diversification by the following maximization:

$$\max_{\mathbf{x}} \frac{1}{T} \sum_{i=1}^{T} U\left[\sum_{i=1}^{n} x_i R_{ti} \right] \qquad (8.6)$$

In the square brackets, we have the return on a portfolio when a proportion x_i is invested in security i, and U is the utility corresponding to this portfolio. Thus, for each year, we have the utility of the return of this hypothetical portfolio. Summing the utility of all years and dividing by T, we derive the average utility. If each year is assigned an equal probability, we obtain the expected utility. By the maximization process, we find the optimal investment proportions, namely, the portfolio that maximizes the expected utility when the empirical distributions are assumed to be the true distributions. Of course, this maximization can be repeated for various utility functions and for various sets of data.

2. Having the expected utility calculated by stage 1, we can calculate the certainty equivalent $W_1^\bullet$ by solving the following equation:[31]

$$U(W_1^\bullet) = EU(R_P(1)), \qquad (8.7)$$

---

[31] For other results corresponding to the loss induced by the employment of the M-V rule, see B. R. D. Tew and C. Witt, "The Opportunity Cost of a Mean-Variance Efficient Choice," *Financial Review*, 1991; and Y. Simman, "The Opportunity Cost of Mean-Variance Investment Strategies," *Management Science*, 1993.

where, R_P (1) is the optimal portfolio obtained by the maximization given by equation (8.6). For example, if one invests, say, $10,000 in a given portfolio, the investor is indifferent regarding a choice between getting the uncertain return of the optimum portfolio or a certain sum, say, $W^\bullet = \$10,500$. Note that 1 denotes that this portfolio and corresponding certainty equivalent are calculated for distribution 1, the true distribution.

3. Using the same empirical data as given in the preceding, first estimate the various parameters: for example, the means, variances, and covariances. Assume that there is some parametric distribution with these parameter estimates. For example, assume a multivariate normal distribution. Then draw a random sample from the multivariate normal distribution with the estimated parameters.[32] Thus, if we have a multivariate normal distribution with, say, $n = 30$, we draw from the multivariate normal distribution n vectors of rates of return, where each vector contains T numbers. Employ the maximization given by equation (8.6) to these n vectors to find the optimal investment proportions under the assumption of a multivariate normal distribution. Obviously, relying on a single sample drawn from a multivariate distribution is noisy; therefore, we suggest repeating this procedure M times and obtaining the average optimal investment proportion in each asset, when the average is calculated across the M samples from the multivariate normal distribution.

4. Using the optimal (average) investment proportions obtained with the M samples, we calculate the expected utility of this portfolio and the certainty equivalent exactly as done before. By this, we have the following equation:

$$U(W_2^\bullet) = EU(R_P(2)).$$

The number 2 indicates that this is the portfolio obtained by the second method, namely, by assuming some parametric distribution. Portfolios 1 and 2 are obtained by two different methods: Portfolio 1 is

---

[32] For some distributions, an analytical solution is possible, whereas for others it is very complicated. To have a uniform treatment for all distributions, we employ the same sampling method for all parametric distributions under consideration.

obtained by employing the empirical distribution, which by assumption is the true distribution, and portfolio 2 is obtained by assuming that the distribution is parametric (i.e., a multivariate normal distribution). Both the parametric and the empirical distributions have the same parameters, which are the sample parameters. Because in deriving portfolio 2, we assume some parametric distribution that deviates from the empirical distribution, which is assumed to be the true distribution, we expect to incur some loss. Indeed, it is suggested to measure the monetary loss resulting from this assumption by the difference in the two certainty equivalents:

$$\text{Monetary Loss} = W_1^* - W_2^* \geq 0. \qquad (8.8)$$

The closer the parametric distribution to the empirical distribution, the smaller the expected loss.

We report in the following the goodness of fit to normality and the economic loss, given by equation (8.8) of sixteen assets, when these assets are the indexes of the stock markets of sixteen countries (see Table 8.8 for the list of countries included). The period covered is 1980–2004, when the density function of monthly rates of returns are considered. Comparing the empirical density to the normal density, most, albeit not all, empirical distributions are more peaked than the normal distribution and have heavier tails. The "peakedness" is most prominent in two empirical distributions: that of the Canadian Stock Market Index and that of the Singapore Market Index. This evidence of peakedness and fatter tails conforms to the previous reported deviations of empirical distributions from normality.

Table 8.8 presents the statistical significance tests, where the null hypothesis is that the empirical distributions are not significantly different from normal. Several statistical tests were conducted on each individual index as well as on the multivariate distribution. For example, with the Kolmogorov-Smirnov test, in nine of the sixteen tests, the normality is rejected at a 5 percent significance level (see Table 8.8). When the null hypothesis is that the sixteen assets are distributed multivariate normal, the null is rejected even at 0.1 percent; namely, the joint empirical distribution is significantly different from the multivariate normal distribution.

Table 8.9 reports the economic loss when normality is assumed, as calculated by equation (8.8). Here it is assumed that once the investor

Table 8.8. *Normality Goodness-of-Fit Tests*

Asset	Kolmogorov-Smirnov D 0.069	Pr > D	Anderson-Darling A-sq Statistic	Pr > Pr-sq
U.S. Market Index	0.069	<0.010	1.288	<0.005
U.K. Market Index	0.041	>0.150	0.834	0.033
Australia Market Index	0.056	0.021	1.276	<0.005
Belgium Market Index	0.050	0.069	1.586	<0.005
Canada Market Index	0.069	<0.010	1.832	<0.005
France Market Index	0.049	0.079	1.241	<0.005
Germany Market Index	0.057	0.018	1.590	<0.005
Hong Kong Market Index	0.066	<0.010	1.571	<0.005
Italy Market Index	0.046	0.117	0.554	0.156
Japan Market Index	0.054	0.034	0.919	0.021
Netherlands Market Index	0.071	<0.010	1.220	<0.005
Norway Market Index	0.034	>0.150	0.513	0.201
Singapore Market Index	0.088	<0.010	3.358	<0.005
Spain Market Index	0.047	0.106	1.000	0.013
Sweden Market Index	0.031	>0.150	0.364	>0.250
Switzerland Market Index	0.053	0.036	0.796	0.041

Note: Two normality univariate goodness-of-fit statistics for monthly rates of returns (%) on the 16 risky assets in the empirical analysis: Kolmogorov-Smirnov and Anderson-Darling. For each statistic, the value and the corresponding p-value are reported. Note that when the probability is less than the predetermined significance level, the normal distribution is rejected. Dates are reported by Fama and French and cover the period between January 1980 and December 2004.

maximizes expected utility when the joint empirical distribution of the seventeen assets is the correct distribution (note that the Treasury bills index is added to the sixteen stock indexes). The table reports the loss corresponding to utility functions with various degrees of risk aversion. For example, with $\gamma = 2$, an optimal diversification provides per $10,000 investment, a certainty equivalent of $10,119.238, whereas when one assumes a multivariate normal distribution in seeking the optimal diversification, the certainty equivalent is a little lower, $10,113.415. Looking at the various cases, the loss is only a number of dollars, varying in the range of $5.460 to $5.823.

The astonishing result is that despite the strong rejection of the multivariate normal distribution, the loss is negligible: less than $6! Thus, we have a large discrepancy between the statistician's and the economists' conclusions: The statistician strongly rejects normality, whereas the economist would probably say, no big deal, you can

All 16 Market Indexes

Security	$U(X) = X^{1-y}/(1-y)$, $y = 2$		$U(X) = X^{1-y}/(1-y)$, $y = 3$		$U(X) = X^{1-y}/(1-y)$, $y = 6$		$U(X) = X^{1-y}/(1-y)$, $y = 9$	
	Empirical	Normal	Empirical	Normal	Empirical	Normal	Empirical	Normal
T-bill	0.00%	0.00%	0.00%	1.48%	38.28%	22.50%	58.74%	40.97%
US	0.00%	4.41%	4.64%	7.13%	10.10%	11.53%	7.34%	15.36%
UK	0.00%	2.77%	0.00%	5.56%	0.00%	3.43%	0.00%	1.25%
Aus	0.00%	3.58%	0.00%	5.52%	0.00%	3.20%	0.00%	3.92%
Bel	29.31%	15.86%	33.09%	15.46%	21.48%	14.56%	14.32%	10.44%
Can	0.00%	0.06%	0.00%	44.00%	0.00%	0.43%	0.00%	0.26%
Fra	0.00%	1.19%	0.00%	1.00%	0.00%	0.14%	0.00%	0.78%
Ger	0.00%	0.37%	0.00%	8.00%	0.00%	0.02%	0.00%	0.07%
HK	11.27%	14.81%	7.15%	9.76%	4.35%	6.89%	6.68%	3.98%
Ita	0.00%	10.05%	0.00%	7.56%	1.17%	3.81%	0.59%	2.20%
Jap	0.00%	2.03%	0.00%	1.41%	0.00%	1.84%	0.00%	0.58%
Nth	0.00%	3.53%	3.50%	6.27%	1.14%	6.54%	0.00%	2.05%
Nor	0.00%	2.02%	0.00%	1.56%	0.00%	1.49%	0.00%	0.63%
Sin	0.00%	1.49%	0.00%	1.04%	0.00%	1.37%	0.00%	0.33%
Spa	17.81%	13.61%	17.86%	11.77%	8.89%	10.71%	5.24%	5.59%
Swe	41.61%	23.83%	33.77%	22.60%	14.60%	10.14%	10.08%	10.30%
Swi	0.00%	0.37%	0.00%	0.64%	0.00%	1.42%	0.00%	1.29%
Expected Utility	-0.98822	-0.98879	-0.48967	-0.49023	-0.19237	-0.19290	-0.11836	-0.11887
Certainty Equivalent*	10,119.238	10,113,415.000	10,104,899.000	10,099.116	10,078.106	10,072.580	10,068.478	10,063.015

*The certainty equivalent is per $10,000 investment.

Note: The empirical distribution of returns and the normal distribution are employed to solve for the optimal portfolio strategy that maximizes expected utility from terminal wealth given the assumed distribution of returns. The investable universe consists of the U.S. market index as the market indexes of 15 other countries and the risk-free security (U.S. Treasury bill, or T-bill) and cover the period between January 1980 and December 2004. The optimal portfolio weights for each distribution, as well as the resulting expected utility and the certainty equivalent, are reported. The portfolio weight corresponding to each asset is the optimal proportion of wealth (%) invested in that asset.

continue to assume normality and employ the M-V rule because the induced loss is less than \$6 per \$10,000 of invested capital.

So far, it is assumed that the investor diversifies in seventeen assets, particularly in sixteen international markets. Nonetheless, many investors invest only in one market, so it is interesting to measure the loss when investors diversify between one risky market and the riskless asset, namely Treasury bills. Table 8.10 provides the economic loss in such a case.

The reported figures in this table refer to diversification between Treasury bills and the U.S market index. As can be seen, when normality is assumed, the loss is merely about \$2 per \$10,000 when $\gamma = 2$, and this loss is close to zero when $\gamma = 9$. Even better results are obtained with the logistic distribution assumption. It is close to zero with $\gamma = 9$ and a fraction of \$1 for $\gamma = 2$. Because the M-V is also optimal for the logistic distribution, one can safely employ the M-V rule: the economic loss is negligible and in some cases even close to zero, despite the strong rejection of the parametric distribution.

8.8. NORMAL DISTRIBUTION: IS MARKOWITZ'S EFFICIENT SET TOO BIG?

We have proved that when the distributions are normal, the M-V rule is optimal; hence, it can be safely employed. In the previous sections, we examine whether the distributions are normal, and we measure the economic loss when deviations from the normal distribution take place. However, the M-V rule is criticized, intuitively rather than theoretically, even in the case of a normal distribution, casting doubt on the assertion that the M-V rule is optimal in the case of normal distributions. In the following, we discuss this criticism and reconcile this criticism with the assertion (and proof) that the M-V rule is optimal. We show that the difference between the two approaches regarding the size and content of the efficient set is not theoretical but practical: those who suggest that Markowitz's efficient set is too big simply claim that some preferences do not exist in practice and, hence, some segment of the M-V efficient set can be relegated to the inefficient set because in practice no investor will select a portfolio from the suggested relegated segment.

Table 8.10. *Horse Race Between Six Parametric Distributions, One Risky Asset, and One Riskless Asset*

Distribution	Market Proportion	T-bill Proportion	Expected Utility	Certainty Equivalent*
Panel A: $U(X) = X^{1-y}/(1-y)$, $y = 2$				
Empirical	100.00%	0.00%	-0.99091	10,091.732
Logistic	98.83%	1.17%	-0.99093	10,091.489
Lognormal	83.25%	16.75%	-0.99131	10,087.639
Normal	90.91%	9.09%	-0.99111	10,089.673
Skew Normal	93.37%	6.63%	-0.99105	10,090.269
Student's t	92.66%	7.34%	-0.99107	10,090.099
Skew-t	93.03%	6.97%	-0.99106	10,090.189
Panel B: $U(X) = X^{1-y}/(1-y)$, $y = 9$				
Empirical	33.01%	66.99%	-0.11919	10,059.648
Logistic	33.75%	66.25%	-0.11919	10,059.642
Lognormal	47.38%	52.62%	-0.11941	10,057.388
Normal	34.49%	65.61%	-0.11919	10,059.625
Skew Normal	32.75%	67.25%	-0.11919	10,059.647
Student's t	25.69%	74.31%	-0.11925	10,059.087
Skew-t	35.85%	64.15%	-0.11920	10,059.562

*The certainty equivalent is per $10,000 investment.

Note: The empirical distribution of returns, as well as the different parametric distributions, is employed to solve for the optimal portfolio strategy that maximizes expected utility from terminal wealth given the assumed distribution of returns. The investable universe consists of the U.S. market index and the risk-free security (U.S. Treasury bill) and covers the period between January 1980 and December 2004. The optimal portfolio weights for each distribution, as well as the resulting expected utility and the certainty equivalent, are reported. The portfolio weight corresponding to each asset is the optimal proportion of wealth (%) invested in that asset.

The intuitive objection to the M-V rule even in the normal case was first published by Baumol[33] and many years later, in a more general expected utility framework, by Leshno and Levy.[34] Because both raise a criticism that is similar in nature, we relate to both criticisms in this section.

Suppose the following ideal situation exists favoring the M-V: distributions are normal and risk-averse investors maximize expected utility. In this case, the M-V criterion is optimal. Even in this theoretically ideal case for the M-V rule, academics point to a drawback of the M-V analysis that, if valid, casts doubt on the M-V efficiency analysis and therefore casts doubt on the validity of the CAPM.

To show that the M-V rule may lead to a paradox, Baumol gives an example of a possible choice of one of two prospects, such as follows:

	Prospect *G*	Prospect *F*
Mean, μ	5	50
Standard Deviation, σ	1	2

It is obvious that the M-V rule cannot determine dominance between these two prospects; yet Baumol claims that all rational investors will choose prospect *F*, because even with the relatively very low return observed with investment *F*, and the relatively very large return observed in *G* (say, ten standard deviations to the left with prospect *F* and ten standard deviations to the right with prospect *G*, an event with close to zero probability), the investor will end up being better off by choosing *F*. Of course, there is no need for such an extreme example to show that the M-V efficient set may also contain portfolios that, for all practical purposes, are inefficient.

Thus, Baumol claims that some of the M-V efficient portfolios should be relegated to the inefficient set. In the preceding example, unlike Markowitz, Baumol would claim that prospect *G* is inefficient. However, following Baumol, if one adjusts the M-V rule to eliminate a portion or several portions of the M-V efficient set, there is a risk that the tangency portfolio will be eliminated, which results in some ambiguous implications to the validity of the CAPM.

[33] W. J. Baumol, "An Expected Gain Confidence Limit Criterion for Portfolio Selection," *Management Science*, 1963.

[34] M. Leshno and H. Levy, "Preferred by All and Preferred by Most Decision Makers: Almost Stochastic Dominance," *Management Science*, 2002.

Whereas Baumol's rule is based solely on intuition, Leshno and Levy (2002) suggest new rules, called almost stochastic dominance (ASD) and almost M-V (AMV), denoted by SD^* and $M\text{-}V^*$ rules, respectively. These rules avoid paradoxes like the one described already. However, recall that Baumol published his article before the CAPM was published; hence, he analyzed the implications relevant to the M-V efficient set. Leshno and Levy, who published their article in 2002, also analyzed the implications relevant to the CAPM. Moreover, regarding normal distributions, they show that there are cases where neither F nor G dominates the other, yet they suspect that in practice such dominance exists. To understand this more clearly, consider the following two normal distributions:

$$G \sim N(\mu, \sigma) = N(1, 1)$$
$$F \sim N(\mu, \sigma) = N(10, 2)$$

Although neither FSD nor M-V dominance exists, Leshno and Levy claim that after removing economically irrelevant preferences, FSD^* and $M\text{-}V^*$ dominance of F over G exists.

As Figure 8.7a plainly shows, there is no dominance between the two distributions F and G; yet, presumably, all "reasonable" investors will select Prospect F. Leshno and Levy claim that the SD rules are established for *all* possible *mathematical* preferences, whereas in practice, many of these preferences do not fit any realistic investor; hence, they are *economically* irrelevant. This concept introduces the contradiction between the mathematical decision rule (e.g., FSD) and investors' realistic choices. To overcome this difficulty of the SD rules, as well as the M-V rule, Leshno and Levy developed new rules that eliminate irrelevant preferences. These new rules reveal a preference for option F, in the preceding example, over option G, and this preference holds true for 100 percent of the investors, when some pathological preferences are eliminated.

Leshno and Levy analyze the FSD rule, whereas Baumol focuses on the M-V rule. However, if the distributions are normal, then the M-V and FSD rules coincide.[35] Hence, Leshno and Levy, like Baumol, eliminate a segment from the M-V efficient frontier, which may affect

---

[35] Actually, SSD and M-V coincide in the normal case. However, FSD and M-V coincide only in the case of two prospects with equal variance.

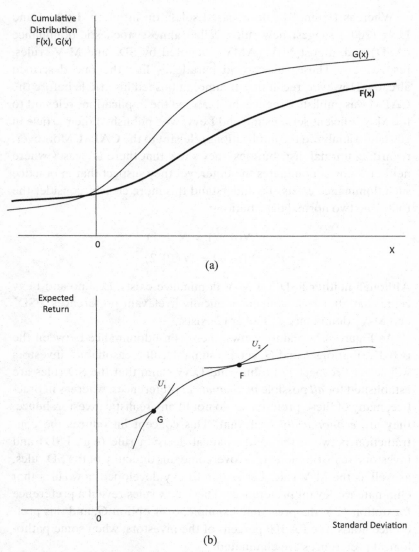

Figure 8.7. (a) No First-Degree Stochastic Dominance (FSD) and No Mean-Variance (M-V) Dominance by either F or G, but F Dominates G by FSD* and M-V*. (b) Portfolios F and G in the M-V Space: Utility U_1 Is M-V Relevant, while It Is M-V* Irrelevant.

the validity of the CAPM, especially if the market portfolio is located on the relegated segment. In terms of Figure 8.7b, this implies that whereas, according to the M-V both F and G are efficient, according to the M-V*, G is inefficient because the preference that tangents point G, in practice, does not actually exist.

Thus, the difference between the approaches of Makowitz and Baumol is that Markowitz allows all possible risk-averse preferences, including those that give a very high utility weight to the outcome left to the intersection point of the two cumulative distributions in Figure 8.7a, yet Baumol implicitly claims that such preferences do not exist in practice.

We show herein that although Baumol as well as Leshno and Levy relegate some segment of the M-V efficient set to the inefficient set, and despite the fact that the market portfolio may be eliminated from the efficient set, when the riskless asset prevails, the CAPM is, once again, intact. Thus, the M-V efficiency analysis may be affected by Baumol's and Leshno and Levy's reduction in the efficient set, whereas the CAPM is not. Let us elaborate.

Baumol suggests the following investment rule instead of the M-V rule:

F dominates G if

> a) $E_F (x) \geq E_G (x)$

and

> b) $L_F (x) = E_F (x) - k\sigma_F \geq L_G (x) = E_G (x) - k\sigma_G$ (8.9)

where k is larger than 1.

As can be seen, the risk index is the lower floor L, rather than the standard deviation. Of course, the higher the value L, the lower the risk involved with the investment under consideration. By taking the first derivative of L with respect to E, it can easily be shown that the lower portion of the M-V efficient set is relegated to the inefficient set according to Baumol's criterion. Namely, $\partial L/\partial E < 0$ should hold true on the M-V efficient frontier, which after some algebraic manipulations reduces to $\partial E/\partial \sigma < k$. Thus, the lower the value k, the larger is the segment of the frontier that is relegated to the inefficient set. From this analysis, it is clear that it is possible that the market portfolio, which according to the CAPM is located on the efficient

frontier, will be inefficient by Baumol's rule. Therefore, as per Baumol's suggestion, the Markowitz efficient set is divided into two segments: segment bc, which is Baumol's efficient set, and segment ab,
which is Baumol's inefficient set. The market portfolio m, theoretically, can be located on either bc or ab (see Figure 8.8).

In Figure 8.8a, portfolio m is located on what remains from the efficient set, whereas in Figure 8.8b, it is not. Let us now add the riskless
asset. If the tangency portfolio m is located on segment bc, the CAPM
trivially also holds true with Baumol's analysis; the relegated segment
is irrelevant because portfolio m remains on the efficient segment (see
Figure 8.8a).

Now we turn to the less trivial case, presented in Figure 8.8b. In
this case, the tangency portfolio m is located on the inefficient frontier; hence, it is inefficient. We show in the following that with the
riskless asset, portfolio m is always efficient, regardless of whether or
not it is relegated to the inefficient asset in the case where the riskless
asset does not prevail. First, note that the inefficient set, according
to Baumol, contains the segment where the derivative $\partial E/\partial\sigma > k$.
Therefore, the lower part of the efficient frontier may be inefficient.
Suppose that segment ab in Figure 8.8b is inefficient and segment bc
is efficient; hence, when the riskless asset does not prevail, portfolio
m is inefficient.

We turn now to the case with a riskless asset. The M-V efficient set
becomes line rr' of Figure 8.8b, represented by the capital market line
(CML) formula:

$$\mu_p = r + \frac{\mu_m - r}{\sigma_m}\sigma_p, \tag{8.10}$$

where p stands for portfolios located on the CML represented by line
rr'. According to Baumol, the efficient set is still defined by the derivative $\partial E/\partial\sigma < k$. However, on the CML, the derivative is constant and
is represented by

$$\frac{\mu_m - r}{\sigma_m} = \text{constant}. \tag{8.11}$$

There are two potential possibilities:

1) On the CML, the derivative $\partial L/\partial E > k$ (which also implies
   that $\partial E/\partial\sigma > k$). Namely, as we move to the right on the CML,

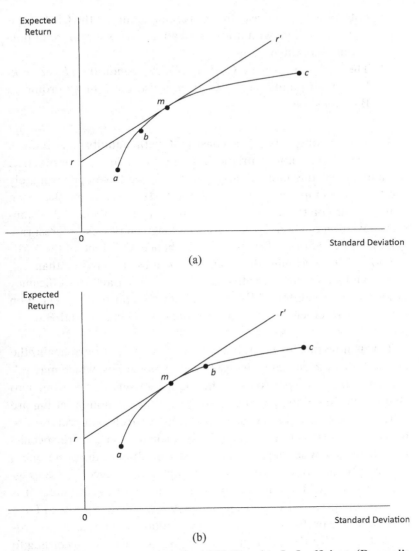

Figure 8.8. (a) Segment *ab* of the M-V Frontier Is Inefficient (Baumol's Rule), and Portfolio *m* Remains on the Baumol's Efficient Set (Segment *bc*). (b) Segment *ab* Is Inefficient According to Baumol's Rule, and Portfolio *m* Is Located on the Inefficient Set.

both E and L increase; therefore, each point on the CML dominates all points with a lower mean, a case where infinite borrowing is optimal.

2) The derivative on the CML fulfills the condition $\partial E/\partial\sigma < k$.
Hence, all points on the CML are also efficient according to
Baumol's rule.

Of course, only case 2 is consistent with equilibrium. Indeed,
case 2, which does not contradict equilibrium, holds true in practice.
To understand this more clearly, recall that we have approximately
the following empirical estimates of the CML parameters: the mean
annual return on the market portfolio is about 12 percent with a standard deviation of about 20 percent. The long-run riskless interest rate
is about 4 percent (see Ibbotson, 2007); hence, the slope of the CML
is about 0.40. Recalling that Baumol's k must be greater than 1.0,
it is obvious that the derivative requirement for Baumol's efficiency
holds true on the CML ($\partial E/\partial\sigma < k$); hence, all portfolios located on
the CML are efficient according to Markowitz-Sharpe and Baumol
alike.[36]

Let us now turn to Leshno and Levy's claim that once again, the
classic M-V efficient set includes too many portfolios, which may relegate the tangency portfolio to the inefficient set. This is similar to
Baumol's claim; however, the analysis and the economic setting are
different. Leshno and Levy suggest eliminating irrelevant preferences;
hence, the market portfolio may be inefficient. To be more specific,
they define a new set of preferences that is a subset of the preferences
assumed by the M-V analysis. For example, preference U_1 (see Figure 8.7b) is considered irrelevant by Leshno and Levy, whereas it is
a legitimate preference according to M-V analysis. Leshno and Levy
may eliminate preference U_1 because portfolio F dominates G according to the M-V* rule, although no such dominance exists according to
the M-V rule.

---

[36] It is interesting to note that without the riskless asset, portfolio m may be theoretically inefficient. However, as at this point the slope is equal to the CML's slope, with
the existing empirical estimates of the various parameters, we find that portfolio m
is efficient.

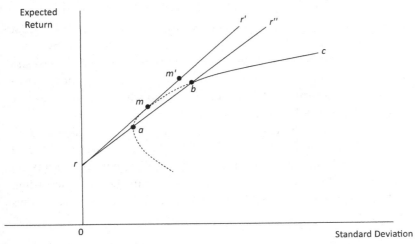

Figure 8.9. The Mean-Variance (M-V) and the M-V* Efficient Frontiers: *m* is on the M-V* Inefficient Segment (Left to Point *b*).

To understand this claim better, refer back to Figure 8.7a, where neither *F* nor *G* dominates the other according to M-V, although *F* may dominate *G* according to MV* (for more details, see Leshno and Levy, 2002). As in the case of Baumol, Leshno and Levy also suggest the possibility that the market portfolio is relegated to the inefficient set. Although this is the case when the riskless asset is not available, once again, its existence "rescues" the CAPM, even in Leshno and Levy's framework (see Figure 8.9).

The segment below point *b* may be relegated by Leshno and Levy to the inefficient set according to the M-V* rule. Hence, portfolio *m* may be inefficient. Yet, when one adds the riskless asset, portfolio *m* or some combination of *m* with the riskless asset becomes efficient. This is because for any portfolio located on a line below *rr'* (i.e., located on *rr''*), there is a portfolio on *rr'* with the same variance and a higher mean; hence, it is dominated by SD, as well as by M-V (recall that normal distributions are assumed). Furthermore, because SD implies SD* (and M-V implies M-V*; see Leshno and Levy, 2002), the dominance also holds true according to Leshno and Levy's rules. Thus, all portfolios located below *rr'* are M-V* inefficient.

Unlike the case of Baumol, in the case of Leshno and Levy, not all portfolios located on rr' are necessarily efficient. It is possible that portfolio m is inefficient because portfolio m' dominates it by MV*. However, because m' is a linear combination of m and the riskless asset, all investors will end up holding a combination of m and the riskless asset. As a result, the CAPM is also valid when investors employ either the SD* or M-V* rule.

Finally, even if the riskless asset does not exist, according to both Baumol and Leshno and Levy, the optimal portfolio will be selected from the reduced M-V frontier, and in equilibrium Black's (1972) zero beta CAPM holds true. This also occurs because according to Baumol's criterion and M-V*, all interior portfolios are always inefficient.

8.9. SUMMARY

It has been proven in previous chapters that if distributions are normal, with the additional assumption of risk aversion, the M-V rule is optimal. The following questions related to the M-V rule are discussed in this chapter:

1. Is there a theoretical or an empirical justification for the normality assumption?
2. If normality is rejected, what is the economic loss induced by the employment of the M-V rule in portfolio selection?
3. If normality exists, is Markowitz's efficient set too big?

When the price changes are independent and identically distributed (i.i.d.) and the number of transactions is very large, by the central-limit theorem, the distribution is normal.[37] However, because empirical distributions of price changes are more peaked and have heavier tails than the normal distribution, it is suggested that the log of price changes are i.i.d., leading to the stable Paretian distribution (Mandelbrot). If the parameter α of the Paretian distribution is equal to 2, the Paretian distribution of the log-return collapses to the

---

[37] See L. J. B. A. Bachelier, *Le Jeu, la chance, et le hazard*, E. Flammarion, Paris, 1914, chaps. xviii–xix.

normal distribution. Statistical tests reveal that this parameter is smaller than 2, rejecting the normality assumption. However, even if $\alpha = 2$, the distribution of log of terminal wealth and not of wealth is normally distributed, and because utility is defined on wealth and not on log of wealth, the M-V rule is not optimal even in this case.

Empirically, it is found that the distributions of various assets are more peaked and have heavier tails than the normal distribution has. Moreover, most statistical tests of goodness of fit reject the normal distribution. However, there is no agreement on the theoretical distribution that fits best the empirical distribution. This disagreement is explained by the fact that different researchers employ various sets of data, and particularly various investment horizons. The investment horizon is crucial for goodness-of-fit tests as well as for portfolio selection, as the various parameters vary in a nonlinear manner with the investment horizon. In particular, all pairwise correlations approach zero as the investment horizon approaches infinity.

For an investment horizon shorter than one year, the logistic distribution, which is more peaked and has heavier tails than the normal distribution has, dominates as the best fit to empirical distributions corresponding to various assets. For logistic distributions (which belong to the elliptical family of distributions), the M-V rule is optimal. Thus, we have empirical justification for the logistic distribution and theoretical justification for the M-V rule, despite the rejection of normality. Yet, for longer investment horizon, the fit of the logistic is not good enough to justify the employment of the M-V rule.

Despite the strong rejection of normality, and the rejection of the logistic distribution in some cases, the M-V rule serves as an excellent approximation to expected utility maximization. For various degrees of risk aversion, we have an astonishing result: the loss of using the M-V rule when normality is rejected is negligible – less than $6 per $10,000 of investment!

Finally, even if normality exists, Markowitz's efficient set may be too large because it includes portfolios that practically no investor holds. Accepting this argument, which is practically oriented (and hence has a practical rationale but no theoretical justification), a segment of the efficient set is relegated to the inefficient set without affecting the M-V analysis and the implied CAPM.

298   *The Capital Asset Pricing Model in the 21st Century*

In sum, the M-V rule is very robust: it can be justified by the logistic distribution, which, unlike the normal distribution, fits the empirical distribution nicely. Moreover, it can be used even without the theoretical justification because the economic loss of employing the M-V rule rather than expected utility is negligible.

9

Prospect Theory and Expected Utility

9.1. INTRODUCTION

In a series of laboratory experiments, Kahneman and Tversky[1] (K&T) find that the subjects participating in these experiments do not choose among various prospects by the expected utility paradigm, as one would predict. Moreover, experimental studies reveal that in the domain of negative outcomes, risk seeking characterizes the subjects' choices, which is in contradiction to the risk-aversion assumption, an assumption that is usually made in the derivation of the Mean-Variance (M-V) rule and the Capital Asset Pricing Model (CAPM). In this chapter, we focus on Prospect Theory (PT) as suggested in K&T's 1979 article, and in Chapter 10, we discuss the advances and modifications suggested to the original theory. The main difference between the original model and the advanced model, known as Cumulative PT (CPT; see Chapter 10), refer to the way decision weights are determined. Also, in the advanced model, estimates of the value function and the decision weights function are provided. As we shall see in these two chapters, each decision weight method has its pros and cons, and the modified version does not have a clear advantage over the original version. In Chapter 11, we analyze the M-V rule and the CAPM within the PT paradigm. Surprisingly, we show that under a wide range of conditions, both the common investment decision rules and the CPT, the modified PT model, can coexist.

---

[1] D. Kahneman and A. Tversky, "Prospect Theory: An Analysis of Decision Under Risk," *Econometrica*, 1979.

The seminal PT article by K&T, which was published in 1979, has had a monumental impact on economic and financial research. Actually, it constitutes a landmark in the development of new research fields, nowadays known as *behavioral finance* and *behavioral economics*. Moreover, new journals have been established that are completely devoted to experimental economics and to behavioral finance and behavioral economics.

The fact that a contradiction within expected utility can exist was known before the seminal PT article was published. For example, Allais[2] showed in 1953 that with prospects involving relatively large sums of money, decision making by expected utility reveals paradoxes in choices. This claim was backed by a commonsense argument rather than by supporting empirical or experimental findings.

Roy[3] strongly objects to the expected utility paradigm and suggests the "Safety-First Rule," which is based on the principle of avoiding a disaster. However, Roy just presents his beliefs but does not prove them empirically or experimentally. Furthermore, most of the article by Roy is devoted to the mathematics of the M-V efficient frontier rather than to arguments against expected utility. Edwards[4] claims that subjects employ decision weights rather than objective probabilities, a claim that has become a central building block of PT.

Another article, published by Markowitz[5] as early as 1952, contains another fundamental ingredient of PT. Markowitz advocates that investors make decisions based on gains and losses rather than on total wealth. He also advocates that the utility curve in the negative domain is steeper than the segment of the utility in the positive domain, a characteristic called later by K&T *loss aversion*.[6] K&T, who acknowledge the early contribution of Markowitz write:

[2] M. Allais, "Le Comportement de l'Homme Rationnel devant le Risque: Critique des Postulats et Axiomes de l'Ecole Americaine," *Econometrica*, 1953.
[3] A. D. Roy, "Safety First and the Holding of Assets," *Econometrica*, 1952.
[4] W. Edwards, "Subjective Probabilities Inferred from Decisions," *Psychological Review*, 1962. Fellner introduced the concept of decision weighting in his 1961 book. For more details, see W. Fellner, *Probability and Profit – A Study of Economic Behavior along Bayesian Lines*, Homewood, IL: Irwin, 1965.
[5] H. M. Markowitz, "The Utility of Wealth," *Journal of Political Economy*, 1952.
[6] See also F. Mosteler and P. Nogee, "An Experimental Measure of Utility," *Journal of Political Economy*, 1951.

Markowitz was the first one to propose that utility be defined on gains and losses rather than on final asset positions, an assumption which has been explicitly accepted in most experimental measurement of utility.... Markowitz also noted the presence of risk seeking in preferences among positive as well as negative prospects, and he proposed a utility function which has convex and concave regions in both the positive and the negative domains. (p. 276)

The article by Markowitz was published in 1952, around the time when the Expected Utility Theory (EUT) gained power in economic research; hence, it did not have the strong effect that the first PT article had when it was published in 1979, just after many anomalies in the stock market were discovered. Moreover, the article published by Markowitz has not been backed by formal experiments and has not been followed by a critical mass of other articles advocating a contradiction to the EUT; hence, it did not have the momentum that PT had. Furthermore, Markowitz published in the same year[7] his seminal M-V article, which implicitly assumes expected utility maximization with risk aversion, which seemingly contradicts his other article, which raised objections to EUT. In our view, the powerful M-V article weakened the argument of the one that cast doubt on the validity of the expected utility paradigm.

Moreover, the previous articles showing that investors sometimes behave irrationally have been published mainly in psychological journals and hence had virtually no effect on economists. Yet the PT article by K&T had a tremendous influence on research in economic and finance because of the following characteristics:

1. The 1979 PT article is comprehensive, including many more behavioral elements that are not included in previous studies. Some of these behavioral elements contradict the expected utility paradigm, which was the central paradigm in economic research.
2. Unlike the previous articles, which described choices and were published in psychological journals, the first PT article was published in *Econometrica*, which is one of the most important academic journals in economics. Hence, it drew the attention of economists.

[7] H. M. Markowitz, "Portfolio Selection," *Journal of Finance*, 1952.

3. The hypotheses postulated in the PT study are experimentally tested; hence, the hypotheses are confirmed, at least by laboratory findings.
4. The 1979 article was followed by many more articles on this topic; many of these articles were published by K&T themselves. Thus, a critical mass of research questioning the expected utility paradigm has been established.
5. Other researchers employed PT to explain some paradoxes, for example, the Allais paradox, the equity premium puzzle, and many more unexplained market phenomena. These studies constitute a "stamp of approval" of economists on the importance of PT.

Realizing that the assumptions made in most classic economic models asserting that individual investors are always making investment decisions that maximize some objective, generally maximizing expected utility, do not hold in practice, researchers have begun to explore a new avenue. This research field reveals experimentally and empirically that investors are sometimes not "rational, efficient machines" that always maximize some objective function successfully. For example, non-economic factors such as sentiment become important in explaining many financial phenomena, which are classified as *market anomalies*. Mood, weather conditions, seasons of the year, and particularly the number of daylight hours were revealed to be important factors affecting the investors' decision making and choices and, hence, affecting market prices of risky assets.

Indeed, a recent book by Akerlof and Shiller,[8] *The Animal Spirit*, shows that rational economic models cannot explain many economic phenomena: one rather needs sentiment, mood, and other factors not considered by traditional economic models to explain these phenomena. They write:

To understand how economies work and how we can manage them and prosper, we must pay attention to the thought patterns that animate people's ideas and feelings, their animal spirit. (p.1)

---

[8] G. A. Akerlof and R. J. Shiller, *Animal Spirit: How Human Psychology Drives the Economy, and Why It Matters for Global Capitalism,"* Princeton University Press, Princeton, NJ, 2009.

Such development in research could not take place without the PT article and many other psychological articles that followed it.

Finally, whereas the expected utility paradigm provides a normative theoretical model that asserts how people should behave (hence leading to many theoretical models), PT is a descriptive model that reveals how people actually do behave and what axioms of the EUT are contradicted. Hence, it is very difficult to build economic models based on PT, for example, equilibrium risk–return relationship, performance measures, and so forth. Thus, there is a fear that PT asserts what is wrong in the present rational economic models but does not offer a well-organized substitute. The difference between the existing models and PT and the response to this fear are best summarized in the last few sentences in the 1992 article by Tversky and Kahneman:[9]

Prospect Theory departs from the tradition that assumes the rationality of economic agents; it is proposed as a descriptive, not a normative, theory. The idealized assumption of rationality in economic theory is commonly justified on two grounds: the conviction that only rational behavior can survive in competitive environment, and the fear that any treatment that abandons rationality will be chaotic and intractable. Both arguments are questionable. First, the evidence indicates that people can spend a lifetime in a competitive environment without acquiring a general ability to avoid framing effects or to apply linear decision weights. Second, and perhaps more important, the evidence indicates that human choices are orderly, although not always rational in the traditional sense of this word. (p. 317)

9.2. PROSPECT THEORY AND EXPECTED UTILITY

According to EUT, the following three fundamentals hold; PT casts doubt on the validity of these fundamentals.

Expectation: Investors maximize expected utility given by

$$EU(x) = \sum_{i=1}^{n} p_i U(x_i),$$

where the pair (p_i, x_i) stands for the probability and the corresponding outcome. By PT, investors do not employ the objective probabilities; hence, paradoxes emerge as long as it is assumed that choices rely on objective probabilities.

---

[9] A. Tversky and D. Kahneman, "Advances in Prospect Theory: Cumulative Representation of Uncertainty," *Journal of Risk and Uncertainty*, 1992.

Asset integration: A given prospect x is accepted if

$$EU(w + x) > U(w),$$

where w stands for the current assets held. By PT, people do not integrate assets from various sources, and they make decisions based on *changes* in wealth (gains and losses) rather than *total* wealth.

Risk aversion: The utility function is concave. Although risk aversion is not necessary in expected utility framework, it is commonly employed in various economic models. By PT, a segment of the utility function with risk seeking also exists.

Based on experimental results, K&T observe that the choices made by the subjects participating in the laboratory study contradict these three foundations of expected utility and of economic models, which are based on expected utility with risk aversion. We discuss the PT criticisms of each of the preceding three expected utility ingredients in the following sections.

a) Prospect Theory and Expected Utility Maximization

We first show evidence indicating that investors do not make investment decisions, at least in some specific cases, by the expected utility model. We present here the choices in two experiments from which one may conclude that people employ decision weight rather than objective probabilities, contradicting the expected utility paradigm. K&T extend Allais' paradox and show that choices with expected utility reveal paradoxes; hence, expected utility maximization does not provide a satisfactory model for decision making. The subjects participating in the experiment face problems 1 and 2 as specified here:

Problem 1: Choose between A and B given by (note that the currency is not important for these experiments, thus we do not specify it) the following:

A:	2,500 with probability 0.33	B: 2,400 with certainty
	2,400 with probability 0.66	
	0 with probability 0.01	

Most subjects (82%) selected prospect B.

Problem 2: Choose between C and D given by the following:

C:	2,500 with probability 0.33	D: 2,400 with probability 0.34
	0 with probability 0.67	0 with probability 0.66

Most subjects (83 percent) selected prospect C.

Like in Allais' paradox, the choices given reveal a paradox, if indeed the choices are made by the EUT criterion. However, although Allais advocates that the paradox occurs with very large sums of money, K&T show that the paradox exists also with moderate sums of money.

To proceed with the demonstration of the paradoxes of expected utility, without loss of generality, we assume that $U(0) = 0$. This condition can always be achieved by conducting a linear transformation of the utility function under consideration. To see the inconsistency of the choices when expected utility is employed, recall that the choice of prospect B in problem 1 implies that

$$U(2,400) > 0.33U(2,500) + 0.66U(2,400) + 0.01U(0)$$
$$\Rightarrow 0.34U(2,400) > 0.33U(2,500)$$

and the choice of prospect C, by the same subjects, in problem 2 implies that

$$0.34U(2,400) < 0.33U(2,500).$$

Thus, most of the choices of prospect B in problem 1 and most of the choices of prospect C in problem 2 reveal a contradiction in choices in the expected utility paradigm, an inconsistency that is similar to the one shown by Allais, called *Allais's paradox*.[10] The explanation for this paradox, like in Allais' paradox, is well known in the literature as the *certainty effect*. In problem 1, investors face one certain outcome (prospect B), and they overweight this certain outcome. Alternatively, under prospect A in problem 1, there is a probability of 0.01 for a zero outcome. However, participants in such experiments subjectively

---

[10] See Allais, 1953, *op. cit.*

overweight this probability, say to 0.05, to strengthen the decision to choose prospect B, hence avoiding a possible situation of no gain at all, which exists in prospect A but not in prospect B. This idea led to the development of the concept of decision weights; namely, investors do not employ objective probabilities but rather subjective values called decision weights. We extend the discussion on decision weights later in this chapter.

The decision weights play an important role in the decision-making process, particularly when one of the prospects guarantees a certain outcome and the other prospect has a zero outcome with a small probability, as given in the example. It has been found that with positive outcomes, subjects tend to select the certain prospect to avoid the possible situation of having a zero outcome if the alternative uncertain prospect is selected. With negative prospects (losses), the opposite is true: Subjects tend to select the prospect with zero loss with a small probability rather than the prospect with the sure loss. Because there is little chance of avoiding the loss with the uncertain prospect, the subjects select this prospect, hoping for the zero outcome and avoiding a situation with a sure loss.

However, in some cases, it is difficult to disentangle the certainty effect from the preference. Problems 3 and 4 to follow illustrate cases in which choices can be explained by the certainty effect as well as by preferences.

Problem 3 (positive outcomes): Choose between prospects A and B, given by the following:

A: 4,000 with probability 0.80	B: 3,000 with certainty
0 with probability 0.20	

K&T found that 80 percent of the 95 subjects selected the certain prospect, prospect B. These choices of the certain prospect can be explained either by the assertion that subjects overweight the value of the certain outcome to make a choice that allows them to escape from the possibility of obtaining a zero outcome or by the existence of risk aversion in the positive domain of outcomes, with no need for the certainty effect as an explanatory factor.

The opposite holds with respect to losses, as demonstrated in problem 4.

Problem 4 (negative outcomes): Choose between prospects A and B given by the following:

A: –4,000 with probability 0.80	B: –3,000 with certainty
0 with probability 0.20	

In this problem, 92 percent of the subjects selected prospect A, which gives them a chance to avoid a loss altogether. The choices can be explained by risk seeking or risk aversion with the certainty effect.

In sum, with gains, the subjects select the prospect with the lower mean outcome and prefer the certain prospect despite its lower mean, which is consistent with risk aversion, and the certainty effect is not needed to explain choices. With losses, they prefer the prospect with the higher mean loss because it has also a possibility of losing nothing, a feature subjects appreciate; hence, they select this prospect despite the higher mean loss. In the negative domain, the choices can be explained by risk seeking (with no need for the certainty effect) or by risk aversion and the certainty effect.

In sum, the experiment results reveal inconsistent choices within expected utility paradigm, leading to the conclusion that at least in some cases, the subjects probably employ decision weights; hence, they do not choose among prospects by the expected utility maximization. This occurs particularly in cases where one prospect is certain and the other prospect has one zero outcome.

Additionally, a certainty effect is observed. When the two prospects under consideration are positive (gains), the subjects tend to choose the certain prospect despite its lower mean. The opposite result takes place with negative prospects (losses): the subject tends to avoid the sure loss and choose the prospect with a higher mean loss, which also offers a small chance to avoid loss altogether.

The interpretation of the experimental results is that subjects select the prospect by some function $\sum w(p_i)U(x_i)$ and not by $\sum p_i U(x_i)$, where $w(p_i)$ is the weight assigned to probability p_i. However,

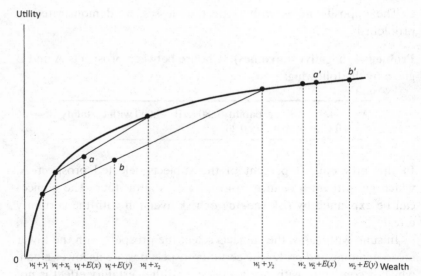

Figure 9.1. The Expected Utility of Two Prospects at Two Initial Wealth Levels.

with objective probabilities paradoxes emerge, whereas with decision weights, these paradoxes may vanish.

b) Asset Integration

According to the EUT, the value of the prospect depends on the level of the initial wealth. Therefore, for two prospects, x and y, it is possible that the same investor will rank these two prospects differently at two hypothetical levels of initial wealth. Thus, for two levels of wealth w_1 and w_2, we may have the following:

$$EU(w_1 + x) > EU(w_1 + y) \quad \text{and} \quad EU(w_2 + x) < EU(w_2 + y).$$

For example, suppose the investor who considers choosing between portfolios x and y selects portfolio x. After the decision is made, the same investor wins the big prize in the national lottery. Then, according to EUT, this investor may decide to switch to portfolio y, simply because he or she has become richer. Figure 9.1 demonstrates how, within expected utility paradigm, the change in initial wealth may change the preference between the two prospects. Suppose that prospect y has a higher mean and a higher dispersion than prospect x, as demonstrated in Figure 9.1. Then, at wealth level w_1, the expected utility of $w_1 + x$ is larger than the expected utility of $w_1 + y$, and the opposite holds for wealth level w_2. To facilitate the graphical presentation, and without loss of generality, we choose a utility function that is first concave and then becomes linear, or almost linear, at a relatively large wealth level. Each prospect has two possible outcomes with means of Ex and Ey, respectively. As can be seen from the left part of the figure, before winning the lottery and becoming rich, prospect x is preferred because point a is above point b, implying that the expected utility of $w_1 + x$ is larger than the expected utility of $w_1 + y$ (note that the expected utility is found by the intersection point of the perpendicular rising from the expected monetary value and the chord on the utility function). However, with wealth level w_2, the opposite is true because point b' is above point a'. To have a transparent and a simple presentation, the relevant lines corresponding to wealth level w_2 are omitted. However, we can safely determine that point b' is above point a' because we assume a linear, or an almost linear, utility function in this region, and by construction, the expected value of y is larger than the expected value of x.

Of course, such a reverse preference is only due to change in the initial wealth, which is the reference point in the expected utility calculation. By PT, such a change in preference is impossible because investors make decisions based on change of wealth (gains and losses) rather than on total wealth. Namely, the investors do not integrate the change of wealth (gains and losses) with the initial wealth. Such a claim is in severe contradiction to expected utility paradigm, claiming that income from all sources should be integrated, as demonstrated in Figure 9.1. K&T base their claim on subject choices. They conduct the following experiment, whose results conform to their hypothesis asserting that subjects do not integrate income from all sources:

Problem 5 (assets integration): In addition to whatever you own, you are given 1,000. You are now asked to choose between prospects A and B, given by the following:

A:	1,000 with probability 0.50	B: 500 with certainty
	0 with probability 0.50	

They find that 84 percent of the 70 subjects participating in this experiment selected prospect B. Then, with 68 subjects, they conduct the following experiment, given by problem 6.

Problem 6 (assets integration): In addition to whatever you own, you are given 2,000. You are now asked to choose between prospects C and D, given by the following:

C: −1,000 with probability 0.50 0 with probability 0.50	D: −500 with certainty

This experiment reveals that 69 percent of the choices were prospect C.

A simple calculation shows that should the subjects integrate all sources of wealth, they would not change their choices, as in both experiments given in problems 5 and 6, because they face the same two choices given by E (= A = C) and F (= B = D):

A = C = E: 2,000 with probability 0.50 1,000 with probability 0.50	B = D = F: 1,500 with certainty

The fact that the subjects did not make the same choices in the preceding two experiments but rather switched from prospect B in the first experiment to prospect C in the second experiment, indicates that most of them made the decisions based on change of wealth rather than on total wealth. Otherwise, they should not have changed their choices, which in terms of total wealth are the same in both experiments. Thus, by PT, in contrast to EUT, people do not integrate all sources of income, but rather they consider the marginal changes in their wealth resulting from their choices; namely, they consider only the gains and losses.

We turn now to the third main point of PT, which does not contradict EUT but rather contradicts the risk-aversion assumption made in virtually all economic models, particularly in equilibrium models, which are developed within expected utility paradigm.

c) Risk Aversion

Employing the certainty equivalent approach, K&T conducted a simple experiment aimed at analyzing the shape of the typical preference. Based on the subjects' choices, they conclude that risk aversion characterizes preferences in the positive domain and risk seeking prevails in the negative domain.

Let us go back to experiments 3 and 4 to show the implication of the finding regarding the shape of the preferences. By experiment 3, most subjects prefer to get 3,000 with certainty rather than 4,000 with probability 0.80 and zero with probability 0.20. Because the expected value of the uncertain prospect is 3,200 (i.e., greater than 3,000), it is advocated by PT that risk aversion prevails in the positive domain of outcomes. This result, which is consistent with the risk-aversion assumption made by most models in economics and finance, is illustrated in Figure 9.2a. The expected utility of the risky prospect is given by point *a* in Figure 9.2a, and the certainty equivalent of this risky prospect is *x'*, where

$$0.80U(4{,}000) + 0.20U(0) = U(x').$$

The investor with this preference is indifferent about getting the certainty equivalent or the risky prospect because both yield the same expected utility. However, 3,000 is larger than the certainty equivalent, so they prefer to get the certain prospect rather than the uncertain prospect.[11]

However, it is important to emphasize that a risk averter will not always prefer the certain prospect. If we replace the 3,000 in the previous experiment by a certain value smaller than *x'*, the uncertain prospect would be selected. Thus, the choice depends on the degree of risk aversion as well as the size of the certain outcome. Therefore, if, in this experiment, the certain outcome would be increased, say to 3,150, we would expect that an even a higher proportion of the subjects would choose the certain prospect. Graphically, we find that point *b* is

---

[11] In the graphical analysis corresponding to the risk-seeking and the risk-aversion segments of the preference function, it is assumed that in each domain of outcomes, the preference is well behaved, namely, that there are no inflection points.

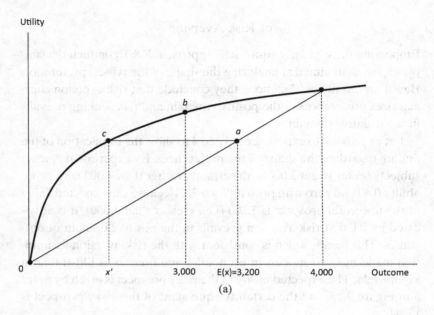

(a)

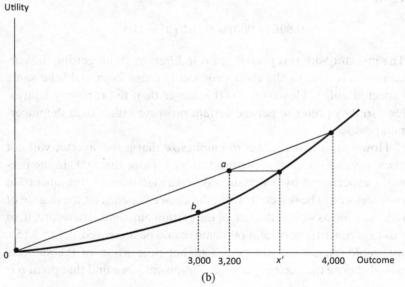

(b)

Figure 9.2. Choices with Positive Prospects. (a) Risk Aversion. (b) Risk Seeking.

located above point *a* (see Figure 9.2a), implying that the certain outcome of 3,000 is preferred to the uncertain prospect. This can occur only when the preference is concave (i.e., only with risk aversion). To see this claim, let us look at Figure 9.2b representing risk seeking. With this preference, the uncertain prospect should be preferred because point *a* is located above point *b*. In other words, the certainty equivalent of the risky prospect is equal to 3,200, and because the certain prospect provides only 3,000, the uncertain prospect is preferred.

Thus, we conclude that if a subject prefers the certain prospect, he or she must be a risk averter. However, the opposite conclusion, asserting that risk aversion implies the choice of the certain prospect, is invalid. Therefore, the fact that most subjects selected the certain prospect (which has a lower mean than the mean of the risky prospect) implies by PT that risk aversion must prevail, at least for those subjects who selected the certain prospect. However, recall that this conclusion is valid only when we use the objective probabilities and not the decision weights. We elaborate on this issue later in this chapter.

With choices in the negative domain (losses), risk seeking prevails. In experiment 4, the subject must choose between losing 3,000 with certainty or losing 4,000 with probability 0.80 and neither losing nor gaining with probability of 0.2. Most subjects prefer the uncertain prospect with a higher expected loss, which leads to the conclusion that risk seeking prevails in the negative domain. This result is demonstrated graphically in Figure 9.3a. Point *a* is located above point *b*, yielding a higher expected utility; hence, the choice of the risky prospect can be explained by a risk-seeking preference.

With risk aversion (see Figure 9.3b), the choice of the risky prospect is impossible because point *c* is above point *d*; hence, the certain prospect should be preferred. The fact that most subjects preferred the uncertain prospect with a higher average loss than the loss corresponding to the certain prospect implies that risk aversion in the negative domain cannot exist.

In sum, risk seeking is necessary to explain most choices in the negative domain, and risk aversion is necessary in explaining most choices in the positive domain. Yet, recall that these conclusions rely on the fact that objective probabilities rather than decision weights are employed. Namely, in the various calculations of the certainty

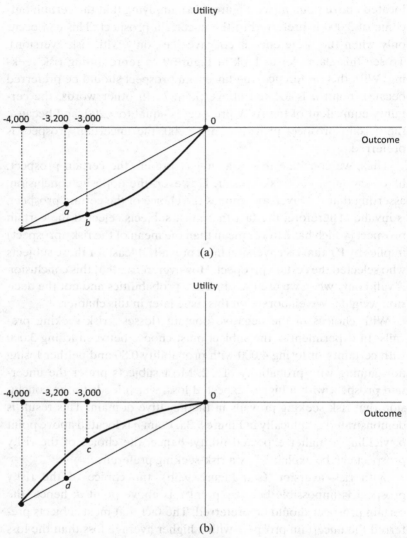

Figure 9.3. Choices with Negative Prospects. (a) Risk Seeking. (b) Risk Aversion.

equivalent and in drawing the chords in Figures 9.2 and 9.3, the objective probabilities are employed. With decision weights, one can explain the choices with all types of preferences, and no decisive conclusion can be made regarding the shape of the preference.

Take, for example, the aforementioned two positive prospects and assume the following risk-seeking preference: $U(x) = x^2$. Then the expected utility of the certain and uncertain prospects are given by the following:

Certain prospect: $3,000^2 = 9,000,000$

Uncertain prospect: $0.80 * 4,000^2 + 0.20 * 0 = 12,800,000$.

Hence, with objective probabilities and risk seeking, one cannot explain the choices of the certain prospect because the uncertain prospect has a higher expected utility. However, suppose that $w(0.80) = 0.50$. Then, with decision weights, we have the same expected value for the certain prospect. However, the expected value of the uncertain prospect will be $0.50*16,000,000 = 8,000,000$, which is smaller than the utility of the certain prospect. Thus, with decision weights, the choices of the certain prospect, with positive prospects, can be explained by both concave and convex functions alike. From this example, we conclude that the risk aversion in PT is quite different from that in EUT: While in EUT risk aversion implies concavity of the preference, this is not necessarily so with PT. Indeed, in the 1992 article by Tversky and Kahneman,[12] they explain the difference between EUT and PT regarding this issue:

Although the present theory can be applied to derive the value function from preferences between prospects, the actual scaling is considerably more complicated than in utility theory because of the introduction of decision weights. For example, decision weights can produce risk aversion and risk seeking even with a linear value function. (1979, p. 280)

And they add:

In expected utility theory risk aversion and risk seeking are determined solely by the utility function. In the present theory, as in other cumulative models, risk aversion and risk seeking are determined jointly by the value function and by the capacities, which in the present context are called weighting functions for short. (p. 302)

So far, we present evidence revealing that observed choices contradict some fundamental characteristics of EUT. We next discuss in more

[12] See Tversky and Kahneman, 1992, *op. cit.*

detail the value function and the decision weights function as advocated by PT.

9.3. THE VALUE FUNCTION

In this section, we discuss attitude toward risk as well as *loss aversion*, which is related to the steepness of the various segments of the value function.

a) The Shape of the Value Function

The value function is similar to the utility function, yet it is different because it is defined in terms of change of wealth rather than total wealth. Also, it does not strictly reflect the risk attitude because either risk aversion or risk seeking may prevail, even with a linear value function, because the decision weights also affect attitude toward risk (see preceding quotes). Thus, unlike with the utility function, with the value function, the relationship between the shape of the value function and the attitude toward risk is not clear-cut.

As we see in the following discussion, despite the difficulty of disentangling the preference and decision weights, we can deduce the shape of preference from choices, as long as the decision weight of a given probability is constant and independent of the other outcomes of the distribution; for example, $w(0.25)$ is identical for all outcomes with a probability of 0.25. Indeed, this property exists in PT but not in CPT, which we discuss in Chapter 10. Problem 7 is constructed with the purpose of discovering the shape of the value function despite the previously mentioned difficulties.

Problem 7: Choose between prospects A and B, given by the following:

A: 6,000 with probability 0.25	B: 4,000	with probability 0.25
0 with probability 0.75	2,000	with probability 0.25
	0	with probability 0.50

Most of the subjects (82 percent of the 68 subjects) selected prospect B. From these choices, with $V(0) = 0$, we can assert that for most subjects, the following holds:

$$w(.25)V(6000) < w(.25)V(4,000) + w(.25)V(2,000).$$

Because by PT $w(0.25)$ is a constant number across all prospects, it is canceled out and we therefore have

$$V(6,000) < V(4,000) + V(2,000).$$

From this inequality, for well-behaved functions, we can conclude that the value function is concave in the positive domain.

Similarly, when the subjects had to choose between C = (−6,000) with probability 0.25 and D = (−2,000 with probability 0.25, or −4,000 with probability 0.25), most of the subjects selected prospect C, implying by the same argument as before that

$$V(-6,000) > V(-2,000) + V(-4,000).$$

Hence, for well-behaved value functions, we can conclude that the value function is convex in the negative domain of outcomes.

b) Loss Aversion

By PT, as claimed also by Markowitz,[13] the segment of the value function corresponding to the negative outcomes is steeper than the segment of the value corresponding to the positive outcomes. This property is called *loss aversion*, and it stems from the observation that most people find the symmetrical bet given by $(x, 0.50, -x, 0.50)$ unattractive. Figure 9.4 demonstrates this bet with various value (or utility) functions. First recall that the expected value of this prospect can be found graphically by the perpendicular raising from the mean outcome, which is zero in this example, and the chord connecting the value of $-x$ and $+x$ on the value function.

Figure 9.4a demonstrates a linear value function in which the expected utility (value) of this function is given by point a; hence, the investor is indifferent about accepting or rejecting this prospect, which represents a fair game. In Figure 9.4b, the expected utility is given by point a, located above zero; hence, $EV(X) > V(0)$. Therefore, with this preference, which is steeper in the positive domain than in the negative domain, this prospect is attractive and hence should be selected. In contrast, in Figure 9.4c, the segment of the preference

---

[13] H. M. Markowitz, 1952, *op. cit.*

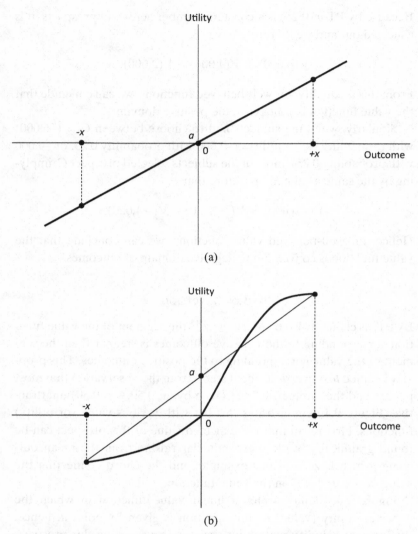

Figure 9.4. Preference and the Attractiveness of a Fair Game. (a) Linear Preference: Indifferent. (b) Preference Steeper in the Positive Domain: Attractive. (c) Preference Steeper in the Negative Domain (Prospect Theory Preference): Unattractive. (d) Preference Steeper in the Negative Domain (Markowitz Preference): Unattractive.

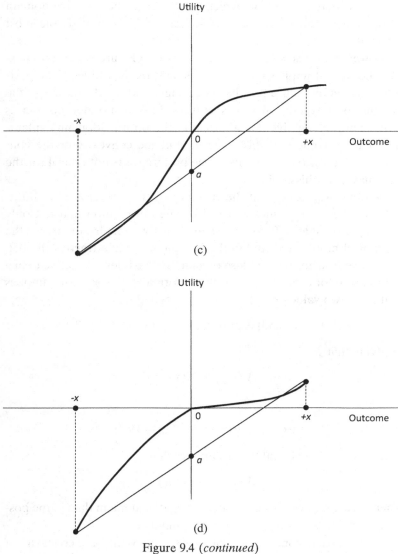

Figure 9.4 (*continued*)

corresponding to the negative domain is steeper than the segment corresponding to the positive domain, and because point *a* is located below zero, the prospect under consideration is unattractive. It has been found that most investors would consider this prospect unattractive; therefore, Figures 9.4a and 9.4b are ruled out by PT, and it is advocated that Figure 9.4c, which is steeper in the negative domain of outcomes than in the positive domain of outcomes, is the most relevant.

However, at this point, we should note that Figure 9.4d is also possible because it implies that the bet is unattractive. Indeed, the preference given by Figure 9.4d has been suggested by Markowitz as the one that best explains investors' choices. In sum, a preference that is steeper in the negative domain than in the positive domain explains the unattractiveness of this prospect, but the convexity or the concavity of the various segments of the preference is not crucial for the explanation of this choice.

Another way to look at the steepness of the preference at different domains of outcomes is based on the observation that not only do people consider a fair game as unattractive but also the larger the amount of money involved in the bet, the more unattractive the bet. For example, a 50:50 bet to lose or gain $10,000 is less attractive than a bet of 50:50 for a gain or loss of $100. Formally, this assertion implies that if for two values x and y with $x > y \geq 0$, then

$$(y, 0.50, -y, 0.50) \text{ is preferred to,} \quad (x, 0.50, -x, 0.50),$$

implying that

$$V(y) + V(-y) > V(x) + V(-x).$$

Hence,

$$V(-y) - V(-x) > V(x) - V(y).$$

Setting y and $V(y)$ equal to zero implies that

$$V(x) < -V(-x).$$

Therefore, the curve is steeper in the negative domain than in the positive domain, as shown in Figures 9.4c and 9.4d.

To draw some conclusion regarding the convexity and concavity of the preference in the various domains, let y approach x.[14] Using the preceding inequalities, it implies that $V'(x) < V'(-x)$, provided that

[14] Although there are different approaches to investigate the shape of preference, implying that different approaches to define loss aversion exist, in this chapter we discuss the argument and technique suggested by Tversky and Kahneman, 1992, *op. cit.*

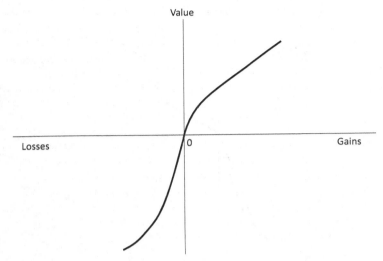

Figure 9.5. The Prospect Theory Value Function.

the derivatives exist. However, it is worth noting that the inequality regarding these two derivatives may conform also to the preference given in Figure 9.4d.

Figure 9.5 demonstrates the value function as advocated by PT. As can be seen, risk aversion prevails in the positive domain and risk seeking in the negative domain.[15] The curve is steeper in the negative domain than in the positive domain. The values on the horizontal axis are changes of wealth rather than wealth and are thus denoted by gains and losses.[16]

Does PT advocate that initial wealth is completely irrelevant for decision making? Actually, the initial wealth is also relevant but not as much as in EUT. The value function of PT is actually $V(w, x)$ rather than $V(x)$ when x denotes change of wealth (gains/losses) and w denotes the initial wealth. This is much different from $U(w + x)$ of expected utility, when the two sources of income are integrated.

---

[15] For a survey revealing risk seeking in choices between negative prospects, see P. C. Fishburn and G. A. Kochenberger, "Two-Piece von Neumann-Morgenstern Utility Functions," *Decision Sciences*, 2007.

[16] One of the earliest experimental studies that reveals that preference is not concave in the whole domain was conducted by Swalm. See R. O. Swalm, "Utility Theory – Insight into Risk Taking," *Harvard Business Review*, 1966.

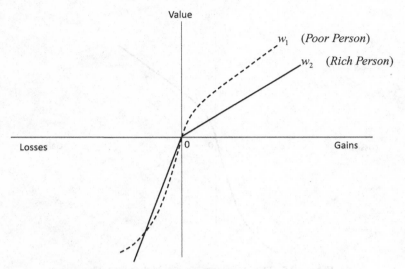

Figure 9.6. The Value Function for Two Levels of Wealth.

K&T speculate that the richer the person, the flatter the value function, and the value of a very rich person becomes close to a linear function. However, they claim that the certainty equivalent of the prospect ($1,000, 0.50, 0, 0.50) is for most people $400 to $500; hence, the value function with one argument $V(x)$ provides a satisfactory approximation to the true function $V(w, x)$. Figure 9.6 illustrates the value function for two levels of wealth. The figure clearly reveals that the slope corresponding to the higher wealth level is smaller. To make this point as transparent as possible, assume we have a rich person and a poor person. Furthermore, assume that the rich person has a linear preference, with two segments; see the preference denoted by w_2 in Figure 9.6. This means that the richer the person, the less premium he or she is willing to pay to get rid of a given risk and the less he or she is willing to pay to participate in a game, which involves only losses.

Finally, by PT, the value function given in Figure 9.5 describes the values derived from changes in wealth in most but not in all cases. For example, suppose that an individual needs $100,000 to purchase a house. Then the utility will reveal a steep rise in the preference near this critical value. Similarly, the preference may reveal a steep increase in risk aversion near the critical loss, which compels him or her to sell the house. This, in turn, implies that the value function may have more segments than the two shown in Figure 9.5. In fact, this PT argument is similar to the one employed by Friedman and Savage[17] explaining the several segments in their suggested utility function.

In sum, the value function has the following properties:

1. It is a function of changes of wealth (losses and gains) and not of total wealth. Consequently, investors do not integrate all sources of income.
2. Although the initial wealth may affect the curvature of the value function, it is generally ignored in PT because a good approximation is obtained by relying solely on change of wealth. However, in principle, the larger the wealth, the flatter the value function.
3. Risk aversion prevails in the positive domain, and risk seeking prevails in the negative domain.
4. The segment corresponding to the negative domain is steeper than the segment corresponding to the positive domain.
5. The value function at zero change of wealth is equal to zero, $V(0) = 0$, which is the reference point of the value function.
6. Finally, at some specific cases (buying or selling a house), the value function may have some more inflection points; these are the critical values, which may change from one individual to another.

9.4. THE DECISION WEIGHT FUNCTION

Decision weights in various forms are suggested in the literature as a substitute to the objective probabilities. The two main approaches to incorporate decision weights into the decision-making process are the one suggested by PT and the one that relies on the cumulative distribution, or the rank of the outcomes in the cumulative distribution. Each approach has its pros and cons. We discuss in the following the decision weights suggested by PT and, in Chapter 10, we discuss the other weighting methods.

---

[17] M. Friedman and L J. Savage, "The Utility Analysis of Choices Involving Risk," *Journal of Political Economy*, 1948.

The fact that decision weights play the same role as the probabilities in expected value calculation makes one wonder whether one can treat decision weights as probabilities. By PT, although decision weights are similar with some respect to the subjective probabilities suggested by Savage,[18] they are actually not probabilities. They do not obey the probability axioms; particularly the sum of the decision weights covering all possible mutually exclusive events is not necessarily equal to 1. This does not imply that probabilities and decision weights are not positively correlated. There is no question that the decision weights are affected by the objective probabilities. It is unlikely that an event with an objective probability of 0.1 will have a higher decision weight of an event with a probability of 0.9. Yet decision weights are not probabilities, and they reflect, on top of the objective probabilities, the desirability of the prospect under consideration.

Let us demonstrate this idea with the famous Allais paradox. Suppose that one has to choose between prospect A and prospect B. Prospect A provides $1 million with certainty, and prospect B provides $0, $1 million, and $5 million with probabilities of 0.01, 0.89, and 0.1, respectively. The fear of ending with a zero cash flow if prospect B rather than prospect A is selected may increase the decision weights corresponding to the zero outcome from 0.01 to say 0.20, such that prospect B will be undesirable compared with prospect A. In this respect, the decision weights reflect not only the objective probability but also the desirability of the prospect: the person who makes the choice is made afraid by the possibility that if prospect B is selected, he or she may get nothing. In contrast, the alternative, if prospect A is selected, is to get $1 million with certainty. This possible regret induces the subject to increase the decision weight, as explained previously, until prospect B becomes unattractive relative to prospect A and, consequently, prospect A is selected.[19]

---

[18] L. J. Savage, *The Foundation of Statistics*, Wiley, New York, 1954.
[19] It is interesting to note that decision weights are employed even if the probabilities are clearly stated. Ambiguity regarding the probabilities a fortiori may enhance the role of decision weights. For example, Ellesberg has shown that people prefer to bet on an urn that contains equal numbers of red and green balls rather than on an urn that contains red and green balls in unknown proportions. Thus, the ambiguity may induce people to employ decision weights and to prefer one option to the

The decision weights, as suggested by PT, have several important characteristics:

1. For two probabilities, $p_1 = p_2$, we have $w(p_1) = w(p_2)$, where w stands for decision weight.
2. For extreme probabilities of zero and 1, the decision weight is equal to the probability. Namely, $w(0) = 0$ and $w(1) = 1$.
3. The decision weight of small probabilities tends to be larger than the objective probability; namely, $w(p) > p$ if p is relatively small.

Whereas the first two characteristics are based simply on logical considerations, the third property is based on the following experimental observations of K&T, given in problems 8 and 9 as follows:

Problem 8: Suppose you have to choose between prospect A with an outcome of 5,000 with probability 0.001 or a zero outcome with probability 0.999 and prospect B providing 5 with certainty. Which prospect would you choose?

Most subjects (72 percent of the 72 subjects participating in this experiment) selected prospect A. From this result, we can conclude the following:

$$w(.001)V(5,000) > V(5) \Rightarrow w(.001) > V(5)/V(5,000)$$

Given that in the positive domain the value function is concave, we must have that $V(5)/V(5,000) > 0.001$; therefore, $w(0.001) > 0.001$. We turn now to an experiment corresponding to the negative domain.

Problem 9: Suppose you have to choose between prospect A with an outcome of $-5,000$ with probability 0.001 or a zero with probability 0.999 and prospect B, with a certain outcome of -5. Which prospect would you choose?

Most (83 percent) of the choices were prospect B. Thus, for the typical choice, the following holds:

$$V(-5) > w(.001)V(-5,000) \Rightarrow w(.001) > V(-5)/V(-5,000).$$

other, where rationally they should be indifferent between the two options. See D. Elleberg, "Risk, Ambiguity and Savage Axioms," *Quarterly Journal of Economics*, 1961.

Note that the inequality is reversed because we divide by a negative value (recall that V $[-5,000]$ is negative; see Figure 9.5). Because the value function is convex in the negative domain, we have $V(-5)/V(-5,000) > 0.001$, which finally yields that $w(0.001) > 0.001$.

To summarize, for small probabilities, regardless of the sign of the outcomes, the decision weights tend to be larger than the objective probabilities. Because some probabilities are overweighted, does it imply that the sum of the decision weights is larger than 1? Not really! By PT, it is suggested that just the opposite holds, as given by point 4 as follows:

4. Subcertainty: It is claimed by PT that typically the sum of the decision weights is smaller than 1, despite the overweight given to small probabilities. This assertion is based on the results of the experiments given in problems 1 and 2 given previously. Let us elaborate.

By the choices in problem 1, we can conclude that the following holds:

$$V(2,400) > w(.66)V(2,400) + w(.33)V(2,500)$$
$$\Rightarrow [1 - w(.66)]V(2,400) > w(.33)V(2,500)$$

and from the choices in problem 2, we conclude that the following holds:

$$w(.33)V(2,500) > w(.34)V(2,400).$$

From these two inequalities, the following emerges:

$$1 - w(.66) > w(.34). \quad \text{Namely, } w(.34) + w(.66) < 1$$

Thus, typically the sum of the probabilities is smaller than 1. Because small probabilities are overweighted, it must be that some other probabilities are underweighted. This result explains why decision weights are not probabilities.

9.5. THE PROS AND CONS OF PROSPECT THEORY
DECISION WEIGHTS

In this section, we discuss some of the characteristics of PT decision weights and their implication to other decision-making studies.

a) Drawback: First-Degree Stochastic Dominance Violation

First-degree stochastic dominance (FSD; see Chapter 3) is nothing but a reflection of the monotonicity axiom, asserting that the more wealth a person has, the better off he or she is (more precisely, he or she cannot be worse off). Virtually all researchers, economists, and experimental psychologists alike agree with FSD. In fact, in some of the formulations of EUT, FSD is used as one of the axioms.[20] Unfortunately, PT's decision weights may violate FSD – a severe drawback. To verify such possible violation, some numerical examples are sufficient.

Consider the two prospects, F and G, given in Table 9.1. With objective probabilities, F dominates G by FSD, because we have (see part 1 of the table), $F(x) \leq G(x)$ for all values x, and there is at least one strict inequality (see, for example, $x = 90$). Now we turn to part 2 of the table, where decision weights are determined, for example, by the following formula: $w(p) = p^2$, where p is a probability and not a cumulative probability. This is a legitimate probability-weighting formula. However, we stress that this example is chosen for its simplicity, and the FSD violation can be demonstrated with many other decision-weighting functions.

With the decision weights in this specific case, we no longer have a probability function because the sum of the decision weights is smaller than 1. We can handle this issue by normalizing the decision weights such that the sum will be 1. This normalization is presented in part 3 of Table 9.1. As can be seen from this part of the table, the two cumulative distributions intersect; hence, the FSD of prospect F over prospect G that exists with objective probabilities is violated. To be more specific, although we have with objective probabilities that

[20] See P. C. Fishburn, "Nontransitive Measurable Utility," *Journal of Mathematical Psychology*, 1982.

Table 9.1. *Prospects A and B*

1. With Objective Probabilities

F		G	
Return	Probability (p)	Return	Probability (p)
90	1/10	90	2/10
100	7/10	100	6/10
110	2/10	110	2/10

2. With Decision Weights

F		G	
Return	Decision Weights $[w(p)]$	Return	Decision Weights $[w(p)]$
90	1/100	90	4/100
100	49/100	100	36/100
110	4/100	110	4/100

3. With Normalized Decision Weights

F•		G•	
Return	Cumulative Probability with Normalized Decision Weights	Return	Cumulative Probability with Normalized Decision Weights
90	1/54	90	4/44
100	49/54	100	40/44
110	1	110	1

$F(x) \leq G(x)$ for all values x, with the decision weights, we have for the value $x = 100$ that $F^\bullet(100) = 50/54 > G^\bullet(100) = 40/44$ (where $F^\bullet$ and $G^\bullet$ are the normalized distributions); hence, the FSD dominance is violated.

To show the FSD violation, it is not necessary that the sum of the decision weights be equal to 1. Even a simpler example of the FSD possible violation, with no need for employing normalization of the cumulative distributions, is given by the following example. Consider the following two prospects:

Prospect A: (5, 8, 10 with equal probability of 1/3)
Prospect B: 10 with certainty

It is obvious that prospect B dominates prospect A by FSD with objective probabilities, implying that for all nondecreasing utility functions, $E_B U(x) \geq E_A U(x)$. Suppose now that we have the following decision weights, $w(1/3) = 1/2$ and $w(1) = 1$. Then, for the linear utility function (as well as many other utility functions), we have

$$EU_A(x) = 1/2(5 + 8 + 10) = 11.5 > E_B U(x) = 10.$$

Thus, for at least one utility function, prospect A is preferred over prospect B; therefore, the FSD of prospect B over prospect A is violated.

K&T have realized this drawback and suggested that in the editing stage of all relevant prospects, all those that are inferior by FSD rule will be eliminated. With such a procedure, there is no risk that the FSD inferior prospect will be selected. However, in a subsequent study, they suggest another weighting system, one that guarantees no FSD violation. We discuss the advanced weighting method in Chapter 10.

b) Some Advantages

PT decision weights, as suggested in the 1979 article, have also some clear advantages over other suggested weighting methods:

1. With the suggested method, one has the flexibility to assign various decision weights to various events. For example, one may assign $w(p) > p$ to small probabilities and $w(p) \cong p$ for relatively moderate and large probabilities. Such flexibility does not exist with some other methods that suggest a strict formula to calculate the decision weights.
2. For $p_i = p_j$, we have $w(p_i) = w(p_j)$, and hence equal probabilities are assigned equal decision weights, which has an intuitive appeal. Again, this property is not maintained with some other weighting methods. This is particularly important to empirical studies, in which each observation is assigned an equal probability.
3. With equally likely outcomes, the employment of decision weights does not affect choices. For example, suppose that one faces two empirical distributions of rates of return. Each

distribution contains, say, ten annual rates of returns. Furthermore, suppose that an investor prefers one distribution over another with the objective distribution. Then we claim that with decision weights also, the choice will not be changed. This is a desired property because with equally likely outcomes, there is no one extreme low probability; hence, there is no reason to change the choice. To see this claim, suppose that with objective probabilities, prospect A, for a given utility (or value function), is preferred over prospect B. Then we have the following:

$$\sum\nolimits_{i=1}^{n} (1/n)U(x_i)/A > \sum\nolimits_{i=1}^{n} (1/n)U(x_i)/B.$$

With decision weights, which are identical for all probabilities $1/n$, we have

$$\sum\nolimits_{i=1}^{n} w(1/n)U(x_i)/A > \sum\nolimits_{i=1}^{n} w(1/n)U(x_i)/B,$$

when $/A$ and $/B$ denotes values corresponding to prospects A and B, respectively. Both $1/n$ and $w(1/n)$ are constant numbers, so the preference of prospect A over prospect B does not depend on these values. Thus, if A yields a higher expected value with objective probabilities, the same is true also with decision weights, despite the fact that decision weights are not probabilities.

Finally, the fact that decision weights do not change choices in the equally likely outcomes has a great practical advantage. In most cases that are outside of the realm of textbooks, particularly with investments in the stock market, probabilities are unknown; hence, it is common to take a sample of *ex-post* observations and to assign an equal probability to each observation. This is the common method for calculating beta, variance, and other parameters needed for portfolio selection. In this important case, employing PT decision weight, does not change the choice – an important result.

9.6. SUMMARY

As early as 1953, Allais demonstrated that choices in the expected utility framework reveal some paradoxical results. Edwards, in 1962, suggested that people employ decision weights rather than objectives probabilities. In 1952, Markowitz suggested that investors make investment decisions based on *change* of wealth (gains and losses) rather than on *total* wealth and that the reference point is zero, with a risk-seeking segment as well as a risk-aversion segment.

Although there were many objections to expected utility in the early 1950s, only with the publication of the PT article by Kahneman and Tversky in 1979 did the criticism to expected utility gain momentum. Nowadays, completely new interrelated fields of research, called *behavioral finance* and *behavioral economics*, have been developed. The main idea of these research fields is that investors are not always rational in their investment decision making, and the deviations from rationality are systematic. Moreover, sentiment and mood affect the investment decision making, which, of course, contradicts EUT, which assumes investors are rational.

PT's experiments reveal the following main results:

a) Investors do not integrate all sources of income and, hence, make decisions based on change of wealth (gains and losses) rather than on total wealth.

b) People employ decision weights rather than objective probabilities.

c) The value (utility) function is convex in the negative domain (risk seeking) and concave in the positive domain (risk aversion). Thus, the value function is S-shaped.

d) The segment of the value function corresponding to the negative domain is steeper than the segment corresponding to the positive domain (loss aversion).

The decision weight function, which is a function of the probability under consideration, is also affected by the desirability of the prospect. For example, if a prospect has a zero outcome with a relatively small probability, and the alternative prospect has a certain positive outcome, generally investors increase the decision weight assigned to the probability of the zero outcome to avoid a choice that may end up with zero outcome.

The decision weights suggested by PT may lead to a violation of FSD, an obvious drawback. However, it has the advantage of flexibility in determining the decision weights. Moreover, in the equally likely outcomes case, there is no extreme low probability; thus, it is intuitively expected that decision weights will not affect choices. Indeed, this is the case with PT's decision weights. This advantage is particularly important in empirical studies, where generally the same probability is assigned to each *ex-post* observation. In this case, decision weights, which are not probability measures and may not add up to 1, do not affect the choice – a clear-cut advantage of the suggested method. In the next chapter, we analyze other suggested models for the formulation of decision weights.

10

Cumulative Decision Weights

No Dominance Violation

10.1. INTRODUCTION

From the discussion of the observed experimental choices in the laboratory, particularly from the Allais paradox (see Chapter 9), it is obvious that, at least in some cases, people employ decision weights (DWs) rather than objective probabilities. However, as we demonstrated in Chapter 9, although the employment of DWs may resolve some expected utility paradoxes, it may create other paradoxes, such as First-degree Stochastic Dominance (FSD) violation. This implies a rejection of the monotonicity axiom, implying that a person may prefer less wealth than more wealth, an unacceptable situation. Thus, the expected utility model reveals some paradoxes and the Prospect Theory (PT) model may violate FSD. Therefore, a more satisfactory model that avoids the two types of paradoxes is needed.[1]

With respect to the FSD violation, one must distinguish between a predicted FSD violation, obtained with a theoretical model, and an experimentally or an empirically observed FSD violation. The observed experimental or empirical FSD violations may be induced by two factors: DWs and bounded rationality. The DWs' effect on FSD violations, in PT framework, is discussed in Chapter 9. The

---

[1] The accumulated body of evidence that expected utility is inadequate in describing human behavior led researchers to look for other models, which resolves some of the paradoxes. See, for example, P. C. Fishburn, *Nonlinear Preference and Utility Theory*, The Johns Hopkins University Press, Baltimore, 1988; M. J. Machina, "Choices Under Uncertainty: Problems Solved and Unsolved," *Economic Perspectives*, 1987; and C. F. Camerer, "An Experimental Test of Several Generalized Utility Theories," *Journal of Risk and Uncertainty*, 1989.

bounded rationality FSD violations may be due to the complexity of the prospects under consideration; that is, people cannot comprehend the complicated distributions of rates of return of the two prospects under consideration and hence do not select rationally among the various prospects. In this chapter, we discuss these two sources of potential FSD violations. However, one should keep in mind that a violation of FSD in choices induced by bounded rationality might exist regardless of whether objective probabilities or DWs are employed. Thus, DWs and bounded rationality may join forces, operating in the same direction and resulting in an FSD violation.

Virtually no researcher is ready to accept a theoretical model that allows preferring less wealth to more wealth, that is, that allows for an FSD violation. Therefore, efforts have been made by several researchers to modify the DW structure that has been suggested by PT, a modification that guarantees no FSD violations.

Indeed, several studies suggest shifting from probabilities to DWs by making some transformation on the cumulative probability function of returns rather than a transformation on each individual probability, hence the term *cumulative DWs*. By the suggested cumulative DW models, the transformation on the cumulative distribution is monotonically increasing; thus, it ensures that if prospect F dominates prospect G by FSD with objective probabilities, then prospect F also dominates prospect G when the probabilities are replaced by DWs. The advantages of the suggested cumulative DW methods are apparent in their simplicity and in that they guarantee no FSD violation. In addition, unlike the DWs determined by PT, those determined by a transformation of the cumulative probability function can also be employed with continuous random variables – a technical advantage.

The disadvantage of the earlier suggested cumulative DWs method (first suggested by Quiggin[2] in 1982) is that it does not distinguish between transformation of probabilities in the positive and the negative domain. The possibility of distinguishing between the weighting model in the negative and the positive domains was suggested

---

[2] J. Quiggin, "A Theory of Anticipated Utility," *Journal of Economic Behavior and Organization*, 1982. See also M. E. Yaari, "The Dual Theory of Choice Under Risk," *Econometrica*, 1987, and D. Schmeidler, "Subjective Probability and Expected Utility without Additivity," *Econometrica*, 1989.

a decade later by Cumulative Prospect Theory (CPT) DWs (see Tversky and Kahneman[3]). Yet another remaining disadvantage that virtually all cumulative DW methods share is that with these methods there is no freedom to assign some unique DW to a particular event because the DW assigned to each event is technically derived from the cumulative DW function. Therefore, in Section 10.5, we suggest in the spirit of Rank-Dependent Expected Utility (RDEU) and CPT DW methods another DW function that on the one hand does not violate FSD and on the other hand provides more freedom in the determination of the DW, which may be dependent on the prospects under consideration.

Kahneman and Tversky suggest two alternative ways to avoid FSD violation:

a) *The noncumulative method:* This method employs the noncumulative DWs as suggested in their original 1979 article, but it involves editing in the first stage, before a choice is made. In the editing process, all FSD inferior prospects are eliminated. This procedure cannot be applied to continuous random variables because a DW is attached to each event separately. However, a specific DW can be assigned to each event, so the DW is not obtained as a technical result derived from some cumulative function.

b) *The cumulative method*: This method employs a cumulative transformation of probabilities to DWs, as advocated in their CPT study. This method, like the previously suggested methods, guarantees no FSD violation. Moreover, unlike the previous methods, it has the flexibility to have different transformation formulas corresponding to the negative and the positive domains of outcomes. In addition, the suggested procedure is applicable to both discrete and continuous random variables.

In this chapter, we discuss the various suggested methods to transform probabilities into DWs. We demonstrate the pros and cons of each method by means of numerical examples. From the discussion of

---

[3] A. Tversky and D. Kahneman, "Advances in Prospect Theory: Cumulative Representation of Uncertainty," *Journal of Risk and Uncertainty*, 1992.

the various methods for determining the DW, it emerges that one cannot find one method that fits all situations. Presumably, the DWs are situation dependent, and one method cannot fit all situations. Moreover, as we shall see in Section 10.5 of this chapter, the DWs, as suggested by CPT, although they avoid FSD violations, may also lead to unreasonable DWs, particularly in the case of equally likely outcomes. Finally, we also discuss in this chapter the FSD violations that are due to bounded rationality. The bounded rationality has nothing to do with DWs, as it is shown in this chapter that FSD violations are expected even with objective probabilities. Moreover, the more complicated the choices are, the more FSD violations occur.

10.2. RANK-DEPENDENT EXPECTED UTILITY

The RDEU is a model that assumes that investors maximize expected utility with a transformation of the probabilities into DWs, where the transformation is done on the cumulative probability rather than on the individual probabilities. Quiggin[4] was the first to suggest transforming the cumulative probabilities into DWs. Several other studies that follow the pioneering suggestion of Quiggin have a common feature: on the one hand, they employ DWs; on the other hand, they guarantee no FSD violation. Of course, the transformation suggested by Quiggin can be employed with PT's value function and with a utility function alike.

The basic idea of transforming a cumulative probability function is as follows: Define the cumulative distributions of the two prospects under consideration as $F(x)$ and $G(x)$. Define the two new transformed prospects that are derived from the two prospects under consideration as $F^{\bullet}(x)$ and $G^{\bullet}(x)$. The relationship between these distributions is as follows:

$$F^{\bullet}(x) = T[F(x)]$$
$$G^{\bullet}(x) = T[G(x)],$$

where T is a monotonic nondecreasing function of the cumulative probabilities with $T(0) = 0$ and $T(1) = 1$. Because of the monotonicity assumption, we have $T' \geq 0$.

---

[4] See Quiggin, 1982, *op. cit.*

In the discrete case, RDEU suggests the following probability transformation: with

$$V(w, p) = \sum_{i=1}^{n} U(x_i) w_i(p_i),$$

where

$$w_i(p_i) = T\left(\sum_{j=1}^{i} p_j\right) - T\left(\sum_{j=1}^{i-1} p_j\right)$$

$$= T[F(x_i)] - T[F(x_{i-1})] \tag{10.1}$$

for the lowest possible value denoted by 1, we have $w_1(p_1) = T(p_1)$, and $w_i(p_i)$ is the DW assigned to the outcome with probability p_i, which is derived from the cumulative distribution transformation.

Note that $V(w, p)$ denotes the expected utility with DWs. Of course, this general formulation collapses to the classic expected utility when $T[F(x)] = F(x)$; hence, the DW of each probability is equal to the probability itself. Similarly, this formula also provides the expected value of PT when the utility function is replaced by the value function. However, the unique feature of this formulation is that the DWs are derived from the cumulative distributions and not directly from the individual probabilities, as done in the original PT; hence, by the monotonicity of the transformation, no FSD violation can occur. Namely, if $F(x) \leq G(x)$ for a given value x, we also have $F^{\bullet}(x) \leq G^{\bullet}(x)$ because the transformation is monotonic; therefore, FSD is not violated.

Example: Suppose the two prospects under consideration are given by

    $G(x)$: 1, 2, and 3 with an equal probability of 1/3
    $F(x)$: 2, 3, and 5 with probabilities of 1/2, 1/4, and 1/4, respectively

It is easy to see that F dominates G by FSD. Figure 10.1a provides the cumulative distributions F and G and, as can be seen from this figure, F dominates G by FSD because the two distributions do not intersect, and F is located below G.

Now consider the following monotonic transformation:

$$F^{\bullet}(x) = T[F(x)] = [F(x)]^2,$$

and similarly,

$$G^{\bullet}(x) = T[G(x)] = [G(x)]^2.$$

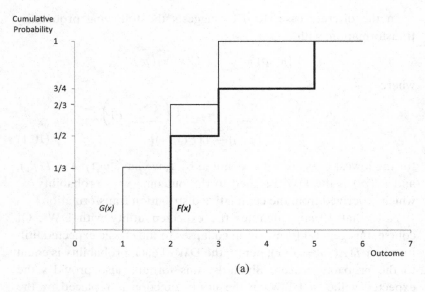

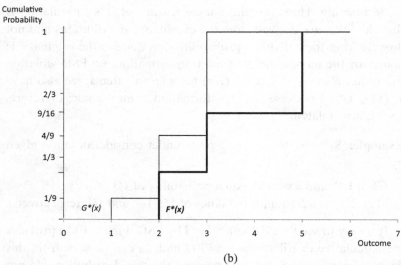

Figure 10.1. Cumulative Distributions of Prospects *F* and *G*. (a) With Objective Probabilities. (b) With Decision Weights.

Table 10.1 provides the statistical data corresponding to the two distributions *F* and *G*. The table also provides the transformed distributions *F*• and *G*•. Let us explain how the individual DWs are calculated. We illustrate the calculation with distribution *G*, and the

Table 10.1. *Cumulative Decision Weights with Monotonoic Transformation*

Prospect G				
x_i	$P(x_i)$ $G(x_i)$	$G^* = T[G(x_i)] = [G(x_i)]^2$		$W_i\,(P_i) = T[G(x_i)] - T[G(x_{i-1})]$
1	1/3 1/3	1/9		1/9
2	1/3 2/3	4/9		3/9
3	1/3 1	1		5/9
Prospect F				
x_i	$P(x_i)$ $F(x_i)$	$F^* = T[F(x_i)] = [F(x_i)]^2$		$W_i\,(P_i) = T[F(x_i)] - T[F(x_{i-1})]$
2	1/2 1/2	4/16		4/16
3	1/4 3/4	9/16		5/16
5	1/4 1	1		7/16

DWs corresponding to distribution F are calculated in a similar way. At the first step, we calculate the DW corresponding to the largest outcome, which is $x = 3$ in our specific case. In calculating the DW with this method, one can start at any point x_0, with a cumulative probability $F(x_0)$. For simplicity, we start herein from the largest possible outcome and, by iteration, solve step by step for the DW assigned to each outcome.

Using equation (10.1), the DW of the probability 1/3 corresponding to the outcome $x = 3$, with the preceding assumed transformation, is given by the following:

$$w(1/3) = [G(3)]^2 - [G(2)]^2 = 1^2 - (2/3)^2 = 5/9.$$

Now let us turn to the second largest value, which is $x = 2$ in our example, to obtain

$$w(1/3) = [G(2)]^2 - [G(1)]^2 = (2/3)^2 - (1/3)^2 = 3/9.$$

Finally, for the probability corresponding to the lowest outcome $x = 1$, we have

$$w(1/3) = [G(1)]^2 = (1/3)^2 = 1/9.$$

These DWs are given in Table 10.1a. In a similar way, the DWs corresponding to prospect F are calculated (see Table 10.1b). Using these DWs, we can draw the distributions F^* and G^*, which are similar to the original distributions with one exception: the DWs substitute for the objective probabilities. As expected, these two distributions do not intersect and F^* dominates G^* by FSD. Thus, we have illustrated by a simple numerical example that if F dominates G by FSD, this dominance is intact also with DWs as long as the DWs are calculated by a monotonic transformation conducted in the cumulative probability, like the one employed in the calculations in Table 10.1. Of course, similar results are obtained with other monotonic transformations; for example, $T[F(x)] = \sqrt{F(x)}$, and so forth.

Finally, note that the DW corresponding to each outcome depends on the rank of this outcome in the distribution. For example, in rolling a die, although the numbers 1 and 6 have the same probability of 1/6, each observation will get a different DW that depends on its ranking in the distribution; hence the term *rank-dependent expected utility*.

So far, we have one formula for the transformation of all probabilities regardless of whether they correspond to positive or negative outcomes. However, Tversky and Kahneman advocate that investors typically behave differently in the positive and the negative domains. Therefore, it may be that $w(p)$ may vary for the same probability of, say, $p = 1/3$ and for the same rank of the outcome within the distribution, depending on whether this probability corresponds to negative or positive outcome. Thus, it is possible that the assigned DW formula depends not only on the probability but also on the sign of the income. For example, for the distribution $(-1, 2, 3)$ with an equal probability to each outcome, the weight given to 1/3, corresponding to the outcome $x = -1$, may be different from the DW assigned to the probability of 1/3, corresponding to the outcome $x = 1$, in the following distribution $(1, 2, 3)$ with an equal probability of 1/3. With the RDEU DWs, the rank of the outcome in the distribution and its probability determine the DW, but not the sign of the outcome. Tversky and Kahneman consider the irrelevance of the sign of the outcome in the determination of the DW as a drawback. Therefore, they suggest another weighting method, which on the one hand does not violate FSD, and on the other hand takes into consideration the signs of the various outcomes.

10.3. CUMULATIVE PROSPECT THEORY DECISION WEIGHTS

Realizing the objection to a theoretical model that violates FSD, Tversky and Kahneman[5] suggest CPT as a modification to their original PT. The main contribution of the suggested modification is with

---

[5] See Tversky and Kahneman, 1992, *op. cit.*

respect to the DWs: they are determined such that FSD is not violated. Additionally, in this study, they conduct experiments, which allow them to estimate the parameters of the value function as well as the parameters of the DW function. However, unlike the previous studies, which suggest transforming the cumulative distributions into DWs, they suggest transforming the probabilities corresponding to negative and positive outcomes of the distribution separately.[6]

Here we demonstrate CPT's DWs that correspond to mixed prospects. When we have positive or negative prospects rather than mixed prospects, only the positive or the negative DW formula is applied, respectively. To explain the DW method suggested by Tversky and Kahneman, assume that we face a distribution of outcomes when n of the outcomes are positive and m of the outcomes are negative. The probabilities of all outcomes ranked by their size is given by

$$p_{-m}, \ldots \ldots p_{-2}, p_{-1}, p_{+1}, p_{+2}, \ldots \ldots \ldots p_{+n},$$

where p_{-m} corresponds to the lowest (negative) outcome and p_{+n} corresponds to the highest (positive) outcome.

Then, by CPT, the DWs are determined as follows:

$$w_n^+(p_n) = T^+(p_n)$$
$$w_i^+(p_i) = T^+(p_i + \cdots + p_n) - T^+(p_{i+1} + \cdots + p_n)$$
$$\text{for } 0 \leq i \leq n - 1, \tag{10.2}$$

where p_i is the probability of the ith outcome, and these are ordered from the smallest to the largest; $w_i^+(p_i)$ is the DW corresponding to the ith probability calculated with the transformation of the cumulative distribution, where the transformation is denoted by T. The superscript $+$ emphasizes that in this way we calculate the DWs corresponding to the probabilities of positive outcomes only. Note that with CPT we have to start the calculation with the largest possible value and then by iteration solve for the DW assigned to each observation.

---

[6] See also L. R. Duncan and P. C. Fishburn, "Rank- and Sign-Dependent Linear Utility Models for Finite First-Order Gambles," *Journal of Risk and Uncertainty*, 1991.

Regarding the negative outcomes, by CPT we have

$$w_m^-(p_{-m}) = T^-(p_{-m})$$

and

$$w^-(p_i) = T^-(p_{-m} + \cdots\cdots + p_i) - T^-(p_{-m} + \cdots\cdots + p_{i-1})$$

$$\text{for } 1 - m \leq i \leq 0 \qquad\qquad\qquad (10.3)$$

where the superscript – emphasizes that we are dealing with DWs corresponding to probabilities of negative outcomes only. Unlike the calculation corresponding to the positive outcomes, with negative outcomes, we start the calculations with the smallest possible outcome and then by iteration calculate the DW corresponding to each negative outcome.

The transformation function T^+ and T^- corresponding to the positive and the negative outcomes may be identical, but this is not necessarily so. Finally, with mixed prospects, which contain negative as well as positive outcomes, formulas (10.2) and (10.3) are employed simultaneously. In a case of a positive prospect (i.e., all outcomes are positive) or a negative prospect (i.e., all outcomes are negative), only the + DWs formula or the – DWs formula is employed.

The following demonstrates the transformation of probabilities into DWs as suggested by CPT by means of an example, and then we contrast it with the decisions obtained by the RDEU model.

An example: The example given here is taken from Tversky and Kahneman.[7] Suppose you roll a die and x denotes the outcome. If the number is even, you receive \$x$, and if the number is odd, you pay \$x$. Thus, you have the following distribution of outcomes:

For even numbers: [(0, 1/2), (2, 1/6), (4, 1/6), (6, 1/6)]
For odd numbers: [(0, 1/2), (–1, 1/6), (–3, 1/6), (–5, 1/6)]

Let us explain. The positive branch of the distribution includes 2, 4, and 6, with a probability of 1/6 each, summing to 1/2. We then add an outcome of zero with probability 1/2 so that the probabilities sum to 1. The negative branch is obtained in a similar manner. Note that adding a zero outcome to the two branches does not change choices, because by CPT the value function at point zero is equal to zero.

---

[7] See Tversky and Kahneman, 1992, *op. cit.*

To demonstrate how the DWs are calculated, we must add a transformation function T. As selected before, let us select the arbitrary transformation

$$T\left(\sum p_i\right) = \left(\sum p_i\right)^2, \tag{10.4}$$

where the DW of the relevant probabilities is calculated by equations (10.2) and (10.3). We start with the positive branch of outcomes. We have the following:

For outcome $x = 6$: $w(1/6) = T(1/6) = (1/6)^2 = 1/36$.

For outcome $x = 4$: $w(1/6) = T(2/6) - T(1/6) = 4/36 - 1/36 = 3/36$.

For outcome $x = 2$: $w(1/6) = T(3/6) - T(2/6) = 9/36 - 4/36 = 5/36$.

Similarly, for the negative outcomes we have the following:

For outcome $x = -5$: $w(1/6) = T(1/6) = 1/36$

For outcome $x = -3$: $w(1/6) = T(2/6) - T(1/6) = 4/36 - 1/36 = 3/36$

For outcome $x = -1$: $w(1/6) = T(3/6) - T(2/6) = 9/36 - 4/36 = 5/36$

In the preceding calculation, for simplicity and without loss of generality, we assume that the same transformation T is employed in the negative and the positive domain of outcomes; thus, we employ the same transformation T, with no need to employ T^+ and T^-. Table 10.2 provides a summary of the DWs as calculated by CPT DWs (see equations (10.2) and (10.3)) and by RDEU (see equation (10.1)), where in both cases we employ the same probability transformation given by equation (10.4).

A few observations from the two different DWs obtained by the two methodologies are worth noting:

a) The sum of the DWs as determined by the RDEU model is equal to 1. The sum of CPT DWs is generally different from 1 (in our specific case, it is smaller than 1). Thus, one can treat the RDEU model DWs as probabilities, but CPT DWs, in general, cannot be interpreted as probabilities. Note that the results reported in Table 10.2 correspond to the specific selected probability transformation function, but the property discussed is intact for other transformations as well: RDEU DWs can be interpreted as probabilities but CPT DWs, generally, cannot.

Table 10.2. *Rank-Dependent Expected Utility (RDEU) and Cumulative Prospect Theory (CPT) Decision Weights: Mixed Prospects with the Transformation* $T[\bullet] = [\bullet]^2$

Outcome	Probability	CPT Decision Weights	RDEU Decision Weights
−5	1/6	1/36	$(1/6)^2 - 0 = 1/36$
−3	1/6	3/36	$(2/6)^2 - (1/6)^2 = 3/36$
−1	1/6	5/36	$(3/6)^2 - (2/6)^2 = 5/36$
2	1/6	5/36	$(4/6)^2 - (3/6)^2 = 7/36$
4	1/6	3/36	$(5/6)^2 - (4/6)^2 = 9/36$
6	1/6	1/36	$1 - (5/6)^2 = 11/36$
Sum of Decision Weights		18/36	1

b) A symmetrical DW structure is obtained for the negative and the positive outcomes with CPT DWs. This is a technical result related to our specific example and not a necessary result. With different transformation functions corresponding to the negative and positive outcomes, this symmetry vanishes. Indeed, as we shall see, Tversky and Kahneman suggest a different transformation formula for negative and positive outcomes.

Let us now compare the DWs of CPT and RDEU for nonmixed prospects. Table 10.3a and 10.3b demonstrate the calculations for positive and negative prospects, respectively.

The following conclusions can be drawn from Table 10.3:

a) When one compares only positive or only negative prospects, the sum of the DWs under the two DW calculation methods is always equal to 1. Consequently, the DWs of CPT, under nonmixed prospects, can also be treated as probabilities.
b) With negative prospects, and with the same probability transformation formula, the DWs as determined by the two methods under consideration are identical. However, with positive prospects, the DWs as calculated by the two methods are very different.

The preceding discussion and the numerical examples reveal that there is more than one method to avoid FSD violation. However, the employment of RDEU and CPT to calculate DWs reveals that very different DWs are assigned to the various outcomes by these two

Table 10.3. *Cumulative Prospect Theory (CPT) and Rank-Dependent Expected Utility (RDEU) Decision Weights with Positive and Negative Prospects, with the Transformation $T[\bullet] = [\bullet]^2$*

		a. Positive Prospect	
Outcome	Probability	CPT Decision Weights (eq. (10.2))	RDEU Decision Weights (eq. (10.1))
1	1/6	$1 - (5/6)^2 = 11/36$	1/36
2	1/6	$(5/6)^2 - (4/6)^2 = 9/36$	3/36
3	1/6	$(4/6)^2 - (3/6)^2 = 7/36$	5/36
4	1/6	$(3/6)^2 - (2/6)^2 = 5/36$	7/36
5	1/6	$(2/6)^2 - (1/6)^2 = 3/36$	9/36
6	1/6	$(1/6)^2 - 0 = 1/36$	11/36
Sum		1	1

		b. Negative Prospect	
Outcome	Probability	CPT Decision Weights (eq. (10.2))	RDEU Decision Weights (eq. ((10.1))
–6	1/6	$(1/6)^2 - 0 = 1/36$	1/36
–5	1/6	$(2/6)^2 - (1/6)^2 = 3/36$	3/36
–4	1/6	$(3/6)^2 - (2/6)^2 = 5/36$	5/36
–3	1/6	$(4/6)^2 - (3/6)^2 = 7/36$	7/36
–2	1/6	$(5/6)^2 - (4/6)^2 = 9/36$	9/36
–1	1/6	$1 - (5/6)^2 = 11/36$	11/36
Sum		1	1

methods, even when the same probability transformation formula is employed, let alone when different formulas are employed to transform probabilities by the two suggested methods.

Which DWs are the correct ones? This question should be addressed experimentally or empirically. We next turn to the estimates of the DWs and the value functions as have been found experimentally.

10.4. THE VALUE AND THE DECISION WEIGHT FUNCTIONS AS SUGGESTED BY CUMULATIVE PROSPECT THEORY

Based on the observed subjects' choices, Tversky and Kahneman[8] estimate the value (utility) function and the DW function. They suggest that the typical subject maximizes an S-shape value function and

[8] *Op. cit.*, 1992.

employs a reverse S-shape DW function. They suggest the following model of choices:

a) *The value function*: People maximize the expected value of the following function:

$$V(x) = \begin{cases} x^{\alpha} & \text{if } x \geq 0 \\ -\lambda(-x^{\beta}) & \text{if } x < 0 \end{cases} \qquad (10.5)$$

where x denotes the change in wealth and the experimental parameter estimates are $\alpha = 0.88$, $\beta = 0.88$, and $\lambda = 2.25$.[9] Note that this is an *S-shape* function revealing risk seeking for losses and risk aversion for gains, contradicting the concave-shape preference advocated by economic models, which rely on Expected Utility Theory (EUT; see Figure 9.5). Also note that by this model, investors maximize the expected value of the aforementioned function, when the argument of the function is the *change* of wealth, rather than total wealth. Thus, it is assumed that $EV(x)$ is maximized and not $EV(W + x)$ when W is the initial wealth and x is the change of wealth, implying that zero wealth is the reference point.

b) *Loss aversion*: The parameter λ has been experimentally estimated to be greater than 1. This implies that the segment of the value function in the negative domain is steeper than the segment in the positive domain, a characteristic well known as *loss aversion*. This finding, according to our view, is one of the most important robust contributions of PT to the theory of choices because it explains people's behavior and suggests solutions to several economic puzzles, for example, the equity premium puzzle pointed out by Mehra and Prescott.[10] The value function under PT and under CPT is the same, as described by Figure 9.5 in Chapter 9.

---

[9] Numerous studies provide different estimates of the parameters of the value function. However, we focus in this chapter on the original estimates as provided by Tversky and Kahneman.

[10] R. Mehra and E. Prescott, "The Equity Premium: A Puzzle," *Journal of Monetary Economics*, 1985. For a solution of this puzzle with loss aversion, see S. Benartzi, and R. H. Thaler, "Myopic Loss Aversion and the Equity Premium Puzzle," *Quarterly Journal of Economics*, 1995. See also A. Tversky and D. Kahneman, "Loss Aversion in Riskless Choice: A Reference Dependent Model," *Quarterly Journal of Economics*, 1991.

However, based on experimental results, the advances in PT suggest a parameterization of the S-shape function.

c) Inventors do not use objective probabilities but rather use DWs given by the following function:

$$T^+(F) = \frac{F^\gamma}{[F^\gamma + (1 - F)^\gamma]^{1/\gamma}}$$

$$T^-(F) = \frac{F^\delta}{[F^\delta + (1 - F)^\delta]^{1/\gamma}} \tag{10.6}$$

where the experimental parameter estimates are $\gamma = 0.61, \delta = 0.69$, and F is the cumulative distribution. The transformed probability at any point $F(x)$ is given by the T function, which has different parameters for the positive and the negative domain of x. Thus, for a given value of the outcome x, $F(x)$ is calculated (with objective probabilities), then the function T is calculated. Having the function T corresponding to two subsequent values of F, one can calculate the implied DW assigned to each individual probability (in the discrete case), as done in the construction of Tables 10.2 and 10.3 previously presented.

Figure 10.2 demonstrates the DW function as estimated by Tversky and Kahneman. First, note that $T(0) = 0$ and $T(1) = 1$. The 45° line is the hypothetical line describing a case in which the DWs are equal to the objective probabilities. By CPT DWs, the curves that describe the DW functions are above the straight line at the beginning; after the intersection point, the opposite holds: the transformation curve is below the straight line. Also note that the transformation curves corresponding to the negative and the positive outcomes are very similar in their shape.

10.5. THE VARIOUS DECISION WEIGHTS: FORMULAS AND ESTIMATES

This section is devoted to DWs and to a new suggested method to determine DW, called prospect-dependent decision weights (PDDW).

As we have seen in Chapter 9, DW is one factor that induces possible deviations from the expected utility paradigm. The DW employment explains the Allais paradox and relates strongly to the

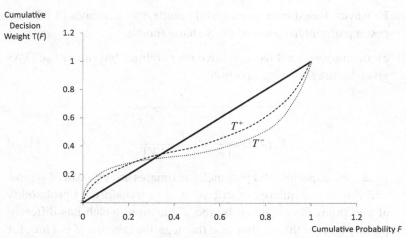

Figure 10.2. Cumulative Prospect Theory Decision Weight Function. *Source:* A. Tversky and D. Kahneman, "Advances in Prospect Theory: Cumulative Representation of Uncertainty," *Journal of Risk and Uncertainty*, 1992 (with minor changes in notation).

certainty effect phenomenon observed in experimental choices. It is claimed that the employment of DW allows the investor to justify the choice or, more precisely, helps the investor make a choice with which he or she can live peacefully. Indeed, DWs are not probabilities; rather, they reflect probabilities as well as preferences.

To quantify the DW, several researchers conducted experiments aiming to estimate these values. The formulas suggested by these various researchers for the DW function, as well as the obtained estimates, are quite different from each other. This should not surprise us because the obtained DW estimates are a function of the prospects under consideration in each experiment. We suggest in this section that there is no justification to provide estimates of the DWs because they are situation dependent. Specifically, the DWs attributed to a probability, of, say, 0.1 corresponding to the lowest possible outcome may be different from one experiment to another, depending on the alternative prospects under consideration.

We show here the difference corresponding to the various DW methods and suggest another new DW method; this method does not suffer from the drawbacks of the existing DW methods. Yet, also, the new suggested method, called PDDW, does not violate FSD.

There are DW models that may violate FSD and models that guarantee no such violation. Early studies on the effect of DW on the decision-making process were conducted by Edwards[11] in 1962. Yet, only in 1979, when Kahneman and Tversky published their famous PT article, did DWs become central to economics and finance research. Fishburn[12] and others pointed out that PT's DW may lead to an FSD violation, that is, to the violation of the monotonicity axiom. Because no violation of FSD is considered essential to economic models, PT's DWs are unaccepted. Indeed, Tversky and Kahneman themselves suggest a modification of their original model called CPT. This theory is similar to PT in many respects, but it determines the DW in such a way that FSD is not violated. Quiggin[13] was first to suggest the RDEU, by which DWs are employed in such a way that FSD is not violated (see also Machina[14]). Nowadays, it is accepted that a system of DW should be established with a constraint that FSD is not violated. Therefore, in this section, we follow this "no FSD violation" principle.

The main contribution of DW is in explaining choices in practice, to explain subjects' behavior in experimental tests, and particularly to explain choices that contradict the principle of expected utility maximization. Because the experimental choices are from a set of possible prospects, it is natural that the prospects under consideration (like in the Allais paradox) affect the DW employed by subjects; hence, the DWs are expected to be prospect dependent. The drawback of the existing DW already mentioned, particularly the formulas that determine the DWs, is that they ignore the other prospects that compete with the specific prospect under consideration.

Thus, with the most common decision-weighting methods – namely, CPT and RDEU – the DWs are not taking into account the alternative under consideration. However because the employment

[11] See W. Edwards, "Subjective Probabilities Inferred from Decisions," *Psychological Review*, 1962.

[12] P. C. Fishburn, "On Handa's 'New Theory of Cardinal Utility' and the Maximization of Expected Utility," *Journal of Political Economy*, 1978.

[13] See J. Quiggin, "A Theory of Anticipated Utility," *Journal of Economic Behavior and Organization*, 1982, and *Generalized Expected Utility Theory: The Rank-Dependent Model*, Kluwer Academic Press, Boston, MA, 1993.

[14] M. J. Machina, "Review of Generalized Expected Utility Models: The Rank-Dependent Model," *Journal of Economic Literature*, 1994.

of DW by itself is derived from psychological motives, it is reasonable that the structure of two (or more) prospects under consideration play an important role in determining the DW, $w(P)$, which implies that the alternative prospect, like in the Allais paradox, affects the DW. In other words, any DW function that is estimated based on a given pair of prospects is relevant only to this pair; therefore, one cannot write down a generalized DW function. The DWs rather change from one pair of choices to another; hence, they are prospect dependent. We first illustrate this issue with two examples and then provide a more general comparison of the existing DW models and the new suggested PDDW model.

Example 1: A Choice between Two Prospects
Suppose an investor considers two sets of choices, A and B, as follows:
Choice A

$$F = \left\{ \begin{array}{l} -\$1 \text{ million with probability } 0.01 \\ +\$5 \text{ million with probability } 0.99 \end{array} \right\},$$

$$G = \left\{ +\$1 \text{ million with probability } 1 \right\}$$

Choice B

$$F = \left\{ \begin{array}{l} -\$500, -\$480, -\$460, \ldots \$20, \$40 \ldots .\$1,460, \$1,480, \$1,500 \\ \text{each outcome with a probability } 0.01 \end{array} \right\},$$

$$G = \left\{ +\$400 \text{ with probability } 1 \right\}$$

The probability of 0.01 in set A is very meaningful because it implies a big loss, particularly with a possible regret of not winning the $1 million of prospect G. The probability of 0.01 of, say, losing $500 in set B is not very meaningful because the –$500 outcome is not dramatically different from other outcomes. Yet, by CPT and RDEU, the same DW is assigned to 0.01 in both cases. Thus, by CPT and RDEU, we have $w_F(0.01)$ of set A (corresponding to loss of $1 million) = $w_F(0.01)$ of set B (corresponding to –$500); hence, $w(0.01)$ is determined independently of the alternative prospect under consideration. However, set A is very similar to the Allais paradox, and to avoid the situation of not winning the $1 million for sure, people may employ a DW $w(0.01) > 0.01$ (and maybe also $w(0.99) < 0.99$), which justifies the rejection of F. In addition, the size of the possible loss may affect the DW. However, in set B, $w(0.01)$, corresponding to –$500, may be close to $p = 0.01$ because choosing either F or G does not make a dramatic change in the possible obtained cash flow. In other words, in choice A, severe regret may affect the DW, a regret that does not exist in choice B: thus, different DWs are expected in these two choices.

Whereas CPT and RDEU models of DW ignore the alternative choice (and for this reason in the preceding example, $w(0.01)$ is the same for both A and B; see, equation (10.6) to follow), we suggest a model that allows us to have $w_F(0.01) \cong 0.01$ in set B and at the same time to have $w_F(0.01) > 0.01$ in set A. We emphasize that PDDW allows a dependency on the alternative prospect (or prospects), but it does not force it. However, such dependency is called for to explain choices such as those in cases A and B. Thus, the PDDW model, which is prospect dependent, allows us to distinguish between the DW of sets A and B, a case that does not prevail with the other existing DW models. Finally, this distinction of the DW by the PDDW model is not due to the "certainty effect." If G in set A is replaced by $500,000 and $1.5 million, each with an equal probability, we still expect to obtain similar choice, implying that $w(0.01) > 0.01$.

Example 2: A Choice between More Than Two Prospects
We claim in the following that the DWs are determined by *all* alternative prospects from which the subject has to choose. To demonstrate this concept, it is sufficient to discuss the following three prospects: F, G, and H:

$$F: \left\{ \begin{array}{l} -\$1 \text{ million with probability } 0.01 \\ \$5 \text{ million with probability } 0.99 \end{array} \right\}$$

$$G: \left\{ \begin{array}{l} -\$1.2 \text{ million with probability } 0.01 \\ \$6 \text{ million with probability } 0.99 \end{array} \right\}$$

$$H: \left\{ \begin{array}{l} \$1 \text{ million with probability } 0.5 \\ \$2 \text{ million with probability } 0.5 \end{array} \right\}$$

If the subjects face only the pair (F, H), the hypothesis (as in example 1) is that like in a Allais paradox, most subjects would choose H. The same result is expected if the subject has to choose only from the pair

(G, H).[15] Thus, like in example 1, one needs $w(0.01) \gg 0.01$ and/or $w(0.99) \ll 0.99$ (with and without loss aversion) to explain the choice of H from the pair (F, H) or the choice of H from the pair (G, H). Now suppose that the choice is only from the pair (F, G). In this case, there is no need for a "flight from a loss" because F and G have very similar outcomes. Thus, in a choice between F and G, we expect to have $w(0.01) \cong 0.01$ and $w(0.99) \cong 0.99$; therefore, in such a case, DWs are not needed and probably are not employed in making choices. This is quite different from CPT and RDEU models of DW where $w(0.01)$ is the same regardless of the two prospects under consideration. Finally, suppose the subjects have to choose one prospect from $\{F, G,$ and $H\}$. Here, a flight from a loss implies that $w(0.01) \gg 0.01$ and/or $w(0.99) \ll 0.99$; otherwise, F or G may be selected.

Let us formalize the claim asserting that DWs are prospect dependent: Suppose that there is a vector of prospects F and prospect G. Prospect G contains an outcome x with a probability $p(x)$. We claim that the DW corresponding to $p(x)$ is determined by x, $p(x)$, as well as by F. Namely, instead of writing $w(p(x))$, we write the DW as follows: $w[p(x), x, G, F]$. Thus, the DW depends on $(p(x), x)$ corresponding to G, as well as other prospects F under consideration.

Finally, note that to justify the choice of H, one needs in the preceding example, that $w(0.01)$ is much greater – or $w(0.99)$ is much smaller – than the one estimated by CPT; see equation (10.6). This only emphasizes our point: $w(p)$ as estimated by CPT is relevant to the pair of distributions employed to estimate it, but it cannot be employed in other situations, such as in the preceding example. Therefore, we can impose some restrictions on $w(p)$ but cannot have one equation for $w(p)$ that fits all situations. To elaborate: The CPT and RDEU models of DW have the advantage of not violating FSD, but they also have the following three drawbacks that the suggested PDDW model overcomes:

a)   Left Tail Irrelevance (LTI)
b)   CPT's Fixed Mathematical DW Formula
c)   Irrelevancy of the Alternative Prospects

We now elaborate on each of these issues.

---

[15] Note that unlike the example in the Allais paradox, the outcome of prospect H does not have to be certain. Namely, the same analysis is intact if H is replaced by H' yielding a certain amount (e.g., $1.5 million with probability 1).

a) Left Tail Irrelevance

The DWs of both CPT and RDEU are determined in a nonflexible manner; consequently, for a given accumulated probability, the same weight is assigned to all outcomes, which are below the corresponding value. Namely, the structure of the left-tail distribution does not affect the total weight allocated to the left-tail outcomes. Although this DW scheme guarantees no FSD violation, it induces the LTI paradox, or the left-tail unreasonable DW. To demonstrate the LTI issue, assume for simplicity first that $x > 0$. Consider two distributions, F and G, as follows:

F: $x = 1, 2, 3, 4, 5, 6, 7, 8$, with equal probability of $\frac{1}{8}$
G: $x = 1, 2$, with an equal probability of $\frac{1}{2}$

By the DWs of both RDEU and CPT, $T(P)$ is determined only as a function of P, where P is the *cumulative* probability, regardless of the structure of outcomes and probabilities corresponding to the left tail of the distribution. To illustrate, suppose that $T(P = \frac{1}{2}) = 0.60$. Then, in this example, the same 0.60 DW is spread over all the preceding outcomes; that is, over $x = 1, 2, 3$, and 4 in distribution F, and is assigned also to $x = 1$ in distribution G. Furthermore, suppose now that F' replaces F, where F' is given by $x = 1, 2, \ldots 50$ with a probability 0.01 assigned to each outcome, and $x = 100$ with a probability of $\frac{1}{2}$. Still, the value $T(P = \frac{1}{2}) = 0.60$; therefore, this weight is spread over the first fifty values. The same result is obtained when we change the probabilities, for example, as follows: We get in prospect $x = 1$ with $p(x) = 0.01$, $x = 4$ with $p(x) = 0.49$, and $x = 5, 6, 7$, and 8 with a probability of $\frac{1}{8}$. Thus, the changes in outcomes and probabilities do not change the cumulative DW given by $T(P) = 0.60$. This insensitivity of the cumulative DW to the structure of the distribution is obviously a drawback.

Thus, in this specific example, the structure of F (or G) corresponding to $F \leq \frac{1}{2}$ (i.e., the left tail of the distribution) does not affect the "total" DW allocated to this portion of the distribution. We may have a symmetrical distribution, a skewed distribution, small or large probabilities; yet, in all cases, in this example, a DW of 0.60 is allocated to the "left tail."

So far, we have assumed that $x > 0$. However, this drawback of the existing DW models is even more serious when we also allow large negative outcomes with a very small probability. Moreover, if the lowest observation is $-\$10^6$ or $-\$5$ with probability 0.1, $w(0.1)$ will be the same, an undesired characteristic of CPT and RDEU's DW models. Of course, this example illustrates the left tail drawback with a specific point, $T(\frac{1}{2}) = 0.60$, but the same drawback holds for any value $T(P)$. We call this undesired property of the main DW models the *left tail irrelevance.*

b) Cumulative Prospect Theory's Unreasonable Decision Weights: The Equally Likely Outcome Case

Whereas the RDEU method of probability transformation, $T(F)$, is not specific regarding its values (apart from $T'(P) > 0$ and $T(0) = 0$, $T(1) = 1$), the CPT DW method of Tversky and Kahneman is more specific. As shown in equation (10.6), they estimate the function $T(P)$ separately for negative outcomes and separately for positive outcomes. The formula in equation (10.6) depends on the cumulative probability function, not on the alternative prospect under consideration. However, as we shall see, the disadvantage of such a fixed formula is that it suggests in some cases unreasonable DW. We suggest a DW method that has some advantages over the existing methods.

Although most researchers support the reverse S-shape DW function, various estimates of the parameters of the DW are suggested. (See, for example, Camerer and Ho,[16] Wu and Gonzales,[17] and Abdellaoui.[18]) Prelec[19] states a set of axioms from which he derives several DW functional forms, $w(P)$. With his main formula for DW, he obtains the following DW function:

$$w(P) = \exp\{-(-\ln P)^{\alpha}\}, \quad (0 < \alpha < 1). \tag{10.7}$$

[16] C. F. Camerer and T. H. Ho, "Violations of Betweeness Axiom and Nonlinearity in Probability," *Journal of Risk and Uncertainty*, 1994.

[17] G. Wu and R. Gonzales, "Curvature of the Probability Weighting Function," *Management Science*, 1996.

[18] M. Abdellaoui, "Parameter Free Elicitation of Utility and Probability Weighting Functions," *Management Science*, 2000.

[19] D. Prelec, "The Probability Weighting Function," *Econometrica*, 1998.

This function also has no flexibility and, as for a given cumulative probability P, $w(P)$ is determined regardless of the left tail distribution.

Thus, in all the aforementioned studies, the weighting function has an inverse S-shape; therefore, generally, the DWs in the center of the distribution are smaller than the objective probabilities, and the opposite holds with regard to the left and right ends of the distribution. These properties conform to the strong experimental support revealing that in some situations, especially in the case of "long shots," relatively large DWs rather than objective probabilities are employed. Indeed, formula (10.6) was estimated by Tversky and Kahneman mainly with bets of small probabilities (e.g., 0.1). There is no doubt that equation (10.6) provides the best estimate of the DW function based on the specific choices presented to the subjects in Tversky and Kahneman experiments. However, as claimed previously, DW should be prospect dependent; therefore, we cannot apply their DWs to other choices. Specifically, it is not reasonable to generalize this formula and apply this probability weighting formula to other bets (e.g., bets with relatively large probabilities, such as $p \geq 0.25$) and particularly to equally likely outcome bets with n positive outcomes, such as $p_i = 1/n$ when $n = 2, 3, 4, \ldots$.

To illustrate why equation (10.6) is valid for some choices but not for other choices, we will provide an example revealing that when employing equation (10.6) in the case of equally likely outcomes, the CPT DW may lead to results that are very hard to accept. Consider the case when $n = 4$ with $p_i = \frac{1}{4}$, as follows:

Outcome (in $)	-2,000	-1,000	+3,000	+4,000
Probability	1/4	1/4	1/4	1/4
Viscusi's decision weight	1/4	1/4	1/4	1/4
CPT decision weight $w(p)$	0.29	0.16	0.13	0.29
Prelec's decision weight	0.29	0.16	0.16	0.29
PT decision weight $w^*(P)$	$w(\frac{1}{4}) = c$	$w(\frac{1}{4}) = c$	$w(\frac{1}{4}) = c$	$w(\frac{1}{4}) = c$

As can be seen from this example, CPT determines DWs that are very difficult to accept: the probability of $3,000 decreases from 0.25 to 0.13, and the probability of $4,000 increases from 0.25 to 0.29. Assigning to $4,000 a DW more than double (!) the DW assigned to $3,000 has no experimental support or an intuitive explanation. A similar argument is intact with Prelec's DW. This extreme DW does not occur with PT because in our example, we would have in this case the same DW to all outcomes.

Similarly, the Prospective Reference Theory of Viscusi,[20] determines that $w(\frac{1}{4}) = \frac{1}{4}$ in the uniform-probability case. This example illustrates that equation (10.6) may be valid for the specific experiment of Tversky and Kahneman but may yield unreasonable DWs in other situations. Hence, assuming a rigid DW function is problematic because the DW formula may dramatically change from one experiment to another. This is the main idea of the PDDW model presented next.

c) Irrelevancy of the Alternative Prospects

The DWs of PT, CPT, Prelec, and RDEU are determined by the probability function of a given prospect but not by the probability function of the alternative prospects under consideration. Similarly, objective probabilities in expected utility framework are *not* affected by the alternative prospects under consideration. In practice, subjective DWs may be affected by the alternative prospects. This is particularly relevant if the alternative prospect provides a certain outcome that creates the "certainty effect." We have already demonstrated this issue with two examples. Because the prospect dependency is the main advantage of the suggested PDDW, we further illustrate this idea by adding the following example. Suppose that one faces two sets of choices denoted by A and B:

$$
A \begin{cases} F = -\text{\$1 million with probability 0.01 and \$5 million} \\ \quad \text{with probability 0.99} \\ G = \quad \text{\$1 million with probability 1} \end{cases}
$$

$$
B \begin{cases} F = -\text{\$1 million with probability 0.01 and \$5 million} \\ \quad \text{with probability 0.99} \\ G' = -\text{\$1.1 million with probability 0.01, \$3 million with} \\ \quad \text{probability 0.49, and \$10 million with probability 0.5} \end{cases}
$$

[20] W. K. Viscusi, "Prospective Preference Theory; Toward an Explanation of Paradoxes," *Journal of Risk and Uncertainty*, 1989.

By the existing methods of determining DW (see the preceding discussion, particularly equation [10.6]), $w_F(0.01)$ is determined independently of the alternative prospect under consideration; see equation (10.6). However, intuitively, in the comparison of F and G corresponding to set A, the subject may employ $w_F(0.01) > 0.01$ to justify the selection of G, which avoids a possible loss and provides a certain outcome of $1 million. This reasoning does not hold with the comparison of F and G' of set B because in both F and G' there is a similar loss (−$1 million and −$1.1 million, respectively) with a probability of 0.01. Thus, it is reasonable to assume that the subject will assign the same DW in such a case; hence, $w_F(0.01) \cong w_G(0.01)$ is possible. By the PDDW model (suggested in Section 10.6), the DWs are affected by the two alternative prospects under consideration. Therefore, the DWs are *dependent* on the alternative prospect under consideration. Namely, in the first case (see set A), $w_F(0.01) = w_F(0.01, F, G)$, and in the second case, $w_F(0.01) = w_F(0.01, F, G')$; thus, contrary to equation (10.6), the DW of 0.01 of F may be different in the two cases.

In the following section, we show that the PDDW model suggests a method for determining DWs in a way that resolves the preceding problem (a)–(c).

10.6. THE SUGGESTED PROSPECT-DEPENDENT DECISION WEIGHTS MODEL

The DWs of the CPT, the RDEU, and the PDDW modeld are constructed in such a way that guarantees no FSD violation. However, there is a basic difference between PDDW and the other two procedures of establishing the DW. By CPT and RDEU, for cumulative probability P corresponding to two distributions F and G, we must have $T_F(P) = T_G(P)$, where $T(P)$ is the cumulative DW corresponding to P. Thus, if for a given value P, $Q_F(P) > Q_G(P)$, then also $Q_{F*}(T(P)) > Q_{G*}(T(P))$, where $Q_F(P)$ and $Q_G(P)$ are the Pth quintile of distributions F and G, respectively (i.e., the original distributions) and Q_{F*} and Q_{G*} are the quintiles of the distributions with DW.[21] This type

---

[21] As for CPT generally, $\sum w \neq 1$, for the sake of the discussion, we assume a non-mixed gamble where $\sum w = 1$; hence, we can use the concept of a cumulative distribution.

of DW technique guarantees that if $Q_F(P) \geq Q_G(P)$ for all values P then also $Q_{F*}(P) \geq Q_{G*}(P)$ for all values P, ensuring that FSD is not violated.

Thus, by the CPT and the RDEU models, in establishing the DWs we look horizontally at the cumulative distributions, F and G. Yet, with the PDDW model, we employ a different DW procedure: we look at the same two cumulative distributions vertically rather than horizontally. Suppose that for two cumulative probabilities, P_1 and P_2, corresponding to distributions F and G, respectively, we have $Q_F(P_1) = Q_G(P_2)$, where $P_1 \geq P_2$. By PDDW, we employ DW such that $T_F(P_1) \geq T_G(P_2)$, where $T_F(P_1)$ and $T_G(P_2)$ are the cumulative DWs corresponding to P_1 and P_2, respectively. Thus, also by this DW model, FSD is not violated because if F is below G, also the transformed distribution F is below the transformed distribution G. Note that by looking at the cumulative distributions F and G vertically rather than horizontally, we may have for a given P that $T_F(P) \neq T_G(P)$, which is impossible under CPT and RDEU. The possibility of having $T_F(P) \neq T_G(P)$ under the PDDW model provides a wide range of possible DWs, which is not available under CPT and RDEU models, allowing the DW to be prospect dependent. This property is illustrated graphically and with a numerical example in the following section.

Figure 10.3 demonstrates the difference among RDEU, CPT, and PT DWs and PDDW DWs. Suppose that we start with F and G such that F dominates G by FSD. For simplicity, F and G are drawn as two straight lines (a uniform distribution), but the analysis is general for any type of distribution. Figure 10.3 demonstrates the two distributions, $F*$ and $G*$, denoting F and G but with DWs rather than objective probabilities, with CPT's, RDEU's, and PT's DWs, as well as the suggested PDDW. For simplicity, in our example, we are confined to the positive domain (the same is true for x $\lesssim$ 0). Figure 10.3a focuses on the general RDEU DWs of Quiggin.[22] We first draw F and G (with FSD of F over G) and then draw $F*$ and $G*$ when, for demonstration purposes, we select the specific example of $T(P) = P^2$, which is a legitimate transformation in the RDEU framework (the same phenomenon exists with all other monotonic functions $T(\cdot)$ as long as $T'(\cdot) \geq 0$). As we can see from Figure 10.3a, for a given P_o, for both

---

[22] See Quiggin, 1982 and 1993, *op. cit.*

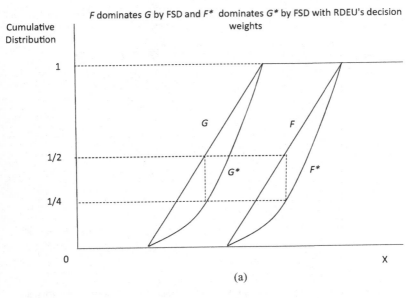

(a)

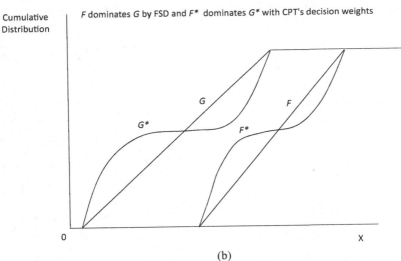

(b)

Figure 10.3. *F* and *G* and the Corresponding Distributions *F** and *G** with Various Decision Weights. (a) With RDEU Decision Weights. (b) With CPT Decision Weights. (c) With PT Decision Weights. (d) With PDDW Decision Weights.

Cumulative
Distribution

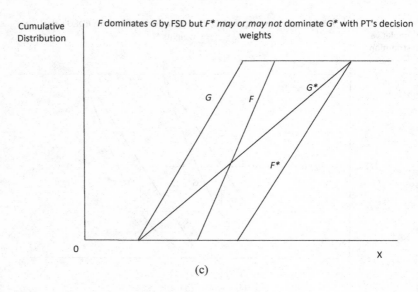

F dominates G by FSD but *F* may or may not* dominate G* with PT's decision weights

(c)

Cumulative
Distribution

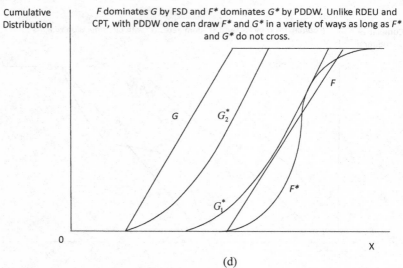

F dominates G by FSD and F* dominates G* by PDDW. Unlike RDEU and CPT, with PDDW one can draw F* and G* in a variety of ways as long as F* and G* do not cross.

(d)

Figure 10.3 (*continued*)

F and G, the transformation $T(P) = P^2$ induces the same decrease in F^* relative to F and in G^* relative to G. For example, for $P_o = \frac{1}{2}$, both F and G are reduced to $T(\frac{1}{2}) = \frac{1}{4}$ (see Figure 10.3a). Thus, with RDEU, unlike PDDW (as we shall see), it is impossible, for example, to have $T_F(\frac{1}{2}) = \frac{1}{4}$ and $T_G(\frac{1}{2}) \neq \frac{1}{4}$.

Figure 10.3b demonstrates the effect of CPT DWs on F and G. As in RDEU also with CPT, for the same level P_o, F and G should be changed such that $T_F(P_o) = T_G(P_o)$ must hold. This property of CPT and RDEU imposes a restriction on the derived DW of each individual outcome (in the discrete case); hence, it does not allow much flexibility. Therefore, the interaction between the outcomes and the DW is restricted. This example indicates that both RDEU and CPT DW models are very rigid. Figure 10.3c demonstrates F^* and G^* constructed with PT's 1979 paper DW. Although in Figure 10.3c, F^* and G^* do not cross, as is well known, with PT FSD may be violated; hence, F^* and G^* may cross (see Figure 10.3c).

In contrast to Figures 10.3b and 10.3c, with PDDW (see Figure 10.3d), one can choose DWs that shift G to G_1^*, to G_2^*, or to any G_i^*, as long as it does not cross F^*, which is the distribution corresponding to F with DW. Because of the flexibility of the PDDW method, one can assign (albeit does not have to) to an equal probability of two outcomes, say, 0.01, the same DW, which is generally impossible under CPT and RDEU. Of course, under PDDW, one can choose CPT's or RDEU's DW as a specific case because the transformations given in Figures 10.3a and 10.3b do not contradict the PDDW model.

We now formulate the PDDW model. By the suggested procedure, the only restriction of the PDDW model is that FSD is not violated. Under this only constraint, a wide range of possible DWs is possible, which allows us to change DW from one situation to another, to determine the DW as a function of the alternative prospect under consideration, to assign equal DWs to equal probabilities, and to have CPT and/or RDEU DW as a specific case.

Suppose that the subject faces two prospects, F and G, and has to choose one of them. F and G are given as follows:

$$F: \{(x_1, p_1), (x_2, p_2)\dots(x_n, p_n)\}$$

$$G: \{(y_1, q_1), (y_2, q_2)\dots(y_m, q_m)\}$$

where x and y denote the *ranked* outcomes and $x_1 < x_2 \dots < x_n$, and $y_1 < y_2 \dots < y_m$, and p_i and q_i are the corresponding probabilities. First, take all values x and y and rank them such that we get one vector of ranked values $z_1, z_2 \dots z_{n+m}$, when $z_1 < z_2 \dots < z_{n+m}$. Note that the vector z has $n + m$ elements because it is composed of both

variables x and y. Thus, to each value z_k, $k = 1, 2, \ldots n + m$, we have
the corresponding probability taken from F or G, and the corresponding DWs. Suppose F dominates G by FSD. Namely, $F(z) \leq G(z)$ for all
values z (with at least one strong inequality), where F and G are the
two cumulative distributions. In terms of the vector z_{n+m}, this FSD
relationship can be rewritten also as

$$\sum_{i=1}^{j} q_i(z_i) \geq \sum_{i=1}^{j} p_i(z_i) \tag{10.8}$$

for all $j = 1, 2 \ldots n + m$, with a strict inequality for at least one
value z_i (see Levy[23]). Note that in condition (10.8), when $z_i \neq x_i$, then
$p_i = 0$, and when $z_i \neq y_i$ then $q_i = 0$. Condition (10.8) implies that F is
located (weakly) below G because the total accumulated probability
corresponding to F is smaller (or equal) to the accumulated probability corresponding to G, up to any value z_i. Hence, F dominates G by
FSD.[24]

We now turn to the needed restriction on the DWs corresponding
to the PDDW model. The PDDW DW scheme fulfills the following
three restrictions:

(a) $w_i((p_i), F, G) \geq 0$
(b) $\sum_{i=1}^{m} w_i(q_i(z_i), F, G) = \sum_{i=1}^{n} w_i(p_i(z_i), F, G) = 1$

These two conditions guarantee that $w(p)$ can be considered as a
probability measure. Condition (c) guarantees no FSD violation.

(c) If for any point j_o
(c1) If $\sum_{i=1}^{j_o} q_i(z_i) \geq \sum_{i=1}^{j_o} p_i(z_i)$ holds, then also with DW (c2)
holds:
(c2) $\sum_{i=1}^{j_o} w_i(q_i(z_i), F, G) \geq \sum_{i=1}^{j_o} w_i(p_i(z_i), F, G) \tag{10.9}$

Obviously, because of condition (b), we must have an equality in (c2)
for $j_o = n + m$ because the sum of the DWs of F and G must be

[23] H. Levy, *Stochastic Dominance: Investment Decision Making under Uncertainty*,
Springer, 2nd edition, 2006.
[24] Intuitively, $\sum_{i=1}^{j} p_i(z_i) \leq \sum_{i=1}^{j} q_i(z_i)$ for all j (with a strict inequality for at least
one value j) implies that for F, probabilities are shifted from low values z_i to higher
values z_i, relative to the distribution G, and because the preference is monotonic, F
dominates G by FSD. Actually, this condition is equivalent to the well-known FSD
condition, $F(x) \leq G(x)$, for all values x.

equal to 1. However, if FSD prevails, the condition (c1) => (c2) guarantees that the employment of DW does not violate FSD.

As explained previously, by CPT and RDEU, we look horizontally at the cumulative distribution and determine, for the cumulative probability P, the DW $w(P)$. By PDDW, we look vertically for the cumulative probability up to any point z_{jo} and determine the cumulative DWs up to this point. As we shall see in the forthcoming example, comparing the cumulative distribution vertically rather than horizontally is not merely a technical difference; it has an economic implication because it affects the flexibility that one has in employing DWs.

By condition given in equation (10.9), if F is below G at point z_{jo}, also with DW, F^* is below G^* at this point. Similarly, if F is above G at z_{jo}, the same holds with F^* and G^*. Therefore, it must be that if $F(z_{jo}) = G(z_{jo})$, also $F^*(z_{jo}) = G^*(z_{jo})$. This means that if F and G intersect n times, F^* and G^* also intersect n times. This property is shared also with RDEU's and CPT's DW schemes because if F and G intersect at cumulative probability P, also F^* and G^* intersect at this point because $F^*(P) \equiv T_F(P) = T_G(P) \equiv F^*(P)$. However, at any point apart from the intersection points of F and G, the PDDW scheme is very different from the other DW models because it allows much more flexibility in the determination of the DW of each outcome (see forthcoming example).

The PDDW scheme is a generalization of both RDEU and CPT DW schemes, in the sense that these two weighting methods are obtained as a specific case of PDDW scheme. Let us elaborate. With RDEU, we have the following three properties:

1. If F and G cross each other n times, F^* and G^* also cross each other exactly n times.
2. If $n = 0$ (no intersection of F and G), one prospect dominates the other by FSD, and this dominance is intact also with F^* and G^*, that is, with DW.
3. Suppose that for two values x_1 and x_2, where $x_1 < x_2$, we have $F(x_1) = G(x_2)$. Namely, F and G do not cross either at x_1 or at x_2. Then, by RDEU, also $F^*(x_1) = G^*(x_2)$, where F^* and G^* are the transformed distributions (see Figure 10.3a).

In the PDDW framework, properties 1 and 2 also hold. However, regarding property 3, by PDDW, we may have $F^*(x_1) \neq G^*(x_2)$. By PDDW (see equation [10.9]), we only require that if one distribution is below the other distribution at some value z_o, the same must hold with DW. Hence, if $x_1 < x_2$ and $F(x_1) = G(x_2)$, the condition $F^*(x_1) = G^*(x_2)$ may be fulfilled as a specific case of PDDW, but it is not required. Thus, the RDEU transformation $T(\cdot)$ is a specific case of the PDDW scheme, where specific DWs are selected such that the condition given by equation (10.9) holds, and also $F^*(x_1) = G^*(x_2)$ holds.

The PDDW model is also a generalization of the CPT's DW scheme. In the case of non-mixed prospects, with only positive or only negative outcomes, the CPT DW can be interpreted as a probability measure – and thus as a special case of RDEU – and therefore as a special case of PDDW. However, in the case of mixed gambles, under CPT, we may have $\Sigma w_i \lessgtr 1$. In this case, one can modify PDDW such that it is comparable to CPT and can be shown as a generalization of it.[25]

We now turn to a numerical example that illustrates the difference in the various DW models and reveals that the PDDW model is a generalization of CPT and RDEU DW models.

---

[25] The PDDW can be written in a more generalized form without condition (b). In this case, $w_i(p_i)$ is not necessarily a probability measure, which is in line with CPT's DW. In this case, eq. (10.9) should be changed such that

$$(\text{c2}) \qquad \sum_{i=1}^{j_0} w_i\,[q_i(z_i), F, G] \geq \sum_{i=1}^{j_0} w_i\,[p_i(z_i), F, G]$$
$$\text{for all } j = 1, 2, n + m - 1$$

and for the value $j = n + m$, we have condition

$$(\text{c3}) \qquad \sum_{i=1}^{n+m} w_i\,[q_i(z_i), F, G] \leq \sum_{i=1}^{n+m} w_i\,[p_i(z_i), F, G].$$

This guarantees that if $w_i(p_i) = 0$ for all values z_i, for the last value $i = n + m$ (which must belong to F because F dominates G by FSD), there is a very large DW, which guarantees that the FSD is not violated. This change in the inequality sign in (c3) is not needed when condition (b) is required because it is automatically fulfilled with an equality for $i = n + m$. However, with $\sum w_i \neq 1$, we may have a strict inequality in (c3) for the value $i = n + m$. Thus, the formulation of PDDW is general because we may have $\sum w_i \neq 1$, which is in CPT framework, but also we may have $\sum w_i = 1$, which is in RDEU framework. Note that regardless of the formulation, if F dominates G, we require that $\sum w_i\,(F) \geq \sum w_i\,(G)$.

Table 10.4. *Various Decision Weights*

Prospect F				
Outcome:	1	2	3	4
Probability p:	0.01	0.01	0.40	0.58
Possible PDDW: $w(p)$: Option (1)	0.05	0.05	0.30	0.60
Option (2)	0.05	0.10	0.35	0.50
CPT decision weights (see eq. (10.6))	0.09	0.04	0.41	0.46
Prelec's decision weights (see eq. (10.7))	0.05	0.03	0.41	0.51
Prospect Theory decision weights	C_0	C_0	C_3	C_4

CPT, Cumulative Prospect Theory; PDDW, Prospect-Dependent Decision Weights.

Example: Let F and G be as follows:

G: $x = 1, 2, 3, 4$, with an equal probability of $\frac{1}{4}$

F: $(1, \frac{1}{100})$, $(2, \frac{1}{100})$, $(3, \frac{40}{100})$, $(4, \frac{58}{100})$.

It is easy to verify that F dominates G by FSD. For the simplicity of the exposition and without a loss of generality, suppose that with G we have $w_i(p_i) = p_i = \frac{1}{4}$ for all i; namely, the DWs are equal to the objective probabilities. How much can one change the probabilities of F by the PDDW method such that the FSD will not be violated? To answer this question, we adhere to condition (c), that is, to the vertical DW method. By condition (c) of PDDW, we must have the following three constraints:

$$0 \le w_1(\tfrac{1}{100}, 1) \le \tfrac{1}{4}$$
$$0 \le w_2(\tfrac{1}{100}, 2) \le \tfrac{1}{2} - w_1(\tfrac{1}{100}, 1)$$
$$0 \le w_3(\tfrac{40}{100}, 3) \le \tfrac{3}{4} - w_1(\tfrac{1}{100}, 1) - w_2(\tfrac{1}{100}, 2) \qquad (10.10)$$

and by condition (b), the following must hold:

$$w_4(\tfrac{58}{100}, 4) = 1 - \sum_{j=1}^{3} w_i.$$

With these constraints (which provide a wide spectrum of possible DW), the FSD of F over G is not violated because conditions (a)–(c) given previously are fulfilled. By CPT (see equation (10.6)), we have the following weights (see Table 10.4): $w_1(0.01) = 0.09$, $w_2(0.01) = 0.04$, $w_3(0.40) = 0.41$, and $w_4(0.58) = 0.46$. It is easy to see that CPT's DWs fulfill the conditions given in equation (10.10), demonstrating that CPT's DWs are a specific case of PDDW scheme.

Let us now return to the available flexibility in the determination of the DWs by PDDW, which does not characterize the other DW models. For example, one may select by PDDW the two alternative sets of DWs given in Table 10.4, corresponding to F, consistent with equation (10.10) and still keep the FSD dominance of F and G. As before, we assume that with prospect G, $w(\frac{1}{4}) = \frac{1}{4}$ and F is given by the several DWs corresponding to the various models (see Table 10.4).

In the previous example, we provide two possible sets of DWs corresponding to PDDW, whereas in CPT (or by Prelec's Method), such flexibility is not possible, and only one set of DW is possible. In the PDDW DW set labeled as option (1), equal probability events (0.01) are assigned the same DW, which does not occur with CPT's DW. In set (2), we have different DWs corresponding to equally likely events. Of course, one can choose an infinite number of sets of possible vectors of $w(p)$ that fulfill conditions (a), (b), and (c) of PDDW. As we can see, with PT, we must have the same DW to the values $x = 1$ or $x = 2$ (denoted by c_0), but there is a flexibility in the determination of the level c_0 as well as in the determination of c_3 and c_4. Thus, the PDDW method has even more flexibility than that offered by PT, and at the same time, it maintains the no-FSD-violation property of CPT and RDEU.

Finally, assume that in the preceding example, F is replaced by F' where F': $(-100, 1/100), (2, 1/100), (3, 40/100), (4, 58/100)$. Obviously, neither F' nor G dominates the other by FSD. In such a case, the subjects may change the DW corresponding to 0.01. Yet, by replacing $(1, 1/100)$ of F by $(-100, 1/100)$ of F', $w(0.01)$ of RDEU is unchanged. However, by PDDW, which is prospect dependent, one can increase the DW of 0.01. Thus, by the PDDW model, it is possible that $w(1, 1/100)$ is equal to, say, 0.02 and $w(-100, 1/100)$ is equal to, say, 0.20, a flexibility that is induced by the vertical DW method, which, in turn, allows the dependency of the DW on the prospects under consideration.

10.7. FIRST-DEGREE STOCHASTIC DOMINANCE VIOLATIONS DUE TO BOUNDED RATIONALITY

Theoretically, FSD violations may be induced by the assumed theoretical model, in particular due to the assumed DWs employed by investors, DWs that may violate FSD. Experimentally and empirically, FSD violation may be induced also by human errors. CPT and other cumulative DW models guarantee no theoretical FSD violation. However, in practice, the prospects may be relatively complicated, suggesting that FSD violations may occur. Thus, by this argument, it is possible that rational investors employ DWs that do not violate FSD; however, in some cases, they do not comprehend the advantage of the FSD superior prospect and mistakenly choose the inferior prospect, resulting in an observed experimental FSD violation. Moreover, it is possible that once the subjects realize the FSD relation between the two prospects under consideration, they may change their decision after administering their error. In such a case, we say that investors are rational, but their rationality is bounded. Finally, even if investors do not employ DWs at all (which probably takes place with equal probability outcomes), FSD violation may occur due to bounded rationality.

In experiments, when subjects face uncertain prospects, it is difficult to figure out whether the observed FSD violations are due to the employment of DWs, which contradict monotonicity, or whether these violations are due to human errors (bounded rationality). One way to disentangle these two issues is to conduct experiments in which FSD prevails but the degree of complexity of choices varies. If the proportion of FSD violations increases with the degree of complexity, we tend to conclude that the FSD violation phenomenon is due to bounded rationality rather than to the employment of DWs.[26]

In a series of experiments, Levy[27] presents the subjects with choices, which gradually increase with the degree of complexity. We briefly describe these experiments and the corresponding results.

---

[26] Although it is commonly accepted that DWs should not violate FSD, not all researchers agree with this assertion. In a series of studies, Birnbaum and Navarrete advocate that subjects employ DWs, which in some cases predict FSD violations. They suggest Configural Weight models in which people weigh probabilities of various branches of outcomes in a way that is predicted to lead to FSD violation. For more details, see M. H. Birnbaum and J. B. Navarrete, "Testing Descriptive Utility Theories: Violations of Stochastic Dominance and Cumulative Independence," *Journal of Risk and Uncertainty*, 1998.

[27] H. Levy, "First-Degree Stochastic Dominance Violations: Decision Weights and Bounded Rationality," *Economic Journal*, 2008.

Experiment 1:
In the first and most transparent FSD case, the subjects had to choose between two prospects, F and G, with the following characteristics:

F		G	
Outcome in $	Probability	Outcome in $	Probability
-500	1/3	-500	1/2
$+2,500$	2/3	$+2,500$	1/2

There were $n = 25$ subjects, all undergraduate business students. Because a straightforward FSD holds in this case, and because the subjects face a very simple comparison with only two outcomes under each prospect, not surprisingly, 100 percent of the choices were F, which dominates G by FSD, implying no FSD violations. It seems that in this case, neither DW nor bounded rationality affects choices.

Experiment 2:
In the second experiment, the choice is a little more complicated; the subjects had to choose between F and G given by:

F		G	
Outcome in $	Probability	Outcome in $	Probability
-100	1/2	-100	1/4
$+400$	1/2	-75	1/4
		$+400$	1/2

Obviously, G dominates F by FSD. However, to see this dominance transparently, one needs to split the first outcome of F and write it as $\{(-100, 1/4), (-100, 1/4)\}$ instead of $(-100, 1/2)$. We find experimentally that to discover FSD with no splitting, as presented to the subjects, is more difficult to grasp, because we observe in this experiment many FSD violations.

Table 10.5 presents the various groups of subjects and their choices. Unlike in experiment 1, in experiment 2 when the FSD setting is slightly more difficult, there is a substantial number of FSD violations. The lowest proportion of FSD violations is made by group II, which is composed of mutual fund managers and financial analysts (7.1 percent FSD violations). It is interesting to note that the existence of a monetary payoff, or the degree of knowledge of the subject in EUT and

Table 10.5. *The Choices in Experiment 2 (%)*

Group	Subjects	No. of Subjects, n	Choice of Prospect F	G	Total
I	Undergraduate business students, no monetary payoff	58	15.5	84.5	100
II	Mutual funds managers and financial analysts, **no** monetary payoff	42	7.1	92.9	100
III	Second-year MBA students, no exposure to FSD criterion with monetary payoff	23	11.7	87.3	100
IV	Second-year MBA students, all studied FSD **with** monetary payoff	27	22.2	77.8	100
V	Advanced MBA students and Ph.D. candidates: all studied expected utility and FSD, **with** monetary payoff	15	13.3	86.7	100
Total	Aggregate across all groups	165	15.2	84.8	100

FSD, First-Degree Stochastic Dominance.
Source: H. Levy, "First Degree Stochastic Dominance Violations: Decision Weights and Bounded Rationality," *The Economic Journal*, 2008.

Stochastic Dominance Theory, did not affect the results much. Overall, we have 7.1 to 22.2 percent FSD violations, with an average across all groups of 15.2 percent FSD violations. A possible explanation for the selection of the FSD inferior option by about 15 percent of the subjects may be related to the *framing effect*: prospect G is characterized by two possible negative outcomes, and prospect F has only one negative outcome. Of course, splitting the -100 of F to two outcomes of -100, each with a probability of 1/4, would eliminate this framing effect.

To summarize experiments 1 and 2, with a simple FSD dominance, there are no FSD violations, and with a little more complicated FSD case, when splitting of the probability is needed for having a transparent FSD, we observe 15.2 percent FSD violations across all subjects. Finally, note that in experiment 2, we have choices in line with Birnbaum's[28] recipe for an FSD violation, albeit not so complicated as the one suggested by him, which may explain why we got only 15.2 percent FSD violations.

[28] See footnote 26.

Levy[29] conducts more experiments in which the degree of difficulty to detect the FSD preferred prospect continued to increase. The main result, which for brevity sake is not reported here, is that the more complicated the choice, the more FSD violations are observed. These FSD violations also exist with large probabilities and with equally likely observations, cases where it is unlikely that DWs play a major role in making choices; hence, the FSD violations are attributed to bounded rationality.

Thus, an FSD violation may be due to the employment of DWs, which are not in the spirit of CPT, RDEU, or PDDW DWs, or due to bounded rationality, which has nothing to do with the DW formula.

10.8. SUMMARY

Allais' paradox, as well as other more formal and extensive experiments, reveal a contradiction within the EUT. These paradoxes paved the way for other competing theories where DWs, which are not linear in probability, play a central role. The DWs of the PT, discussed in Chapter 9, may solve paradoxes like Allais' paradox, but unfortunately they may induce FSD violations, implying that investors prefer less wealth to more wealth. This is, of course, an unacceptable property, which has led to the development of other DW models that do not contradict FSD.

Quiggin's RDEU and Tversky and Kahneman's CPT suggest DWs that theoretically do not violate FSD. Whereas the RDEU's DWs do not distinguish between negative and positive prospects, CPT's DWs are determined separately for the negative and the positive domains of outcomes and hence provide more flexibility. In particular, they allow different attitudes regarding DWs when gains and, alternatively, losses are involved. Moreover, Tversky and Kahneman estimate the value (utility) function as well as the DW function and suggest several parameter estimates to represent the typical decision maker participating in their experiments. They suggest an S-shape preference, which is steeper in the negative domain relative to the positive domain, and a reverse S-shape DW function, revealing that

---

[29] *Op. cit.*, 2008.

small probabilities are overweighted and relatively large probabilities are underweighted.

Both RDEU and CPT suggest that DW be determined independently of the alternative prospect under consideration, and in the equally likely outcome, both suggest in some cases unreasonable DWs. Therefore, we suggest the PDDW method, which does not violate FSD and overcomes some of the drawbacks of the existing DW methods.

Experimental studies reveal the existence of FSD violations. Does it imply that DWs that violate FSD (like those of the original PT) are employed? Not necessarily! There are two possible explanations for the FSD-violation phenomenon: the observed FSD violations may imply that investors employ DWs that violate FSD; yet it is also possible that investors employ DWs that do not violate FSD (or do not employ DWs at all), but they violate FSD as a result of bounded rationality.

It has been reported in several experiments that there is a solid ground to the hypothesis that choices are affected by bounded rationality, explaining the observed FSD violations. Thus, human limitations rather than DWs account for the observed FSD violations. This conclusion is supported by the fact that in simple choices, we find no FSD violations, and as the choices become more complex, the percentage of errors (FSD violations) increases.

11

The Mean-Variance Rule, the Capital Asset Pricing Model, and the Cumulative Prospect Theory

Coexistence

11.1. INTRODUCTION

In deriving the Mean-Variance (M-V) rule and the Capital Asset Pricing Model (CAPM), one assumes explicitly or implicitly normal distributions of returns and risk aversion. With these assumptions, it emerges that the variance of the portfolio's return is the measure of the investment's risk. In Chapter 8, we saw that although normality of returns is statistically rejected, the economic loss from assuming normality when the distributions are actually not normal is relatively small. Moreover, in Chapter 4, we saw that even if the distributions of returns are not normal, the M-V rule can be employed as an approximation to expected utility, as long as risk aversion is assumed. Furthermore, it was shown empirically in Chapter 4 that the choices made by the M-V rule are almost fully correlated with the choices made by direct expected utility maximization for a wide set of risk-averse utility function.

Considering the relatively small economic loss involved as a result of the normality assumption, in this chapter we assume that the M-V and the CAPM are derived based on this normality assumption, within the expected utility framework, rather than as an approximation to expected utility. However, even in this framework, as we saw in Chapters 9 and 10, the M-V and the CAPM are questionable for the following reasons:

a) By the Prospect Theory (PT), people maximize a value function, which is defined on *change* of wealth (gains and losses)

372

rather than on *total* wealth; by expected utility, the M-V rule and the CAPM are defined on total wealth.

b) To derive the M-V rule and the CAPM, risk aversion is needed, whereas by PT, the value function has a *risk-seeking* segment. The risk- seeking segment of preference is steeper than the risk-aversion segment, implying *loss aversion*.

c) Adopting the modified version of the PT, called Cumulative Prospect Theory (CPT), people employ *cumulative decision weights*. Thus, the cumulative distribution of returns is transformed, and in calculating the expected value (utility), the transformed distribution rather than the original distribution is employed. This seems to be a "deathblow" to the M-V rule and the CAPM because even if the original distribution of returns is normal, generally the transformed distribution is not. Moreover, although the normal distribution is symmetric, implying that skewness is equal to zero, the transformed distribution may be skewed, thus relying only on the mean, and variance may be misleading because there is ample evidence that investors like positive skewness and dislike negative skewness.

For the preceding reasons, it would seem that the CPT paradigm and the M-V rule plus the CAPM paradigm cannot coexist. Moreover, the fact that Markowitz and Sharpe won the Noble Prize in Economics in 1990 for developing the M-V rule and the CAPM, and Kahneman won the Noble Prize in Economics in 2002 for introducing the PT, emphasizes the seeming contradiction between these two paradigms and makes it even more uncomfortable for researchers. If one adopts PT, it seems the M-V and the CAPM should be abandoned. If one employs the M-V and the CAPM, the important evidence regarding subjects' choices, as clearly shown in PT experiments, are ignored.

Nonetheless, as we see in this chapter, under some very weak restrictions, both paradigms can coexist, quite an astonishing (and encouraging) result. The M-V efficient set is only slightly modified when people make investment decisions by CPT, despite the aforementioned three deviations of this theory from the Expected Utility Theory (EUT). Thus, we show in this chapter that even if the transformed distribution is not normal anymore, the M-V analysis and the

CAPM are intact, as long as the decision weight function is cumulative, as advocated by rank-dependent expected utility (RDEU) and by CPT. Namely, the two paradigms coexist as long as the First-degree stochastic dominance (FSD) rule is not violated.

In this chapter, we discuss each of the preceding factors that induce conflict between EUT and PT. We first show that when diversification is not allowed (e.g., comparing two real projects), indeed, PT and the M-V rule may lead to contradictory results, even when decision weights are not employed, let alone when decision weights also affect choices. However, more important, we show that in the more relevant case, when diversification is allowed (e.g., financial assets), the two paradigms, PT and the M-V efficiency analysis, yield almost the same efficient frontier, and when a riskless asset is added, these two paradigms yield the same frontier; therefore, the CAPM is also intact. Then we show that when decision weights that do not violate FSD are employed on the distributions of the various portfolios under consideration, the M-V, the CAPM, and CPT can still coexist, which is quite an astonishing result, given that PT and EUT severely contradict each other. Thus, the CAPM is intact in both EUT and CPT paradigms.

Finally, recall that some of the results reported in this chapter relate to the M-V rule and CPT, and some of the results relate to the CAPM and CPT. However, the results reported here are intact also for all the extensions of the CAPM discussed in Chapter 6, provided the models do not hinge onto concavity of preference. Specifically, the results are intact for the zero beta model, the segmented CAPM, and the Arbitrage Pricing Theory (APT). The results are not valid for the consumption base models, the Intertemporal CAPM (ICAPM), and the consumption CAPM, which are based on the maximization of expected utility of consumption of concave functions. The reason for the contradiction of these models with CPT is that by CPT, preference is not concave in the whole range of outcomes.

11.2. GAINS AND LOSSES VERSUS TOTAL WEALTH

In this section, we analyze the effect of the initial wealth on the M-V efficient frontier and on the CAPM.

a) The Wealth Effect on the Mean-Variance Efficient Frontier

The value function of PT is defined on gains and losses, whereas the utility function is defined on total wealth. We saw in Chapters 9 and 10 that the level of wealth affects the optimal choice in the expected utility framework, but it does not affect choices in the PT framework. Hence, choices in PT, in principle, are different from choices in the EUT framework. Because the M-V rule and the CAPM are derived within the EUT framework, one may suspect that these portfolio selection models will not be valid in the PT framework. We show in this section that despite this difference regarding the role that wealth plays in investment decision making, the M-V efficiency analysis and the CAPM are intact, even when the initial wealth is ignored in the decision-making process. We shall see in this chapter that the equilibrium prices of the various assets may be affected by the assumed initial wealth, but the general risk–return CAPM linear relationship is intact regardless of the assumed initial wealth.

Before advancing to show this claim, we should stress that we focus here only on one difference between the two competing paradigms, the initial wealth, assuming that apart from this factor, there are no other factors that might induce a discrepancy between the two paradigms. Later in the chapter, we analyze the other main factors that may induce differences between the two paradigms, as well as the combined effect.

By the M-V rule, prospect x dominates prospect y if the following holds:

$$E(w + x) \geq E(w + y) \quad \text{and} \quad \sigma(w + x) \leq \sigma(w + y) \quad (11.1)$$

and there is at least one strict inequality. Note that because the M-V rule is derived within expected utility paradigm, the criterion for choice is based on total wealth, which is composed from the initial wealth, w, and the change of wealth, denoted as x and y, under the two choices, respectively. However, equation (11.1) holds if and only if equation (11.2) holds, where

$$E(x) \geq E(y) \quad \text{and} \quad \sigma(x) \leq \sigma(y). \quad (11.2)$$

Thus, if one prospect dominates the other by the M-V rule with initial wealth, the dominance exists also with changes in wealth, that is, with

gains and losses. This implies that the asset composition of the M-V
efficient set suggested by Markowitz (see Chapters 4 and 5) is unaffected by the initial wealth. Therefore, this specific difference between
expected utility and PT does not induce any changes in the M-V efficient set.

However, one nagging question still exists: Why is it that the
M-V efficient set, which is derived within the expected utility
paradigm, is unaffected by the initial wealth, but the expected utility
itself is affected by the initial wealth? The answer to this seeming puzzle is actually simple: The M-V optimal choice from the efficient set,
as expected by EUT, *is* affected by the initial wealth, but the efficient
set is not. Thus, with a change in wealth, the investor may move on
the M-V efficient frontier, although the frontier itself *is* unchanged.
In addition, as we shall see soon, the linear risk–return relation of
the CAPM, which relies on the market portfolio derived from the
M-V efficient set, under the assumption that the riskless asset is available, is intact, even though equilibrium prices may be affected by the
inclusion or exclusion of the initial wealth in the optimal portfolio-
choice process. In sum, initial wealth affects the optimal choice but
not the M-V efficiency analysis and not the CAPM risk–return linear
relation.

Two wealth variables affect expected utility and the optimal M-V
choice. To see this, recall that the utility is given by

$$U(W - w + w(1 + R)),$$

where W is the investor's initial total wealth, w is the wealth invested
in the market, and R stands for the rate of return on the investment.
We saw, in Chapter 5, that w does not affect the M-V efficient frontier;
so, for simplicity, the derivation of the M-V frontier is done for a \$1
investment. However, the optimal investment, taken from the M-V
frontier, is given by the tangency of the indifference curve with the
M-V frontier. Because the indifference curve depends on the initial
wealth, W, the choice of the optimal M-V portfolio is affected by the
initial wealth.

Figure 11.1 demonstrates the assertion that the M-V efficient set is
unaffected by the initial wealth; yet, in choosing the optimal portfolio
from the efficient set, the initial wealth cannot be ignored. Curve *ab*

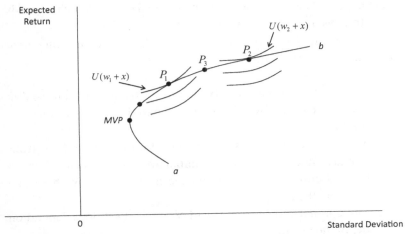

Figure 11.1. Mean-Variance Efficient Frontier with Initial Wealth.

denotes the M-V frontier, and the segment MVP-*b* denotes the M-V
efficient set. The compositions of all portfolios located on the frontier are unaffected by the initial wealth. This conclusion stems from
equations (11.1) and (11.2) and from the fact that minimization of
the portfolio's variance for a given mean return is unaffected by the
assumed initial wealth (see Chapter 5). However, the utility function
is affected by the initial wealth; hence, also, the indifference curves
are determined by this wealth. Indeed, with the same risk-averse utility function, say, U_0, we have $U_0(W - w + w(1 + R))$, and with normal
distributions of returns, the indifference map of curves corresponding
to this preference in the M-V space[1] is affected by the initial wealth,
as demonstrated in Figure 11.1. For example, for initial wealth W_1, the
optimal portfolio is P_1, and for the same person, with a wealth level
W_2, the optimal portfolio is P_2. If one would ignore the initial wealth,
as recommended by PT, but still rely on the M-V analysis, a given
investor would stick to one portfolio, say, portfolio P_3, regardless of
the wealth level. However, by the employment of the M-V analysis

---

[1] With normal distributions and risk aversion, the indifference curves can be written in
terms of the mean and variance, and they are as depicted in Figure 11.1. For more
details, see J. Tobin, "Liquidity Preferences as Behavior toward Risk," *Review of
Economic Studies*, 1958.

within expected utility framework, the optimal choice, which depends on the total wealth, does vary with the wealth level.

Before we turn to the wealth effect on the CAPM, let us summarize the results we have so far:

a) Choices by expected utility should be based on total wealth, whereas choices by PT should be based only on changes in wealth.

b) The asset compositions of portfolios located on the M-V frontier are independent of the initial wealth and hence can be derived either with or without the initial wealth, without any effect on the results.

c) The optimal choice from the M-V efficient set does depend on the initial wealth.

d) The main conclusion is as follows: Markowitz's efficiency analysis is focused on the derivation of the M-V frontier, not on the optimal selection from the frontier (because the utility function is unknown anyway). Therefore, accepting the evidence of PT, asserting that people care about change of wealth rather than total wealth, does not affect the M-V efficiency analysis. Thus, the fact that PT relies on change of wealth and that expected utility relies on total wealth affects expected utility choices but does not affect the M-V analysis, which is the same in both frameworks.

b) The Wealth Effect on the Capital Asset Pricing Model

The capital market line (CML) is an extension of the M-V efficiency analysis when borrowing and lending is allowed. Thus, the analysis is exactly as before, with a similar conclusion: The efficient set is not affected by the initial wealth, but the optimal choice from the CML is affected by this wealth. Figure 11.2 illustrates this assertion. Portfolio M is the market portfolio, and portfolios P_1 and P_2 are the optimal portfolios for the same investor for two hypothetical levels of initial wealth, W_1 and W_2, respectively. By PT, the initial wealth is irrelevant. Consequently, the same optimal portfolio, say, portfolio P, is selected regardless of the level of the initial wealth. Thus, by the M-V rule, derived within EUT, the CML frontier (which is a straight line when

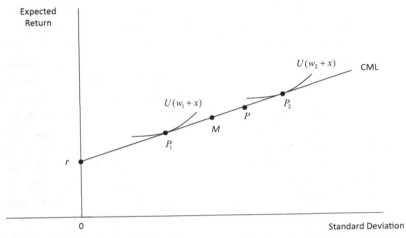

Figure 11.2. The Choice of a Portfolio from the Capital Market Line with Initial Wealth.

the riskless asset is available) is unaffected by the initial wealth, but the choice of the optimal portfolio from the CML is affected by the initial wealth level. In this respect, adding the riskless asset does not change the result we discussed regarding Markowitz's M-V efficiency analysis.

Both with and without the initial wealth, all investors select a portfolio that is a mix of portfolio M and the riskless asset; therefore, the Separation Theorem applies, and one can use the technique described in Chapter 5 to derive the CAPM equilibrium risk–return linear relation. In sum, the CAPM is intact also when one adopts the PT's assertion that people make investment decisions based on change of wealth rather than on total wealth. Moreover, we shall show that CPT investors also select their optimal portfolios from the M-V efficient set.

Does this conclusion imply that equilibrium prices are unaffected by the investor's initial wealth? Absolutely not. The risk–return linear relationship is unaffected by the initial wealth, but equilibrium asset prices may be affected by the initial wealth. The reason for this conclusion is that the initial wealth may affect the location of the tangency point of the indifference curves with the CML (see Figure 11.2). The farther to the right the location of the typical investor's tangency point, the more wealth is invested in the market portfolio and, for a given supply of stocks, the higher the equilibrium price. Thus, for a given end-of-period distributions of the value of the various firms, with higher prices, the means of the rates of return on the various assets decrease; hence, a CML with a smaller slope is obtained (not shown in Figure 11.2). This effect is not different from the effect of an increase in the money invested in the stock market for a given supply of risky assets on asset pricing. However, it is important to emphasize here that, by EUT, wealth affects the location of the tangency points of the indifference curves (and hence affects equilibrium prices), and by PT, wealth does not affect the tangency point. Yet including or excluding the initial wealth from the analysis does not affect the main result: All investors select their portfolios from the CML; therefore, when this element of CPT is incorporated, the CAPM is intact, regardless of the assumed initial wealth.

11.3. RISK AVERSION VERSUS THE S-SHAPE VALUE FUNCTION

To derive the M-V rule and the CAPM, risk aversion is assumed. In contrast, PT advocates that the preference is S-shaped, with a risk-seeking segment in the negative domain, casting doubt on the validity of the variance as a measure of risk. In this section, we show that when diversification is not allowed or not possible, indeed the two models, the CAPM and PT, may yield contradictory results. However, in the more relevant case in which diversification is allowed, the two models yield almost the same results, and when we add the riskless asset, the two models yield identical results, implying that the M-V and the CAPM are also intact, with an S-shape preference with a risk-seeking segment. To analyze choices with risk aversion and with an S-shape preference, we need to employ the stochastic dominance rules and, in particular, the prospect stochastic dominance (PSD) rule discussed in Chapter 3. Let us elaborate.

a) Diversification Is Not Allowed

Suppose that investors have to choose between prospect F and prospect G, but diversification between the two prospects is not allowed. We subsequently show that in this case, it is possible that F

dominates G by the M-V rule but not by the PSD rule, and the opposite may also hold: F may dominate G by PSD but not by M-V. In such a case, one must decide which assumption regarding preference is more reasonable because the two paradigms may lead to contradictory decisions.

To show this claim, recall that prospect F dominates prospect G by PSD (i.e., for all S-shape preferences) if and only if the following holds:

$$\int_{y}^{x} [G(t) - F(t)]dt \geq 0 \tag{11.3}$$

for all $y \leq 0$ and $x \geq 0$ and there is at least one strict inequality when F and G are the cumulative distributions of the two options under consideration. We also employ, in the proof of this claim, the following equation, which relates to the difference between the means of the two prospects (see Chapter 3):

$$E_F(x) - E_G(x) = \int_{-\infty}^{+\infty} [G(x) - F(x)]dx. \tag{11.4}$$

The following discussion is intact with no constraint on the distributions, and it holds a fortiori for the specific case when normality is assumed. Levy and Levy[2] demonstrate the possible contradictions with precise parametric calculations, but here, for simplicity, we rely on a graphical explanation with no precise calculations. Let us demonstrate the two possible contradictory cases:

1. *F dominates G by M-V but not by PSD*: Figure 11.3a illustrates this case. First note that F is steeper than G; hence, it has a lower variance than that of G. Second, by equation (11.4), the mean of F is higher than that of G. (Note that graphically the + area is larger than the absolute value of the − area.) Thus, F dominates G by the M-V rule. However, we also have (when the numbers are selected arbitrarily for demonstration of such possibility):

$$\int_{0}^{+\infty} [G(x) - F(x)]dx = +2 - 6 = -4 < 0$$

---

[2] H. Levy and M. Levy, "Prospect Theory and Mean-Variance Analysis," *Review of Financial Studies*, 2004.

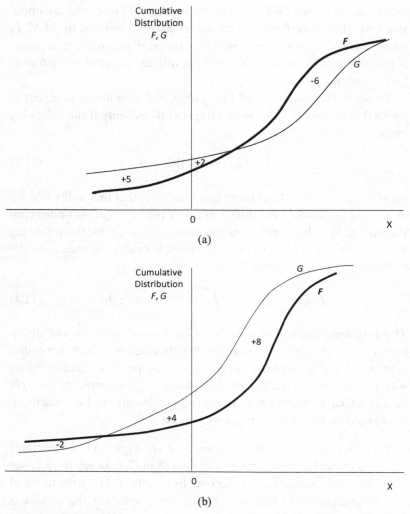

Figure 11.3. Contradiction between Mean-Variance (M-V) and Prospect Stochastic Dominance (PSD) in Choices. (a) *F* Dominates *G* by M-V but Not by PSD. (b) *F* Dominates *G* by PSD but Not by M-V.

and hence equation (11.4) does not hold; therefore, *F* does not dominate *G* by PSD.

2. *F dominates G by PSD but not by M-V*: Figure 11.3b demonstrates this case. First note that although the mean of *F* is higher

than that of G (+8 +4 −2; see equation (11.4)), as illustrated graphically, F is flatter than G; thus, it has also a higher variance. Therefore, F does not dominate G by the M-V rule. However, the integral given by equation (11.3) is positive for all values $y < 0 < x$ (+4 is larger than the absolute value of –2); hence, F dominates G by PSD.

Figure 11.4 demonstrates these results in the M-V space. Figure 11.4a demonstrates the preceding results, where F dominates G by the M-V rule, yet some investor with an S-shape preference exists who prefers prospect G. Thus, from the PT's point of view, prospect G is mistakenly eliminated from the efficient set by the M-V rule. This corresponds to case (a) in Figure 11.3. Figure 11.4b reveals the opposite case: by PT, prospect G is eliminated to the inefficient set, where some M-V investors may prefer G over F; hence, the elimination of G by PT to the inefficient set would be considered a mistake from the M-V investor's point of view.

So far, the results are quite discouraging because the two paradigms may lead to contradictory choices, implying that one must have a stand regarding which theory is the correct theory. As we shall see, in the most relevant case, when diversification is allowed (i.e., a diversification between prospects F and G is allowed), there is no need to take a stand because both theories lead to the same efficient set, despite the fact that one theory assumes risk aversion and the other theory assumes a preference that includes a risk-seeking segment.

b) Diversification between Risky Assets Is Allowed

To analyze this important case, we make the following assumptions, which are generally needed in the M-V and CAPM analyses: Normal distributions of returns and portfolios can be formed without any restrictions. Furthermore, we rule out the possibility of a perfect correlation between any two assets, so Markowitz's nondegenerated M-V efficient set can be derived. The relationship between the PSD and the M-V efficient sets is summarized in theorem 1, taken from the article by Levy and Levy.[3]

---

[3] See Levy and Levy, 2004, *op. cit.*

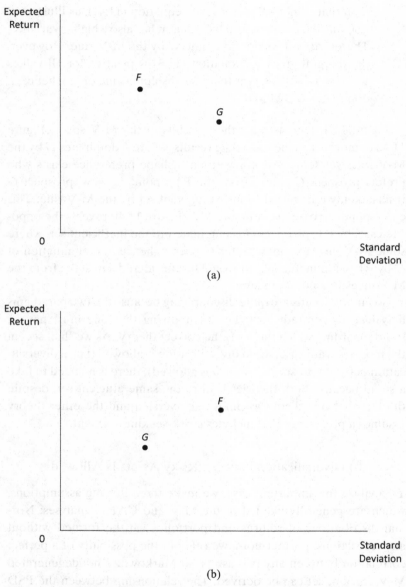

Figure 11.4. Contradiction between Mean-Variance (M-V) and Prospect Stochastic Dominance (PSD) in Choices in the M-V Space. (a) *F* Dominates *G* by M-V but Not by PSD. (b) *F* Dominates *G* by PSD but Not by M-V.

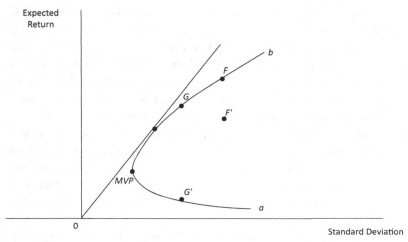

Figure 11.5. The Mean-Variance and Prospect Stochastic Dominance Efficient Sets.

Theorem 1: Suppose that the distributions of returns are normal and objective probabilities are employed in decision making. Then the PSD efficient set is a subset of the M-V efficient set, and the PSD efficient set is smaller than the M-V efficient set by at most the segment located between the minimum variance portfolio and the point of tangency between the frontier and the line raising from the origin.

Proof: Figure 11.5 presents the M-V frontier and the M-V efficient set and, as we explain soon, also the PSD efficient set. First, note that the well-known result asserts that curve *ab* is the M-V frontier and that segment MVP-*b* is the M-V efficient set. To prove the claim given in this theorem, we first show that all PSD efficient portfolios must be located on the segment MVP-*b* or on some parts of this curve. Namely, with normal distributions, an interior prospect cannot be PSD efficient. In addition, noninterior prospects located on the segment MVP-*a* also cannot be PSD efficient. To see this claim, consider two prospects, F and F', when one is interior and one is located on the efficient frontier, vertically above it. Because F has a higher mean than F' and the same variance, and because the distributions of returns are by assumption normal, F dominates F' by FSD (see equation 3.3

in Chapter 3). This means that F dominates F' for all nondecreasing preferences; hence, such a dominance exists also for all S-shape preferences. In other words, $FSD \Rightarrow PSD$. As for any M-V interior prospect, there is a prospect located on the M-V efficient frontier that dominates it by FSD and, therefore, also by PSD, all PSD efficient prospects must be located on the M-V frontier, or on some parts of this curve, but are definitely not interior to this curve. By the same token, PSD efficient portfolios cannot be located on the segment MVP-a of the frontier because, for any portfolio located on this segment, there is a portfolio located on segment MVP-b, directly above it, that dominates it by FSD and, hence, also by PSD. For example, prospect G dominates prospect G' by FSD and, hence, also by PSD.

So far, we have shown that the PSD efficient set cannot be curve MVP-a, or a subset of this curve, implying that all PSD efficient portfolios must be somewhere on curve MVP-b. However, as we will show, the PSD efficient set could be smaller than the M-V efficient set. To show this, note first that as one moves on the efficient frontier from point MVP to point b, both the mean and the variance increase. Thus, in the analysis that follows, we compare two prospects where one has a higher mean and a higher variance than the other does.

Consider Figure 11.6. In both Figures 11.6a and 11.6b, distribution F has a higher mean and a higher variance than distribution G. Assuming that both F and G are located on the M-V efficient set, this implies that F is located to the right of G on the M-V efficient frontier. Recall that two normal distributions intersect at most once, and the one with the lower variance cuts the other distribution from below, as demonstrated in these two figures.

The two figures demonstrate a different location of the intersection points of the two cumulative normal distributions, once in the positive domain and once in the negative domain. As we shall see, the location of the intersection point is of crucial importance for the determination of the dominance relation. However, in both figures, because F has a higher mean than G, the $+$ area is larger than the $-$ area (see equation (11.4)).

In the specific case demonstrated in Figure 11.6a, the intersection point x_0 is located in the positive domain. We claim that with $x_0 > 0$, neither distribution F nor distribution G dominates the other by PSD. G does not dominate F because it has a lower mean, and a higher (or

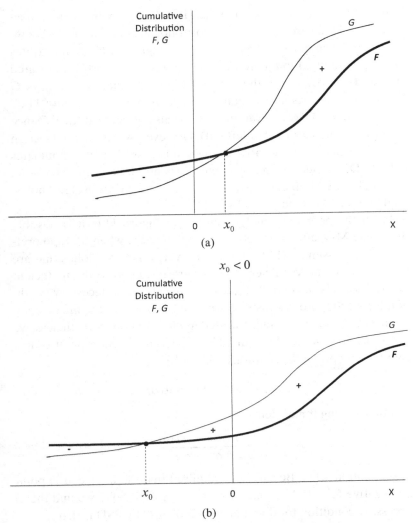

Figure 11.6. The Cumulative Normal Distributions with $E_F > E_G$ and $\sigma_F > \sigma_G$.

equal) mean is a necessary condition for a PSD dominance. F does not dominate G because for any value $0 < x < x_0$, we have

$$\int_o^x [G(x) - F(x)] < 0.$$

See Figure 11.6a and equation (11.3). Thus, if the intersection point x_0 is located in the positive domain, both F and G are PSD as well as M-V efficient.

We turn now to the case where the intersection point is in the negative domain, a case where some portfolios located on the M-V efficient frontier may be inefficient by PSD. Figure 11.6b demonstrates such a possibility. First, note that as required from portfolios located on the M-V efficient set, the mean of F is larger than the mean of G (the positive area is larger than the negative area); see Figure 11.6b and equation (11.4). The variance of F is also larger that the variance of G (hence, it has a thicker left tail). However, when the intersection point is located in the negative domain, it is possible that F dominates G by PSD, although such dominance does not exist by the M-V rule. Indeed, Figure 11.6b demonstrates a case where equation (11.3) holds, implying that F dominates G by PSD.

From the preceding analysis and from Figure 11.6, it is possible that some M-V efficient portfolios are inefficient when S-shape preferences are assumed (PSD rule). However, which portfolios that are located on the M-V efficient frontier are relegated to the inefficient set by PSD? To answer this question, recall that a necessary condition for a PSD of one prospect over the other is that the intersection point x_0 is negative, as demonstrated in Figure 11.6b. Nonetheless, we saw in Chapter 4 (see Section 4.6) that the intersection point of two cumulative normal distributions is given by

$$(x_0 - \mu_F)/\sigma_F = (x_0 - \mu_G)/\sigma_G,$$

and that solving for x_0 yields

$$x_0 = \frac{\mu_G \sigma_F - \mu_F \sigma_G}{\sigma_F - \sigma_G}$$

(see equation 4.15). Because it is required that the intersection point be negative for a PSD dominance of F over G to hold, we find that a necessary condition for dominance of F over G by PSD is that

$$\mu_G \sigma_F - \mu_F \sigma_G < 0 \Rightarrow \mu_F/\sigma_F > \mu_G/\sigma_G, \tag{11.5}$$

where the right-hand side of equation (11.5) asserts that the slope of portfolio F, with a line raising from the origin, must be higher than the corresponding slope of portfolio G. Thus, the slope condition given in equation (11.5) is a necessary condition for dominance of F over G by PSD. This condition implies that, at most, a lower part of the M-V efficient set is relegated to the PSD inefficient set.

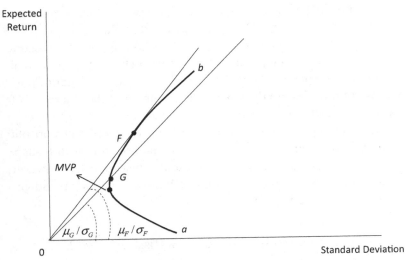

Figure 11.7. The Prospect Stochastic Dominance and Mean-Variance Efficient Sets.

The slope necessary condition for the PSD dominance is demonstrated graphically in Figure 11.7. Consider two portfolios, F and G, located on the M-V efficient set. As can be seen, the slope connecting portfolio F with the origin is larger than that corresponding to portfolio G, and because F has a higher mean and a higher variance than G, F may dominate G by PSD. We say "may dominate" because we have a necessary condition for dominance (see equation (11.5)), but not a sufficient condition for a PSD dominance. To assert safely that such dominance takes place, we need to show that in addition to the necessary condition, the condition given by equation (11.3) also holds.

In sum, any portfolio located on the M-V efficient set may dominate by PSD another portfolio located on the same set, if the dominating portfolio has a higher mean, a higher variance, and a higher slope with the line raising from the origin. Therefore, at most, the segment MVP-F, which is M-V efficient, may be PSD inefficient (see Figure 11.7). Thus, the M-V efficient set is MVP-b, and the PSD efficient set is at least the segment Fb and may include some part of the segment MVP-F. Thus, by PSD, the lower segment of the M-V efficient set may be relegated to the inefficient set. Finally, it is interesting to note that the PSD possible relegation of the lower part of the efficient set to the inefficient set is similar to the result suggested by Baumol.[4]

The good news emerging from this analysis is that by relaxing the risk-aversion assumption and assuming S-shape preferences, all investors still choose from the M-V efficient set, and no interior portfolio is optimal, despite the risk-seeking segment of the S-shape preference. The bad news is that a conflict in choices may exist between the two paradigms: M-V investors may have an optimal portfolio located on the segment MVP-*F*, whereas the investors with S-shape preferences may relegate this portfolio to the inefficient set. However, even this relatively nonsevere conflict between the two paradigms vanishes once we add the riskless asset.

c) Diversification Is Allowed and a Riskless Asset Exists

With diversification and without the riskless asset, we have shown that the M-V and the PSD efficient sets are closely related. Now we show that when we follow the CAPM's assumption and allow also riskless borrowing and lending, the M-V and PSD efficient sets coincide. Thus, if an S-shape preference is assumed, all investors select the optimal portfolio from the CML; hence, the Separation Theorem holds, implying that the CAPM is intact. This claim is summarized in theorem 2.

Theorem 2: Suppose the distributions are normal and that riskless borrowing and lending are allowed. Employing objective probabilities, the M-V and the PSD efficient sets coincide. Therefore, all S-shape investors select their optimal portfolio from those located on the CML, and the CAPM is also intact with S-shape preferences.

Proof: The proof is a simple extension of theorem 1, when a riskless asset whose rate of return is positive is allowed. Figure 11.8 presents the CML: All portfolios located on line *rr'* are M-V efficient. Because all distributions are by assumption normal, all mixes of the riskless asset and portfolio *m* are also normal. Therefore, any two distributions corresponding to two portfolios located on the CML cross only once. Take, for example, portfolios *G* and *F*. Portfolio

---

[4] W. J. Baumol, "An Expected Gain Confidence Limit Criterion for Portfolio Selection," *Management Science*, 1963.

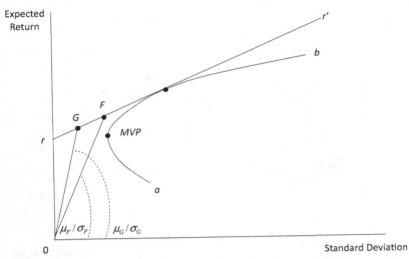

Figure 11.8. The Mean-Variance and Prospect Stochastic Dominance Efficient Set with a Riskless Asset.

G does not dominate portfolio F by PSD because F has a higher mean, and a necessary condition for dominance by FSD is that the dominating prospect will have a higher mean. However, portfolio F does not dominate portfolio G, because it has a lower slope, namely, $\mu_F/\sigma_F < \mu_G/\sigma_G$ (see Figure 11.8), and the necessary condition for dominance given in theorem 1 does not hold. By the same token, any two portfolios located on line rr' do not dominate each other by PSD; therefore, the M-V and the PSD efficient sets coincide.

So far, we have seen that accounting for two elements of PT, the change of wealth rather than total wealth argument, and the S-shape preference rather than the risk-aversion assumption do not affect the M-V analysis much. Moreover, when riskless borrowing and lending are allowed, the PT and the M-V rule choices coincide, leading to the Separation Theorem and the CAPM. This is quite a surprising result because it implies that the CAPM is intact even when preference is not concave. However, although all investors will select their portfolio from the CML, to guarantee an equilibrium, one may impose an upper bound on borrowing to make sure that infinite borrowing does not take place, even if it is optimal for some S-shape preference.

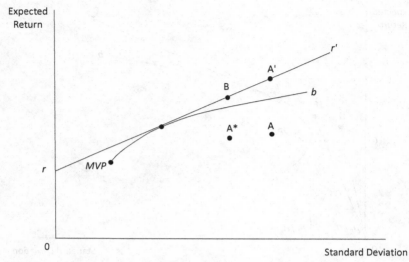

Figure 11.9. The Efficient Set with Decision Weights that Do Not Violate First-Degree Stochastic Dominance.

We turn now to the third fundamental element of PT: the decision weights.

11.4. CUMULATIVE DECISION WEIGHTS, MEAN-VARIANCE, AND THE CAPITAL ASSET PRICING MODEL

There are several suggestions in the literature regarding the desired structure of the decision weights as well as regarding the experimental estimates of the decision weights that subjects employ. If one adheres to the decision-weights method suggested by the original 1979 PT article, as we have already seen in Chapter 9, the FSD rule may be violated. Specifically, this implies that the M-V rule may also be violated because it may affect the various parameters of the distribution in an unequal manner.

Because the decision weights suggested in the original PT paper violate FSD (and, of course, may violate M-V), in this section we focus on the modified decision-weights models – the cumulative form of the decision-weights models. Thus, in this section, we analyze the impact of all possible decision weights on the M-V rule and on the CAPM as long as these decision weights do not violate FSD. In the next section, we analyze the pros and cons of several decision-weight models and compare the implied decision weights as estimated by the various methods.[5]

Figure 11.9 presents the M-V efficient set and the CML, in the case where in calculating the various parameters, objective probabilities are employed and where distributions are assumed to be normal.

It is well known in the financial literature that every risk averter who maximizes expected utility will select his or her optimal portfolio from the CML. Now let us introduce S-shape preferences and cumulative decision weights, analyzing the effect of these two factors on choices and on the CAPM. We perform the analysis in two stages: first with objective probabilities and second with decision weights.

a) S-Shape Preference with Objective Probabilities

The results with objective probabilities have already been discussed, but we repeat them here in different formulation that helps to introduce decision weight into the analysis.

Suppose one accepts that investors are not risk averse in the whole domain but rather have an S-shape preference as suggested by PT. Thus, the investor maximizes:

$$\text{Maximize } EU_s \left[\sum x_i R_i + \left(1 - \sum x_i \right) r \right], \qquad (11.6)$$

where U_s is an S-shape preference, R_i is the return on the ith risky asset, x_i is the investment proportion in the ith risky asset, and r is the riskless interest rate. As one maximizes the expected utility with a risk-seeking segment, one may claim that an interior M-V portfolio may be selected, say, portfolio A (see Figure 11.9). We claim that such a choice does not maximize the expected utility of an S-shape preference as long as normality is assumed. To see this, compare portfolios A and A'. Because both have the same variance and portfolio A' has a higher mean, for normal distributions A' dominates A by FSD. Thus, the expected utility of A' is higher than (or equal to) the expected utility of A, for all possible nondecreasing preferences, and specifically for all S-shape preferences. Therefore, portfolio A cannot be the solution to equation (11.6). By the same token, and with objective probabilities, one can prove that the solution to equation (11.6)

---

[5] Note that PT's decision weights cannot be employed in the continuous case, whereas decision weights that are based on cumulative distributions can be employed both in the discrete as well as the continuous cases.

must yield a portfolio located on the CML, suggesting that the CAPM is intact also for all S-shape choices as long as the distributions of returns are normal.

b) S-Shape Preferences with Monotonic Decision Weight Functions

We are ready now to add one more dimension of PT: We assume that in addition to the S-shape preferences, subjects also employ a monotonic decision-weight function. The shape of the decision-weight function is not important now, and the only requirement is that, if prospect F dominates prospect G by FSD with objective probabilities, such dominance is intact also with decision weights. Namely, in the spirit of cumulative decision weights, we require that FSD is not violated by the employment of decision weights. Thus, we require that

$$F(x) \leq G(x) \quad \text{for all values } x \Rightarrow T[F(x)] \leq T[G(x)] \text{ for all values } x.$$

Obviously, if the function T is a monotonic with $T' \geq 0$, FSD is not violated. We claim also that with this monotonic decision-weight function, the CAPM is intact on one condition: investors first select the portfolio (e.g., a mutual fund, an exchange traded fund, and so forth) and then employ the decision weight function on the selected portfolio, not on each individual asset before the portfolio is composed.[6]

---

[6] If investors first employ decision weights on each individual asset and only in the second stage compose the optimal portfolio by considering the transformed distribution of each asset, the CAPM is not intact. To see this, suppose that portfolio A is given if Figure 11.9 is the optimal selected portfolio for some S-shape preference after first transforming the probabilities of each asset by a monotonic decision-weight function. We cannot say that portfolio A' dominates portfolio A by FSD because after transforming the probability of each asset in portfolio A, the distribution of returns on portfolio A is not normal anymore. Hence one cannot determine FSD situations by the M-V rule for the equal variances case. However, such decision-weight methodology is unaccepted for two reasons. First, with objective probabilities, portfolio A may be located at some other point, say, point A*, and because portfolio B (with objective probability) is located vertically above it, B dominates A* by FSD. Hence, selecting portfolio A with decision weights (employed on each individual asset) rather than portfolio B violates FSD. This is an unaccepted procedure because FSD violations are not allowed. Second, with thousands of available assets, it does not make sense that decision weights are employed on each individual asset. With the readily available mutual funds and ETFs, it makes more sense that if decision weights are employed, they are employed on the available portfolios, a case where the CAPM is intact.

To show that the CAPM is intact with monotonic decision weights also, suppose, once again, that portfolio A is selected with S-shape preferences and with a monotonic decision-weight function (see Figure 11.9). We claim that this solution cannot be optimal within the PT framework because portfolio A′ dominates portfolio A with objective probabilities by FSD, and because monotonic decision weights do not violate the FSD dominance, portfolio A′ dominates portfolio A with this monotonic decision-weights function also. Thus, for any portfolio located below the CML, there is a portfolio located vertically above it, which dominates it by FSD, with objective probabilities as well as with monotonic decision weights.

In sum, for S-shape preferences with a monotonic decision-weight function, for any selected portfolio below the CML, there is a portfolio located vertically above it on the CML that dominates it by FSD; hence, the dominance is intact also for all S-shape preferences. Therefore, all CPT's investors will choose the optimal portfolio from those located on the CML, and thus the Separation Theorem and the resulting CAPM are intact. Finally, note that this result is intact not only with CPT's decision-weight function but with all monotonic decision-weight functions that do not violate FSD.

So far, we have proved that for any portfolio located below the CML there is a portfolio located on the CML that dominates it by FSD. However, it does not imply that all portfolios located on the CML are efficient with S-shape preferences and with decision weights. For example, it is possible that with decision weights, portfolio A′ dominates portfolio B by PSD (see Figure 11.9). Thus, in contrast to the M-V efficient set, which includes all portfolios located on the CML, with PT efficiency analysis, it is possible that a certain segment of the CML is inefficient. This result should have no effect on the CAPM, however, because all PT investors select some portfolio located on the CML and, therefore, select a mix of portfolio m and the riskless asset, which is a necessary condition to derive the CAPM.

In Figure 11.9, we draw the CML with objective probabilities. However, as the objective probabilities of each portfolio are transformed, the efficient set in the M-V space, when the various parameters are calculated with decision weights, may take a different form. Figure 11.10 demonstrates the CPT efficient set in terms of decision weights and in terms of objective probabilities. Line rr' presents all

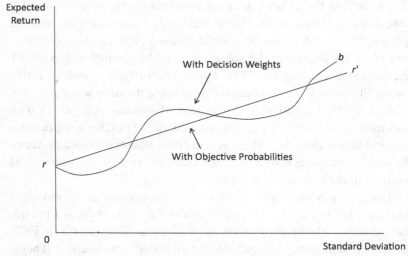

Figure 11.10. The Cumulative Prospect Theory Efficient Set with Objective Probabilities and with Decision Weights.

CPT efficient portfolios stated in terms of objective probabilities. Curve *rb* presents the same efficient set stated in terms of decision weights rather than objective probabilities. Although these curves are not necessarily continuous, we can safely determine that for each efficient portfolio located on line *rr'*, there is a corresponding portfolio located on curve *rb*. Finally, note that point *r* is located on the two efficient sets because it is assumed that decision weights are not employed on the certain income.

11.5. CAPITAL ASSET PRICING MODEL WITHIN EXPECTED UTILITY AND WITHIN CUMULATIVE PROSPECT THEORY[7]

We have seen in the previous sections of this chapter that if choices are made based on losses and gains rather than total wealth, when preferences are S-shaped and when DW functions that do not violate FSD are employed, the M-V efficiency analysis and the CAPM are

---

[7] For a more detailed analysis of the coexistence of CAPM and CPT, see H. Levy, E. D. De Giorgi, and T. Hens, "Two Paradigms and Nobel Prizes in Economics: A Contradiction or Coexistence?," *European Financial Management*, forthcoming.

intact. Of course, this assertion is valid as long as the other assumptions needed to prove the CAPM hold. Specifically, normality of the distribution of returns plays a central role in proving this assertion.

The preceding conclusion implies that the CAPM holds, but it does not imply that equilibrium prices of risky assets are unaffected by switching regimens. For example, if suddenly all investors change their taste and instead of being risk averters (as assumed by the classical derivation of the CAPM), they make choices based on a S-shaped preferences, as assumed by CPT, we still have the same CAPM linear relation between mean and risk, but the various parameters – the price of unit of risk as well as equilibrium prices – may change. Namely, we have equilibrium, but a different one, that depends on the assumed decision-making regimen. In this section, we collect all the results discussed in this chapter and analyze their implications to the M-V, CAPM, and price of risk.[8]

To integrate all the results corresponding to the CAPM and CPT, and to analyze the effect of CPT on equilibrium asset pricing, let us first analyze the constraints that should be imposed on the CPT's preferences, constraints not discussed by CPT. Recall that so far, we have analyzed the effect of observed experimental subjects' behavior on the M-V efficiency analysis and on the CAPM. We now analyze the constraints that should be imposed on CPT's preference by the observed subject's behavior, revealing that symmetric fair games are usually rejected.

To analyze the needed constraint, let us first repeat the prospect value function discussed in Chapter 9, given by

$$V(x) = \{x^\alpha \text{ if } x \geq 0 \quad \text{and} \quad -\lambda(-x)^\beta \text{ if } x < 0\}, \quad (11.7)$$

---

[8] Although to the best of our knowledge this chapter is the first to provide a complete integration between the CAPM and CPT, there are several studies dealing with various aspects of investment decision within PT or CPT frameworks. See S. Benartzi and R. Thaler, "Myopic Loss Aversion and the Equity Premium Puzzle," *Quarterly Journal of Economics*, 1995; N. Barberis, M. Huang, and T. Santos, "Prospect Theory and Asset Prices," *Quarterly Journal of Economics*, 2001; and A. Berkelaar, R. Kouwenberg, and T. Post, "Optimal Portfolio Choice Under Loss Aversion," *Review of Economics and Statistics*, 2004. The closest paper to the material discussed in this chapter is by H. Levy and M. Levy, "Prospect Theory and Mean–Variance Analysis," *Review of Financial Studies*, 2004.

Table 11.1. *Experimental Findings for the Value Function Parameters*

	α	β	λ
Kahneman et al. (1990)			2+
Tversky and Kahneman (1991)			2+
Pennings and Smidts (2003)			1.8
Tversky and Kahneman (1992)	0.88	0.88	2.25
Camerer and Ho (1994)	0.37	0.37	
Wu and Gonzalez (1996)	0.52	0.52	
Abdellaoui (2000)	0.89	0.92	
Abdellaoui et al. (2005)	0.91	0.96	

Source: M. Levy, "Loss Aversion and Price of Risk," *Quantitative Finance*, 2010.

where Tversky and Kahneman[9] estimate the various parameters as follows: $\alpha = \beta = 0.88$ and $\lambda = 2.25$. Such a function implies risk seeking in the negative domain, risk aversion in the positive domain, and loss aversion because $\lambda > 1$ implies that the risk-seeking segment is steeper than the risk-aversion segment of the value function.

Although there is wide agreement that loss aversion prevails (see also Markowitz[10]), not all researchers agree on the various CPT parameters of the decision-weight function and those of the value function. We focus here on the diversity of estimates of the parameters of the value function. Table 11.1 summarizes the various estimates of the parameters of the value function. As can be seen from this table, all the loss-aversion parameters, λ, are greater than 1, implying the existence of loss aversion. However, regarding α and β, the range of parameters is very wide, from 0.37 up to 0.96. Despite this wide range of the estimates, one result is very interesting: in each study, the two parameters are either equal to each other or very close to each other. Thus, we can safely conclude that $\alpha \approx \beta$.

Is there a rationale for the identity of these two parameters? M. Levy[11] was the first to show that this result is actually expected. Moreover, he shows that if these two parameters are not equal, then a fair game will not be rejected, contrary to the observed behavior of

[9] See Tversky and Kahneman, 1992, *op. cit.*
[10] H. M. Markowitz, "The Utility of Wealth," *Journal of Political Economy*, 1952.
[11] M. Levy, "Loss Aversion and the Price of Risk," *Quantitative Finance*, 2010.

people. Thus, he suggests imposing a constraint on the S-shape value function stemming from the fact that fair games are generally rejected and that loss aversion exists. To show this claim, consider a stock that costs \$1 and gives an uncertain payoff of either \$0.50 or \$1.50 with an equal probability. Thus, purchasing this stock is like participating in a fair symmetric game, which most investors reject. However, with the PT value function, he or she shows that if $\alpha \neq \beta$, the fair game will be accepted, and the only case where, as expected, a fair game is rejected is when $\alpha = \beta$. To elaborate:

When, $\alpha > \beta$, purchasing N stocks yields an expected value of

$$EV(x) = 1/2(.5N)^{\alpha} - 1/2\lambda[-(-0.5N)]^{\beta}. \qquad (11.8)$$

(Recall that purchasing the stock costs \$1, and we assume for simplicity that the cash flow occurs immediately, so no discounting is required.) From this equation, and for $\alpha > \beta$ and for a finite λ, it is obvious that purchasing an infinite number of stocks is optimal; thus, the investor would be willing to participate in a fair symmetric game. Because fair games are generally rejected, Levy rules out such a possibility.

When $\alpha < \beta$, one can find the optimal number of stocks that should be purchased by taking the derivative of equation (11.8) and equating it to zero. Such a procedure yields

$$0.5^{\alpha} \alpha N^{\alpha-1} = 0.5^{\beta} \lambda \beta N^{\beta-1}.$$

Therefore, the optimal number of stocks that should be purchased is

$$N^* = 2\left(\frac{\alpha}{\lambda\beta}\right)^{1/(\beta-\alpha)} > 0.$$

Because it can be easily verified that this solution provides a maximum rather than a minimum, once again we find that it is optimal to take a fair game, an unacceptable result.

Thus, the only possibility left is that $\alpha = \beta$. In this case, we have

$$EV(x) = 1/2(0.5N)^{\alpha} - 1/2\lambda(-(-0.5N))^{\alpha} = 1/2(1-\lambda)0.5^{\alpha}N^{\alpha}.$$

With loss aversion ($\lambda > 0$), the value of this function is monotonically decreasing with N; hence, the optimal solution is $N = 0$, namely, rejecting the fair game.

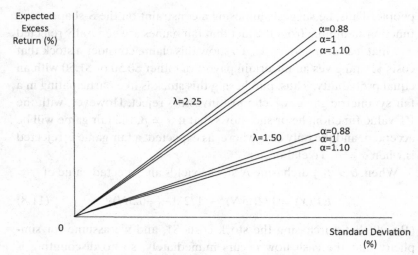

Figure 11.11. The Capital Market Line under Various Parameters of the Cumulative Prospect.

Using the needed constraint $\alpha = \beta$, and assuming loss aversion ($\lambda > 1$) and a normal distribution of returns, M. Levy has shown that the CML is a function of the various parameters of the CPT value function. This result is approximated in Figure 11.11.

A few conclusions can be drawn from this analysis:

a) The CML's general shape is unaffected by moving from the expected utility regimen to the CPT regime.

b) The CML is affected by the various CPT parameters. Because the slope of the CML changes with changes in these parameters; it implies that the price of risk also changes. Therefore, the CAPM asset pricing also changes despite the fact that a similar mean-return linear equilibrium relation exists, both in expected utility and in CPT regimens.

c) The CML is highly sensitive to the loss-aversion parameter but not to α and β.

Thus, the Separation Theorem and the linear CAPM relation exist both in CPT and expected utility regimens, but the price of risk and equilibrium prices of risky assets may change across regimens.

11.6. SUMMARY

In this chapter, we have analyzed and compared CPT, M-V, and the CAPM. Because the M-V and the CAPM have been developed within expected utility theory, we also contrast CPT with expected utility. In such a comparison of two fundamental paradigms, one needs to keep in mind that expected utility is a normative theory, whereas CPT is a descriptive theory; it is not surprising, therefore, that contradictions between these two theories exist.

Contrasting CPT on the one hand and M-V analysis and the CAPM on the other hand is crucial because both theories are widely used: The M-V model and the CAPM occupy a significant portion of virtually all finance textbooks and are also widely used by financial institutions and practitioners. The CPT is a research field that has gained momentum, bringing about the development of new research fields called behavioral economics and behavioral finance in the last two decades. If contradictions between these two paradigms exist, one has to take a side because one cannot use one paradigm without refuting the conflicting evidence provided by the other paradigm.

By CPT, several observed experimental phenomena are documented. The following are the three most important findings:

a) Subjects make choices by considering change of wealth (gains and losses) rather than total wealth.
b) Subjects employ decision weights rather than the objective probabilities.
c) Preference has an S-shape with a risk-seeking segment in the negative domain of outcomes and a risk-averse segment in the positive domain of outcomes. In addition, the curve is steeper in the negative domain than in the positive domain, a property well known as loss aversion.

The findings given in a) and b) directly contradict EUT. The finding given in c) does not contradict expected utility in general, but it contradicts virtually all economic models that assume risk aversion in the whole domain of outcomes. In particular, it casts doubt on the variance employed in the CAPM as a measure of risk.

In this chapter, we obtain quite astonishing results: The CPT and the M-V and the CAPM can coexist, despite the fact that expected utility and CPT are in contradiction and despite the fact that the M-V and the CAPM are derived within expected utility paradigm. This strong conclusion is intact as long as the distribution of returns is normal. However, the normality assumption is a very weak assumption because we have seen in Chapter 8 that making a choice "as if" the distributions are normal where in fact they are not normal is involved with a negligible financial loss.

The M-V and the CAPM are intact with CPT because of the following arguments:

a) *Initial wealth:* First, note that the M-V analysis is invariant to the assumed initial wealth. Thus, the composition of all efficient portfolios is the same stated in terms of change of wealth and in terms of total wealth. Similarly, the CML is unaffected by the initial wealth. Although the tangency point of the indifference curve and the CML is affected by the initial wealth, still we have a Separation Theorem and the CAPM follows.

b) *S-shape preference:* Relying on objective probabilities (rather than decision weights), having an S-shape preference (or value function) may induce a reduction in the M-V efficient set, but investors with such preference will not select a portfolio that is interior to the M-V efficient set. Moreover, when the riskless asset exists, the M-V efficient set is identical to the PT S-shape preferences efficient set, and the Sharpe-Lintner CAPM follows also within the CPT. When the riskless asset does not exist, the zero beta model follows within CPT.

c) *Decision weights:* Finally, when the cumulative decision-weight function, which does not violate FSD, is added to the analysis, we find that the M-V analysis and the CAPM are intact despite the fact that the transformed probability functions are not normal anymore.

Considering all three differences between expected utility and CPT reveals that whereas expected utility and CPT are two contradictory paradigms, the M-V and the CAPM can coexist with both paradigms. This conclusion is valid as long as the DW functions do not violate FSD, as indeed required by CPT and other decision-weight models. Some important extensions of the CAPM that have been discussed in

Chapter 6 (e.g., zero beta model, segmented CAPM, and APT) also coexist with CPT.

Finally, although the CML slope, the price of risk, and the assets equilibrium prices generally change by shifting from the expected utility regimen to the CPT regimen, the separation theorem and the CAPM linear risk–return relation remains intact. Therefore, one can integrate the main ingredients of CPT's observed people's behavior into finance without losing the main two models: the M-V efficient analysis and the CAPM. Contrary to what one would expect, accepting CPT makes the CAPM even stronger because it is robust to drastic changes in the assumptions that underline it. The M-V efficiency analysis and the CAPM can be safely employed because these two models are robust to the new experimental evidence of CPT. However, one should remember that although the linear risk–return relation is intact in both models, and beta is the risk index, the equilibrium prices and the price of risk may be different under CPT and under the classic CAPM.

References

M. Abdellaoui, "Parameter Free Elicitation of Utility and Probability Weighting Functions," *Management Science*, 2000.

A. Admati, "A Noisy Rational Expectation for Multi-Asset Securities Markets," *Econometrica*, 1985.

G. A. Akerlof and R. J. Shiller, *Animal Spirit: How Human Psychology Drives the Economy, and Why It Matters for Global Capitalism*, Princeton University Press, NJ, United States, 2009.

S. S. Alexander, "Price Movements in Speculative Markets: Trends of Random Walks," *Industrial Management Review*, 1961.

M. Allais, "Le Comportement de l'Homme Rationnel devant le Risque: Critique des Postulats et Axiomes de l'Ecole Americaine," *Econometrica*, 1953.

K. Arrow, *Aspects of the Theory of Risk Bearing*, Yrjo Jahnssonin Saatio, Helsinki, 1965.

K. J. Arrow, *Essays in the Theory of Risk Bearing*, North-Holland, Amsterdam, 1971.

A. B. Atkins and E. A. Dyl, "Transaction Costs and the Holding Periods for Common Stocks," *Journal of Finance*, 1997.

D. Avramov and T. Chordia, "Pricing Stock Returns," *Journal of Finance*, 2006.

Babson College: http://libguides.babson.edu taken from the Library Guides of Babson College in Wellesley, MA, USA.

L. J. B. A. Bachelier, *Le Jeu, la chance, et le hazard*, E. Flammarion, Paris, 1914, chaps. xviii–xix.

R. W. Banz, "The Relationship Between Return and Market Value of Common Stocks," *Journal of Financial Economics*, 1981.

B. Barber and T. Odean, "Trading Hazardous to Your Wealth: The Common Stock Investment Performance of Individual Investors," *Journal of Finance*, 1999.

B. M. Barber and T. Odean, "Boys Will Be Boys: Gender, Overconfidence, and Common Stock Investment," *Quarterly Journal of Economics*, 2001.

N. Barberis, M. Huang, and T. Santos, "Prospect Theory and Asset Prices," *Quarterly Journal of Economics*, 2001.

O. E. Barndorff-Nielsen, T. Mikosch, and S. I. Resnick, *Levy Process – Theory and Application*, Springer-Verlag, New York, 2001.

S. Basu, "Investment Performance of Common Stocks in Relation to their Price-Earning Ratios: A Test of the Efficient Market Hypothesis," *Journal of Finance*, 1977.

W. J. Baumol, "An Expected Gain Confidence Limit Criterion for Portfolio Selection," *Management Science*, 1963.

S. Benartzi and R. Thaler, "Myopic Loss Aversion and the Equity Risk Premium Puzzle," *Quarterly Journal of Economics*, 1995.

J. B. Berk, "Necessary Conditions for the CAPM," *Journal of Economic Theory*, 1997.

A. Berkelaar, R. Kouwenberg, and T. Post, "Optimal Portfolio Choice Under Loss Aversion," *Review of Economics and Statistics*, 2004.

M. J. Best and R. R. Grauer, "Capital Asset Pricing Compatible with Observed Market Value Weights," *Journal of Finance* 1985.

B. Biais, P. Bossaerts, and C. Spatt, "Equilibrium Asset Pricing Under Heterogeneous Information," EFA 2004 Maastricht Meetings Paper No. 5083; 13th Annual Utah Winter Finance Conference; AFA 2003, Washington, DC, Meetings.

M. H. Birnbaum and J. B. Navarrete, "Testing Descriptive Utility Theories: Violations of Stochastic Dominance and Cumulative Independence," *Journal of Risk and Uncertainty*, 1998.

F. Black, "Capital Market Equilibrium with Restricted Borrowing," *Journal of Business*, 1972.

F. Black, M. C. Jensen, and M. Scholes, "The Capital Asset Pricing Model: Some Empirical Tests," in M. C. Jensen, ed., *Studies in the Theory of Capital Markets*, Praeger, New York, 1972.

F. Black and M. Scholes, "The Pricing of Options and Corporate Liabilities," *Journal of Political Economy*, 1973.

M. E. Blume, J. Crockett, and I. Friend, "Stock Ownership in the United States: Characteristics and Trends," *Survey of Current Business*, 1974.

M. E. Blume and I. Friend, "The Asset Structure of Individual Portfolios and Some Implication to Utility Functions," *Journal of Finance*, 1975.

Z. Bodie, A. Kane, and A. J. Marcus, "*Investments*," 9th ed., McGraw-Hill, 2010.

P. Bossaerts and C. Plott, "The CAPM in Thin Experimental Financial Markets," *Journal of Economic Dynamics &Control*, 2002.

R. A. Brealey, S. C. Myers, and F. Allen, *"Principles of Corporate Finance,"* 10th ed., McGraw-Hill, 2011.

D. T. Breeden, "An Intertemporal Asset Pricing Model with Stochastic Consumption and Investment Opportunities," *Journal of Financial Economics,* 1979.

S. Brodrick, Bank Rate: www.bankrate.com.

J. Y. Cambell, M. Lettau, B. G. Malkiel, and Y. Xu, "Have Individual Stocks become More Volatile? An Empirical Exploration of the Idiosyncratic Risk," *Journal of Finance,* 2001.

C. F. Camerer, "An Experimental Test of Several Generalized Utility Theories," *Journal of Risk and Uncertainty,* 1989.

C. F. Camerer and T. H. Ho, "Violations of Betweeness Axiom and Nonlinearity in Probability," *Journal of Risk and Uncertainty,* 1994.

G. Chamberlain, "A Characterization of the Distributions That Imply Mean-Variance Utility Functions," *Econometrica,* 1983.

N. F. Chen, R. Roll, and S. A. Ross, "Economic Forces and Stock Market," *Journal of Business,* 1986.

P. H. Cootner, "Stock Prices: Random vs. Systematic Changes," *Industrial Management Review,* 1962.

P. DeMarzo and C. Skiadas, "Aggregation, Determinacy, and Informational Efficiency for a Class of Economics with Asymmetric Information," *Journal of Economic Theory,* 1998.

A. S. Dexter, J. N. Yu, and W. T. Ziemba, "Portfolio Selection in a Lognormal Market When the Investor Has a Power Utility Function: Computational Results." In M. A. H. Dempster (ed.), *Stochastic Programming,* Academic Press, New York, 1980.

D. Duane, Practical Stock Investing: www.practicalstockinvesting.com.

L. R. Duncan and P. C. Fishburn, "Rank- and Sign-Dependent Linear Utility Models for Finite First-Order Gambles," *Journal of Risk and Uncertainty,* 1991.

P. H. Dybvig and S. A. Ross, "Differential Information and Performance Measurement Using a Security Market Line," *Journal of Finance,* 1985.

L. H. Ederington, "Mean-Variance as an Approximation to Expected Utility Maximization," working paper, Washington University, St. Louis, 1986.

W. Edwards, "Subjective Probabilities Inferred From Decisions," *Psychological Review,* 1962.

D. Ellsberg, "Risk, Ambiguity and Savage Axioms," *Quarterly Journal of Economics,* 1961.

J. L. Evans and S. H. Archer, "Diversification and Reduction in Dispersion: An Empirical Analysis," *Journal of Finance,* 1968.

E. F. Fama, "The Behavior of Market Prices," *Journal of Business,* 1965.

E. Fama, *Foundation of Finance*, Basic Books, New York, 1976.

E. Fama and J. D. MacBeth, "Tests of the Multi-Period Two-Parameter Model," *Journal of Political Economy*, 1974.

E. F. Fama and K. R. French, "The Cross–Section of Expected Stock Returns," *Journal of Finance*, 1992.

F. Fama and K. R. French, "Common Risk Factors in the Return on Stocks and Bonds," *Journal of Financial Economics*, 1993.

W. Fellner, *Probability and Profit – A Study of Economic Behavior along Bayesian Lines*, Homewood, IL: Irwin, 1965.

W. E. Ferson and C. R. Harvey, "The Risk and Predictability of International Equity Returns," *Review of Financial Studies*, 1993.

Financial Times: http://markets.ft.com.

P. C. Fishburn, "On Handa's 'New Theory of Cardinal Utility' and the Maximization of Expected Utility," *Journal of Political Economy*, 1978.

P. C. Fishburn, "Nontransitive Measurable Utility," *Journal of Mathematical Psychology*, 1982.

P. C. Fishburn, *Nonlinear Preference and Utility Theory*, The Johns Hopkins University Press, Baltimore, 1988.

P. C. Fishburn, "Rank- and Sign-Dependent Linear Utility Models for Finite First-Order Gambles," *Journal of Risk and Uncertainty*, 1991.

P. C. Fishburn and G. A. Kochenberger, "Two-Piece von Neumann-Morgenstern Utility Functions," *Decision Sciences*, 2007.

S. M. Focardi and F. J. Fabozzi, "Fat Tails, Scaling, and Stable Laws: A Critical Look at Modeling External Events in Financial Phenomena," *Journal of Risk Finance*, 2003.

M. Friedman,"The Methodology of Positive Economics," in *Essays in Positive Economics*, Chicago and London, University of Chicago Press, 1953.

M. Friedman and L. J. Savage, "The Utility Analysis of Choices Involving Risk," *Journal of Political Economy*, 1948.

X. Gabaix, P. Goplkrishnan, and V. Plerou, "A Theory of Power-Law Distributions in Financial Market Fluctuations," *Nature*, 2003.

M. Gibbons, S. Ross, and J. Shanken, "A Test of the Efficiency of the Market Portfolio," *Econometrica*, 1989.

Google: www.google.com/finance.

B. Gray and D. French, "Empirical Comparisons of Distributional Models for Stocks Index Returns," *Journal of Business*, 1990.

R. C. Green, "Positively Weighted Portfolios on the Minimum Variance Frontier," *Journal of Finance*, 1986.

R. C. Green and B. Hollifield, "When Will All Mean-Variance Efficient Portfolios Be Well Diversified?" *Journal of Finance*, 1992.

J. Hadar and W. Russell, "Rules for Ordering Uncertain Prospects," *American Economic Review*, 1969.

P. Handa, S. P. Kothari, and C. Wasley, "The Relation between the Return Interval and Betas: Implication for the Size Effect," *Journal of Financial Economics*, 1989.

G. Hanoch and H. Levy, "The Efficiency Analysis of Choices Involving Risk," *Review of Economic Studies*, 1969.

G. Hanoch and H. Levy, "Efficient Portfolio Selection with Quadratic and Cubic Utility," *Journal of Business*, 1970.

L. P. Hansen and S. F. Richard, "The Role of Conditioning Information in Deducing Testable Restrictions Implied by Dynamic Asset Pricing Models," *Journal of the Econometric Society*, 1987.

B. Hansson, "Risk Aversion as a Problem of Conjoint Measurement," *Decision, Probability, and Utility*, eds. P. Gardenfors and N. E. Sahlin, Cambridge University Press, 1988.

C. R. Harvey, J. C. Liechty, M. Liechty, and P. Muller, "Portfolio Selection with High Moments," *Working Paper*, Duke University, 2002.

C. R. Harvey and A. Siddique, "Conditional Skewness in Asset Pricing," *Journal of Finance*, 2000.

Ibbotson Associates, *Stocks, Bonds, Bills, and Inflation, 2001 Yearbook*, Ibbotson Associates, Chicago.

Ibbotson Associates, *Stocks, Bonds, Bills and Inflation, 2007 Yearbook*, Ibbotson Associates, Chicago.

R. Jagannathan and Z. Wang, "The Conditional CAPM and the Cross-Section of Expected Returns," *Journal of Finance*, 1996.

M. C. Jensen, "The Performance of Mutual Funds in the Period 1945–1964," *Journal of Finance*, 1968.

D. Kahneman and A. Tversky, "Prospect Theory of Decisions Under Risk," *Econometrica*, 1979.

G. Kaplanski and H. Levy, "Sentiment and Stock Prices: The Case of Aviation Disasters," *Journal of Financial Economics*, 2009.

M. G. Kendall, "The Analysis of Economic Time-Series," *Journal of the Royal Statistical Society* (Ser. A), 1953.

M. Kendall and A. Stuart, *The Advanced Theory of Statistics*, Griffin, London, 1983.

Y. Kroll, H. Levy, and H. M. Markowitz, "Mean-Variance versus Direct Utility Maximization," *Journal of Finance*, 1984.

H. A. Latané, "Criteria for Choice among Risky Ventures," *Journal of Political Economy*, 1959.

M. Leshno and H. Levy, "Preferred by All and Preferred by Most Decision Makers: Almost Stochastic Dominance," *Management Science*, 2002.

D. Levhari and H. Levy, "The Capital Asset Pricing Model and the Investment Horizon," *Review of Economics and Statistics*, 1977.

H. Levy, "Portfolio Performance and the Investment Horizon," *Management Science*, 1972.

H. Levy, "Stochastic Dominance Among Log-Normal Prospects," *International Economic Review*, 1973.

H. Levy, "Equilibrium in an Imperfect Market: A Constraint on the Number of Securities in the Portfolio," *American Economic Review*, 1978.

H. Levy, "A Test of the CAPM via a Confidence Level Approach," *The Journal of Portfolio Management*, 1981.

H. Levy, "The Capital Asset Pricing Model: Theory and Empiricism," *The Economic Journal*, 1983.

H. Levy, "Risk and Return: An Experimental Analysis," *International Economic Review*, 1997.

H. Levy, *Stochastic Dominance: Investment Decision Making Under Uncertainty*, 2nd edition, Springer, Unites States, 2006.

H. Levy, "First Degree Stochastic Dominance Violations: Decision Weights and Bounded Rationality," *Economic Journal*, 2008.

M. Levy, "Positive Optimal Portfolios Are All Around," *Working Paper*, Hebrew University, 2009.

M. Levy, "Loss Aversion and the Price of Risk," *Quantitative Finance*, 2010.

H. Levy and M. Levy, "Prospect Theory and Mean-Variance Analysis," *Review of Financial Studies*, 2004.

M. Levy and H. Levy, "The Small Firm Effect: A Financial Mirage?," *Journal of Portfolio Management*, 2011.

H. Levy, M. Levy, and G. Benita, "Capital Asset Pricing with Heterogeneous Beliefs," *Journal* of *Business*, 2006.

H. Levy and R. Duchin, "Asset Return Distribution and the Investment Horizon," *Journal of Portfolio Management*, 2004.

H. Levy, E. D. De Giorgi, and T. Hens, "Two Paradigms and Nobel Prizes in Economics: A Contradiction or Coexistence?," *European Financial Management*, forthcoming.

H. Levy and H. M. Markowitz, "Approximating Expected Utility by a Function of Mean and Variance," *American Economic Review*, 1979.

M. Levy and R. Roll, "The Market Portfolio May be Mean/Variance Efficient After All," *Review of Financial Studies*, 2010.

H. Levy and M. Sarnat, *Portfolio and Investment Selection: Theory and Practice*, Prentice-Hall, New York, 1983.

H. Levy and G. Schwarz, "Correlations and the Time Interval Over Which The Variables are Measured," *Journal of Econometrics*, 1997.

J. Lewellen and S. Nagel, "The Conditional CAPM Does Not Explain Asset-Pricing Anomalies," *Journal of Financial Economics*, 2006.

J. Lintner, "Security Prices, Risk and the Maximal Gain from Diversification," *Journal of Finance*, 1965.

J. Lintner, "Security Prices and Risk: The Theory of Comparative Analysis of AT&T and Leading Industrials," paper presented at the Conference on the Economics of Public Utilities, Chicago, 1965.

J. Lintner, "The Aggregation of Inventors Diverse Judgment and Preferences in Purely Competitive Markets," *Journal of Financial and Quantitative Analysis*, 1969.

M. J. Machina, "Choices Under Uncertainty: Problems Solved and Unsolved," *Economic Perspectives*, 1987.

M. J. Machina, "Review of Generalized Expected Utility Models: The Rank-Dependent Model," *Journal of Economic Literature*, 1994.

B. Mandelbrot, "The Variation of Certain the Speculative Prices," *Journal of Business*, 1963.

H. M. Markowitz, "Portfolio Selection," *Journal of Finance*, 1952.

H. M. Markowitz, "The Utility of Wealth," *Journal of Political Economy*, 1952.

H. M. Markowitz, *Portfolio Selection: Efficient Diversification of Investment*, Wiley, New York, 1959, Yale University Press, New Haven, 1970, Basil Blackwell 1991.

H. M. Markowitz, *Portfolio Selection: Efficient Diversification of Investment*, Yale University Press, New Haven, 1970.

H. M. Markowitz, "Investment for the Long Run: New Evidence for an Old Rule," *Journal of Finance*, 1976.

H. M. Markowitz, "Foundation of Portfolio Theory," *The Journal of Finance*, 1991.

H. M. Markowitz, "Portfolio Theory: As I Still See It," *Annual Review of Financial Economics*, 2010.

H. M. Markowitz, D. W. Reid, and B. V. Tew, "The Value of a Blank Check," *Journal of Portfolio Management*, 1994.

R. Mehra, and E. Prescott, "The Equity Premium: A Puzzle," *Journal of Monetary Economics*, 1985.

R. C. Merton, "An Analytical Derivation of the Efficient Portfolio," *Journal of Financial and Quantitative Analysis*, 1972.

R. C. Merton, "Intertemporal Capital Asset Pricing Model," *Econometrica*, 1973.

R. C. Merton, "A Simple Model of Capital Market Equilibrium with Incomplete Information," *Journal of Finance*, 1987.

M. Miller and M. Scholes, "Rates of Return in Relation to Risk: A Reexamination of Some Recent Studies," in M. Jensen, editor, *Studies in the Theory of Capital Markets*, Praeger, New York, 1972.

A. Moore, "A Statistical Analysis of Common Stock Process," unpublished Ph.D. dissertation, Graduate School of Business, University of Chicago 1962.

J. Mossin, "Equilibrium in a Capital Asset Market," *Econometrica*, 1966.

R. Naes and B. A. Ødegaard, "The Link Between Investor Holding Period and Liquidity," *Working Paper*, 2007.

R. Naes and B. A. Ødegaard, "Liquidity and Asset Pricing: Evidence on the Role of Investor Holding Period," EFA Athens Meeting Paper, 2009.

T. Odean, "Do Investors Trade too Much?" *American Economic Review*, 1999.

R. R. Officer, "The Distribution of Stock Return," *Journal of the American Statistical Association*, 1972.

M. F. M. Osborne, "Brownian Motion in the Stock Market," *Operation Research*, 1959.

R. Owen and R. Rabinovitch, "On the Class of Elliptical Distributions and their Applications to the Theory of Portfolio Choice," *Journal of Finance*, 1983.

J. W. Pratt, "Risk Aversion in the Small and in the Large," *Econometrica*, 1964.

D. Prelec, "The Probability Weighting Function," *Econometrica*, 1998.

L. M. Pully, "A General Mean-Variance Approximation to Expected Utility for Short Holding Periods," *Journal of Financial and Quantitative Analysis*, 1981.

L. M. Pully, "Mean-Variance Approximation to Expected Logarithmic Utility," *Operation Research*, 1983.

J. Quiggin, "A Theory of Anticipated Utility," *Journal of Economic Behavior and Organization*, 1982.

J. Quiggin, "A Theory of Anticipated Utility," *Journal of Economic Behavior and Organization, 1982, and Generalized Expected Utility Theory: The Rank-Dependent Model*, Kluwer Academic Press, Boston, MA, 1993.

M. Rabin, "Risk Aversion and Expected Utility Theory: A Calibration Theorem," *Econometrica*, 2000.

M. R. Reinganum, "Misspecification of Capital Asset Pricing; Empirical Anomalies Based on Earnings' Yield and Market Values," *Journal of Financial Economics*, 1981.

Reuters: www.reuters.com.

R. Roll, "A Critique of the Asset Pricing Theory's Tests: Part I: On Past and Potential Testability of Theory," *Journal of Financial Economics*, 1977.

A. D. Roy, "Safety-First and the Holding of Assets," *Econometrica*, 1952.

S. Ross, "The Capital Asset Pricing Model (CAPM), Short Sales Restrictions and Related Issues," *Journal of Finance*, 1977.

S. A. Ross, "Mutual Fund Separation in Financial Theory," *Journal of Economic Theory*, 1978.

M. Rothschild and J. Stiglitz, "Increasing Risk: I. A Definition," *Journal of Economic Theory*, 1970.

Rutgers: ttp://newarkwww.rutgers.edu.

P. A. Samuelson, "The Fundamental Approximation Theorem of Portfolio Analysis in Terms of Means, Variances and Higher Moments," *Review of Economic Studies*, 1970.

L. J. Savage, *The Foundation of Statistics*, Wiley, New York, 1954.

D. Schmeidler, "Subjective Probability and Expected Utility without Additivity," *Econometrica*, 1989.

W. F. Sharpe, "A Simplified Model for Portfolio Analysis," *Management Science*, 1963.

W. F. Sharpe, "Capital Asset Prices: A Theory of Market Equilibrium," *Journal of Finance*, 1964.

W. F. Sharpe, "Capital Asset Prices with and without Negative Holdings," *Journal of Finance*, 1991.

W. F. Sharpe, *Raleigh News Observer*, February, 23, 1992.

W. F. Sharpe, "Expected Utility Asset Allocation," *Financial Analysts Journal*, 2007.

Y. Simman, "The Opportunity Cost of Mean-Variance Investment Strategies," *Management Science*, 1993.

R. O. Swalm, "Utility Theory-Insight into Risk Taking," *Harvard Business Review*, 1966.

B. R. D. Tew and C. Witt, "The Opportunity Cost of a Mean-Variance Efficient Choice," *Financial Review*, 1991.

G. Tintner, *The Variate Difference Method*, Bloomington, IN, 1940.

J. Tobin, "Liquidity Preference as Behavior towards Risk," *Review of Economic Studies*, 1958.

J. Tobin, "The Theory of Portfolio Selection," in F.Y. Hahn and F. P. Berchling, eds., *The Theory of Interest Rates*, MacMillan, London, 1965.

J. Treynor, "Towards Theory of Market Value of Risky Assets," Unpublished paper, 1962.

J. L. Treynor, "How to Rate Management Investment Funds," Harvard *Business Review*, 1965.

A. Tversky and D. Kahneman, "Loss Aversion in Riskless Choice: a Reference Dependent Model," *Quarterly Journal of Economics*, 1991.

A. Tversky and D. Kahneman, "Advances in Prospect Theory: Cumulative Representation of Uncertainty," *Journal of Risk and Uncertainty*, 1992.

Value Line: www.valueline.com.

W. K. Viscusi, "Prospective Preference Theory: Toward an Explanation of Paradoxes," *Journal of Risk and Uncertainty*, 1989.

J. von Neumann and O. Morgenstern, *Theory of Game and Economic Behavior*, 3rd ed., Princeton University Press, NJ, 1953.

G. A. Whitmore, "Third Degree Stochastic Dominance," *American Economic Review*, 1970.

J. T. Williams, "Capital Asset Prices with Heterogeneous Beliefs," *Journal of Financial Economics*, 1977.

G. Wu and R. Gonzales, "Curvature of the Probability Weighting Function," *Management Science*, 1996.

M. E. Yaari, "The Dual Theory of Choice Under Risk," *Econometrica*, 1987.

YAHOO: http://finance.yahoo.com.

W. E. Young and R. H. Trent, "Geometric Mean Approximation of Individual Securities and Portfolios Performance," *Journal of Financial and Quantitative Analysis*, 1969.

G. Zhou, "Asset Pricing Under Alternative Distributions," *Journal of Finance*, 1993.

Name Index

Abdellaoui, Mohammed, 354, 405
Admati, Anat, 172, 405
Akerlof, George A., 302, 405
Alexander, Sidney S., 250, 405
Allais, Maurice, 39, 42, 45, 300, 305, 330, 405
Allen, Franklin, 19, 407
Archer, Stephen H., 9, 407
Arrow, Kenneth J., 35, 45, 85, 96, 106, 405
Atkins, Allen B., 225, 405
Avramov, Doron, 178, 405

Bachelier, Louis Jean-Baptiste Alphonse, 243, 244, 248, 296, 405
Banz, Rolf W., 203, 204, 205, 405
Barber, Brad M., 165, 225, 405, 406
Barberis, Nicholas, 397, 406
Barndorf-Nielsen, Ole Eiler, 406
Basu, S., 205, 406
Baumol, William J., 288, 289–292, 294, 295, 296, 390, 406
Bekaert, G., 178
Benartzi, Shlomo, 43, 225, 269, 346, 397, 406
Benita, Golan, 173, 410
Berk, Jonathan B., 89, 255, 406
Berkelaar, Arjan, 397, 406
Bernoulli, 24, 44
Best, Michael J., 221, 406
Biais, Bruno, 173, 406
Birnbaum, Michael H., 367, 369, 406
Black, Fischer, 158–159, 186, 196–199, 207, 247, 296, 406
Blume, Marshall E., 165, 406
Bodie, Zvi, 19, 406

Bossaerts, Peter, 173, 236–237, 406
Brealey, Richard A., 19, 407
Breeden, Douglas T., 171, 407
Brodrick, Sean, 18, 407

Cambell, John Y., 9, 407
Camerer, Collin F., 333, 354, 407
Chamberlain, Gary, 89, 255, 407
Chen, Nai-Fu, 183, 407
Chordia, Tarun, 178, 405
Constantinides, G., 4
Cootner, Paul H., 250, 407
Cramer, G., 24, 44
Crockett, Jean, 165, 406

DeMarzo, Peter, 172, 407
Dempster, M. A. H., 95
Dexter, A. S., 95, 407
Duane, D., 412
Duchin, Ran, 258, 260, 261, 263, 264, 277, 410
Duncan, Luce R., 341, 407
Dybvig, Philip H., 178, 407
Dyl, Edward A., 225, 405

Ederington, L. H., 95, 407
Edwards, Ward, 300, 330, 349, 407
Ellsberg, Daniel, 324, 407
Evans, John L., 9, 407

Fabozzi, Frank J., 257, 408
Fama, Eugene F., 4, 199–200, 201, 205, 206, 207, 211, 213, 214, 236, 237, 250–255, 256, 284, 407, 408
Fellner, William John, 300, 408

415

Subject Index

abnormal profit, recorded with small firms, 203
abnormal return, 229
abnormal small firm return, 175
Absolute Risk Aversion (ARA)
  corresponding quadratic utility function, 40
  increasing, 40
  increasing degree of, 114
  losing ground, 43
  measure of risk aversion, 36
academia, role of M-V and CAPM in, 18–21
academic journals
  editors selecting articles for, 22
  sample, 21
additive return, starting with, 227
additivity of returns, not prevailing, 228
additivity property, researchers tempted by, 228
adjusted beta, 13, 14–15
aggregate market price of risk, 151
aggressive stock, 146, 229, 231
Allais paradox, 39, 42, 305, 324, 347
Almost M-V (AMV), 289
Almost Stochastic Dominance (ASD), 289
alpha
  of CAPM, 4, 7, 10
  measuring abnormal profit (or loss), 7
  multivariate test by GR&S, 207–209
  negative indicating underperformance, 13
alternative prospects, 356–357

American Medical Systems Holdings Inc., 10
Anderson-Darling goodness of fit test, 284
Animal Spirit, The, 302
annual return distribution, estimating, 275
annual variance, changing, 266
anomalies, in empirical studies of CAPM, 3
approximation
  finding quality of the suggested, 98
  with portfolios, 112
approximation function, analyzing theoretically, 94
ARA. *See* Absolute Risk Aversion (ARA)
arbitrage, implying First degree Stochastic Dominance (FSD), 183
Arbitrage Pricing Theory (APT), 179–183
  assumptions for deriving, 180
  CAPM as a possible equilibrium solution, 157
  intact without normality, 157
  justifying Three-Factor Model, 4
  relying on linear return generating process, 185
  results intact for, 374
  validity under Prospect Theory, 183
arbitrage profit, 180
asset composition of the M-V efficient set, 376
asset integration, 304, 308–310